CULTURE AND COSMOS
http://www.CultureAndCosmos.org

Culture and Cosmos is published twice a year, in northern spring/summer and autumn/winter, in association with the Sophia Centre for the Study of Cosmology in Culture, University of Wales Trinity Saint David.
Contributions and editorial correspondence should be addressed to:
Editors@cultureandcosmos.org

Editor: Dr. Nicholas Campion, the Editor of *Culture and Cosmos*, University of Wales Trinity Saint David, Lampeter, Ceredigion, Wales, SA48 7ED, UK.
E Mail **n.campion@uwtsd.ac.uk**
Deputy Editor: Dr. Jennifer Zahrt
Editorial Board: Dr. Silke Ackermann, Professor Anthony F. Aveni, Dr. Giuseppe Bezza, Dr. David Brown, Professor Charles Burnett, Dr. Hilary M. Carey, Dr. John Carlson, Dr Patrick Curry Professor Robert Ellwood, Dr. Germana Ernst, Dr. Ann Geneva, Professor Joscelyn Godwin, Dr. Dorian Greenbaum, Dr. Jacques Halbronn, Robert Hand, Dr Jarita Holbrook, Professor Michael Hunter, Professor Ronald Hutton, Dr Peter Kingsley, Dr. Edwin C. Krupp, Dr. J. Lee Lehman, Dr. Lester Ness, Professor P. M. Rattansi, Professor James Santucci, Robert Schmidt, Dr. Fabio Silva, Dr. Lorenzo Smerillo, Professor Richard Tarnas, Dr. Graeme Tobyn, Dr. David Ulansey, Robin Waterfield, Dr. Charles Webster, Dr. Graziella Federici Vescovini, Dr. Angela Voss, Dr. Paola Zambelli, Robert Zoller.
Copy Editor: Kathleen White
Web: Dr. Frances Clynes

Contributors Guidelines: Please see http://www.cultureandcosmos.org/submissions.html

Copying: Apart from fair dealing for the purposes of research or private study, or criticism or review, as permitted under the Copyright, Designs and Patents Act 1988, no part of this publication may be reproduced, stored or transmitted in any form or by means without the prior permission of the Publisher.

Front cover: See Lilan Laishley, 'South Indian Ritual Dispels Negative Karma in the Birth Chart', Fig. 2. *Yantra* of Navagraha, in this issue.

Published by Culture and Cosmos, Dr Nicholas Campion, Faculty of Humanities and the Performing Arts, University of Wales Trinity Saint David, Lampeter, Ceredigion, Wales, SA48 7ED, UK.

© Culture and Cosmos 2017
Printed by Lightning Source.

The Sophia Centre

http://www.uwtsd.ac.uk/sophia

The Centre for the Study of Cosmology in Culture is an academic centre within the Faculty of Humanities and the Performing Arts at the University of Wales Trinity Saint David.

The Centre's academic goals are

- 'to pursue research, scholarship and teaching in the relationship between astrological, astronomical and cosmological beliefs and theories, and society, politics, religion and the arts, past and present' and
- 'to undertake the academic and critical examination of astrology and its practice'.

The Centre's wider goal is stated in its title – to 'study cosmology in culture'. In a traditional sense, a cosmology is a world view, an understanding of the cosmos which informs individual and social action and ideology. The Centre promotes research in the subject area, holds seminars and conferences, publishes scholarly material, is associated with Sophia Centre Press and supervises PhD students.

The Centre's teaching is focused on the MA Cultural Astronomy and Astrology. For further information see
http://www.uwtsd.ac.uk/ma-cultural-astronomy-astrology

CELESTIAL MAGIC

A special issue of *Culture and Cosmos*
Vol. 19 nos. 1 and 2
Spring/Summer and Autumn/Winter 2015

Copyright © 2017 Culture and Cosmos
All rights reserved

Published by Culture and Cosmos
& Sophia Centre Press
England

www.cultureandcosmos.org

In association with the
Sophia Centre for the Study of Cosmology in Culture,

University of Wales Trinity Saint David,
Faculty of Humanities and the Performing Arts
Lampeter, Ceredigion, Wales, SA48 7ED, UK

British Library Cataloguing in Publication Data
A catalogue card for this book is available from the British Library

All rights reserved. No part of this book may be reproduced or utilized in any form or by any means, electronic or mechanical, including photocopying, recording or by any information storage and retrieval system, without permission in writing from the Publishers.

ISSN 1368-6534

Printed in Great Britain by Lightning Source

Culture and Cosmos

Culture and Cosmos

CONTENTS

Nicholas Campion, *Editorial* — 1

THEORY

Mike Harding
The Meanings of Magic — 9

José Manuel Redondo
The Celestial Imagination: Proclus the Philosopher on Theurgy — 25

PRACTICE

Liz Greene
The God in the Stone: Gemstone Talismans in Western Magical Traditions — 47

Claire Chandler
Investigating the Magical Practice found in PGM (Greek Magical Papyri) XIII — 87

M. E. Warlick
Alchemy and the Transgendering of Mercury — 99

Karen Parham
Teleological and Aesthetic Perfection in the Aurora Consurgens — 115

TRANSFORMATION AND ASCENT

Alison Greig
Angelomorphism and Magical Transformation in the Christian and Jewish Traditions — 129

Christine Broadbent,
*Celestial Magic as the 'Love Path':
The Spiritual Cosmology of Ibn 'Arabi I* — 145

Hereward Tilton
Bells and Spells: Rosicrucianism and the Invocation of Planetary Spirits in Early Modern Germany — 167

Joscelyn Godwin
Astral Ascent in the Occult Revival 189

Sue Lewis
The Transformational Techniques of Huber Astrology 207

RITUAL

Jane Burton
Ancient Necromantic Rituals in Contemporary Celestial Magic 225

Lilan Laishley
South Indian Ritual Dispels Negative Karma in the Birth Chart 251

NOTES ON CONTRIBUTORS 272
BACK ISSUES 277

CULTURE AND COSMOS

www.CultureAndCosmos.org

Editor Nicholas Campion
Vol. 19 No. 1 and 2 Autumn/Winter and Spring/Summer 2015
ISSN 1368-6534

Published in Association with
The Sophia Centre for the Study of Culture in Cosmology,
Faculty of Humanities and the Performing Arts
University of Wales Trinity Saint David
http://www.uwtsd.ac.uk/sophia

Editorial

The papers in this volume of *Culture and Cosmos* were originally presented at the 2013 University of Wales Trinity Saint David/ Sophia Centre conference on Celestial Magic. As is well known, the annual Sophia Centre conferences explore the variety of topics covered by the umbrella term 'cultural astronomy and astrology', as explored through the research and teaching of the Sophia Centre, including the MA in Cultural Astronomy and Astrology. The purpose of the conference was to explore aspects of the relationship between the theories and practices of magic and astrology. Arriving at a single definition of astrology is difficult enough, but magic is equally problematic: as Owen Davies wrote, 'Defining "magic" is a maddening task'.[1] We know the origins of the word. 'Magic' is derived from the Greek mageia, which originally referred to the ceremonies and rituals performed by a magos. In the mid–fifth century BCE Herodotus wrote about the magi as a priestly caste.[2] The magi then performed their most celebrated task over four hundred years later by presenting their gifts to the infant Christ, participating (in Christian theology) in the transformation of the entire world to a new phase of existence. But what actually is the practice to which the magi gave their name?

---

[1] Owen Davies, *Magic: A Very Short Introduction* (Oxford: Oxford University Press, 2012), p. 1.
[2] Herodotus, *The Histories*, trans, Aubrey de Sélincourt (Harmondsworth, Middlesex: Penguin, 1972), 1.132.

Definitions of magic vary. Ronald Hutton wrote that it may be conceived of as 'embracing any formalised practices by human beings designed to achieve particular ends by the manipulation and direction of supernatural power or of spiritual power concealed within the natural world'.[3] Manipulation is the key in this view, suggesting that the actor, the magician can be separate to the thing being acted on. A different slant places the magician within the system. For example, according to Rachel Elior, magic consists of those practices specifically concerned with 'developing and maintaining', through the application of human intention, 'the system of bonds and relationships between the revealed and concealed worlds'.[4] For once in such questions there is fair agreement between the academic specialists and the skeptics. For example, *The Sceptic's Dictionary*, considering the term 'magical thinking', rather than 'magic', contains the following passage:

> magical thinking involves several elements, including a belief in the interconnectedness of all things through forces and powers that transcend both physical and spiritual connections. Magical thinking invests special powers and forces in many things that are seen as symbols.[5]

Magical thinking is a participative mode of thought where participation can be understood as a basic human awareness of the interrelatedness of all things in the world. Ariel Glucklich extends this discussion:

> Magic is based on a unique type of consciousness: the awareness of the interrelatedness of all things in the world by means of simple but refined sense perception. This awareness can be called 'magical consciousness' or less ambiguously, the 'magical experience'... Magic does not seek to 'fix' an objective world; it addresses an awareness of a bind that is neither subjective no objective. It straddles the line between the perceiver and the world because the two are part of a unified system, a mental ecology.[6]

---

[3] Ronald Hutton, *Witches, Druids, and King Arthur* (London: Hambledon, 2003), p. 106.
[4] Rachel Elior, 'Mysticism, Magic, and Angelology: The Perception of Angels in Hekhalot Literature', *Jewish Quarterly Review*, Vol. 1 (1993): pp. 3–53, on p. 16.
[5] Robert Carroll, 'Magical Thinking' in The Sceptic's Dictionary, http://skepdic.com/astrolgy.html [accessed 14 November 2016].
[6] Ariel Glucklich, *The End of Magic* (New York: Oxford University Press, 1997), p. 12.

The concept of magic as mental ecology takes us far away from any assumptions that it has to be overtly occult, esoteric or mystical. What I would term 'mundane magic' is developed by Yannik St. James, Jay M. Handelman, and Shirley F. Taylor. In the abstract to their paper on 'Magical Thinking and Consumer Coping', they wrote:

> The analysis of interview and blog narratives of consumers attempting to lose weight reveals how they adopt practices imbued with magical thinking in the form of creative persuasion, retribution, and efficient causality. Magical thinking allows participants to construct a space of uncertainty and ambiguity that transforms impossibilities into possibilities, thus sustaining their hope in the pursuit of goals. In so doing, consumers demonstrate a chimerical agency where they creatively blur fantasy and reality to cope with cultural expectations of control.[7]

Given that the assumption of a binary distinction between fantasy and reality may raise more problems than it solves, the notion of magic as an act of will then is firmly embedded in the mundane world. The writer William Burroughs would have agreed. He wrote that

> Since the word 'magic' tends to cause confused thinking, I would like to say exactly what I mean by 'magic' and the magical interpretation of so-called reality. The underlying assumption of magic is the assertion of 'will' as the primary moving force in this universe–the deep conviction that nothing happens unless somebody or some being wills it to happen. To me this has always seemed self-evident. A chair does not move unless someone moves it. Neither does your physical body, which is composed of much the same materials, move unless you will it to move. Walking across the room is a magical operation. From the viewpoint of magic, no death, no illness, no misfortune, accident, war or riot is accidental. There are no accidents in the world of magic. And will is another word for animate energy.[8]

---

[7] Yannick St. James, Jay M. Handelman, and Shirley F. Taylor, 'Magical Thinking and Consumer Coping', *Journal of Consumer Research*, Vol. 38, no. 4 (December 2011), pp. 632–49, on p. 632.
[8] William Burroughs, 'Rock Magic: Jimmy Page, Led Zeppelin, and a Search for the Elusive Stairway to Heaven' *Crawdaddy,* 1975, http://arthurmag.com/2007/12/05/willima-burroughs-onled-zeppelin/ [accessed 18 October 2014]

For Burroughs magic is a fundamental quality of life. Our ability to walk across a room may be an act so necessary to our survival that it is considered the very opposite of magic as an exceptional phenomenon, but Burroughs reminds that the fact that we can walk across a room, even that we are here at all as reflexive, consciousness beings, is remarkable. So where does that leave celestial magic? For Burroughs the act of travelling to the Moon in 1969 would be likely magical. But let's consider astrology in particular. Many historians look at classical astrology as belonging to the same suite of activities as divination and magic. For example Bertrand Lançon (echoing Hutton's definition of magic as manipulation) wrote that in the Roman world,

> Nature worked on man and, by magic, men could take action in return and alter their destiny. So they assiduously visited diviners, magi and astrologers in order to lift curses, know their future or read their horoscope.[9]

The most mundane application of astral magic is for personal advantage, and personal advantage was often best served by medicine, and the use of amulets, talismans and sigils. This example from a Greek text makes the point:

> Another amulet for the foot of the gouty man: You should write these names on a strip / of silver or tin. You should put in on a deerskin and bind it to the foot of the man named, on his two feet: 'THEMBARATHEM OUREMBRENOUTIPE / AIOXTHOU SEMMARATHEMMOU NAIOOU, let NN, whom NN bore, recover from every pain which in his knees and two feet'. You do it when the moon is [in the constellation] Leo.[10]

The key point here is one of timing. The Moon is in Leo for around two and a half days every month: all other aspects of the healing ritual are therefore enclosed within a framework in which time is qualitative as much as quantitative, and magical actions can only be effective at certain times.

---

[9] Bertrand Lançon, *Rome in Late Antiquity* (Edinburgh: Edinburgh University Press 2000), p. 96.

[10] Hans Dieter Betz, *The Greek magical papyri in translation, including the Demotic Spells* (Chicago: Chicago University Press, 1992), xiv.1003–14, p. 244.

No matter how powerful the magician, a ritual will be ineffective if performed at an inauspicious moment.

From the Islamic world the tenth/eleventh century text known as the *Picatrix* was translated into Latin in the thirteenth century, and included remedies such as this means of gaining relief from a scorpion sting:

> Carve a picture on a stone of Besoar in the hour of the Moon and while the Sun is in the first degree of it and the ascendant is Leo or Aquarius. Mount the stone on a golden ring and stamp it with resin of Kundur in the designated hour and with the Moon in Scorpio. Give the bitten person a dose of it and he will be cured from his ailment.[11]

Such remedial magic constituted one sub-genre of the wider practice. Magic designed to facilitate the soul's ascent might be another. From the turn of the nineteenth to twentieth centuries we find this example from the practices of the Hermetic Order of the Golden Dawn. One ritual designed to facilitate astral travel held in 1900, began as follows:

> We sat in a semi-circle at the north side of the Altar, facing the South, when Mars was in Virgo at the time. Deo Date then made the Invoking Hexagrams of Mars around the room, and the Pentagram of Virgo and the Mars symbol towards the South.[12]

Is astral magic, or astrological magic if we prefer, distinct from astrology as an interpretative and predictive practice based on the use of horoscopes? It certainly has a separate existence to judge from much of the literature: the vast majority of modern western astrological texts concentrate on the reading of horoscopes, rather than activity, whether magical or otherwise. But what if all astrology is magic? This is certainly the way skeptics see it. As Robert Carroll wrote, 'In all forms, astrology is a manifestation of magical thinking'.[13] While Carroll's absolutist statement 'in all forms' is

---

[11] Anon. *Ghayat Al-Hakim. Picatrix: The Goal of the Wise*, trans. Hashem Atallah, (Seattle: Ouroboros Press, 2002), chap V, p. 40. Bezoar is an antidote obtained from goats or antelopes and kundur is incense.

[12] R. A. Gilbert, *The Golden Dawn, Twilight of the Magicians: The Rise and Fall of a Magical Order* (Wellingborough: Aquarian Press, 1983), p. 132. See also Alex Owen, *The Place of Enchantment: British Occultism and the Culture of the Modern* (Chicago: University of Chicago Press, 2004), pp. 156–57.

[13] Robert Carroll, 'Astrology' in *The Sceptic's Dictionary*, http://skepdic.com/astrolgy.html [accessed 14 November 2016].

easy to falsify (there is no necessity for magical thinking in the financial astrologer's plotting of financial graphs in relation to planetary cycles), the general definition of magical thinking is surely compatible with many modern western astrologers' definitions of astrology, particularly what Carroll called the 'belief in the interconnectedness of all things'.[14] For example, Charles Carter, one of the most influential astrologers in the English-speaking world from the 1930s to the 1960s wrote 'Astrology is the science of certain cryptic relations between the celestial bodies and terrestrial life'.[15] Regarding the consideration of magic as action, as proposed by William Burroughs, the following statement was written by the popular American astrologer Donna Cunningham in 1978:

> To believe that you are being buffeted by Pluto or held back by some bad aspect is very short-sighted. What you should see from the various chapters in this book is that every difficult thing in the chart can lead us to positive, constructive insights and actions that will help us move along on the spiritual path. We generally grow through the mastery of the adverse circumstances, inner conflicts and difficult times that we go through. With that in mind, you can regard difficult aspects, transits, and sign placements as opportunities to grow. The true usefulness of a chart, as I see it, is to get a better perspective on yourself, to appreciate your own individuality and potential, and to work toward your most positive expression of self. Your chart is only an instrument panel where you take readings on the course of your life. YOU ARE THE PILOT.[16]

This is stirring stuff; a call to action and a complete rejection of any assumption that fate has to be passively accepted. Like Burroughs, Cunningham talks about an act of will taking place in the mundane world, rather than the manipulation of occult forces. While it be absurd to argue that all astrology is magical, for to do so would be to exclude all other possibilities, it seems clear that some astrology is magical. But, then, if William Burroughs is correct, is anything *not* magical?

---

[14] Robert Carroll, 'Magical Thinking' in The Sceptic's Dictionary, http://skepdic.com/astrolgy.html [accessed 14 November 2016].

[15] Charles Carter, *The Principles of Astrology*, revised edn., (London: Theosophical Publishing House, 1963 [1925]), p. 13.

[16] Donna Cunningham, *An Astrological Guide to Self-Awareness* (Reno: CRCS, 1978), p. 9.

The Themes in this Volume

All the papers published here deal with the human relationship with the sky, for that is the brief of *Culture and Cosmos*. Faced with the task of organizing the papers into themes, it became clear to me that one practice pervaded most of the submissions: alchemy. And one process was dominant: transformation. Magic is then above all a practice, a word which reminds us that it has practical consequences. And that consequence, our contributors conclude, is personal transformation. Such transformation may take us closer to the divine, or make us more self-aware, or may enhance good fortune. But it always locates the individual within the transformative process, rather than apart from it.

We begin with two papers which I have categorized as 'Theory'. Michael Harding muses on the meaning of magic in relation to Wittgenstein and Heidegger, while José Manuel Redondo takes us back to the Platonism of Late Antiquity on which so much of the European tradition is based.

We then move on to 'Practice', beginning with Liz Greene's sweeping account of 'Gemstone Talismans in Western Magical Traditions', Claire Chandler's examination of one text in the collection we know as the 'Greek Magical Papyri'. M. E. Warlick then focuses on the alchemical 'Transgendering of Mercury', and Karen Parham considers the key alchemical text, the *Aurora Consurgens*.

The section on 'Transformation and Ascent' represents a different kind of practice. Alison Greig begins with an exploration of 'Angelomorphism and Magical Transformation in the Christian and Jewish Traditions', and Christine Broadbent moves to Islamic mysticism in her paper on 'Celestial Magic as the "Love Path": The Spiritual Cosmology of Ibn 'Arabi'. Hereward Tilton moves into the early modern world in his study of 'the Invocation of Planetary Spirits in Early Modern Germany', and Joscelyn Godwin in his paper on 'Astral Ascent in the Occult Revival'. Sue Lewis completes this section with a paper on a little known (outside the community of students and practitioners of modern western astrology) school of astrology, popularly known as 'Huber Astrology'.

Finally, staying in the modern world, we conclude with two papers on 'Ritual', Jane Burton's research into the magical rituals of modern spirit mediums and witches, and Lilan Laishley's observations on rituals designed to dispel negative karma in modern Indian astrology.

It is hoped that this volume will provide a valuable addition to the scholarly literature on astrology and magic. It also contributes to our understanding of the emerging discipline of cultural astronomy in both the ancient and modern worlds.

*

Finally I would like to give my deep thanks to Dr Liz Greene, my friend and colleague. Liz was a guest lecturer on the MA in Cultural Astronomy and Astrology at Bath Spa University from 2002, a member of staff at the University of Wales Lampeter/ University of Wales Trinity Saint David from 2007–13, and my partner in the conception and organisation of this conference.

Dr Nicholas Campion,
University of Wales Trinity Saint David.

The Meanings of Magic

Mike Harding

Abstract: This paper explores at how the word 'magic' may be used, drawing mainly on the work of Wittgenstein. Beginning with his critique of Frazer's *The Golden Bough*, the attitudes of science, spirituality and psychotherapy towards magic and ritual and astrology are discussed, and a key passage in *The Tractatus* is used to challenge orthodox concepts of causality and explanation. The idea of 'real magic' as opposed to trickery is addressed via Heidegger's paper *On the Essence of Truth*, and the paper closes with a reflection on a current scientific suggestion that factors previously considered to be permanent might prove to be variable with time.

As I do not knowingly practice magic, and have not made a formal study of those claiming to be magicians, I will confine myself to looking at how the word *magic* might be used, and will draw mainly on the work of Wittgenstein, who had something of a way with words. So let's start with how it has been applied in the context of this conference.

In bringing us together, the organizers have generously created a broad church – or coven – which accords well with academic requirements to 'embrace diversity' and 'acknowledge difference'. In the call for papers, 'magic' was loosely defined as 'the attempt to engage with the world through the imagination or psyche, in order to obtain some form of knowledge, benefit or advantage. Celestial magic engages with the cosmos through stellar, planetary or celestial symbolism, influences or intelligences'. From this we can deduce that an understanding of magic may lie in the imagination or the psyche, which are then used to engage with the cosmos in various ways. Thus one has to ask, do scientists also use their imaginations to engage with cosmic forces in the search for knowledge and to gain advantage? Most theories that attempt to explain the fundamentals of our earthly existence are pinned to the geometry of the cosmos, and rest on the concomitant assumption that universal laws might be found there. To what extent are scientists doing something similar to what astrologers do, but from a different perspective? Might this throw light on why science tends to be so hostile towards astrology? No one put this hostility more clearly than the late John Maddox in his capacity as editor of *Nature*. In his editorial 'Defending Science Against Anti-Science' he asked, with reference to astrology:

> ...Would other professionals, lawyers or accountants say, be as tolerant of public belief that undermined the integrity of their work – and, potentially, their livelihood.[1]

Professional rivalry is admitted, although choosing lawyers and accountants as exemplars of probity might be further questioned. However, *Nature* now has a new editor, and has more recently published an intriguing paper which has more than a whiff of magic about it, and to which I will return at the close.

But first to Wittgenstein, who exhorts us to 'describe, not explain'.[2] He saw his philosophy as a form of therapy: we are to be cured of the confusions with which language endows us, and need to listen carefully to how it frames our perceptions. In his *Remarks on Frazer's Golden Bough* he declares that 'Magic always rests on the idea of symbolism and of language',[3] and in language there is deposited 'a whole mythology'.[4] By this he means that the words we use are far from self-evident; they draw upon much that the speaker has not considered. He continues: 'Simple though it may sound, we can express the difference between science and magic if we say that in science there is progress, but not in magic. There is nothing in magic to show the direction of any development'.[5] By this I understand that magic has not *formally* developed over the centuries, as has science. Furthermore, Wittgenstein states, 'Frazer says it is very difficult to discover the error in magic and that this is why it persists for so long'.[6] Here attention is drawn to Frazer's claim that magic is essentially erroneous but Frazer can't identify *why*. It's odd to assert that an error exists if it can't be stated. Wittgenstein amplifies this with 'Frazer's account of the magic and religious notions of men is unsatisfactory: it

---

[1] John Maddox, 'Defending Science Against Anti-Science', *Nature* 368, no. 6468 (1994): p. 185.
[2] Ludwig Wittgenstein, *Remarks on the Philosophy of Psychology*, Vol. 1 (Oxford: Blackwell, 1980), p. 6.
[3] Ludwig Wittgenstein, *Remarks on Frazer's Golden Bough*, trans. A.C. Miles, ed. Rush Rhees (Norfolk: Brynmill, 1995), p. 4e.
[4] Wittgenstein, *Remarks on Frazer*, p. 10e.
[5] Wittgenstein, *Remarks on Frazer*, p. 13e.
[6] Wittgenstein, *Remarks on Frazer*, p. 2e.

makes these notions appear as mistakes... but none of them was making a mistake except where he was putting forward a theory'.[7]

For Wittgenstein, error lies in the manner in which we theorise our experience. Thus if people dance to create rain there is no error; only if they were to claim that the stamping of feet *caused* rain in some mechanical way would we have a reason to question that assertion. He is particularly harsh with Frazer's theories, which are

> '... much more savage than most of his savages, for these savages will not be so far from any understanding of spiritual matters as an Englishman of the twentieth century. His explanations of the primitive observances are much cruder than the sense of the observances themselves'.[8]

This raises an important point for all of us with regard to engaging with spiritual practices from an academic perspective. Wittgenstein did not *study* spirituality, he practiced it, and it is embedded in much of his philosophy.[9] While it is beyond the remit of this paper to elaborate more fully here, Monk's biography draws out one of Wittgenstein's essential concerns: that 'scientific' thinking bedevils the atheist and the orthodox theologian equally. Both seek a logical proof for God's existence, one in order to deny, the other for confirmation. Thus both commit the same error of seeking to engage with transcendent concepts while omitting to note the obvious: that what lies outside of human language cannot be captured from within it. Only faith remains. For as Wittgenstein put it, 'not how the world is, is mystical, but that it is'.[10] In short, Wittgenstein was talking about mysticism from personal experience. Frazer was not. Indeed, while Wittgenstein goes into some detailed criticism of the *Golden Bough*, he concludes that Frazer was someone 'who cannot imagine a priest who is not basically an English parson of our times with all his stupidity and feebleness'.[11]

Perhaps not the most phenomenological of remarks, but it does remind us that when we attempt to infer what might be 'meant' by the actions of

---

[7] Wittgenstein, *Remarks on Frazer*, p. 1e.
[8] Wittgenstein, *Remarks on Frazer*, p. 8e.
[9] Ray Monk, *Ludwig Wittgenstein: The Duty of Genius* (London: Vintage Books, 1990), pp. 117, 410; Norman Malcolm, *Wittgenstein: A Religious Point of View?* (London: Routledge, 1993), pp. 7–23.
[10] Ludwig Wittgenstein, *Tractatus Logico-Philosophicus* (1921; New York and London: Routledge and Kegan Paul, 2001), para. 6.44.
[11] Wittgenstein, *Remarks on Frazer*, p. 5e.

12 The Meanings of Magic

people from other cultures, or previous ages, we are simultaneously describing the attitudes of our own and seeing them though the lens of what makes sense to us. To some extent this is unavoidable, as clearly we can't make sense of what does not make sense to us, and the language we use inevitably sets up the manner in which we engage with the unfamiliar, as indeed happens when all attempts are made to explain something that lies outside our ken, including magic and the attempts of psychoanalysts to describe the complexities of mental life. What pictures do we draw on at such moments?

For example, from childhood Freud was fascinated by Egyptian artefacts and his language frequently draws on archaeological metaphors.[12] In his paper 'The Aetiology of Hysteria', Freud likened the search for the causes of mental distress to an archaeologist having to 'uncover what is buried, clear away the rubbish'.[13] Thus in each person there are assumed to be hidden memories, unconscious desires, latent thoughts, and so on which apparently follow a clear developmental sequence of psycho-sexual stages, much of which are repressed in a conjectured unconscious. This approach is more fully discussed in the paper 'A Mighty Metaphor: The Analogy of Archaeology and Psychoanalysis' by Donald Kuspit, in which the manner in which Freud's use of *hidden* (or occult) is employed.[14] While objects can be hidden, either deliberately or by the sands of time, *concepts* are another matter. However useful Freud's ideas might be he was, at the very least, mixing his metaphors or, as Wittgenstein describes (see below), confusing one language game with another. Freud did not 'discover' the unconscious. It is not a buried thing, but a theoretical model used to support his *interpretation* of everyday events. For Freud and his followers an interpretation magically transforms a thought or a desire into an object, the assumed roots of which needs to be explored and plundered for its treasures, much like Tutankhamen's tomb. For Wittgenstein, the suggestion that meanings are 'hidden' from the observer ultimately

---

[12] Elliott Oring, *The Jokes of Sigmund Freud: A Study in Humor and Jewish Identity* (New York: Rowman & Littlefield Publishers, 2007), p. 87.

[13] Sigmund Freud, James Strachey, Anna Freud, and Carrie Lee Rothgeb, *The Standard Edition of the Complete Psychological Works of Sigmund Freud: Introductory Lectures on Psycho-analysis*, Vol. III (London: Hogarth Press and the Institute of Psycho-Analysis, 1963), p. 192.

[14] Donald Kuspit, 'A Mighty Metaphor: The Analogy of Archaeology and Psychoanalysis', in *Sigmund Freud and Art: His Personal Collection of Antiquities*, ed. Lynn Gamwell and Richard Wells (London: Thames & Hudson, 1989), pp. 133–52.

devolves to linguistic error. These typically arise from the manner in which phenomena are often described in terms of metaphysics (abstract theories that are presumed to pre-exist and explain the human endeavours under examination) rather than acknowledging the observer's lack of perception, the observer having been captivated by the way in which *a priori* descriptions skew the phenomena. Norman Malcolm's *Wittgenstein: Nothing is Hidden* both includes and extends Wittgenstein's thought on this matter.[15]

In practice, the therapist may be as unaware as the patient as to the *meaning* of the patient's behaviour, but that is quite another matter. To make behaviour explicit is not to look for something *hidden*, but to reinterpret the significance of what the patient is openly describing week after painful week. Just as in the first to second centuries CE, Claudius Ptolemy was able to produce predictions of planetary movement from what would be seen today as a hopelessly confused view of the cosmos, so can Freud's observations be useful; but this no more proves his theories of the hidden than, as Wittgenstein observed, the actor actually feels 'inside' what his character expresses on stage.[16] The suggestion that the unknown is *hidden* or *occult* just because it is not understood is a good example of the tendency to invent a story about what can clearly be seen in terms of what can't be seen, and then using the unseen to explain the visible. In doing so it returns the search for individual meaning to an 'explanation' that, magically, was assumed to pre-exist its occurrence. This is another example of a confusion of language games, where the language of science – which legitimately posits 'hidden causes' (genes, viruses, etc.) to explain physical manifestations – has been unthinkingly employed by psychologists to examine mental life, a move that Wittgenstein claims can only 'lead us into darkness'.[17]

In psychotherapy, descriptions of familiar events can have their individual usage suddenly stripped away by the therapist when they are differently described in terms of a theory (a view) about them; new possibilities then emerge when experienced through the lens of a new language. At such moments our world changes, for language comprises our world.[18] Might a therapist's interpretation – a form of words – be ex-

---

[15] Norman Malcolm, *Wittgenstein: Nothing is Hidden* (Oxford: Blackwell, 1989).
[16] Ludwig Wittgenstein, *Last writings on the Philosophy of Psychology*, Vol. 2, (Oxford: Blackwell, 1994), p. 7e.
[17] Ludwig Wittgenstein, *The Blue Book* (Oxford: Blackwell, 1998), p. 18.
[18] Wittgenstein, *Tractatus*, para. 5.6

perienced as magical if the patient's perceptions – and thus their world – is radically transformed as a consequence? Similarly, many Cognitive Behavioural Therapists will ask their patients to think differently about themselves, often giving them specific phrases to use with the aim of changing their perceptions. Are these phrases forms of incantations? Is this magic if it works, for there is no agreement on what is meant by 'thinking'.[19]

In terms of the 'occult' sources that figure in Freud's thought, it is interesting to record that a noted historian of psychoanalysis has drawn attention to the influence that both the Kabala and the interpretation of the Talmud had on Freud, claiming that 'the fundamental principles of dream interpretation used by Freud are already present in the Talmud',[20] and that the Talmudic interpretative tradition, which often draws on word-play and the importance of associations spoken at the time of the interpretation, fully recognised the significance between a dream's manifest and latent meanings.[21]

In *The Psychopathology of Everyday Life* Freud drew attention to possible meanings in everyday events: the forgotten appointment, the slip of the tongue, etc.[22] Freud's interest in language led him to believe that there was an Ur Language that underlay all speech. He believed that speech originally emerged from the cries and gestures of our earliest ancestors' sexual desire, acknowledging the theories of the philologist Hans Sperber.[23] Some of Freud's views on the origins of language have been extensively questioned;[24] however, the mythology of a God-given language is embedded in the creation myths of many cultures, some of which claim that to understand and use such words with insight endows the

---

[19] Ludwig Wittgenstein, *Philosophical Grammar: Part 1, The Proposition, and its Sense*, trans. Anthony Kenny, ed. Rush Rhees (Oxford: Blackwell, 1993), pp. 154–64; Martin Heidegger, 'On the Essence of Truth' in *Basic Writings*, ed. David Krell (London: Routledge, 1996).
[20] David Bakan, *Sigmund Freud and the Jewish Mystical Tradition* (New York: Van Nostrand, 1958), p. 258.
[21] Bakan, *Freud and Jewish Mystical Tradition*, p. 247.
[22] Sigmund Freud, *The Psychopathology of Everyday Life* (London: Penguin Books, 1991).
[23] Michel Arrivé, *Linguistics and Psychoanalysis: Freud, Saussure, Hjelmslev, Lacan and others*, Vol. 4 of *Semiotic Crossroads*, trans. James Leader (Paris: John Benjamins Publishing, 1992).
[24] John Forrester, *Language and the Origins of Psychoanalysis* (London: The MacMillan Press, 1985).

speaker with magical power. But one of Wittgenstein's students, Maurice Drury, who later became a psychiatrist, gave a stern warning. He said of psychotherapy that it comprises

> highly skilled procedures requiring years of apprenticeship. To communicate these skills from one generation to another psychologists have developed their own technical language... The danger arises when one learns the language without mastering the skills it is meant to mediate.[25]

Many folk stories have been written about acolytes who have seized upon magic spells, only to find, at great cost, that they held unconsidered consequences.

Before considering Wittgenstein's concept of language games and the manner in which their various usages can be employed, it is interesting to note Freud's reply to a research paper sent to him by his colleague Wilhelm Fliess, in which Fliess apparently supplied evidence for astrology. Freud wrote to Fliess: 'There is something to these ideas; it is the symbolic presentiment of unknown realities with which they have in common... one cannot escape from acknowledging heavenly influences. I bow before you as honorary astrologer'.[26] Freud apparently destroyed all of Fliess' letters some time after 1904 for reasons that have never been made clear.[27] In his book *Freud and Man's Soul* the psychologist Bruno Bettelheim also drew attention to astrology when discussing Freud's seminal work *The Interpretation of Dreams*, stating 'the English title gives the impression that Freud presented a definitive treatise on dreams; by failing to summon associations with astrology, it does not suggest the parallel between the discovery of the true nature of the universe and the discovery of the true inner world of the soul'.[28] As Derrida observes, from Plato onwards many thinkers espousing a rational understanding of humanity are often beguiled by the language of what, upon further consideration, they might hold

---

[25] Maurice O'Connor Drury, *The Danger of Words* (Bristol: Thoemmes Press, 1996), p. 138.
[26] Jeffrey Mason, ed., *The Complete Letters of Sigmund Freud to Wilhelm Fliess 1887–1904* (Cambridge, MA: Harvard University Press, 1985), p. 200.
[27] Mason, *Letters of Freud to Fliess*, p. 5.
[28] Bruno Bettelheim, *Freud and Man's Soul* (London: Penguin, 1991), p. 70.

16 The Meanings of Magic

second thoughts.[29] Or, as Wittgenstein put it, we risk 'the bewitchment of our intelligence by the means of language'.[30]

Language Games
Wittgenstein claimed that we use words in all sorts of ways, and each usage contains its own mythology, its own practice. Much of his work in *Philosophical Investigations, Part 1* is devoted to giving extensive examples of this central tenet. To report an event is not the same as singing about it, making a joke about it, creating a diagram of it, or praying for an answer to it. There is always the matter of intention; often that intention is to make something happen, as with magic. Wittgenstein used the phrase 'language games' to draw attention to the fact that all games (chess, football, etc.) have their unique rules (which is what makes them games) but also that these rules are not interchangeable. However, in everyday life we tend to favour a singular example (the wish to see everything described in scientific terms, through the lens of psychoanalysis, religion, political theory or the demands of the academy, etc.). Thus we risk being 'bewitched' by language itself and so fail to notice how an understanding of its Mercurial nature can only be understood within each specific context.[31] The act of kissing the picture of a lover or a saint is incomprehensible without a felt sense of what it is to be in love, or to hold a religious view. Neither can sensibly return to any objective explanation, for all such 'explanations' tend to cast their shadows onto the phenomena they seek to examine. When scientists search for a cause, they tend to ignore the fact that causality is not a law which nature obeys, but the form of words in which science states its propositions about nature.

Such statements might initially make sense because they are internally consistent (and thus bewitch us) so we tend to ignore the possibility that the whole premise on which they are based could be flawed, and thus attempt to prove our theses by utilizing the same methodology from which they were created. This is akin to someone buying a second copy of the same newspaper to check the veracity of the first one. Even mathematics is not immune from this (see below). Similarly, much academic research is bedevilled by such assumptions, which generally seek confirmation of an

---

[29] Jacques Derrida, 'Plato's Pharmacy', in *A Derrida Reader: Between the Blinds*, ed. Peggy Kamuf (Hemel Hempstead: Harvester Wheatsheaf, 1991), p. 112.
[30] Ludwig Wittgenstein, *Philosophical Investigations, Part 1* (Oxford: Blackwell, 1997), p. 47.
[31] Ludwig Wittgenstein, *On Certainty* (Oxford: Blackwell, 1998), p. 57.

enquiry without questioning on what *its* initial assumptions lie. And assumptions they are, for they can never be finally grounded. They are recursive arguments that hover, so to speak, over the *unspeakable*. This is one of the central points of the *Tractatus*, to which Wittgenstein often returned: that what we can usefully say about the world rests on what we *cannot* formally articulate. If you like, it rests on an inchoate, embodied sense of the world and ourselves which grounds our being in ways that we cannot ultimately describe. Magic, as a practice with its own mythology, would also fall into this category. It is a well-used word, but to what does it return?

In section six of *The Tractatus* Wittgenstein addresses the issue of cause and explanation stating:

> At the basis of the whole modern view of the world lies the illusion that the so-called laws of nature are explanations of natural phenomena.

So people stop short at natural laws, as did the ancients at God and Fate.

And they both are right and wrong. But the ancients were clearer, insofar as they recognised one clear terminus, whereas the modern system makes it appear as though *everything* were explained.[32]

For Wittgenstein, ancient people, and indeed many who currently hold religious views, acknowledge a terminus. Events and practices are ultimately the way they are because God decreed them so, and thus no further explanations are needed. This is generally unsatisfactory in a more secular world, and while all sorts of conjectured laws are pressed into service to fill the absence of the Deity, they can never hold the authority of what has been removed by their endeavours. In attempting to replace God with science, it has to be acknowledged that there is no way of proving the ultimate veracity of the language game they are using; mathematics itself is an invention that is continually on the move, and thus cannot come to rest on a finite truth. Many forms of mathematics have been created to solve problems that only exist within mathematics, and have no place within the world. As with magic, they 'do' things in their own way and can bring benefits. Their formulae are often as attractive for their beauty to modern physicists as they were for Plato, and the thought of God can still surface in their discussions. Einstein suggested that God did not play dice.[33]

---

[32] Wittgenstein, *Tractatus*, para. 6.371 and 6.372.
[33] Ian Stewart, *Does God Play Dice? The Mathematics of Chaos* (Oxford: Blackwell, 1989), p. 1.

18 The Meanings of Magic

Hawking suggests that his theories might lead to 'knowing the mind of God'.[34] Recently billions of euros have been spent on a search for the God-Particle, which apparently might be located under Switzerland – the traditional source of buried wealth.

But mathematics – the practice of counting and measuring that is the bedrock of science – suggests that it offers a picture of reality, but actually returns to a tautology. The formula that ends with the claim: Therefore X=2, tells us only that 2=2. Worse still, it does not tell us what 2 *is* or why 2+2 might equal 4. Yes, it makes sense, for that is how we have been taught. But we cannot state *why* something makes sense to us without returning to a recursive argument, or 'stopping short' – as did the ancients. While mathematics is incredibly useful and makes possible much of today's world, it cannot establish its fundamental veracity as it always comes to rest on its own practice. To suggest otherwise would return us to a universe in which God is the final arbiter, an argument invariably rejected by secularists.

While any reasonably numerate person can use numbers effectively, even if they couldn't calculate as did the Romans (try multiplying L times MCDXV without first translating it into Arabic notation) how do we make sense of Daniel Tammet, who ascribes his amazing ability for calculation to his diagnosis of high-functioning Asperger Syndrome? Tammet offers this description of how he calculates, for example, the fifth power of 37 (69,343,957, if you want to know) or divides 13 by 97 to some 100 decimal places:

> When I divide one number by another, in my head I see a spiral rotating downwards in larger and larger loops, which seem to warp and curve.. When multiplying I see two numbers as distinct shapes. The image changes and a third shape emerges – the correct answer. The process takes a matter of seconds and happens spontaneously.[35]

While most of us can also arrive at the correct answer 'spontaneously' for simple problems, such as 2 x 50 (even if we would be hard pressed to offer an explanation that did not return to a claim that we 'know' this to be so, which is not an explanation at all, but merely evidences that we do know it), his account, although clearly stated, is mysterious. It is based on a practice that effortlessly bypasses the methods we have been taught. While

---

[34] Stephen Hawking, *A Brief History of Time* (New York: Bantam, 1998), p. 193.
[35] Daniel Tammet, *Born on a Blue Day* (London: Hodden & Stoughton, 2006), p. 4.

we may be tempted to think that, somehow or other, he translates the hard currency of numbers into shifting colours and shapes, this would be mistaking our problem with Roman notation, of having to translate letters into Arabic numbers using an established set of criteria (L=50, M=1000, etc.). What Tammet achieves is of quite a different order, for there is no such public agreement on the shape and colour of numbers. His ability fundamentally questions the essential nature of numbers and how they might be portrayed. Insomuch as he can 'do' something that is, I suspect, incomprehensible to those not similarly gifted, can this be thought of as magical?

The Meanings of Magic
How is this familiar word to be understood when it tends to be applied to the unfamiliar? Are all of us playing the same language game? Do some of us believe that 'real' magic exists – that there are some people who can *actually* cast spells that make things happen – without any form of trickery? Here the word 'believe' already sets something up. It would not make much sense if I asked you whether you believe in tables and chairs; the word 'belief' carries within itself the mythology of 'doubt' that casts its own shadow on the question and turns it into something else. Thus it is probable that a magician is seen as someone who acts out a linguistic role without authenticity. We are seeing an actor who can cast a spell on the audience that echoes the 'spelling' of his role, but is ultimately as false as the greasepaint on his face. If such was the case, then the word *magic* would be synonymous with *fake*, as Frazer suggested, but could not elucidate. Or is magic a word that defines something not fully understood? If so, is the existence of the universe then magical? Are *we* all magical, even if we do not know ourselves completely?

How could we tell?

If we are unsure as to what is true or false (real magic versus a trick played on the gullible, genuine psychotherapy versus quackery, etc.) and could give no reason for this linguistic distinction, as Frazer acknowledged with regard to magic, then the concept of true and false would be meaningless in such situations as no evaluative criteria could be established. Heidegger amplifies this quandary when discussing true gold and false gold.[36]

His discussion proceeds thus: one coin is described as true, the other false. We can compare one coin to another with reference to its description

---
[36] Heidegger, 'Essence of Truth', pp. 120–23.

as being true or false and come to a judgement. All well and good. But how can we come to a judgement as to the veracity of the descriptions that *pre-exist* what they seek to validate? We can compare a thing to its referent – that it does or does not accord to a specific description – but how can we assess the authenticity of the definitions in the first place without returning to the object that, apparently, only gains *its* authenticity from descriptions, when the descriptions themselves contain the essential problem? Are the descriptions true or false? And how would we know except, perhaps, by offering further amplifying clauses which, in their turn, would require yet further substantiation *ad infinitum*?

Now, at least may I make one thing clear. I am not going to wander off into the far reaches of post-modernism and decry 'reality' as a purely linguistic artefact. For me, the concept of authenticity has real value. In terms of this paper there would be a profound difference between magic as a trick – and thus not magic at all – and some form of practice that, inexplicably, has a demonstrable consequence. Nor do I suggest that just because something is meaningful to individuals that it necessarily substantiates the authenticity of their claims. In the course of my work as a psychotherapist I have met two people who held the opinion that they were Jesus Christ. While such claims might emerge from a misunderstanding of the Christian claim that God is within us, having erroneous ideas about ourselves is hardly uncommon. Others have offered examples of what is known as magical thinking: the belief that their thoughts are controlled by rays emitted by the television. Here I would have to ask: to what extent are all our thoughts about the world informed by what we have read or heard? How powerful words can be!

Those holding extreme views of themselves tend to be in thrall to their intense convictions, in the face of which no other opinion counts; in other words, the world is ignored in favour of Cartesian self-reference. Kenny states that Descartes assumed that the mind 'can recognize its own thoughts while holding in suspense the question of the existence of the external world'.[37] As it is precisely the external world (language, culture, etc.) which endows us with all the concepts we believe (or doubt, in Descartes' case) it is clear that the classic Cartesian mind/body split is deeply flawed, although many experiencing delusions or other forms of mental suffering appear to act in the manner Descartes describes, where aspects of the world are assumed to have originated from within themselves.

---

[37] Anthony Kenny, *Wittgenstein* (London: Pelican Books, 1975), p. 16.

For example, many of those diagnosed as suffering from an Obsessive Compulsive Disorder (OCD) have clear rituals – hand-washing, counting, making gestures – that are used to ameliorate their anxiety. While these rituals tend to bring temporary relief, sufferers generally acknowledge the ultimate futility of their actions and are often embarrassed by them. But the idea of cleansing rituals is powerful in many cultures and forms an essential part of innumerable religious practices. In the case of OCD it would seem that the idea of ritual behaviour has somehow lost its mythological roots and become dissociated from a social context, consequently devoid of authentic meaning. Many therapists acknowledge the importance of ritual in their own work: the same time each week, the same room, and so on. Therapeutic time is not linear, but better accords with sacred or mythological time when 'the same' returns, as do the familiar seasons.

I raise these points, not in any way to suggest that magical rites are pathological – although some might be carried out for confused and ultimately useless purposes which might benefit from investigation – but to draw attention to how ritual plays a part in many different language games, of which formal magic is but one.

But what of astrology, a craft that interprets the mathematics of the solar system in its own way? As well as being a psychotherapist, I am also an astrologer. That is, I draw on various models that attempt to make sense of the human subject and the world by using the language game of astrology in ways that are meaningful to me. But I do not indulge in any occult practices. Quite the reverse. All that I have published over thirty years has been written *explicitly* to describe those astrological practices that I find useful, and those that I do not.[38]

While I can explain why I find certain approaches *useful* by supplying examples I cannot demonstrate their ultimate correctness. Such an attempt would miss the point that both Wittgenstein and Heidegger have raised with regard to the impossibility of ultimately measuring *how* we measure. How do we know that the manner in which we perceive, measure, and describe the world is the *correct* way? Again, this would demand access to a God-given injunction: the final terminus that Wittgenstein drew attention to in the *Tractatus*.

---

[38] Michael Harding, *Hymns to the Ancient Gods* (London: Penguin/Arkana, 1992); Michael Harding and Charles Harvey, *Working with Astrology* (Frome: Consider Books, 2004).

There can be no final judge, beyond their applicability in the life of an individual, which is far from unimportant. And if I make a correct prediction, would this be an objective proof of astrology? No. For if asked *how* I had done this, all I could do would be to return to a description of my method. I cannot state why it worked. Yes, I might have an insight that others might miss, just as others may see what I have failed to recognise, but this is true of any discipline. Indeed, all research is beset with disagreement. In this respect Rudiger Safranski, a former student of Heidegger, observed:

> ... nature offers different answers according to how we question it... And all of this is a creative process, since every design of Being produces, materially and spiritually, a world interpreted and organized in a definite way.[39]

The point is that we tend to focus exclusively on what has been revealed, and not on the fact that *the world* is such that this can happen; i.e., ultimately our quandaries lie in what we have taken from the world. The central issue – the fact of Being itself – has been ignored at the moment of its showing, obscured by a 'truth' that is always partial and, like language, is always on the move.

But this, so it appears, is similarly suggested by science.

Cosmic Habituation

A new concept has recently emerged in the field of medical research: Cosmic Habituation. The phrase evolved as a consequence of researchers noting that initial findings were convincingly replicated, but as time went by the significance dropped off. Once, those diagnosed as psychotic who were given certain drugs at the onset of their condition reported real benefit. Today, those experiencing similar distress, and being given the *same* medication for the *first* time, do not respond in the same way as those treated identically in earlier times. It is fundamental to science that, if the same procedures are used in the same circumstances, there should be similar outcomes. But this appears not to be the case. Thus has emerged the remarkable idea that the cosmos is changing in some inexplicable manner. In 2011 the journal *Nature* carried a research paper that drew attention to this phenomenon, subsequently termed Cosmic Habituation.[40]

---

[39] Rudiger Safranski, *Martin Heidegger: Between Good and Evil* (Cambridge, MA: Harvard University Press, 1998), p. 219.

[40] John Schooler, 'Unpublished Results Hide the Decline Effect', *Nature* 470 (2011): p. 437.

Somehow or other, we appear to be living in a world that is time-dependent. When repeated, the same procedures do not produce the same results. This would appear to echo the astrological model which claims that all is in flux; while essential human concerns contain much similarity, how they are expressed in the everyday world shifts within its unique language that, like all languages, does not stay still.

The idea of Cosmic Habitation presents a challenge to the traditional scientific model with its suggestion that, with all on the move, there can be no certain point of departure, and thus little hope for a unified theory of everything: in other words, the idea of a universal meta-language that Wittgenstein so forcibly rejects.

This is equally true for those astrologers who seek the validation of some assumed originating source. As a version of this paper was given at the *Celestial Magic* conference we should end with the thought that, while the act of 'reading the stars' for the purpose of obtaining meaning is of a different order than reading a book, both practices rely on agreed-upon procedures for the interpretation of signs. All forms of language are deeply mysterious. What mystery is taking place as you read this?

The Celestial Imagination: Proclus the Philosopher on Theurgy[1]

José Manuel Redondo

Abstract: This paper focuses on Proclus's *On the hieratic art of the Greeks* – considered as a contemporary philosophical problem – exploring some of its fundamental concepts and images, thus delineating Proclus's notion of theurgy, which he primarily conceived as divine action manifesting in the union between a god and the theurgist, and only secondarily as a technique. These aesthetic experiments of thought or philosophical performances, by means of which a divine self is created, had deep metaphysical, cosmological, psychological, ethical, linguistic and even political and religious implications for Late Antiquity Platonism, and had a profound impact on the development of Renaissance philosophy and magic. Such practices are meant to be understood in the context of the philosophical *paideia* of which it represents its final stage and consummation; they are developed by intricate hermeneutics of a poetic theology operated by very sophisticated conceptions of symbol, analogy and the imagination, all of which are at the base of the celestial-terrestrial correspondences used by theurgists in their hymn singing.

In this paper I present some of the main ideas I have been working on in relation to the problem of theurgy in Late Antiquity and Platonism in general, particularly Proclus's conception of theurgy and specifically in regard to the surviving passages of his text on theurgy (which he called *hieratike techne*), *On the hieratic art of the Greeks*. One of Proclus's most comprehensive definitions of theurgy is as follows:

> theurgic power (*theourgikē dynamis*), which is more excellent than all human wisdom, and which comprehends divination's good (*mantikes agathe*), the

---

[1] Substantial portions of this text have been already published by Brill in José Manuel Redondo, 'The Transmission of Fire: Proclus' Theurgical Prayers', in *Platonic Theories of Prayer*, ed. J. Dillon and A. Timotin (Studies in Platonism, Neoplatonism, and the Platonic Tradition 19) (Leiden: Brill, 2016). I thank the publishers whom kindly gave permission to use this material and re-publish parts of it here.

purifying powers in the accomplishment of the rites, and in short, all such things as are the effects of divine possession (*entheou katakojes energemata*).[2]

While I will make observations regarding philosophical notions expressed in several other texts of his, as well as in Iamblichus's *On the mysteries of the Egyptians* (a necessary reference for Proclus's theurgy), I will focus mainly on the passages from *On the hieratic* that are considered among the most important surviving expositions of ancient philosophy on theurgy. I will also consider fragments of *The Chaldaic Philosophy* and his own hymns.[3] Proclus's Platonic theology and theurgy would become one of the main influences in the development of Renaissance magic as theorized and practiced by philosophers such as Marsilio Ficino.

Allow me then to start by addressing the Muses, as both poets and theurgist do, in order to gain their favour for such an audacious enterprise.[4] I'll quote a few verses from Proclus's own hymn composed to the Muses:

---

[2] Numeni D'Apamea, *Oráculos Caldeos: con una selección de testimonios de Proclo, Pselo y M. Itálico. Fragmentos y Testimonios*, ed. Francisco García Bazán (Madrid: Biblioteca Clásica Gredos, 1991); Proclus, *Platonic Theology* (Frome: The Prometheus Trust, 1999), I.25, 113, 7–10; Proclus, *The Six Books of Proclus on the Theology of Plato*, trans. Thomas Taylor (London: A. J. Valpy, 1816), available at http://www.universaltheosophy.com/pdf-library/1816_Six-Books-of-Proclus-on-the-Theology-of-Plato_vols-1-2.pdf [accessed 30 November 2016]; and Proclus, *Théologie platonicienne*, 6 vols, ed. and trans. H. D. Saffrey and L. G. Westerink, Collection des universités de France (Paris: Les Belles Lettres, 1968–1997), p. 81.

[3] The translations from Proclus's passages *On the hieratic art* are mine. The only translation in English that I know of is found in Brian Copenhaver, 'Hermes Trismegistus, Proclus and the question of a philosophy of Magic in the Renaissance', in *Hermeticism and the Renaissance*, ed. Ingrid Merkel and Allen G. Debus (Washington, DC: Folger Books, 1988), the edition of the Greek taken from Joseph Bidez, *Catalogue des manuscrits alchimiques grecs*, Vol. 6 (Brussels: M. Lamertin, 1928). For Proclus's hymns, see the edition, translation into English and with commentary by R. M. Van den Berg, *Proclus' Hymns: Essays, Translations, Commentary* (Leiden: Brill, 2001). Regarding Proclus's biography (*Vita Procli*) by Marinus, see Mark Edwards, *Neoplatonic Saints. The Lives of Plotinus and Proclus by their Students* (Liverpool: Liverpool University Press, 2000). For passages in Marinus's *Vita Procli* about Proclus's theurgical activities, see Marinus of Neapolis, *Marino de Neápolis: Proclo o De la felicidad*, trans. J. M. Álvarez Hoz and J. M. García Ruiz (Irún: Iralka, 1999), especially paragraphs 17–19, 24, 28–29.

[4] For Proclus, as I will very briefly mention later in the text, both poets and theurgists operate with the same mythological hermeneutics; they are co-

We hymn, we hymn the light that raises man aloft,
on the nine daughters of great Zeus with splendid voices,
who have rescued from the agony of this world, so hard to bear,
the souls who were wandering in the depth of life
through immaculate rites from intellect-awaking books,
and have taught them to strive eagerly to follow the path leading
beyond the deep gulf of forgetfulness, and to go pure to their kindred star
from which they strayed away, when once they fell
into the headland of birth, mad about material lots.
But, goddesses, put an end to my much-agitated desire too
and throw me into ecstasy through the noeric words of the wise.[5]

I. Theurgy in context

It is now becoming a common place in studies on Neoplatonic theurgy to point out how in the last decades the assessment of the ancient Platonists' practice of rituals has changed enormously in some respects; at least in specialized circles this is no longer considered an embarrassing fact for the history of philosophy. In part this has occurred due to pertinent comparative studies between theurgy and diverse Mediterranean and Near-Eastern religious, mystical, magical and divinatory traditions; fields of study which, significantly, have also undergone important changes in the last decades, among them, a growing awareness of the indissoluble link between divination and magic, as well as between divination and religion and between magic and religion.[6] Three aspects – divination, religion and magic – are actually encompassed by what Platonists call theurgy, which is both a philosophical and mystical interpretation of Mediterranean religious traditions (including Greek, Egyptian, Chaldean, Assyrian, Persian) which conceives magic and divination as two facets of a complex activity supposed to be necessarily examined and practiced critically through philosophy but at the same time providing a non-discursive philosophical language in a sense complementary to formal demonstration

---

extensive. Myths have an analogous function to the initiations, that is, to incite and awaken the soul.
[5] Van Den Berg, *Proclus' Hymns: Essays, Translations.*
[6] For a recent and insightful update of this discussion, see Sarah Iles Johnston, *Ancient Greek Divination* (Oxford: Blackwell, 2008), particularly Ch. 5, 'The *Mantis* and the Magician'; interestingly, here, both theurgy and the practices of the *Greek Magical Papyri* are characterized as divinatory magic. For divination as the language of magic, see p. 13 and pp. 166–69. For divination as the instantiation of myths, see p. 114. Proclus's *On Providence*, trans. Carlos Steel (New York: Cornell University Press, 2007), p. 39.

but in another sense superior to it. The significant, important changes in the last decades in diverse fields of study related to research on theurgy belong, at the same time, to what seems to be the start of a major reconsideration or shift in our understanding of Neoplatonism, a category no longer entirely acceptable for the specialists, with at least some of them questioning the pertinence of it, given that it was created by seventeenth century German Protestant theologians to pejoratively identify and separate from Plato those Platonists who were the most severe critics of Christianity, in regard of which Plato was wanted to be seen as their natural (or even providential) precedent. This shift, in its turn, seems to encompass our understanding of ancient Greek philosophy as a whole in general, which, as has been recently suggested in the case of Plato and Aristotle, that they have far more in common with the philosophies of India and China than with modern European philosophy, which claims Greek philosophy as its prestigious ancestor.[7]

To speak of theurgy in late Platonism in general is a useful standardization of modern academic research but which may limit our understanding of what is envisaged as a complex and polyvalent phenomenon which in its different facets is designated by several names: *hietarike techne*, *telestike*, *katharmoi*, mystagogy, theosophy, *hiera hagisteia*, *theagogia*, *he theia episteme*, *hierourgia*, *theon therapeia*, telesiourgy, etc. However, there seems to be lacking a discussion of theurgy as a *philosophical praxis*; that is, not as a religious, magical or even esoteric practice done by philosophers, thus conceived as a complement to philosophy, but as a philosophical practice *per se*. Proclus refers to theurgists (*hoi hieratikoi*) as *palai sophoi*, the *ancient sages* to whom the hieratic art was revealed, thus making of theurgy an equivalent to standard, traditional divine service. Nevertheless this idea seems to be affirmed only by the Platonic philosophers in general. So, I would like to propose that while Proclus seems to consider theurgy as an exercise of both poetic and ritual analogical thinking and living, theurgy itself is conceived in Proclus's philosophy as analogue to the religious, mystical and magical ancient traditions, but is never simply identical to them. This is what we may call a holistic hermeneutical exercise that requires simultaneously both a philosophical understanding of analogy and an analogical understanding of philosophy.

---

[7] Christos C. Evangeliou, *Hellenic Philosophy. Origin and Character* (Bodmin: MPG Books, 2006).

In the Platonism of Late Antiquity, theurgy is conceived according to lengthy and complex argumentative exercises regarding the limitations of reason and language. The goal of theurgy, expressed in mythical form as divinization (*theiosis*), is consummated in the ecstatic union of the soul with its leader or guardian deity, through that which is called psychologically the *one in the soul*, or in the poetics of revelation, the *flower of the intellect* and the *flower of the whole soul*. Such an experience seems to imply the creation, or activation, of a *divine self*, mediated by complex thought and imagination techniques as well as by the ethical practice that purifies both, driven in coordinated fashion by an Eros oriented, at the same time, by Beauty. This is a conception – making a very wide generalization – where the imagination, in a deep and important sense, may be a vehicle of knowledge and even be identified with *nóesis*, primary or essential knowledge. The imagination is represented as the fundamental epistemological activity of the soul, where we perceive both sensation and thought, but also as the foundation of all of our experience as memory.

The imagination has an active role revealing knowledge, but in order to effectively do so it's necessary that the philosopher generates the corresponding state of fitness (*epitedeiotes*) or capacity to receive that knowledge, to transform the imagination into a vehicle of comprehension by means of the ethical reform of his body, his emotions and his thought, but according to an integral conception of thought much broader and deeper than the single exercise of rational discourse, one that causes, integrates and coordinates simultaneously sensation, emotion and reflexivity. This active or creative imagination, subtle vehicle (*ochema pneuma*) of the soul, also pictured as descending from the stars and thus an astral vehicle or celestial imagination, is the faculty of divinization by excellence; the imagination divinizes, if I may put it so; it is hieratic, it is theurgy or divine action, a creative dynamic.[8] Gregory Shaw, whose work has been a landmark towards a different and deeper, more sensible understanding of Neoplatonic theurgy, has pointed out how theurgy for the Platonists is a recreation of demiurgy, the activity of the creator god

---

[8] Regarding the notion of the *ochema pneuma* or astral vehicle (or astral body*)*, see: Francisco García Bazán, *El cuerpo astral* (Barcelona: Ediciones Obelisco, 1993); and the study by John Finamore, *Iamblichus and the Theory of the Vehicle of the Soul*, American Classical Studies 14 (Oxford: Oxford University Press, 1985). Also the article by Robert Christian Kissling, 'The OXHMA-PNEUMA of the Neo-Platonists and the de Insomniis of Synesius of Cyrene', *The American Journal of Philology*, Vol. 43, no. 4 (1922): pp. 318–30.

presented by Plato in the *Timaeus*.⁹ Soul irradiates intelligence and life to bodies like the heavens emanate light and life to our world, thus participating of the divine, the cosmos being eternally created. Proclus's *Eighteen arguments on the eternity of the cosmos* is probably the most representative text of antiquity on this topic and certainly a seminal influence in the debate of the same during the subsequent centuries in the medieval theological traditions. The human being, through soul – his essential nature considered precisely as his soul – participates in that which may be said to characterize divinity: creativity, actualizing his capacity as co-creator and ruler of the cosmos of his experience. But humans may only do this according to their capacity to align with the divine, so to speak.¹⁰ All theurgical acts are done by assimilation and familiarity, not by compulsion.¹¹ Theurgists never believe that they can coerce the gods, as vulgar magicians do, but they are the loving servitors of loving deities, which in their turn are the loving servitors of an utterly transcendent, unknowable and ineffable first god, or first principle, depending whether we refer to a theological or metaphysical discourse or to that which is also represented both as Unity and the Good.

II. Theurgic perspectives

The hieratic arts are contextualized according to several simultaneous philosophical perspectives – theological, cosmological, psychological, literary, etc. – all analogues to each other in several possible ways. Perspectives to which I will point, even if very briefly, by just sketching the main lines; but I'll try to do so by examining a contextualization of the discussion of theurgy as a philosophical practice of some kind, not a religious, magical or even esoteric practice, not essentially. One of the most important of such perspectives is the philosophical notion of *mania* – inspired knowledge, metaphorically termed madness – as referring to something incomprehensible and related to the above mentioned critical consciousness of the Platonists regarding the limits of discursive rationality's formal demonstrations. Like Socrates in the opening passage of *Phaedrus*, the *maniai*, the diverse forms of divine inspiration, as an

---

⁹ Proclus, *Commentary on the Timaeus of Plato*, 2 vols (Frome: The Prometheus Trust, 2006), IV, 847; Gregory Shaw, *Theurgy and the Soul: The Neoplatonism of Iamblichus* (University Park, PA: Pennsylvania State University Press, 1995).

¹⁰ Iamblichus, *On the mysteries, De mysteriis,* translated with introduction and notes by Emma C. Clarke, John M. Dillon and Jackson P. Hershbell (Atlanta, GA: Society of Biblical Literature, 2003); II.11.

¹¹ Iamblichus, *On the mysteries*, III.18.

experience to be lived by the philosopher – not only as a concept – take us away from public places or common notions of our mental *polis*, outside the walls of the city of our ordinary cultural habits.[12] Could we thus conceive theurgy as a kind of *reasonable madness*, a form of ethical symbolical practice of self-knowledge, based on what we may call aesthetic experiments of thought or philosophical performances?[13] If we understand that the forms or ideas, paradigms of virtue for the Platonists, are conceived as analogue to the gods, then ethics may be understood as analogous to ritual practice as the repetition of the paradigmatic, considered as divine (strictly speaking, the divine is the origin of the paradigmatic); as the establishment of a virtue as a habit that incarnates, that expresses in the world, manifesting thus the divine; and as what is just in itself or the idea of justice, for example, through the philosopher's just actions. The just and good human being, in its practice of piety, assimilates to the divine, becoming its living image.[14]

Initiatory rites (*telestike*), for example, seem to be interpreted as, and at the same time, through the ethical perfectioning (*teleo*) of the soul. Philosophically, divination is understood as a practice of self-knowledge, Socrates being the exemplar diviner, he who made his life's work to interpret the Delphic oracle, not just intellectually but mainly, or rather, integrally, by the way he lived.[15] For the Platonists, philosophy is the original activity of the human being, not just the activity of a group of specialists, professionals and bureaucrats; the philosopher is thought of as the paradigmatic human being. Put in a simple formula, we may say that in Platonism, regarding the individual, religion is to be understood as an ethical practice, whereas regarding the community and the state, religion is to be understood as politics, in both cases expressed and practiced along the philosophical discourse in mythical language, or in a mythical mode of

---

[12] Plato, *Phaedrus* (227a), in Plato, *Phaedrus, Diálogos I. Apología. Critón. Eutifrón. Ión. Lisis. Cármides. Hipias Menor. Hipias Mayor. Laques. Protágoras*, introduction by Francisco Lisi, with introduction, translation and notes by J. Calonge Ruiz, E. Lledó Íñigo, and C. García Gual. (Barcelona: Gredos, 2003).
[13] Iamblichus, *On the mysteries*, II.11, 96–97; for *symbolic mystagogy*, see VII.2.
[14] Plato, *Republic* 383c, in Plato, *Diálogos IV. Republic, Timaeus, Critias.* translation and notes by J. Calonge Ruiz. E. Acosta Méndez. F. J. Oliveri, and J. L. Calvo (Madrid: Gredos, 2000).
[15] For Iamblichus, for example, true divination is identified with what he considers to be the true philosophical understanding (See *On the mysteries*, III.31). As for Socrates' mission set by the oracle of Apollo, see Plato's *Apology*, in Plato, *Diálogos I.*

discourse; in this way reifying the celestial script of the cosmic law or *Logos*, which is expressed by the stars.[16]

In the *Timaeus,* Plato distinguishes between secondary or auxiliary causality, which refers to that which is more immediate, and a primary or essential causality which refers not to the *how* but to the *what* and above all the *why*; that is, the end or goal, the reason of being, the meaning or purpose of something.[17] In a very general way, even though it is possible and necessary to distinguish primary and secondary causality in Platonism, they are inseparable and operate simultaneously. According to this model, theurgy can only secondarily be considered a human activity and technique that operates through the network of natural correspondences between the gods and the diverse substances in the realm of secondary or auxiliary causality. Theurgy is then essentially an eternal intelligible activity of the gods and primary causality, in which the human being participates along with cosmological and natural dynamics. Such dynamics are themselves an image, an eternal recreation of divine activity. That is, the cosmos is the result or effect of the god's theurgy and it is the gods that illuminate the philosopher's imagination.[18] In this case, theurgy can be imagined according to a mythological hermeneutics that interprets mythic images simultaneously as representations of metaphysical and ethical dynamics, in their turn conceived as analogous to cosmological dynamics. So it is that the same cosmological activity may be formally reasoned as caused by the intelligible, and reasoned by the imagination (*nous phantastikos*), as originating in the gods. The fundamental analogy is between the forms and the gods. However, to talk of the gods as such presupposes already a poetic theology or mythological hermeneutics, while talking about the forms presupposes coordinated metaphysical and ethical hermeneutics.[19]

---

[16] For late antique Platonists mystical politics, see Dominic J. O'Meara, *Platonopolis: Platonic Political Philosophy in Late Antiquity* (Oxford: Clarendon Press, 2003).

[17] Plato, *Timaeus* 46e,d and 47a,b, in Plato, *Diálogos VI*; Plato, *Philebus* 27a8–9, in Plato, *Diálogos V. Parménides. Teeteto. Sofista. Político*, introduction, translation and notes by Ma. Isabel Santa Cruz. Á. Vallejo Campos, and N. Luis Cordero (Madrid: Gredos, 2000); Plato, *Politicus* 281c-e, in Plato, *Diálogos V*.

[18] See for example, Iamblichus, *On the mysteries*, III.14, and Proclus, *Commentaire sur la Republique (On the Republic)*, trans. and notes J. Festugiere (Paris: J. Vrin, 1970), 1.39, 9–17; 2.167, 2–6 and 17–23.

[19] For Proclus, for example, the analogy between the forms and the gods seems that always stays thus, never are both of those terms completely identified. We may even say that this analogical relationship is metaphysical for Proclus, though

This causality model implies, in its turn, a corresponding twofold model of reason and rationality in dialectical relationship: a primary reason and rationality, *nous poietikos* and *noesis* (an active intellect, cause of our being and of our activity of knowing), and a secondary form of reason and rationality, *nous pathetikos* and *dianoia* (a passive intellect whose activity is reflexive discourse), according to Plotinus's standardization.[20] Again, this model in its turn implies a corresponding twofold model of language: one side of it is based on human convention, whose dynamic, in philosophical usage, must be logical; and the other may be seen as a natural, metaphorical aspect of language whose dynamics are based in

---

not ontological, since the gods, as mythological representations of the *henads* or unities, are as such above being, thus their nature is unknowable; however, they may be known by way of analogy and similarity through their own symbols (*symbola* and *synthemata*), but not by trying to think about them – the gods – through their symbols, but, through their symbols, the theurgist is able to unite with them:

> Since Iamblichus asserts that questions may be discussed, in a philosophical, theological, or theurgical manner, it is possible to see the cosmological description of the Forms as proper to philosophical discourse while an anagogic description would stress the theurgic function of the Forms as *sunthêmata*. In other words, although every soul was created by the Demiurge with harmonic ratios (*logoi harmonikoi*) (*On the Timaeus* I,4,32), and divine symbols (*sumbôla theia*; *On the Timaeus* I,4,32–33), the former where active in all souls by virtue of cosmogenesis while the later remained inactive until awakened in theurgy. Thus, when the *logoi* that constitute the soul's essence where ritually appropriated and awakened in the life of the soul, these *logoi* could then be called *sumbôla* or *sunthêmata* (In Shaw, *Theurgy and the Soul*, pp. 164–65).

[20] A distinction very similar to the platonic *noesis* and *dianoia* (Plato, *Republic*, VI.509d). For Plotinus, see for example the *Enneads*, trans. A. H. Armstrong, The Loeb Classical Library, (London: Harvard University Press, 1984), V.9, 3 and V.9, 5 1–10. However they may be distinguished, their difference is not literal or logical, but in the end, I would say, metaphorical. For Plato, true being is to be apprehended by *noesis* together with *logos* (*Timaeus*, 28a), see Proclus, *Commentary On the Timaeus*, I.341, 13–16; I.248, 1–6. Pierre Hadot observes, regarding discursive reasoning:

> But this is only ratiocination, and ratiocination, always remaining on the plane of consciousness and reflection, does not really allow us to know the levels of divine reality which it distinguishes. It is only a preliminary exercise, a support and a springboard. Knowledge, for Plotinus, is always experience, or rather, it is an inner metamorphosis. What matters is not that we know rationally that there are two levels of divine reality, but that we internally raise ourselves up to this levels, and feel them within us as two different tones of spiritual life (In Pierre Hadot, *Plotinus or The Simplicity of Vision* [Chicago: University of Chicago Press, 1998], p. 48).

affinity and similarity, the expression of a non-linear, erotic, and both a *sub* and *meta-cognitive* dimension. A farfetched description of something that may be understood as simple or unitary, but that analysis, by itself, can't be grasped. Theurgical integral exercises of symbolic exegesis incorporate in a rigorous and systematic way analogy, symbol and metaphor as part of a method of metaphysical reflection that coordinates both poles of thought: formal demonstrative reasoning and intuitive reasoning, which thinks through images in terms of wholes, thus going beyond and at the same time integrating the limitations of discursive reasoning whose virtue is revealed in its capacity to delimitate – its function, in the last stance, corresponding to its capacity to limit itself. Luc Brisson contextualizes the use of myth by the Platonic philosophers as an acknowledgement of the limits of reason which leads not to irrationalism: 'the power of reason paradoxically lies in its ability to recognize its own limits'. It was the philosophers who saved the myths, according to Brisson's formula.[21] On the part of the philosophers, such metaphysical considerations must be coordinated with the study of diverse philosophical, scientific and artistic disciplines just as with the philosopher's own ethical development. This comprehensive or integral coordination of knowledge with life culminates, at the end of both the Platonic curriculum of study and at the end of the curriculum of ethical development, in theological hermeneutics as well as in the theurgical practices.[22] That is, progressively, theurgy is meant as a practice for the intellectually and emotionally mature philosopher.

III. Insider/outsider
Important for the modern study of religions and mysticism is an understanding of the insider/outsider problem, the way scholars understand their own personal position in relation to the topic of their investigation. To me, it seems like an inevitable epistemological problem faced in a research on a theme like theurgy, or some kind of mystical practice, especially when the tradition to which it belongs, in order to be properly understood, appeals to a direct experience of knowledge, of some sort, on the part of

---

[21] Luc Brisson, *How Philosophers Saved Myths: Allegorical Interpretation and Classical Mythology* (Chicago: The University of Chicago Press, 2004), see the Introduction, p. 3.
[22] Marinus's *V.P.* portrays, for instance, such program of integral education. Proclus's life is narrated according to the ground plan of ethical and intellectual development, considered a parallel and necessary complement. Compare with Leendert Gerrick Westerink, ed. and trans., *Anonymous Prolegomena to Platonic Philosophy* (Frome: The Prometheus Trust, 2011); pp. 7–12, 24–27.

the investigator: epistemological problems, then, resulting from the relationship of the subject with the object of his investigation. In my opinion Platonists address these matters very coherently, in a way that may still be significant for contemporary researchers – and it is with this intention that I am addressing this issue. However, from the philosophical perspective, it is not just an epistemological question but also fundamentally a metaphysical problem that should not be separated from its epistemological derivation. Proclus, for example, asserts how the question of being, all the philosophical and scientific considerations, are inextricably related to the discernment of one's own being, knowledge being inseparable from self-knowledge.[23] We are hermeneutical beings, so to speak; we are what we integrally interpret ourselves to be. That is, it may be said that self-knowledge determines what we are as much as what we are, expressed by all that we do, determines our knowledge. As human beings we are always operating from a philosophical stance, continually interpreting ourselves, interpreting reality, whether we acknowledge this or not.

These observations follow some of the main remarks made by Plato in his *Alcibiades* I.[24] It is crucial at the beginning of any philosophical investigation to examine such naturally founded prejudices from where we approach our investigation and which will determinate it as such, ourselves not being aware of it, if we don't first examine where are we starting from: what images and notions do we have about the human being, the universe, about reality? So, beyond theoretical issues, but including them, hermeneutics relate to vital questions; it's an integral vital affair; it is about the way we construct, somehow, our whole experience; it's not just about what and how we think – a mere methodological concern – thinking at the same time that mind is something completely, literally separate or different than body or physical reality, for example. For the Platonists, given its ontological condition, soul, that which we essentially are, soul is simultaneously an *outsider* and an *insider*, both. That is, soul is conceived as double, a double unity: we are both our embodied selves and our own

---

[23] Plato, *Charmides. Alcibiades I y II. Hipparchus. The lovers theages. Minos. Epinomis*, ed. Jeffrey Henderson, trans. W. R. M. Lamb (Cambridge, MA: Harvard University Press, 1955).

[24] Plato, *Alcibiades* I, a dialogue whose authenticity is still today questioned and defended by reputed scholars alike. For several centuries, different Platonic schools considered it the first dialogue to be read, according to certain schemes of study of the dialogues.

selves.[25] Soul is both an insider of the cosmos and an outsider of it; the same way it may be said that we can be both subject and object of ourselves, of our thought. Thus, the human being, structured in the same way as the whole of reality, is considered twofold, in dialogic relationship with himself, a relationship which at the same time is diachronical, that is, temporal: we are our temporal doubles, our temporal unfoldment. Two aspects in dynamic, dialectical relationship, not just two separated or completely different things, the way mind and body, subject and object, are represented in western modern culture, generally speaking.[26] So, if a researcher pretends to be exclusively objective, an *outsider* only, he is sort of pretending not to be human, not to be also a human inside the cosmos, an *insider* (with all the experiences that implies). In the same way, we may say then, that the *insider* is not just an *insider*, as if he could only be that, totally determined by such a condition. The subject may be said to be always in relationship with the object, at the same time being able to observe it or reflect on it, that relationship being ethical; thus the ethical state of the subject determines his epistemological relationship with the object, they are continuous, the same way being and thought, after Parmenides, are identified in Platonism; and in the same way we can say that soul gives continuity between the intelligible and the sensible. Hermeneutics are vital, not just theoretical, because as human beings, belonging to a context – *insider*, we are ethical beings.

---

[25] The polemics of interpretation regarding soul in the Platonic tradition are far too complex to be adequately represented here. Basically, it is Plotinus' presentation, which he recognizes as rather unorthodox (see the *Enneads* IV.8, 8), followed in the main lines by Porphyry, which will trigger severe criticism from later Platonists like Iamblichus and Proclus, who will not accept Plotinus' so called undescended soul; that is, an aspect of soul that never really leaves the intelligible realm when it descends into incarnation (IV.7, 13, 10; Cf. IV.3). For the late Platonists, soul fully descends, even if Iamblichus and Proclus may differ somewhat regarding how this is to be understood. However, in the same vein and in a general way, we can say that all these philosophers share a notion of soul as somehow double, a double unity, even if they differ regarding exactly how this is to be understood and the consequences following. For Plotinus, see for example the *Enneads*, IV.4, 10, 15; IV.8, 4, 30; II.3, 30. For Proclus, see *Elements of Theology*, revised text with translation, introduction and commentary by E. R. Dodds (Oxford: Clarendon, 1992), pp. 211 and 186–191.
[26] For a good introductory overview of Neoplatonists's psychology, epistemology and anthropology see Pauliina Remes, *Neoplatonism* (Stocksfield: Acumen, 2008), Chapters 4 and 5.

It is in this context that we may understand Proclus's proposal of the exercise of several different and simultaneous discourses by the philosopher, both demonstrative and inspired.[27] Discourses understood to be analogous but irreducible to each other, then, none of them in sole possession of truth, or all of them, in their own way, simultaneously true. Ultimate truth, being beyond representation, is a sort of an emptiness, but more an incomprehensible fullness, or unity, regarding which, reason must rationally conclude the impossibility of a rational knowledge about. The only thing that I want to point out right now is that, in my opinion, theurgy, as a divinatory and magical philosophical practice, poses a contemporary philosophical problem since it is concerned with a critical conception of thought and reason and so of philosophy itself, always a contemporary problem. And at the same time it poses a philosophical challenge to both the study of theurgy as much as regarding its practice, both to those who research it and to those who practice it, whether we may be talking about the same subjects or not. To end this excursus, we could, for example, ask ourselves, how distorted a subject of research like theurgy, or divination, may be, when we, as researchers, assume uncritically, as real, a notion of time as a horizontal, linear succession? Our *common* notion of time is also understood, rather literally, as external, historical, instead of a notion of time as cyclical and simultaneous – a perpetual flow of life, also understood as psychological, that which structures our experience – as is implied in theurgical divination, in its turn implying a cosmological conception of the cosmos as eternal.[28]

IV. Belief?

So, given the complexity and richness of the theurgist's exegetical methods, we may ask, did the Platonists *believe* in their gods? Perhaps not like *most of us believe* they did. While theurgists share many technical procedures with religious and magical practitioners, they do not seem to believe in the gods the way many of their contemporaries did. While for an

---

[27] Proclus, *Platonic Theology* I, 4.
[28] In a strict sense, for the Platonists, the cosmos is thought of as perpetual, against the eternity of the forms, the intelligible realm admitting no change. The cosmos is seen as perpetually becoming according to an eternal paradigm. See *Eighteen arguments on the eternity of the cosmos*, 15 (Cf. 5, 7, 13), in H. S. Lang and A. D. Macro, *On the Eternity of the World* (*de Aeternitate Mundi*), Greek text with introduction, translation and commentary by H. S. Lang and A. D. Macro, argument I translated from the Arabic by J. McGinnis (Berkeley, CA: University of California Press, 2001); Proclus, *Elements of Theology*, p. 52.

external observer, theurgists, on one hand, and religious and magical practitioners, on the other, may seem to be performing exactly the same actions, the understanding of theurgists regarding what they do and their motivations for doing so, their experience of it, in general, would be very different, or even exactly the opposite.

I would like to suggest that theurgists believed in the gods the way we may be said to believe in the characters of a movie: in a delimited ritual space, inside the movie theatre, during the projection of the film, we believe, we identify ourselves with several characters; we suffer or delight with them, we live an experience that transforms us both emotionally and intellectually, an experience that acquires a life of its own, its own reality, but once the movie is over no one has to worry about the literal existence or inexistence of the characters. Moreover, the observer of the movie performs an exegesis believing that he sees those characters and scenes that so intensely affect him, in what are but colourful lights (compare with *photos charakteres*) reflected in a screen; light, of course, being one of the favourite metaphors used by the theurgists to describe the nature of the gods.[29] So we watch the movie both with our eyes as with our thought, with our imagination; it is the imagination which gives continuity to the activity of our eyes and thought. The experience of one person with an educated imagination, or perfected thought and sensibility, will differ quite a lot from someone who has not such an education, even when for an external observer they might seem to be performing the same action, watching a movie.

V. On theurgy being astrological

The Platonists' theurgy is astrological.[30] Proclus's text on the hieratic art is probably one of the clearest statements about the said fundamental

---

[29] Traditional symbols and patterns that correspond to each divinity, revealed by the same, as patterns of light, during their apparitions or visions. Proclus, *On Plato's 'Cratylus'*, trans. Brian Duvick (New York: Cornell University Press, 2007), pp. 71, 31, 6–8. Compare to Ruth Dorothy Majercik, ed. and trans., *The Chaldean Oracles* (Leiden: Brill, 1989), f. 146.

[30] Some scholars, after Majercik, *The Chaldean Oracles*, f. 107, affirm that theurgists completely rejected astrology, along with most traditional forms of divination, something which, if very briefly, I suggest in this paper that is not the case, particularly regarding astrology. If I understand correctly, though, certainly theurgists can be very harsh against most traditional forms of divination, they are against the way it is understood and practiced, or rather, misunderstood, especially by professionals. They are very critical with the way astrologers understand and

astrological condition of theurgy. Even when theurgists are very critical of astrology as so poorly understood by common practitioners, reduced to a technical, secondary knowledge, theurgy is astrological in a technical sense since the diverse theurgical practices are supposed to be performed at the appropriate time (*kairon*), be it the purifications and initiations, the hymn singing to the different gods, or the composition, animation and ritual work with them through their living statues, integrating thus the ritual display into the cosmic harmony as an organic expression of it.[31] All the hieratic works are based on celestial-terrestrial correspondences. As a symbol charged with divine presence, every terrestrial substance used in theurgical practice is the counterpart of a celestial element, which is in turn an intelligible expression originating in the gods. 'In heaven are found the terrestrial [things] celestially, according to cause and, reciprocally, in the earth are the celestial [things] in a terrestrial manner' (*en ourano men ta kthonia kat aitian kai ouranios, en te ge ta ourania geinos*).[32] The palm tree resembles the Sun in the same way that the sunflower and the rooster converge or are dynamically attuned with the luminary; the Sun, the sunflower and the rooster moving together co-ordinately (*synkineitai*), their lives being linked in some way. It is sympathy (*sympatheia*) that binds together all the orders (*taxin*; *seiron*) of the cosmos which, presided over by the gods as their guides, stretch from the very first beings to the very last. Angels, demons, souls, animals, plants, minerals – all share certain similar living properties and are full of the breath emanated from the stars (*phosteron aporroiais*); properties which, while being analogously displayed in multiple forms, simultaneously through all the orders of the cosmos have their unity in a god, all participating in the divine whose

---

practice their discipline, which they reduce to a technical procedure of interpreting astral charts instead of understanding it and practicing it theurgically. See Iamblichus, *On the mysteries*, p. 11, for Iamblichus's comments on Porphyry's conceptions on the theurgic art.
[31] In fact, it seems that most magical practices of late antiquity were astrological, in the sense of depending on the right astronomical moment for being done successfully; the *Greek Magical Papyri* are full of diverse examples. See also Plotinus's fourth *Ennead*, particularly IV, 4 for an exposition of the astrological base of magical practice. This was a key treatise for Ficino's own developments of astrological magic theory and practice.
[32] Proclus, *On the hieratic art*, in J. Bidez, *Catalogue des manuscrits alchimiques grecs*. Vol. 6 (Brussels: Lamertin, 1928), p. 32.

presence embraces it all. 'Thus all is full of gods' (*Houto mesta panta theon*) repeats Proclus, after the sage Thales.[33]

Though theurgy may be said to be astrological in a technical, secondary sense, primarily it is astrological in a metaphysical sense, since, for the Platonists, the whole of reality is astrological. Sensible, corporeal experience is the astrological phenomenology of the soul of the cosmos composed by the celestial spheres. Bodies are the results or effects (*apoteles*) of the soul's self-creative contemplation and portrayal in the astral dynamics which, according to a *logos*, mediate between the intelligible and the sensible. The participation or causality of the intelligible to the sensible is one of simultaneity or co-presence (*sympnoia*, Plotinus), the same way that intellection and sensation may be seen to be continuous and simultaneous in the case of the human being.[34] This way, astrological methods, understood in a philosophical context that goes far beyond an

---

[33] Proclus, *On the hieratic art*, p. 40; Thales of Miletus, A 22, in Bidez, *Catalogue des manuscrits alchimiques grecs*, Vol. 6.

[34] Plotinus, *Enneads*, II, 3,7,10–20. In general terms the vision of the cosmos in Neoplatonism is of a unitary whole where it reigns in a single harmony or coordination of all. Plotinus will criticize the causality models that, taken to the letter, view in the intelligible the cause of the sensible as a temporary sequence of cause-effect (VI.7.33). Causality must be understood as inter-dependence, and this is not a doctrine, but a dialectical tool that helps us to think and to understand, against our habits, this relationship. Sara Rappe calls this model 'simultaneous arising or simultaneous manifestation and also co-rising, co-manifestation', thus indicating that while there is still a sequence of events these are not causal sequences in the common sense of the term, but rather the cause and the effect have a reciprocal origin (see Sara Rappe, *Reading Neoplatonism: Non-discursive Thinking in the texts of Plotinus, Proclus, and Damascius* (Cambridge: Cambridge University Press, 2000), p. 37–40). Sensible reality, then, appears as an immediate and necessary expression of the intelligible. We can say that the sensible is the co-presence of the intelligible (Plotinus speaks of *simultaneous coordination*, an idea of causation that suggests rather a notion of resonance and sympathy). The relationship between the sensible and the intelligible is central in Neoplatonic thought, that relationship being operated by soul. In the first line of the tractate *On Fate* (III, 1) Plotinus distinguishes between 'The things that become and those that are', to begin the questioning regarding the causal relationship among them', in Plotinus, *Enneads* (I-VII), trans. A. H. Armstrong (London: The Loeb Classical Library. Harvard University Press, 1984). The things that become, or sensible things, for the Neoplatonic tradition, are assimilated symbolically to the terrestrial, and those that are, or intelligible, assimilated to the celestial, as clearly expressed in Proclus's text on the hieratic art (148.9–11).

understanding of astrology as a technique to interpret an astronomical figure (*sjema*), become, for the Platonists, an ethical tool for the ordering of embodied experience, the coordination of sensation and thought – conscious and unconscious, we could say, with the sensible and the intelligible represented respectively by the earth and the sky, a very, very ancient primal mythological image already by the time of Proclus. This ethical coordination is based on the imitation of the dialectical cosmological rhythm or nature's coordination (the astonishingly beautiful self-regulation of the cosmos, hence an aesthetical/ethical paradigm), a perpetual living image (*eikon*) of the metaphysical eternal dialectical rhythm; a *physiology* for the Platonists, after the *Timaeus*. It is a metaphorical ethical exercise for the cosmization of consciousness[35] based in the application of analogy understood to have not only a discursive reality but mainly a metaphysical one.[36] Theurgists reciprocate natural entities whose living being is imagined or seen with thought as a natural hymn (*hymnos physikos*), like the lotus opening its petals like lips singing to the rising sun.

Proclus, after Plotinus, with his presentation of the chains of orders that extend from the first to the very last beings, all bounded by the henads or gods whom express their will through a heavenly *logos* or celestial writing, seems to echo millennial Babylonian traditions, where the gods have in their hands ropes that bind under their command everything in the lower world.[37] The cosmos is the divine temple, adorned with an extraordinary

---

[35] A notion used by Pierre Hadot in several of his works, where he also defines ancient philosophy as a way of life and a spiritual exercise.

[36] Octavio Paz comments in *Los hijos del limo* (Barcelona: Editorial Seix Barral, 1974), p. 84: 'Si la analogía hace del universo un poema, un texto hecho de consonancias, también hace del poema un doble del universo, doble consecuencia: podemos *leer* el universo, podemos *vivir* el poema. Por lo primero la poesía es conocimiento; por lo segundo acto.' ['If analogy makes of the universe a poem, a text made of consonances, also makes of the poem a double of the universe, double consequence: we can *read* the universe, we can *live* the poem. By the first poetry is knowledge; by the second act.'].

[37] Regarding Babylonian celestial divination, see Francesca Rochberg, 'Elements of the Babylonian contribution to Hellenistic astrology', *Journal of the American Oriental Society* Vol. 108, no. 1 (1988): pp. 51–62; Francesca Rochberg, 'Heaven and Earth. Divine/Human Relations in Mesopotamian Celestial Divination', in *Prayer, Magic and the Stars in the Ancient and Late Antique World*, ed. Scott Noegel, Joel Walker and Brannon Wheeler (University Park, PA: Pennsylvania State University Press, 2003). Francesca Rochberg, *The Heavenly Writing. Divination, Horoscopy, and Astronomy in Mesopotamian Culture* (Cambridge:

altar, the celestial vault wherein are found the stars, statues of the gods whose eternal act of the creation of the cosmos is a ritual act, led by the demiurgic hierophant, dedicated to the god of gods. The whole cosmos is an eternal liturgical activity.

Astrological methods – particularly regarding the ruler of the astral chart (*oikodespotes*) for the knowledge of the *daimon*, for the Platonists, knowledge of the deity leader of the soul – perhaps should be further reconsidered as they may provide a very important key about theurgical procedures. Through the insights that this technique could offer, as preliminary knowledge, at least some pertinent symbols may be gathered for the invocation of the soul's patron deity. Because, while for theurgists' proper knowledge of the tutelary goddess or god would mean a direct contact and further unification with it, to pretend to have knowledge about it just through calculations and discourses would be naive. However, as part of a tradition revealed by the gods themselves, from those astrological techniques understood as a preliminary knowledge will result in what may turn out to be significant symbols of the gods, given all the appropriate correspondences of the gods with all the orders and elements of the cosmos, these being the means to contact with them (as revealed by the gods themselves), a communication that would confirm the pertinence of the symbols used. That is, a direct experience that would rectify and deepen that known only indirectly, in an imperfect way, through the astrological discursive practice of interpretation of a chart; imperfect in comparison with the perfectioning of the soul through the contact and progressive union with its god or divine unity. So, while the technical interpretation of astrological symbolism may be imperfect, it may also be a first step, so to speak, though not a necessary one, since the gods could directly inspire the theurgist as how to proceed without himself having to resort to the investigation of astrological figures, which, for the theurgists,

---

Cambridge University Press, 2004.), and Erica Reiner, *Astral Magic in Babylonia* (Philadelphia: The American Philosophical Society, 1995) as well as Nicholas Campion, *The Dawn of Astrology: A Cultural History of Western Astrology* (London: Continuum Books, 2008), Chapters 3 and 4. Reiner refers to Haphaistio, a Greco-Egyptian astrologer roughly a contemporary of Proclus, as evidence of the continued vitality of Mesopotamian divinatory traditions, somehow influencing or still present in the development of late antiquity astrology, see Reiner, *Astral Magic in Babylonia*, p. 79.

the professional astrologers – the so-called 'experts' in these matters – so superficially understand.[38]

VI. Images, statues and hymns
The theurgists prepared statues of the gods at the same time as preparing themselves to receive divine illumination. That is, theurgical work, consisting in unification, expresses this externally through the mixing together of diverse materials which as signals (*synthemata*) and symbols correspond to the same god, thus forming a unity assimilated to the pre-existing divine unity: theurgists operating simultaneously in an intelligible, discursive, natural and perceptible manner.[39] The assembling and formation of the said images resembles divine manifestation itself, where formless beings take form for us, who are bounded by form. An anthropomorphism, but not operated by the theurgist but secondarily, being primarily operated by the divinities and their messengers (*angeloi*), who move, inspire and teach theurgists when they themselves identify with the former (Proclus uses the same term, *hegemones*, guides, to refer to both gods and theurgists), a union conceived by Proclus as erotic or loving, one of the main analogies used in the text.[40] In an example where the philosopher uses an analogy, the said union is preceded by the warming or preparation of a fit material to be ignited by the loving gods when their fire is transmitted (*pyros diadosis*), the same way as when a heated wick is put near a source of heat and without actually touching it catches fire; that is,

---

[38] Regarding question of the ruler of the astral figure, see Porphyry's *Introduction to the Tetrabiblos,* trans. James Herschel Holden (Tempe, AZ: Fellow of the American Federation of Astrologers, 2009), p. 30, and Iamblichus's *On the mysteries, De mysteriis,* trans. Emma C. Clarke, John M. Dillon and Jackson P. Hershbell (Atlanta, GA: Society of Biblical Literature, 2003), IX; PGM XIII 710–730, IV 36–51; and Ptolemy, *Tetrabiblos,* ed. and trans. F. Robbins (Cambridge: Loeb, 1980). III.10. Also see the works of Antiochus of Athens, Paulus Alexandrinus, Haphaistio of Thebes, Firmicus Maternus and the *Liber Hermetis*, for example, regarding the kind of astrological works known by theurgists. We actually have the so-called Paraphrase on Ptolemy's *Tetrabiblos* as well as an *Introduction to Ptolemy's Tetrabiblos*, both attributed to Proclus, an attribution considered dubious by some.
[39] Iamblichus, *On the mysteries*, V.23.
[40] Following Plato's *Symposium*, where the *hiereon techne* are mentioned in Diotima's speech on Eros as the greatest *daimon*, magician and diviner, in Plato, *Diálogos II. Gorgias. Menéxeno. Eutidemo. Menón. Crátilo*, introduction, translation with notes by J. Calonge Ruiz. E. Acosta Méndez. F. J. Oliveri, and J. L. Calvo (Madrid: Gredos, 2000), 202e–203d.

the ignition, likened to divinization, doesn't depend on a corporeal, external causation but only in a secondary, auxiliary way.[41] This divinization is what theurgy really is, not a technique, which deals with secondary, auxiliary causes, necessary but not sufficient for divinization to happen. Let's keep in mind that, for the Platonists, the problem of the limited conception of theurgy just as a technique is co-relative with the problem of limiting our conception of philosophy just as a rational discursive technique.[42]

Prayer is a gift from the gods, as expressed in the inspired prayers, the improvisations which move theurgists to sing with their souls ablaze. Participation in the divine fire is a compassionate activity of the gods to those whom they love and who reciprocate their love – as expected from any lover – as was said about Proclus's relationship with Athena.[43] An experience both of knowledge or intelligible illumination as well as of psychological heating or an enlivening intensification, in the same way that in fire we may distinguish between light and heat; the simultaneous activity of both what Proclus calls *the flower of the intellect* and *the flower of the whole soul*,[44] the latter of which encompasses the former establishing the unity of the soul in the unity of the gods.[45] It is an experience that may be conceived as simultaneously cyclical, both an ascent of the human and a descent of the divine. In Proclus's complex metaphysics, ontology is encompassed by henadology. The realm of being, that which makes the world intelligible, is subordinated to the henads or divine unities – the gods – which, from beyond existence, bind everything together, giving unity to the All.[46] A two-fold metaphysics mirrored by the human being: 'We are

---

[41] Iamblichus, *On the mysteries*, V.7, and Simplicius, *On Categories* 9, 302, 28–303.

[42] Iamblichus, *On the mysteries*, II.11.

[43] *Life of Proclus*, p. 30, in Mark Edwards, *Neoplatonic Saints. The Lives of Plotinus and Proclus by their Students* (Liverpool: Liverpool University Press, 2000), p. 30, and Marinus of Neapolis, *Marino de Neápolis: Proclo o De la felicidad*, trans. J. M. Álvarez Hoz and J. M. García Ruiz (Irún: Iralka, 1999).

[44] The mind and the heart, put into simple terms. D'Apamea, *Oráculos Caldeos*, p. 4.

[45] Proclus, *On the Timaeus*. I.211, 24–8.

[46] In Late Platonism, the first principle of their metaphysics, regarded as Unity, is also regarded as beyond being or existence; the same way that Plato conceives the first principle, called by him the Good, as beyond being or existence; Plato, *Republic* 509b.

images of intellective essences, but statues of unknown signs'.[47] The gods themselves suffer no passion but their messengers seem to represent the mutual passion, the *sympatheia* or compassion that unites divinities and theurgists in love born from the latter's astonishment and inspiration, ignited by the perception of beauty's splendour irradiated from the cosmos, from our bodies.

To conclude, I would like to point that Marsilio Ficino adapted theurgical practices in fifteenth-century Florence, fully integrating theurgy at the heart of his philosophical system, as much as in his own heart, we could say. He also translated Proclus's text on the hieratic art, rendering his title as *De sacrificio et magia*. Ficino clearly comprehends and emphasizes the essential astrological dimension of the whole of theurgical procedures, as expressed particularly in the third book of his *De Vita*, entitled *De vita coelitus comparanda*. Here, though rather discretely and briefly, he wrote about the need of the philosopher to be able to follow his own star and genius, giving some technical directions regarding how to know about one's guardian spirit in the astrological natal figure, followed by some critical remarks on the same, just as the theurgists did. In other of his works, mainly his commentaries on Plato's *Symposium* and *Phaedrus*, Ficino expanded on the astrological dynamics of *eros* (expounding a notable astrological theory of being in love), which for late Platonists was the base of all theurgical actions.[48] Ficino didn't call his magical practice theurgy, something that would had put him in very much trouble with the Christian church authorities; this is the reason why he chose to present his system as natural magic – as opposed to ritual magic – since it is based on 'just' natural sympathies. Nonetheless he structures his magical practice according to Proclus's theurgical virtues: faith (*pistis*), truth and love (*eros*), by which theurgists are recommended to unite with the gods. The triad of virtues derived respectively from the triad of main divine presences which are the sources of plenitude to all beings are Goodness, Wisdom and

---

[47] D'Apamea, *Oráculos Caldeos,* 5.211, 18–25.

[48] I think that one has to contextualize the whole proposal of the *De Vita* against the mystical project of the divinization of the soul that Ficino presents in his *Platonic Theology*. The practices recommended in the *De Vita* may be seen as the starting point of such a project. Regarding how to follow one's own star and guardian spirit, see Marsilio Ficino, 'De vita coelitus comparanda', in *Three Books on Life*, translated with introduction and notes by Carol V. Kaske and John R. Clark (Tempe, AZ: Center for Medieval and Early Renaissance Studies and the Arizona Board of Regents for Arizona State University, 1998), Chapters 13 and 14. Copenhaver, 'Hermes Trismegistus'.

46 The Celestial Imagination: Proclus the Philosopher on Theurgy

Beauty, the three main ethical principles.[49] Goodness, Wisdom and Beauty, in their turn, are related respectively to the main triad of metaphysical principles: the One-Good, Intellect (*Nous*) and Soul, respectively. Both perspectives – ethical and metaphysical – again in their turn mediated through the astrological symbols of Jupiter, the Sun and Venus respectively, what Ficino calls *the three Graces*, the main working symbols of his magical system, thus making of astrology, as a theurgical practice, an applied metaphysics, that is, ethics: a care of the self as well as a practice of self-realization, a *philosophical praxis* expressed through the splendid poetic language of the stars.

---

[49] For Proclus on this triad of virtues: *Platonic Theology*, 1.25 (113, 10); *On the Alcibiades*, trans. W. O'Neill (The Hague: Martinus Nijhoff, 1971), I.1, 51, 13–52, 2; 1.52, 10–53, 2; *Commentary on Plato's Parmenides*, trans. Glenn R. Morrow and John M. Dillon, with introduction and notes by John M. Dillon (Princeton, NJ: Princeton University Press, 1987), p. 927, pp. 18–29; *Commentary on the Timaeus of Plato*, 2 vols (Frome: The Prometheus Trust, 2006), 1.212, 12–25.

The God in the Stone: Gemstone Talismans in Western Magical Traditions

Liz Greene

Abstract: This paper will explore the perceived connection between gemstones and celestial potencies in particular magical currents in the cultures of the West, and the ritual use of gemstone talismans, amulets, and jewellery to invoke, persuade, learn from, or merge with celestial potencies. Underpinning this magical use of precious and semiprecious stones is the idea of correspondences or sympathies between the divine and the mortal realms, most emphasised through the significance of colour – itself understood, in certain currents of thought, to reflect the importance of sight as the organ of perception of the soul and the bridge to the intermediary world of the imagination in which the forms of gods, daimones, and angels can be envisioned through the mediation of those material objects with which they bear the strongest visual resemblance.

This is a conference about celestial magic, and my paper is about magical gemstones and their links with celestial potencies, as they have been understood in particular Western cultural milieux from antiquity to the present day. There is a more or less general agreement about the term 'celestial': it pertains to the heavens – although, in some instances, not the physical heavens as perceived by the eye or through the telescope. The heavens may also be a locus in the *mundus imaginalis*, teeming with daimonic powers, or a series of supernal palaces with floors and walls made of precious stones;[1] or an aspect of the mind of deity, as in Gnostic texts in which the celestial realms and their inhabitants are hypostatised thoughts of God.[2] But although there may be a general consensus about the

---

[1] See, for example, the descriptions of the gemstone constituents of the heavens in biblical and late antique Jewish *hekhalot* literature and Babylonian cuneiform texts, discussed below.

[2] *The Hypostasis of the Archons*, trans. Roger A. Bullard and Bentley Layton, in *The Nag Hammadi Library in English*, ed. James M. Robinson (Leiden: Brill, 1977), pp. 152–60. See also William Romaine Newbold, 'The Descent of Christ in the *Odes of Solomon*', *Journal of Biblical Literature*, Vol. 31, no. 4 (1912): pp. 168–209.

meaning of 'celestial', there is no agreed academic definition of the term 'magic'. Various perspectives will be offered in the papers given throughout this conference, and the way in which I will be using the word is a heuristic one, in the context of how gemstones have been, and still are, viewed as innately possessing, or amenable to being infused with, special potencies through their relationship with astral powers. I am loosely following an understanding of magic offered by Rachel Elior: it is concerned with initiating, developing, and maintaining 'the system of bonds and relationships between the revealed and concealed worlds'.[3]

Sumpatheia

From 1890 onward, in his ever-expanding revisions of *The Golden Bough*, Sir James Frazer (1854–1941) presented his ideas about 'sympathetic' magic, under which appellation magical gemstones could be said to belong.[4] According to Frazer, sympathetic magic 'commits the mistake of assuming that things which resemble each other are the same'.[5] This 'mistake' rests on the perception of analogies: two apparently unrelated objects, linked through a thematic unity such as colour, shape, or number, are believed to be secretly interconnected and influence each other magically. This type of associative or analogic thinking is certainly involved in the magical lore of gemstones, although whether it is 'mistaken' is a subject of ongoing debate. Frazer does not seem to have given much value to the works of Posidonius, Plotinus, Iamblichus, or Proclus, and never discusses the ancient idea of *sumpatheia* as it is presented in these authors: a living universe connected in all its parts through chains of correspondences, or, as Iamblichus himself, borrowing from Plato's *Timaeus*, put it: 'The universe is a single living being'.[6]

Sumpatheia, or the doctrine of 'sympathies', emerges in Western philosophical contexts as a complex and sophisticated world-view from at

---

[3] Rachel Elior, 'Mysticism, Magic, and Angelology: The Perception of Angels in Hekhalot Literature', *Jewish Quarterly Review*, Vol. 1 (1993): pp. 3–53, on p. 16.
[4] James Frazer, *The Golden Bough: A Study in Magic and Religion* (New York: Macmillan, 1922). For a similar perspective, see also Edward Burnett Tylor, *Primitive Culture: Researches into the Development of Mythology, Philosophy, Religion, Language, Art, and Custom* (London: John Murray, 1871).
[5] Frazer, *The Golden Bough*, 3:1–2.
[6] Iamblichus, *De Mysteriis*, trans. Emma C. Clarke, John M. Dillon, and Jackson P. Hershbell (Leiden: Brill, 2004), 4:12. See Plato, *Timaeus*, trans. Benjamin Jowett, in Edith Hamilton and Huntington Cairns (eds.), *The Collected Dialogues of Plato* (Princeton: Princeton University Press, 1989), 30a–e.

least the fifth century BCE onward, dominating the cultures of late antiquity and the alchemical and magical currents of the Middle Ages and early modern period; and virtually all the extant Western literature we possess on the magical properties of gemstones rests on this idea in its various forms. The Greek word συμπαθεια is a composite word comprised of συν, which means 'with', and παθειν, which means 'to experience' or 'to happen'.[7] *Sumpatheia* thus means 'happening with', or 'experiencing with': two apparently unrelated events, conditions, or objects that occur simultaneously and reflect a shared hidden meaning, root, pattern, or divinity. C. G. Jung coined the term 'synchronicity' to strip the old concept of its religious connotations and render it more acceptable to the psychiatric milieu in which he worked.[8] Another, more poetic presentation of *sumpatheia* in the language of the twentieth century comes from the Welsh writer and occultist Arthur Machen (1863–1947). His comments about landscape can equally be applied to gemstones:

> The things which we distinguish as qualities or values are inherent in the real environment to make the configuration that they do make with our sensory response to them. There is such a thing as a 'sad' landscape, even when we who look at it are feeling jovial... That is not imputing human attributes to... the environment, but giving proper recognition to the other end of a nexus, of which only one end is organised in our own mind.[9]

The analogy of colour, which dominates the lore of magical gemstones, is not as simple as it might have seemed to Frazer. Some scholars, still identified with Frazer's understanding of magic, have suggested that, in the case of gemstone amulets intended for healing, 'the most important colours of stones were those of human organs and secretions'.[10] But humans are

---

[7] For the Greek, see Henry George Liddell and Robert Scott, *An Intermediate Greek-English Lexicon* (1889; repr. Oxford: Oxford University Press, 1999).
[8] For Jung's main discussions on synchronicity, see C. G. Jung, 'Letters on Synchronicity', in CW18, *The Symbolic Life*, trans. R. F. C. Hull (London: Routledge & Kegan Paul, 1975), §1193–1212; C. G. Jung, 'On Synchronicity', in CW8, *The Structure and Dynamics of the Psyche*, trans. R. F. C. Hull (London: Routledge & Kegan Paul, 1969), §969–97; C. G. Jung, 'Synchronicity: An Acausal Connecting Principle', CW8, §816–968.
[9] Arthur Machen, 'The Children of the Pool' (1936), in *Tales of Horror and the Supernatural* (London: John Baker, 1949), pp. 316–35, on p. 334.
[10] Attilio Mastrocinque, 'The Colours of Magical Gems', in *'Gems of Heaven': Recent Research on Engraved Gemstones in Late Antiquity c. AD 200–600*, ed.

visual animals, as evidenced by the disproportionately large area in the neocortex of the human brain devoted to sight; cats, in contrast, have a correspondingly large area dedicated to hearing, and dogs to scent.[11] Our perception of the world around us is ordered and defined by what we see and what we imagine we see, and theories of the nature and importance of sight in the context of both science and philosophy abounded in antiquity. Plato insisted that the power of vision is dependent on the Sun-god's 'influx' of physical light, comparable with the soul's vision of truth through the 'influx' of the wisdom of the same god.[12] Aristotle declared that the visibility of an object depends on the impact of its colour on the movement of the element of air between the object and the eye.[13] Euclid was convinced that sight is achieved through a cone of rectilinear visual rays emanating from the eye to the object.[14] Iamblichus, in the late third century CE, describes how the visions experienced in theurgic rituals show 'what is not body as body to the eyes of the soul by means of the eyes of the body'.[15] Physical vision is thus the conduit through which the soul engages with what is seen and perceives through it what is unseen: the hidden divinity of whom the manifest object is a symbol. As Elliot Wolfson has put it: 'The mystical vision... is at the core metaphorical or analogical, for it seeks to make the spiritual world "perceptible" to the

---

Chris Entwistle and Noël Adams. British Museum Research Publication 177. (London: Trustees of the British Museum, 2011), pp. 62–68, on p. 62.
[11] See Stephen Budiansky, *The Character of Cats* (London: Weidenfeld & Nicholson, 2002), p. 111.
[12] Plato, *Republic* VI:507d–510e, trans. Paul Shorey, in *Plato: Collected Dialogues*, ed. Edith Hamilton and Huntington Cairns (Princeton: Princeton University Press, 1961).
[13] Aristotle, *On the Soul*, II:7.418a29–419a20, trans. J. A. Smith, in *The Complete Works of Aristotle*, ed. Jonathan Barnes (Princeton: Princeton University Press, 1984), Vol. 1, pp. 641–92.
[14] See W. R. Knorr, 'On the Principle of Linear Perspective in Euclid's *Optics*', *Centaurus*, Vol. 34 (1991): pp. 194–95; W. R. Knorr, 'Pseudo-Euclidean Reflections in Ancient Optics: A Re-examination of Textual Issues Pertaining to the Euclidean *Optica* and *Catoptrica*', *Physis*, Vol. 31 (1994): pp. 1–45; A. Jones, 'Peripatetic and Euclidean Theories of the Visual Ray', *Physis*, Vol. 31, no. 1 (1994): pp. 47–76. For a discussion of ancient theories of visual perception, see A. Mark Smith, *Ptolemy and the Foundations of Ancient Mathematical Optics: A Source-Based Guided Study* (Philadelphia: American Philosophical Society, 1999); see also Dimitris Plantzos, 'Crystals and Lenses in the Graeco-Roman World', *American Journal of Archaeology*, Vol. 101, no. 3 (1997): pp. 451–64.
[15] Iamblichus, *De Mysteriis*, II.6 and V.26.

material by relating an object from the latter to the former'.[16] And so Iamblichus declares that 'the eyes of the body' cannot tolerate a vision of the gods except through the mediation of perceptible symbols such as gemstones.

The *caelum*, or 'Azure Vault', as James Hillman calls it, would, as the abode of the gods and the *sumbolon* of the world-soul, inevitably be seen as physically embodied in one or more gemstones in the universal chains of correspondences.[17] This understanding was not limited to the world of Greek philosophy. A Talmudic legend speaks of a magical stone that hung around Abraham's neck:

> When a sick man looked upon it, he was cured. And when Abraham passed away, the Lord sealed it in the planet of the sun.[18]

Abraham's gemstone became enmeshed with other legends and texts, forming a chain of narratives connected by sympathies of colour and meaning. In Exodus, the heavens under God's feet are 'like a pavement of sapphire'; in Ezekiel, the Chariot-Throne of God is 'as the likeness of a sapphire stone'.[19] Abraham's stone, it was said, had first been given to Adam and Eve when they left Paradise, to remind them of the primordial light they had lost.[20] This light, according to an early thirteenth-century Kabbalistic text, is 'in the likeness of blue, which is the completion of all colors'.[21] Later Noah was given the stone to guide him on the Ark: 'When it [the stone] was dim he knew it was day, but when it was bright, he knew

---

[16] Elliot R. Wolfson, *Through a Speculum That Shines: Vision and Imagination in Medieval Jewish Mysticism* (Princeton: Princeton University Press, 1994), p. 66.
[17] James Hillman, 'The Azure Vault: *Caelum* as Experience', in *Alchemical Psychology* (Dallas, TX: Spring Publications, 2010), pp. 318–42. See C. G. Jung, CW14, *Mysterium Coniunctionis*, trans. R. F. C. Hull (London: Routledge & Kegan Paul, 1970), §761–70 for these and other associations with the *caelum*.
[18] *Babylonian Talmud, Bava Batra* I:16, Jewish Virtual Library (2013), at http://www.jewishvirtuallibrary.org/jsource/Talmud/bavabatratoc.html [accessed 1 June 2013]. For an elaboration of this legend, see Howard Schwartz, *Tree of Souls: The Mythology of Judaism* (Oxford: Oxford University Press, 2004), pp. 86 and 332; Howard Schwartz, *Reimagining the Bible: The Storytelling of the Rabbis* (Oxford: Oxford University Press, 1998), pp. 17–18.
[19] Exodus 24:10; Ezekiel 1:26.
[20] *Targum Yonatan* 6:16; see also *Genesis Rabbah* 31:11.
[21] R. Azrael of Gerona, *Perush 'Eser Sefirot 'al Derekh She'elah u-Teshuvah*, cited in Wolfson, *Through a Speculum*, p. 299.

it was night'.[22] In the late antique magical text called *Sefer ha-Razim* or 'Book of Secrets', it is related that Noah was given a book 'by Raziel the angel', and inscribed the divine mysteries revealed in the book 'upon a sapphire stone'.[23] In the late twelfth-century text known as *Sefer ha-Bahir* or 'Book of Brightness', the mysterious blue stone is the primal stone of heaven:

> What is the earth from which the heavens were graven?
> It is the Throne of the Blessed Holy One. It is the Precious Stone and the Sea of Wisdom...
> Why is blue chosen above all other colors?
> Because blue resembles the sea, the sea resembles the sky, and the sky resembles the Throne of Glory. It is thus written: 'They saw the God of Israel, and under His feet was like a pavement of sapphire, like the essence of heaven in clarity.'[24]

The blue gemstone – possibly sapphire, but more likely the stone we now know as lapis lazuli – has an ancient association with the highest divinity and the celestial realm in which he has his abode. While this might seem a simple analogy of colour, colour is not simple, and we still do not fully understand why humans respond psychologically and physiologically to different colours of the spectrum in different ways. Like all symbols that have potency, the legendary blue stone contains a profound paradox. It is the least animate of all things in the world, and the furthest away from heaven, yet in legend it is filled with a living light that speaks of the highest realms of spirit. The blue stone is also called *tzohar*, meaning 'brilliance' or 'radiance'. *Tzohar* can also mean a window.[25] This enigmatic word with its multiple associations is the same as the title of the great Kabbalistic work of the late thirteenth century, the *Zohar*, in which the divinely infused gemstone, whose light is 'like the radiance of the sun from its sheath', is in the possession of R. Shim'on ben Yochai, the

---

[22] Genesis 6:9–11:32.

[23] *Sefer ha-Razim*, trans. Michael Morgan (Chico, CA: Scholars Press, 1983), 5, p. 17.

[24] *Sefer ha-Bahir* 96, in *The Bahir*, trans. Aryeh Kaplan (York Beach, ME: Weiser Books, 1979), pp. 35–36. For an alternative translation, see *The Book of Bahir: Flavius Mithridates' Latin Translation, the Hebrew Text, and an English Version*, ed. Saverio Campanini (Torino: Nino Aragno Editore, 2005), p. 296.

[25] Schwartz, *Tree of Souls*, p. lxxiii.

legendary author of the book:[26] a stone that is also a window and a text, whose letters and words themselves are precious gems that contain the power of the 'primordial light'.

Tradition and modernity
Belief that gemstones 'do something' or 'make something happen' is no less endemic today than it was in antiquity. Even the *Financial Times* has noticed. In a recently published article, the author observes, with ill-disguised irritation: 'In the jewellery business there's more superstition than at the Salem Witch Trials... Mysticism is definitely in the ascendant'.[27] Commercial jewellers often present the magical lore of gemstones in a light-hearted way hedged with disclaimers, as in this example provided by a British company called Pia Jewellery:

> Peach aventurine for friendship. Delicately hued semi-precious stones, believed to bring friends together.[28]

The phrase 'believed to' frees the jeweller from all magical claims, yet the statement nevertheless implies that the gemstone possesses some kind of occult potency. An American website says of the gemstone haematite, a crystalline form of iron oxide, that it

> ...harmonizes mind, body and spirit. It prevents negative energies from entering the aura. This is an excellent stone to wear while doing ritual work.[29]

A one-inch piece of polished haematite from this supplier costs $1.99. This gemstone of ancient lineage, associated in one of the earliest Greek lapidaries with the war-god and his planet, is for sale on the internet at a price that would put Tesco to shame; but haematite is a commonly available gemstone, found wherever iron is mined, and the information offered is not necessarily insincere, any more than when it was offered by the amulet-sellers of antiquity.

---

[26] Daniel C. Matt, trans, *The Zohar*, Vol. 1 (Stanford, CA: Stanford University Press, 2004), 11b, p. 76.
[27] James Sherwood, 'Romancing the Stones', *Financial Times*, 25 March 2006, at http://www.ft.com/cms/s/0/ac3ef5a6-bba4-11da-8f51-0000779e2340.html [accessed 30 April 2016].
[28] Pia Jewellery catalogue, Summer 2013; see www.piajewellery.com [accessed 25 May 2013].
[29] http://www.amerindea.com/gemstones03.html [accessed 2 June 2013].

The perceived relationship between haematite, its magical powers, and its planetary lord, is based on colour. Declared in the second-century BCE lapidary of Damigeron to be the stone of Mars, haematite became the most common gemstone for inscribed magical amulets in the late antique Mediterranean world, even in Christian milieux.[30] Uncut and unpolished, haematite is black, lumpy, and unattractive. But when it is broken, carved, chiselled, or powdered, it turns blood-red, calling to mind the words of Shylock in Shakespeare's *Merchant of Venice*: 'If you prick us, do we not bleed?'[31] The name itself is derived from the Greek *aima*, meaning 'blood'. Haematite's relatively consistent astrological tradition is, however, exceptional; in the main, there is little agreement in older texts about which stone 'belongs to' which planet, sign, star, constellation, or decan, or even whether a stone has any astral associations at all.

The first tradition
Three distinct currents, emerging from different cultural contexts, dominate the traditions surrounding magical gemstones. These traditions have become so entangled over the centuries that they now appear as a homogenous lore. The first is the direct association of a gemstone with a celestial potency. Lists of magical stones appear in a Babylonian work from the second millennium BCE known as 'The Tablet About Stones'.[32] The Babylonian gods inhabit a heaven made of gemstones: the realm of the sky-god Anu is composed of reddish *luludanitu*, speckled with white and black; the middle heaven, in which the god Bel sits enthroned, is of deep blue *saggilmu*; and the lower heaven is made of a translucent bluish-grey stone, upon which are inscribed 'the constellations of the gods'.[33] An Assyro-Babylonian incantation from the ninth century BCE describes an amulet of seven stones, to be worn on the breast of the king; the number

---
[30] See, for example, the vast number of haematite amulets described in Campbell Bonner, *Studies in Magical Amulets, Chiefly Graeco-Egyptian* (Ann Arbor, MI: University of Michigan Press, 1950).
[31] William Shakespeare, *The Merchant of Venice*, in *The Oxford Shakespeare*, ed. W. J. Craig (Oxford: Oxford University Press, 1914), Act III, Scene 1.
[32] See Erica Reiner, *Astral Magic in Babylonia* (Philadelphia: American Philosophical Society, 1995), p. 29 and the references given there. Only a small portion of this tablet remains.
[33] Cited in Francesca Rochberg, *In the Path of the Moon: Babylonian Celestial Divination and Its Legacy* (Leiden: Brill, 2010), p. 347. The same Babylonian text is also cited in Daphne Arbel, *Beholders of Divine Secrets: Mysticism and Myth in the Hekhalot and Merkavah Literature* (Albany, NY: SUNY Press, 2003), p. 77.

suggests that they are planetary, although no gods are explicitly linked with the stones.

> The magnificent stones, the magnificent stones, the stones of abundance and of joy.
> Made resplendent for the flesh of the gods.
> The *hulalini* stone, the *sirgarru* stone, the *hulalu* stone, the *sandu* stone, the *uknu* stone.
> The *dushu* stone, the precious stone *elmeshu*, perfect in celestial beauty...
> Placed upon the shining breast of the king as an ornament.
> Azagsud, high-priest of Bel, make them shine, make them resplendent!
> That they may keep the evil one from the dwelling.[34]

Sadly, we cannot identify any of these stones, although *elmeshu*, 'perfect in celestial beauty', is probably lapis lazuli, a deep blue stone so prized by the Babylonians that, in the absence of local availability, they imported it from India.[35] The technology to facet and 'make shine' the extremely hard form of corundum we now call sapphire was not available in the culture which produced this incantation, nor has any Babylonian sapphire jewellery been found.[36] For the Babylonians, the inherent power of the stones remained dormant until they were 'irradiated', which meant, quite literally, that the stone 'should spend the night under the stars' in order to become impregnated with divine effluence and fulfil its magical potential.[37] That the Greeks and Romans borrowed from Babylonian gemstone lore is evident from Pliny, who, in his *Natural History*, written in the first century

---

[34] Charles Fossey, *La Magie Assyrienne: Étude suivie de Textes Magiques transcrits* (Paris: Ernest Leroux, 1902), 18.a2, p. 301 (translation from the French mine). For the original cuneiform text, see Sir Henry Creswicke Rawlinson, *The Cuneiform Inscriptions of Western Asia, Vol. IV: A Selection from the Miscellaneous Insriptions of Assyria* (London: Trustees of the British Museum/R. E. Bowler, 1875), 4:18:3.
[35] Entwistle and Adam, eds., *Gems of Heaven*. For the unlikelihood of the stone being sapphire, see Tait, *7000 Years of Jewellery*, p. 161; Richard M. Pearl, *Faceted Gems: A Historical Article on the Methods and Equipment Used in Lapidary* (Roche Press, 2011).
[36] See Hugh Tait, ed., *7000 Years of Jewellery* (London: British Museum Press, 2006), p. 161; Richard M. Pearl, *Faceted Gems*.
[37] Reiner, *Astral Magic*, pp. 49 and 53.

CE, lists a number of lost Greek and Babylonian sources.[38] Whatever stones are described in the cuneiform tablets, Babylonian ideas about their magical potency were transmitted not only to the Greco-Roman world, but also to the Jews during their period of captivity, appearing in biblical texts such as those I quoted earlier.

In the Egyptian Old Kingdom in the third millennium BCE, two microcrystalline quartzes, carnelian and red jasper, were associated with blood and the solar life-force; as Bram Stoker succinctly put it at the end of the nineteenth century, 'The blood *is* the life'.[39] This association continues in Etruscan scarab amulets of the fifth century BCE, based on Phoenician and archaic Greek prototypes which were themselves borrowed from Egypt. The Egyptian scarab was a solar creature, linked to the god Khepri, the reborn Sun, whose name means 'He Who Comes Into Being'.[40]

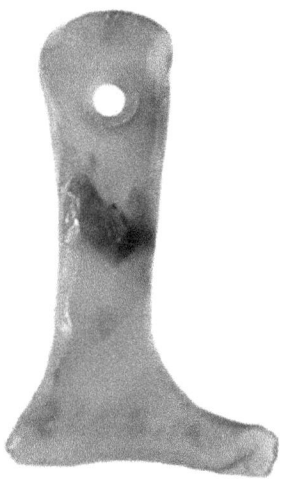

Fig. 1. Carnelian foot amulet fifth to eighth Dynasty, ca. 2465–2100 BCE, Metropolitan Museum of Art; http://www.metmuseum.org/toah/works-of-art/10.130.2355_10.130.2358.

---

[38] Pliny, *Natural History, Books 36–37*, trans. D. E. Eichholz (Cambridge, MA: Harvard University Press, 1962), 9.115; 37.59; 37.25, 34, 90, 114, and 153.
[39] Bram Stoker, *Dracula* (Oxford: Oxford University Press, 1983), p. 234.
[40] See Jan Bergman, 'Ancient Egyptian Theogony', in *Studies in Egyptian Religion: Dedicated to Professor Jan Zandee*, ed. M. S. H. G. Heerma van Voss (Leiden: Brill, 1982), pp. 28–37, on p. 32; Richard H. Wilkinson, *The Complete Gods and Goddesses of Ancient Egypt* (London: Thames & Hudson, 2003), pp. 230–33.

Fig. 2. Khepri scarab pectoral inlaid with carnelian, turquoise, and lapis lazuli with carnelian solar disk; tomb of Tutankhamun, ca. 1327 BCE, Egyptian National Museum, Cairo.

The carnelian foot amulet in Figure 1 was intended to confer speed and power to the limbs of the wearer. The scarab pectoral in Figure 2, found in the tomb of Tutankhamun, underlines the solar significance of the gemstone through the carnelian orb held in the scarab's claws.

The Etruscan scarab amulets of the fifth century BCE, in contrast, were usually engraved with a mythic *historiola*: the figure of Herkle, the Greek Herakles, undergoing one of his Twelve Labours, sometimes with a solar symbol above his head.[41] This carnelian amulet portrays Herkle capturing the Keryneian Hind, the third of the hero's Labours.

---

[41] For the Etruscan scarab amulets, see Larissa Bonfante, 'Etruscan', in *Reading the Past: Ancient Writing from Cuneiform to the Alphabet*, ed. J. T. Hooker (Berkeley, CA/London: University of California Press/British Museum, 1990), pp. 321–78; Nancy T. de Grummond, 'A Scarab Gem from the Etruscan Artisans' Quarter and Sacred Area at Cetamura del Chianti', *Rasenna: Journal of the Center for Etruscan Studies*, Vol. 2, no. 1 (2010): p. 7, at
http://scholarworks.umass.edu/cgi/viewcontent.cgi?article=1013&context=rasenna [accessed 30 April 2016]; Irad Malkin, *The Returns of Odysseus: Colonization and Ethnicity* (Berkeley, CA: University of California Press, 1998), p. 164; Otto Brendel and Francesca R. Serra Ridgway, *Etruscan Art* (New Haven, CT: Yale University Press, 1995), pp. 280–81.

58 The God in the Stone: Gemstone Talismans in Western Magical Traditions

Fig. 3. Etruscan carnelian scarab amulet portraying Herkle slaying a hind, found at a sanctuary at Cetamure del Chianti, ca. fifth century BCE; Museo Archeologico del Chianti Senese.

Eight centuries later, Greco-Egyptian carnelian and red jasper healing amulets like the one below, portraying Herakles battling the Nemean Lion – the first of the hero's Twelve Labours[42] – demonstrate the longevity of the relationship between red gemstones and solar power and heroic strength.

Like the heavenly blue stone in Jewish lore, red quartzes such as carnelian, sard, and red jasper accrued over the centuries a chain of correspondences linking a gemstone, a celestial power, a colour, a bodily organ, a characterological quality, and a mythic narrative. The association of carnelian with Leo, ruled by the Sun, is still found in many contemporary works on gemstones.[43]

---

[42] The order of the Labours varies according to the source. The order provided by Pseudo-Apollodorus' *Bibliotheka*, probably dating from the first-century BCE, is the best-known; for this compendium of Greek myth, see Aubrey Diller, *Studies in Greek Manuscript Tradition* (Amsterdam: Hakkert, 1983), pp. 199–216; R. Scott Smith and Stephen M. Trzaskoma, eds., *Apollodorus' Library and Hyginus' Fabulae: Two Handbooks of Greek Mythology* (Indianapolis, IN: Hacket, 2007). For earlier versions, see Timothy Ganz, *Early Greek Myth: A Guide to Literary and Artistic Sources* (Baltimore, MD: Johns Hopkins University Press, 1993), pp. 374–466.

[43] See, among many others, http://www.birthdaygems.org/jewels-gemstones/carnelian.htm; http://www.shinjyujewelry.com/id182.html [accessed 23 May 2013].

Fig. 4. Greco-Egyptian red jasper amulet portraying Herakles battling the Nemean Lion, ca. first to sixth century CE; Kelsey Museum of Archaeology, 26014.

Most early Greco-Roman lapidaries enumerate the magical properties of gemstones, but offer little in the way of celestial attributions. The oldest extant Greek gemstone treatise, a late fourth-century BCE work by Theophrastus (371–287 BCE) called *On Stones*, is concerned with the physical properties of gems and only refers obliquely to their magical uses, avoiding any discussion of astral connections.[44] Pliny's *Natural History* does describe, albeit with considerable scepticism, the magical properties of the stones; but it offers little in the way of celestial attributions.[45] The first-century CE text known as the Orphic *Lithica* is a religious work, written in the hyperbolic style of late antique poetry; it enumerates the magical attributes of around thirty gemstones, but provides no astral attributions.[46] The collection of Hermetic texts known as *Kuranides*, dated

---

[44] Theophrastus, *Theophrastus on Stones*, ed. and trans. Earle R. Caley and John F. C. Richards (Columbus, OH: Ohio State University, 1956). Theophrastus became head of Aristotle's Peripatetic school of philosophy in Athens after Aristotle withdrew from it before his death in 322 BCE. For biographical material, see the Introduction in Caley and Richards, eds., *Theophrastus On Stones*, p. 3.

[45] Pliny, *Natural History*, Books XXXVI and XXXVII.

[46] This work has not been translated into English. For a French translation, see Robert Halleux and Jacques Schamp, eds. and trans., *Les Lapidaires Grecs* (Paris:

60 The God in the Stone: Gemstone Talismans in Western Magical Traditions

to the fourth century CE, does, like a few other Hermetic treatises, contain a number of planetary attributions.[47] The black stone *kynaedius*, for example, declared to be 'Saturnine', is 'black but bright and shining like glass', apparently referring to the volcanic black glass known as obsidian.[48] But many of the stones are unrecognisable, and the astral associations are neither systematic nor comprehensive.[49]

On the Virtues of Stones, attributed to Damigeron, a Greek author of the second century BCE, is an exception. It only survives in a Latin translation of the first century CE, with many interpolations; only fragments remain of the Greek original. It is in this work that we find the first systematic astrological attributions:

> Seven of the stones belong to seven of the Zodiacal signs... The first stone is called *chrysolithos* and belongs to Leo. The second stone is called *astroselinus* and belongs to Cancer, the third, called haematite, to Aries, the fourth, called *keraunius*, to Sagittarius, the fifth, called *demos*, to Taurus, the sixth, called *arabica*, to Virgo, the seventh, called *ostrachitis*, to Capricorn. These you

---

Les Belles Lettres, 2003), 'Lapidaires Orphique', pp. 1–124, and 'Orphée, *Kérygmes lapidaires*', pp. 125–78. For an early bilingual Greek-Latin edition, see Orpheus, *Orphei Lithica: accedit Damigeron de Lapidibus,* trans. Eugenius Abel (Brussels: Berolini, 1881). See also Ruslan I. Kostov, '*Orphic Lithica* as a Source of Late Antiquity Mineralogical Knowledge', *Annual of the University of Mining and Geology*, Vol. 51, no. 1 (2008): pp. 109–15.

[47] An English translation of the Latin version of *Kuranides* was published in 1685, entitled *The Magick of Kirani, King of Persia, and of Harpocration; Containing the Magical and Medicinal Vertues of Stones, Herbs, Fishes, Beasts, and Birds* (repr. Renaissance Astrology Facsimile Editions, ed. Christopher Warnock, 2005). A more recent English translation of Book One is found in Maryse Waegemann, *Amulet and Alphabet: Magical Amulets in the First Book of Cyranides* (Amsterdam: Gieben, 1987). See also Louis Delatte, *Textes latin et vieux français relatifs aux Cyranides* (Paris: Droz, 1942); David Bain, 'Some Textual and Lexical Notes on Cyranides', *Classica et Medievalia*, Vol. 67 (1996), which on p. 153 n. 11 gives a handy list of the astrological references in the text. For other Hermetic texts in which the three decans of each zodiacal sign are assigned their own gemstones, see Rochberg, *In the Path of the Moon*, p. 157, n. 45.

[48] *Kuranides* I, p. 30.

[49] For the Neoplatonic framework of *Kuranides*, see Garth Fowden, *The Egyptian Hermes: A Historical Approach to the Late Pagan Mind* (Cambridge: Cambridge University Press, 1986), pp. 87–89. See also Brian P. Copenhaver, *Hermetica: The Greek Corpus Hermeticum and the Latin Asclepius in a New English Translation* (Cambridge: Cambridge University Press, 1995), pp. xxxiv–xxxv.

should seek, so that you may have your life in your own safe-keeping at all times, and be ever healthy and carefree.[50]

Damigeron seems to be referring indirectly to the seven planetary rulers of the seven zodiacal signs, and these rulers govern the other five signs as well. But problems begin with the names of the stones. *Chrysolithos*, the gemstone of Leo, means 'golden stone'.[51] It is usually translated as topaz. However, Charles King, a Cambridge scholar writing on gemstone lore in the latter part of the nineteenth century, insisted that *chrysolithos* is yellow sapphire;[52] George Frederick Kunz, an American gemmologist writing in the early twentieth century and citing a seventeenth-century astrological text, suggested that *chrysolithos*, the stone of the Sun, is in fact the 'yellow Brazilian chrysoberyl';[53] Campbell Bonner, one of the most important amulet collectors and cataloguers of the mid-twentieth century, declared that *chrysolithos* is the softer and more easily carved stone we call peridot;[54] and, more recently, the authors of a paper on the archaeology of the Greco-Roman harbour town of Berenike, state, in accordance with Bonner, that *chrysolithos* 'can only be the warm yellowish green peridot'.[55] We still cannot identify Damigeron's Leo gemstone with any accuracy – only that it is golden, as befits its planetary lord.

Some of Damigeron's stones can be safely identified. The Martial haematite still bears its ancient name;[56] *arabica* is probably pearl, as most

---

[50] Damigeron, *De Virtutibus Lapidum: The Virtues of Stones*, trans. Patricia Tahil, ed. Joel Radcliffe (Seattle, WA: Ars Obscura, 1989), p. 4.
[51] Damigeron, *De Virtutibus Lapidum*, XLVII and XLVIII, p. 60.
[52] Charles William King, *The Natural History of Gems or Decorative Stones* (London: Bell & Daldy, 1867), p. 93.
[53] George Frederick Kunz, *The Curious Lore of Precious Stones* (Philadelphia: J.B. Lippincott, 1913), pp. 347–48, citing Henrik Rantzau, *Tractatus de genethliacorum thematum judicia* (Frankfurt: Nicolaus Hoffman, 1633), pp. 46–55.
[54] Bonner, *Studies in Magical Amulets*, p. 205. See also Kostov, 'Orphic Lithica', for the equation of *chrysolithos* with peridot.
[55] Willemina Z. Wendrich, Roger S. Bagnall, René T. J. Cappers, James A. Harrell, Steven E. Sidebotham, and Roberta S. Tomber, 'Bernike Crossroads: The Integration of Information', in *Excavating Asian History: Interdisciplinary Studies in Archaeology and History*, ed. Norman Yoffee and Bradley L. Crowell (Tucson, AZ: University of Arizona Press, 2006), pp. 15–66, on p. 36.
[56] Another example of the association of Mars with haematite can be found in the text known as *The Alexander Romance*, a romanticised biography of Alexander

of the pearls in Damigeron's world came from the Arabian Gulf;[57] and *astroselinus* is probably selenite, a translucent stone related to alabaster. *Ostrachitis* or 'oyster-stone' is the petrified shell of the oyster, possibly reflecting the idea of melothesia: the correspondence between a heavenly body and an organ in the human body, still found today in many astrological texts concerned with *sumpatheia*.[58] According to the traditions of melothesia, Saturn, as lord of Capricorn, governs the skeletal system, giving structure to the human body,[59] and is reflected in the fossilised shell of the oyster, bonelike in its colour and brittle friability.[60] But the Jupiterian *keraunios* or 'thunder-stone' has proven impossible to identify. And the Venusian *demos* – a word which means a tract of land – was unrecognisable even to Damigeron's Latin translator, who declared it to be *ignotus plane*: 'plainly unknown'.

---

the Great, dated to around the first- to third-centuries CE; see Richard Stoneman, trans., *The Greek Alexander Romance* (London: Penguin, 1991), p. 38.

[57] For the Arabian Gulf as the source of pearls, see Theophrastus, *On Stones*, pp. 134–35.

[58] The idea of melothesia is expressed in various texts contemporary with the Latin translation of Damigeron, including Marcus Manilius, *Astronomica*, trans. G. P. Goold (Cambridge, MA: Harvard University Press, 1989), 2.453–65, and Claudius Ptolemy, *Tetrabiblos*, trans. F. E. Robbins (Cambridge, MA: Harvard University Press, 1940), 3:12. For melothesia, see Auguste Bouché-Leclercq, *L'astrologie greque* (Paris: Leroux, 1899), pp. 318–25; H. G. Schipper, 'Melothesia: A Chapter of Manichaean Astrology in the West', in *Augustine and Manichaeism in the Latin West*, ed. Johannes van Oort et al. (Leiden: Brill, 2001), pp. 195–204; Otto E. Neugebauer, 'Melothesia and Dodecatemoria', in *Studia biblica et orientalia, Vol. 3: Oriens Antiquus* (Rome: Pontificio Instituto Biblico, 1959); Erica Reiner, 'Two Babylonian Precursors of Astrology', *Nouvelles Assyriologiques Brèves et Utilitaires* (1993): pp. 21–22; Mladen Popovic, *Reading the Human Body: Physiognomics and Astrology in the Dead Sea Scrolls* (Leiden: Brill, 2007), pp. 164–70.

[59] For this tradition about Saturn, see, among others, Fred Gettings, *The Secret Zodiac: The Hidden Art in Medieval Astrology* (London: Routledge, 1987), p. 137.

[60] See Nathaniel Fish Moore, *Ancient Mineralogy: Or, An Inquiry Respecting Mineral Substances Mentioned by the Ancients, with Occasional Remarks on the Uses to Which They Were Applied* (New York: G. & C. Carvill, 1834), p. 175 and n. 3. Moore, who was Professor of Greek and Latin at Columbia College, New York, points out that Pliny compares this stone with cadmitis, which is identical except for the latter's 'blisters of an azure colour' (Pliny, *Natural History*, 37.10, 151), and that Dioscorides also describes ostrachitis as resembling a shell.

This confusion is not surprising. Every culture assigns its own values and perceptions to the objects of the natural world; some gemstones familiar to us now were unknown in the Mediterranean world; and some, through extreme hardness or brittleness, defied the technology of the time in terms of cutting and polishing.[61] Yet even recently 'discovered' stones can have their own magical traditions within cultures where no transmission of lore from Mesopotamia, Egypt, Greece, Rome, Persia, or India can be demonstrated. It would seem to be the *idea* of the relationship between gemstones and the heavens, rather than a specific association between one stone and one heavenly potency, that exhibits such extraordinary transcultural persistence.

An example is labradorite, a feldspar found primarily around the Arctic Circle. This stone is described in some modern manuals as one of the gemstones of Scorpio; it is called 'the temple of the stars', and is said to confer on the wearer the power to open the mind to hidden realities.[62] The ancient Mediterranean world has, so far, yielded no artefact, amuletic or otherwise, made of labradorite. However, the Inuit of the Labrador Peninsula believe that the wandering spirits of the dead, who appear to the living as the celestial *aurora borealis*, were once trapped within the stone; an Inuit warrior freed most of them with a mighty blow of his spear, but

---

[61] Diamonds, for example, were only obtainable from India with great difficulty before the sixth-century CE, and made their first, and very scarce, appearance in Roman jewellery between the first- and third-centuries CE. See George E. Harlow, 'Following the History of Diamonds', in George E. Harlow, ed. *The Nature of Diamonds* (Cambridge: Cambridge University Press, 1998), pp. 116–35.

[62] See, for example, Barbara Case, *Making Jewelry with Gemstone Beads* (Cincinnati, OH: David & Charles, 2007), pp. 11 and 80, where Case describes labradorite as 'the temple of the stars', reputed to 'enhance our awareness of and attunement to the cycles and rhythms of life'. See also the description of labradorite and its association with Scorpio at http://www.shimmerlings.com/gemstones/labradorite/ [accessed 2 May 2016] where it is said to awaken 'awareness of one's innate magical powers'; http://gemstone-dictionary.com/labradorite.php [accessed 22 May 2013], where labradorite is also associated with Scorpio and is 'a gemstone of destiny because it opens up your psychic abilities by connecting you to the Universal flow of energies that permeates our world and universe'; and http://www.vegaattractions.com/crystals/gems/labradorite.html [accessed 1 June 2013], where it is said to be 'one of the best stones for enhancing the Scorpio personality'.

some of the spirit-lights remained imprisoned.[63] Labradorite only entered Western cultural awareness in 1770, when the Inuit revealed it to the missionaries of the Moravian Church. But in this Arctic world, as in the ancient societies of the Mediterranean, an intimate relationship has developed between stone, colour, celestial potency, and mythic narrative, in a culture entirely unrelated to ancient Western gemstone lore.

With the arrival of Arab learning in the West in the twelfth and thirteenth centuries, new works, from grimoires and alchemical treatises to philosophical expositions and healing compendia, were produced describing the magical attributes of gemstones. Some are replete with magical spells, some are linked with alchemy, some concern the invocation of daimonic and angelic presences, and some are dedicated to healing. Although there is little accord in terms of their allocation to astral potencies, these works concur in the belief that certain gemstones possess 'occult' powers related to the heavens. The world of Renaissance Italy enthusiastically embraced late antiquity's fascination with gemstone amulets, and large collections of surviving Hellenistic gems were amassed by esoterically inclined rulers like Lorenzo de' Medici (1449–1492) and prelates such as Pietro Barbo (1517–1571), later Pope Paul II, who possessed, according to Vasari, over a thousand ancient amulets, intaglios, and cameos, and died from a cold caught from the weight and chill of his rings.[64]

In the late fifteenth century, Marsilio Ficino (1433–1499) encapsulated the Platonic framework of *sumpatheia* by declaring:

> There is nothing so deformed in the whole living world that it has no soul, no gift of soul contained in it. The congruities of these forms, therefore... are

---

[63] For this legend, see Peter Budgell, 'Labradorite: Aurora Borealis Entombed in Stone', *TechnoMine Mining Technology*, 23 April 2007, at http://technology.infomine.com/articles/1/947/labradorite.mineral.labrador/labradorite.aurora.borealis.aspx [accessed 2 May 2016]; *Llewellyn's Magical Almanac* (Woodbury, MN: Llewellyn, 2009), p. 27. Another, slightly different version can be found in Jenifer Altman, *Gem and Stone: Jewels of Earth, Sea, and Sky* (San Francisco: Chronicle Books, 2012), p. 74: 'Labradorite fell from the Northern Lights and... each single specimen holds a blueprint of the universe within itself'.

[64] Patricia Aakhus, 'Astral Magic in the Renaissance: Gems, Poetry, and Patronage of Lorenzo de'Medici', *Magic, Ritual, and Witchcraft*, Vol. 3, no. 2 (Winter 2008): pp. 185–206, on pp. 191–92. See also Laurie Fusco and Gino Corti, *Lorenzo de'Medici, Collector and Antiquarian* (Cambridge: Cambridge University Press, 2006).

what Zoroaster called the divine lure, and Synesius agreed, calling them magic charms.[65]

The World Soul, according to Ficino, generates and animates all the myriad forms of matter, and drawing down celestial 'gifts' requires selecting their 'congruities': objects in natural sympathy with the gifts desired. Wearing, and performing rituals with gemstones with the right planetary 'congruities' facilitate healing and protection. Coral and blue chalcedony, for example, belonging respectively to Venus and Jupiter, 'work against the illusions of the black bile' imposed by Saturn, while the amethyst, also a Jupiterian stone, can protect against lightning.[66] Colours, according to Ficino, 'belong to the stars', and are especially strong in particular gemstones because of their likeness to the heavens.[67]

Drawing on Arab magical texts such as the eleventh-century *Picatrix*, and on various medieval Jewish Kabbalistic works, Henry Cornelius Agrippa (1486–1535), writing early in the sixteenth century, produced *De occulta philosophia*, his great 'junction' text of magic, alchemy, and astrology, synthesising threads from many earlier traditions and providing a cornucopia from which later magi, from his time to the present, have begged, borrowed, and stolen. Agrippa displayed a refreshing pluralism about planetary gemstones, all of which, by his time, could be faceted:

> We must know, that every stone... is not governed by one star alone, but many of them receive influence, not separated, but conjoined, from many stars.[68]

Chalcedony, according to Agrippa, is 'under' Saturn and Mercury, emerald 'under' Jupiter, Venus, and Mercury, and chrysolite 'under' the Sun, Venus, and Mercury. Moreover, each planet 'receives' more than one stone. Jupiter 'receives' not only sapphire, but also aquamarine, emerald, and green jasper, while the Moon 'receives' selenite, pearl, and aquamarine.[69] Some of these associations draw on ancient lapidaries, and some on Arab and Jewish sources. Agrippa resolved the contradictions between the older texts through an inclusiveness that allows multiple

---

[65] Marsilio Ficino, *The Book of Life*, trans. Charles Boer (Dallas, TX: Spring Publications, 1980), p. 87.
[66] Ficino, *The Book of Life*, p. 123.
[67] Ficino, *The Book of Life*, p. 120.
[68] Henry Cornelius Agrippa, *Three Books of Occult Philosophy*, trans. James Freake, ed. Donald Tyson (St. Paul, MN: Llewellyn, 2004), I.32, p. 99.
[69] Agrippa, *Three Books of Occult Philosophy*, I.24, p. 81; I.26, p. 86; I.27, p. 89.

relationships connected by what Jung, in the twentieth century, understood as 'archetypal' themes: Mars, for example, which 'receives' haematite, diamond, and red jasper, rules 'all fiery, red, and sulphurous things', and Mercury rules stones 'which are of divers colours'.[70]

I am going to pass over the alchemical literature from this period, because its rich corpus of writings on planetary gemstones, metals, and soul transformations would merit a separate paper to do the subject any justice. I will only briefly mention Paracelsus (1493–1541), who, in the sixteenth century, demonstrated the ways in which gemstones could be seamlessly incorporated into the framework of the alchemical *opus* through the idea that the heavens are secretly contained within the stones. Gemstones, according to Paracelsus, carry within them the incorruptible spirits of the stars, which must be 'extracted' through various chemical processes in order to reveal their innate perfection and healing powers.

> Precious stones... have the nearest place to the heavenly or sidereal ones in point of perfection, purity, beauty, brightness, virtue, power of withstanding fire, and incorruptibility... It [the incorruptible spirit] should therefore be sought and found in the stones, be recognized in them and extracted from them... For then it is no longer a stone, but an elaborate and perfect metal, comparable to the stars of heaven, which are themselves, as it were, stones separated from those of earth.[71]

From the late seventeenth century onward, belief in the magical power of gemstones began to wane; they became historical artefacts as well as subjects for a more 'scientific' investigation of their nature.[72] But the magical lore of gemstones survived the Enlightenment. A number of important archaeological discoveries in Egypt and the Middle East in the late nineteenth century generated a plethora of new scholarly works on magical amulets, and several important collections of stones were

---

[70] Agrippa, *Three Books of Occult Philosophy*, I.27, p. 89; I.29, p. 94. For planetary themes as archetypes, see C. G. Jung, CW9i.1, *The Archetypes and the Collective Unconscious*, trans. R. F. C. Hull (London: Routledge & Kegan Paul, 1968), §606; Jung, CW14, §308.

[71] Paracelsus, *The Hermetic and Alchemical Writings of Paracelsus*, trans. and ed. A. E. Waite (Chicago: Laurence Scott & Co., 1910), Vol. 1, *Coelum Philosophorum* Part II, pp. 16–18.

[72] See, for example, Robert Boyle, *An Essay About the Origine and Virtues of Gems, Wherein Are Propos'd and Historically Illustrated Some Conjectures About the Consistence of the Matter of Precious Stones, and the Subjects Wherein Their Chiefest Virtues Reside* (London: William Godbid, 1672).

published and analysed.⁷³ Many of these works, as befits their cultural context, are concerned solely with cataloguing ancient examples in important collections.⁷⁴ These catalogues make no magical claims, and there is usually little or no knowledge of astrology demonstrated by the authors.⁷⁵ But other works from this period, emerging from the waters of the occult revival, resurrect the old magical lore. Isidore Kozminsky's *The Magic and Science of Jewels and Stones*, for example, presents the astrological significance of the gemstones as a single ancient tradition, assigning one zodiacal sign to each stone.⁷⁶ Moss agate is 'under the celestial Taurus', and pyrite is 'martial' and 'attached to the zodiacal Scorpio'.⁷⁷ Faced with continuing disagreement about the astral correlations of the stones, Aleister Crowley (1875–1947) adopted Agrippa's pluralistic approach. His list of gemstone attributions deemed suitable for ritual work includes the following:

> Lapis Lazuli is of the blue violet of the highest form of Jupiter... The Amethyst is the violet of Jupiter. The Topaz is of the gold of the Sun. The Emerald is of the green of Venus. Turquoise is the blue of Venus. The Opal has the varied colours attributed to Mercury. Agate has the Mercurial yellow...

---

⁷³ See, as a typical example, Lady Helena Carnegie, ed., *Catalogue of the Collection of Antique Gems Formed by James Ninth Earl of Southesk*, 2 vols (London: Bernard Quaritch, 1908).
⁷⁴ See, for example, J. Henry Middleton, ed., *The Lewis Collection of Gems and Rings in the Possession of Corpus Christi College, Cambridge* (Cambridge: C. J. Clay & Sons, Cambridge University Warehouse, 1892); Charles William King, *The Natural History of Precious Stones and of the Precious Metals* (London: Bell & Daldy, 1867); Carnegie, *Catalogue of the Collection of Antique Gems Formed by James Ninth Earl of Southesk*; Kunz, *The Curious Lore of Precious Stones*; E. A. Wallis Budge, *Amulets and Superstitions: The Original Texts with Translations and Descriptions of a Long Series of Egyptian, Sumerian, Hebrew, Christian, Gnostic and Muslim Amulets and Talismans and Magical Figures, with Chapters on the Evil Eye, the Origin of the Amulet, the Pentagon, the Swastika, the Cross (Pagan and Christian), the Properties of Stones, Rings, Divination, Numbers, the Kabbalah, Ancient Astrology, etc.* (Oxford: Oxford University Press, 1930).
⁷⁵ See Kunz, *The Curious Lore of Precious Stones*; Budge, *Amulets and Superstitions*.
⁷⁶ Isidore Kozminsky, *The Magic and Science of Jewels and Stones* (1922; repr. in 2 volumes, San Rafael, CA: Cassandra Press, 1988).
⁷⁷ Kozminsky, *Magic and Science of Jewels and Stones*, Vol. 2, pp. 28, 74.

The Moonstone is a direct image of the Moon. Pearl and Crystal [rock quartz] are given for the suggestion of purity[78]

Crowley's inclusiveness, limited only by analogies of colour, encouraged the adoption, not only of newly discovered planets such as Uranus and Neptune, but of newly discovered gemstones with no ancient tradition. But the so-called 'tradition' currently offered by many jewellers, in which twelve 'birthstones' are allocated to the twelve zodiacal signs and the twelve months of the year – diamond, for example, is given to April and Aries, emerald to May and Taurus, amethyst to February and Aquarius, and ruby to July and Leo – is actually a list created by the American National Association of Jewellers in Kansas in 1912 for the purpose of promoting expensive precious stones.[79] There *are* older traditions about so-called 'birthstones', which I will discuss later, but they bear no relationship to this list.

The second tradition
The second tradition involving magical gemstones concerns the use of images, words, names, and letters inscribed on the stones, and it is to this tradition that most current scholarly literature is directed. During the 1950s, dedicated gem historians began systematically cataloguing gemstone amulets according to type and cultural provenance.[80] But defining a 'magical' gem, in contrast to one intended purely for 'ornament', is a modern distinction that may be entirely misleading when applied to older cultures; and the frailty of the perceived boundaries between religious, magical, astrological, and medical spheres of human activity is not always acknowledged in the scholarly literature. Many antique gems have been ignored because there are no recognisable magical images, words, or symbols inscribed on them. Given the ubiquity of various forms of magic in antiquity, and the complex ways in which religious ideas and symbols – including astral symbols – were seamlessly integrated into everyday life, this may be entirely anachronistic. As Thales

---

[78] Aleister Crowley, *777 and Other Qabalistic Writings of Aleister Crowley* (York Beach, ME: Weiserbooks, 1977), pp. 102–5.
[79] See, for example, http://www.pledgejewellers.co.uk/guide-to-birthstones.html [accessed 2 May 2016]. The discrepancy between the months and the zodiacal signs, which overlap the last part of one month and the first part of the next, is usually ignored.
[80] See, for example, Bonner, *Studies in Magical Amulets*.

remarked in the sixth century BCE, 'All things are full of gods',[81] and thus all gems, inscribed or not, may reveal a god in the stone.

The astrological dimensions of engraved gemstone amulets have also been overlooked if they do not display overtly zodiacal images. There *are* a few extant amulets where a zodiacal sign seems to be indicated, such as these three late antique stones in the British Museum's collections.

Fig. 5. Astrological gemstone amulets from the British Museum collections.

The green jasper amulet on the left portrays a leaping ram with a lunar crescent and star, and the magical name 'Abrasax'. The yellow jasper amulets in the centre and on the right display a crab; the central amulet portrays a crescent Moon in the crab's right claw, while the amulet on the right has engraved on the reverse *BARCHAI,* a magical name for the Moon-goddess, also found in the Greek Magical Papyri.[82] But when a scene from a mythic historiola is portrayed, it may not be recognised as a reference to a planetary god. Christopher Faraone suggests that 'astrology probably always played a role in the Chnoumis amulets', and it is likely that it played a role in a great many gemstones on which only the figure of a deity is inscribed.[83] The astrological dimension may be oblique or simply implicit, as in the case of a haematite healing amulet in the British Museum

---

[81] Thales, cited in Aristotle, *On the Soul*, 1.5.411a8, Plato, *Laws*, trans. A. E Taylor, in Hamilton & Cairns (eds.), *The Collected Dialogues of Plato*, pp. 1225–1516, 10.899b9, and Iamblichus, *De mysteriis*, I.9.5–6.

[82] For more on these three gemstone amulets, see S. Michel-von Dungern, 'Studies on Magical Amulets', *Recent Research on Engraved Gemstones in Late Antiquity c. AD 200*, no. 600 (2011): pp. 82–83.

[83] Christopher Faraone, 'Text, Image, and Medium: The Evolution of Graeco-Roman Magical Gemstones', in Entwistle and Adam, eds., *Gems of Heaven*, pp. 50–61, on p. 52.

collection, portraying the war-god Ares (Mars) and bearing an inscription stating: 'Ares stopped the liver's pains'.[84]

By late antiquity, engraved gemstone amulets, which seem to have originated in Egypt, had proliferated all over the Roman-ruled world.[85] The sudden popularity of these amulets may be related, not to some sudden conversion to magic, but to a shift from oral to scribal magic, with an accompanying belief in the magical potency of letters, words, and glyphs. Engraving an incantation on a gemstone made it solid, and represented a symbolic re-enactment of the original creation of the world.[86]

An interesting illustration of this emphasis on engraving is a blue chalcedony amulet of the Sun-god with seven rays on his head (Fig. 6), signifying his role as noetic cosmocrator of the seven planets. At the end of each ray is one of the seven Greek vowels, implying a direct link between the planets and their gods, the divine potency of the alphabet, and the kinds of rituals in which the amulet might have been used – including the use of sounds involving the vowels, or what Joscelyn Godwin has called 'vowel-song'.[87] Over five thousand engraved gemstone amulets are known in dozens of private and public collections all over the world, and, given the permissiveness of previous centuries concerning objects stolen from tombs and archaeological sites, a great many more are probably uncatalogued. The chalcedony amulet I have just described is not unique.

---

[84] Haematite Ares amulet, British Museum PE G 112, reproduced in Mastrocinque, 'The Colours of Magical Gems', p. 63. See also Christopher Faraone, 'Text, Image, and Medium', pp. 50–61, on p. 52. Ares is the Greek name for the Roman war-god Mars, after whom the planet is named. The gem is clearly magical, but there is no specific astrological inscription engraved on it. However, there is equally no reason why it is not directly related to the planet as well as its lord and therefore constitutes an example of astral healing magic.

[85] The centre for amulet production seems to have been Alexandria; see Carla Sfameni, 'Magic in Late Antiquity: The Evidence of Magical Gems', in *Religious Diversity in Late Antiquity*, ed. David M. Gwynn and Susanne Bangert (Leiden: Brill, 2010), pp. 435–73, on p. 443.

[86] See Roy Kotansky, 'Incantations and Prayers for Salvation on Inscribed Greek Amulets', in *Magika Hiera*, ed. Christopher A. Faraone and Dirk Obbink (New York: Oxford University Press, 1991), p. 114; Andrew T. Wilburn, *Materia Magica: The Archaeology of Magic in Roman Egypt, Cyprus, and Spain* (Ann Arbor, MI: University of Michigan Press, 2012), pp. 65–66.

[87] For textual support for the late antique association of planets and vowels, and further sources on the correspondences between vowels, sounds, colours, and planets, see Joscelyn Godwin, *The Mystery of the Seven Vowels: In Theory and Practice* (Grand Rapids, MI: Phanes Press, 1991).

The engraved image of the astral divinity is often, but not always, accompanied by magical names, *charactères*, astral symbols, and *voces magicae*. Where Jewish influence predominates, there are no images of divinities; Hebrew letters, angelic and Divine Names, and simple diagrams, such as the *menorah* or seven-branched candelabrum, are inscribed on the

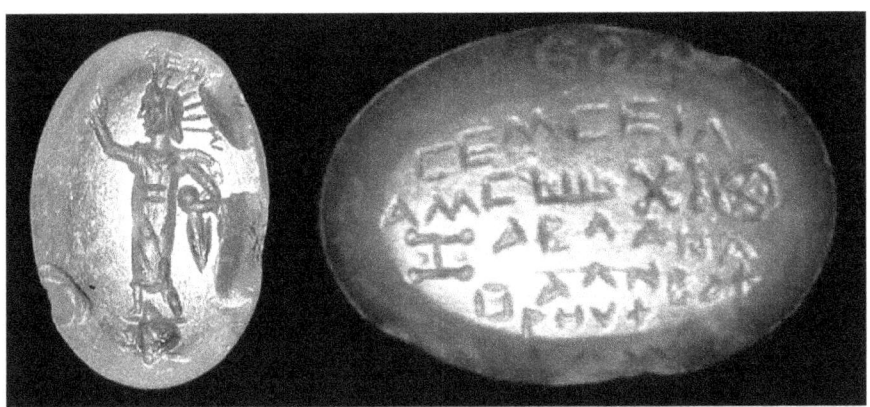

Fig. 6. Blue chalcedony amulet portraying the Sun-god. The reverse displays magical names and *charactères*. Taubman Collection 223, University of Michigan.

stone.[88] The magic of the Roman-ruled late antique world was henotheistic and thoroughly cosmopolitan; and some gemstone amulets combine with enthusiastic promiscuity the image of an Egyptian god, Greek *voces magicae*, astral symbols, and Hebrew Divine Names in a kind of syncretic soup that makes the religious provenance difficult to determine. Particularly popular were hybrid deities combining solar symbolism with names of power such as Abrasax, Iao, and Chnoumis. Amulets bearing such inscriptions were, in the early to mid-twentieth century, mistakenly labelled 'Gnostic'.[89] But Chnoumis was never the exclusive property of the Gnostic sects, nor was Abrasax, a magical name whose Greek letters, read as numbers, total 365, the number of days in the annual solar cycle.

Hybrid solar deities such as Chnoumis – a celestial being portrayed as a serpent with a lion's head crowned with seven rays – are coupled with

---

[88] See Gideon Bohak, *Ancient Jewish Magic: A History* (Cambridge: Cambridge University Press, 2008), pp. 159–61.
[89] See, for example, Campbell Bonner, 'Liturgical Fragments on Gnostic Amulets', *Harvard Theological Review*, Vol. 25, no. 4 (1932): pp. 362–67.

names of power, especially IAO, the Greek rendition of the Hebrew YHVH. The red jasper Chnoumis amulet below (Fig. 7, left), from the third century CE, is inscribed with the name IAO;[90] the serpentine Chnoumis amulet (Fig. 7, centre), portraying the god with seven eggs and twelve rays – presumably the seven planets and the twelve zodiacal signs – is likewise inscribed with IAO;[91] and the haematite cock-headed anguipede or snake-legged being (Fig. 7, right) is inscribed with the names AIEH and IAHIO, both, like IAO, equivalent to the Hebrew YHVH.[92]

Fig. 7. Left, red jasper Chnoumis amulet, third century CE. Centre, serpentine Chnoumis amulet with seven eggs and twelve rays. Right, haematite anguipede, first to sixth centuries CE.

Even early Christian amulets display this kind of syncretism.[93] It is the combination of symbol, writing, and stone, rather than the stone alone, which was perceived as possessing the greatest magical power. Many scholarly works on engraved gemstone amulets are not concerned with the reasons why a particular stone was chosen.[94] This might suggest that any

---

[90] Red jasper Chnoumis, third-century CE, University of Michigan US-AA-SCL-Bonner 46.
[91] Serpentine Chnoumis, first- and sixth-centuries CE, Kelsey Museum of Archaeology 26118.
[92] Haematite anguipede, first- to sixth-centuries CE, Kelsey Museum of Archaeology, 26054.
[93] See, for example, the gemstone amulet engraved with Christ on the cross accompanied by *voces magicae*, illustrated in Sfameni, 'Magic in Late Antiquity', p. 466, Fig. 10.
[94] Exceptions are Mastrocinque, "The Colours of Magical Gems', and Faraone, 'Text, Image, and Medium'.

old stone would do, provided the images and symbols were inscribed correctly. But certain stones do seem to have been favoured for particular purposes and specific astral potencies, even if they were difficult to obtain locally. Some of the *Greek Magical Papyri* (*PGM*) as well as the late antique lapidaries, offer careful instructions on how to engrave and use a particular stone in the context of a ritual.[95] An amulet similar to the Chnoumis amulet shown below (Fig. 8) is described in the late antique lapidary known as the *Lapidary of Socrates and Dionysius*,[96] dating from the third century CE. It is intended to heal stomach problems, and the image should be engraved on blue chalcedony, the 'colour of air'.[97]

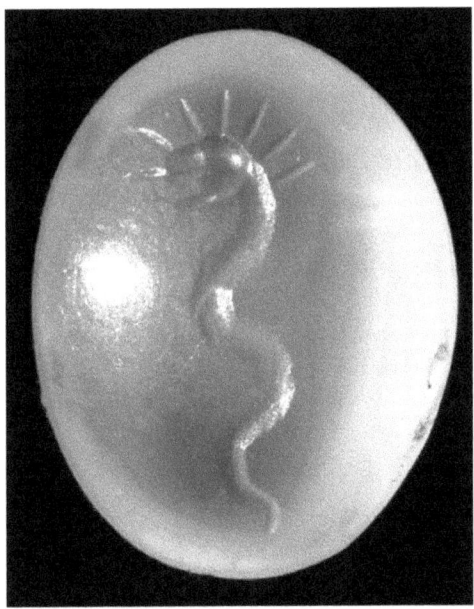

Fig. 8. Blue chalcedony Chnoumis amulet, first to sixth centuries CE.

---

[95] See, for example, Hans Dieter Betz, *The Greek magical papyri in translation, including the Demotic spells*. Vol. 1 (Chicago: University of Chicago Press, 1996), 5.477–58, p. 109, which instructs the adept to engrave on an agate an image of the syncretic Greco-Egyptian deity Sarapis, in order to facilitate divinatory dreams.
[96] For this lapidary, including the original Greek and a French translation, see Halleux and Schamp, *Les Lapidaires Grecs*, pp. 139–77.
[97] *The Lapidary of Socrates and Dionysius*, 35, in Halleux and Schamp, *Les Lapidaires Grecs*, p. 170. For the frequency of this gemstone among Chnoumis amulets, see Bonner, *Studies in Magical Amulets*, p. 60. Blue chalcedony Chnoumis amulet, first- to sixth-century CE, British Museum BMG173.

74 The God in the Stone: Gemstone Talismans in Western Magical Traditions

Engraved gemstone amulets were closely linked to rituals intended to procure the usual material goals,[98] but they were also used in theurgic efforts to transform the soul through a direct experience of divinity. The stones were not static objects that 'did' something if worn; they were dynamic participants in the ritual, ensuring that the god in the stone would join in. This is made clear in the *Greek Magical Papyri*, some of which offer instructions on how to use a particular engraved gemstone in the context of a ritual. For example, *PGM* 5 instructs the adept to engrave on an agate an image of the syncretic deity Sarapis, a god devised during the third century BCE by King Ptolemy I of Egypt to unify the Greek and Egyptian pantheons. Agate, or *achates* in Greek, is a generic term used to describe a number of patterned and striped microcrystalline quartzes, including the spotted green and red jasper known as bloodstone.[99]

The text of *PGM* 5 instructs that the amulet, similar to the one shown in Fig. 9, should be utilised in a ritual in which divinatory dreams are invoked, and that the god's image is accompanied by his magical names.[100]

Many engraved gemstone amulets were intended to cure a particular illness or protect a bodily organ.[101] Chief among the potencies invoked for healing was Chnoumis. His seven-rayed crown suggests that he symbolises the 'Intelligible' or spiritual Sun: the great cosmic life-force embodied on the earthly level by the Sun in the heavens.[102] His amulets are sometimes made of carnelian or red jasper, but they are also often carved from bloodstone, also called 'heliotrope' after the *heliotropium*, a plant whose flower turns its head to follow the Sun, and which was named, along with bloodstone, as the natural *sunthemata* or 'tokens' of solar power by the Neoplatonist Proclus in the fifth century CE.[103] The red flecks in

---

[98] See Carla Sfameni, 'Magic in Late Antiquity', pp. 435–73.
[99] See Faraone, 'Text, Image, and Medium', p. 60 n. 54.
[100] Betz, *PGM* 5.477–58, p. 109.
[101] See Bonner, *Studies in Magical Amulets*, pp. 51–94, consisting of three chapters on medical amulets.
[102] For Chnoumis' association with the first decan of Leo, see Michel-von Dungern, 'Studies on Magical Amulets', p. 83. For the 'noetic' or 'spiritual' Sun in Neoplatonic and Greco-Egyptian magical texts, see, for example, Hans Levy, *Chaldaean Oracles and Theurgy: Mysticism, Magic and Platonism in the Later Roman Empire* (Paris: Institut d'Études Augustiniennes, 2011), pp. 201–4, 409–30; Hans Dieter Betz, *The 'Mithras Liturgy': Text, Translation, and Commentary* (Tübingen: Mohr Siebeck, 2003).
[103] Proclus, *Commentary on Plato's Timaeus*, ed. and trans. Harold Tarrant (Cambridge: Cambridge University Press, 2007), I.3.10, p. 206.

bloodstone may be related, as the name suggests, to blood, and thus to the solar life-force. But the predominantly green colour of this jasper implies that the world of nature, *phusis*, was perceived as the physical vehicle in which this creative cosmic potency is both embedded and embodied.

Fig. 9. Bloodstone amulet with Sarapis and *voces magicae*, first to second centuries CE.[104]

The weaving of mythic narratives continued in Christian contexts. The bloodstone amulet below (Fig. 10), mirroring with precision the bloodstone amulet of Sarapis described above, portrays Christ healing the bleeding woman described in Mark and Luke; quotations from these Gospels are engraved on the amulet.[105]

---

[104] Bloodstone Sarapis amulet, Roman-Egyptian provenance, first to second centuries CE, Yale Babylonian Collection 2492.

[105] Mark 5:25–35 and Luke 8:43–48. Some words from the Gospels are engraved on the amulet as words of power, in much the same manner as the *voces magicae* on the Greco-Egyptian amulets. For another Christian bloodstone amulet, see in Jeffrey Spier, ed., *Picturing the Bible: The Earliest Christian Art* (New Haven, CT: Yale University Press, 2007), on p. 228.

76 The God in the Stone: Gemstone Talismans in Western Magical Traditions

Fig. 10. Christian bloodstone amulet, sixth-century Byzantine from Egypt, Metropolitan Museum of Art 17.190.491.

The stone is the same, but the narrative has changed. The *voces magicae* have become quotations from the Gospels; as Origen declared in the third century CE, 'The name of Jesus is so powerful against the demons that sometimes it is effective even when pronounced by bad men'.[106] The bloodstone, in Christian lore, was believed to be created when drops of blood from Christ's wounds fell on a piece of green jasper lying in the earth beneath the cross.[107] Colour, narrative, celestial potency, image, language, and human suffering and aspiration are woven into a chain of sympathies that, once again, transform the gemstone into a potent intermediary spanning the abyss between revealed and concealed worlds.

---

[106] Origen, *Contra Celsum*, trans. Henry Chadwick (Cambridge: Cambridge University Press, 1965), I.6.

[107] See Brown University. Dept. of Art, and David Winton Bell Gallery (Brown University), *Survival of the Gods: Classical Mythology in Medieval Art* (Providence, RI: Brown University, 1987), p. 169. For earlier sources, see Kunz, *The Curious Lore of Precious Stones*, p. 267. For more on Christian bloodstone amulets, see Jeffrey Spier, 'Medieval Byzantine Magical Amulets and Their Tradition', *Journal of the Warburg and Courtauld Institutes*, Vol. 56 (1993): pp. 25–62.

The third tradition

The last tradition I would like to explore is that of so-called 'birthstones', which, in modern times, have become the most familiar aspect of all magical gemstone lore. Although many people purchasing a ring set with their birthstone might not think of magic, nevertheless the belief that there is some hidden relationship between the date of one's birth, the gemstone, and the zodiac implies that *sumpatheia* is still alive and well, albeit unacknowledged.

In Exodus, written between the tenth and seventh centuries BCE, the Lord gives instructions for a 'breastpiece of decision' that Aaron, the brother of Moses, must wear 'for consecrating him to serve Me as priest'.

> You shall make a breastpiece of decision... Set in it mounted stones, in four rows of stones. The first row shall be a row of carnelian, chrysolite, and emerald; the second row a turquoise, a sapphire, and an amethyst; the third row, a jacinth, an agate, and a crystal; and the fourth row: a beryl, a lapis lazuli, and a jasper... The stones shall correspond to the names of the sons of Israel: twelve, corresponding to their names... Inside the breastpiece of decision you shall place the *Urim* and *Thummim*, so that they are over Aaron's heart when he comes before the Lord.[108]

There is ongoing disagreement about how to translate the names of some of the stones.[109] Moreover, the colours of these stones are not always consistent; garnets, for example, are found in green as well as golden-red and reddish-purple; turquoise can be green, sky-blue, or yellow; and it is unclear which type of jasper is meant as the last of the stones, since this mottled stone can be found in colours that encompass the entire spectrum. We still do not know which gems were utilised in this most important of religious symbols, although many attempts have been made over the centuries to reconstruct the breastpiece. Modern efforts at reproducing the stones of the breastpiece are not limited to Jewish contexts, but range from Mormon replicas to Masonic versions, affirming how this potent symbol still wields its ancient fascination in a wide variety of contemporary cultural milieux. There is, however, general agreement about the function of the 'breastpiece of decision': it was an instrument of divination,

---

[108] Exodus 28:5–22.

[109] For example, the fourth stone, which is called 'turquoise' in the translation of the *Tanakh* I have used above, is given as 'emerald' in the King James Bible, 'carbuncle' in the Septuagint, 'turquoise' in the *New American Standard Bible*, and 'garnet' in *Strong's Dictionary*.

intended to ascertain God's will.[110] The mysterious *Urim* and *Thummim* may have been engraved gemstones used as lots, for divining God's intentions in situations where ordinary human judgement might fail.[111]

Exodus makes no mention of the signs of the zodiac. But in the first century CE, the historian Josephus (37–100 CE) and the Platonic philosopher Philo of Alexandria (20 BCE–50 CE) both insisted on a relationship. Josephus is clear about the correlation between the breastpiece and the zodiac:

> And for the twelve stones, whether we understand by them the months, or whether we understand the like number of the signs of that circle which the Greeks call the Zodiac, we shall not be mistaken in their meaning.[112]

He names the gemstones, but unfortunately his list does not accord with the one given in Exodus,[113] although he offers further insight into the oracular nature of the breastpiece:

> For God declared beforehand, by those twelve stones which the high priest bore on his breast... when they should be victorious in battle; for so great a splendor shone forth from them before the army began to march, that all the people were sensible of God's being present for their assistance. Whence it

---

[110] The *Urim* and *Thummim* are also described as divinatory instruments in 1 Samuel 28:6 and Numbers 27:21. The understanding of the breastpiece as an oracle was also expressed in the so-called 'Letter of Aristeas', a document written in Greek by an Alexandrian Jew called Aristeas to his brother Philocrates, in the third century BCE: 'It was an occasion of great amazement to us when we saw Eleazar engaged on his ministry, and all the glorious vestments, including the wearing of the 'garment' with precious stones upon it... On his breast he wears what is called the 'oracle', to which are attached twelve stones of different kinds, set in gold, giving the names of the patriarchs in what was the original order, each stone flashing its own natural distinctive color.' See *Letter to Aristaeus*, pp. 96–98, trans. R. J. H. Shutt, in *The Old Testament Pseudepigrapha*, Vol. 2, ed. James H. Charlesworth (New York/London: Doubleday, 1985), p. 19. See also the notes by the translator of Exodus in *The Jewish Study Bible*, Jeffrey H. Tigay, who observes on p. 172 that both the breastpiece and the *ephod* are 'involved in ascertaining the divine will', see *The Jewish Study Bible, Tanakh Translation*, ed. Adele Berlin and Marc Zvi Brettler (Oxford: University of Oxford Press, 1999).
[111] See the notes by Jeffrey H. Tigay, the translator of Exodus in *The Jewish Study Bible*, p. 172.
[112] Flavius Josephus, *The Antiquities of the Jews*, 3.7.7, in William Whiston, trans., *Josephus: The Complete Works* (Nashville, TN: Thomas Nelson, 1998), p. 107.
[113] Josephus, *The Antiquities of the Jews*, 3:7.5, pp. 105–6.

came to pass that those Greeks, who had a veneration for our laws... called that breastplate the Oracle.[114]

Philo's approach, in contrast, is unashamedly Platonic. In the treatise entitled *On Dreams*, he describes the High Priest's vestments as symbols reflecting both the cosmos and the human soul:

> For there are, as it seems, two Temples of God, the one is this cosmos, in which the firstborn divine Logos is also High Priest, the other is the rational soul, whose priest is the true man, whose perceptible image is the one who offers the traditional prayers and sacrifices.[115]

The High Priest and his vestments as a 'perceptible image' of the divine Logos tells us something about Philo's understanding of the faculty of sight: what we see is the fleshly garb of the unseen, and the gemstones of the breastpiece are the 'perceptible images' of deity. In *On the Life of Moses*, Philo offers his understanding of the twelve gemstones as symbols of the zodiacal signs:

> The twelve stones on the breast, which are not like one another in colour... what else can they be emblems of, except of the circle of the zodiac?... The twelve stones are of different colors and none of them like to any other. For each of the signs of the zodiac also produces its own particular coloring in the air and earth and water and their phases, and also in the different kinds of animals and plants.[116]

The natural world in all its complexity thus reveals a kaleidoscope of changing colours that reflect the zodiacal cycle, whose twelve 'phases' are also symbolised by the twelve gemstones.

In the two or three centuries following the destruction of the Temple in 79 CE, Jewish *hekhalot* literature reimagined the rituals and vestments of the High Priest as aspects of a heavenly ritual occurring in a *mundus*

---

[114] Josephus, *The Antiquities of the Jews*, 3.8.9, p. 110.

[115] Philo, *On Dreams*, in *Philo: Vol. V*, trans. F. H. Colson (Cambridge, MA: Harvard University Press, 1934), I.214–15f. See also Jutta Leonhardt, *Jewish Worship in Philo of Alexandria* (Tübingen: Mohr Siebeck, 2001), p. 128.

[116] Philo, *On the Life of Moses*, in *Philo: Vol. VI*, trans. F. H. Colson (Cambridge, MA: Harvard University Press, 1935), 2.124. Philo also offers a zodiacal interpretation of the breastpiece in *On the Special Laws*, in Philo: Vol. VII, trans. F. H. Colson (Cambridge, MA: Harvard University Press, 1937), 1.87, and *On Dreams*, 1.214.

imaginalis that was also an inner soul-journey. The Temple, no longer existent in material form, became a visionary sanctuary providing a point of union between heaven and earth.[117] The gemstones of the breastpiece are now dimensions of the vision of the Divine Glory: beryls shine between the wings of the angels and the Throne of God,[118] while the Throne itself, made of lapis lazuli, is 'surrounded by thickets of brightness, emerald and sapphire'.[119] These references, highlighting the mysterious identity between gemstones and deity, were inspired by Ezekiel,[120] whose description of the 'stones of fire', written eight centuries earlier, comprise nine of the twelve stones of the High Priest's breastpiece.[121]

The twelve gemstones entered Christian celestial geography through the *Apocalypse of John*, in which they form the foundations of the walls of the New Jerusalem:

> The first foundation was jasper; the second, sapphire; the third, a chalcedony; the fourth, an emerald; the fifth, sardonyx; the sixth, sard; the seventh, chrysolite; the eighth, beryl; the ninth, a topaz; the tenth, a chrysoprase; the eleventh, a jacinth; the twelfth, an amethyst.[122]

---

[117] For the transformation of the Temple, see Martha Himmelfarb, 'From Prophecy to Apocalypse: *The Book of the Watchers* and Tours of Heaven', in *Jewish Spirituality from the Bible to the Middle Ages*, ed. Arthur Green (New York: Crossroad, 1986), pp. 146–65; Martha Himmelfarb, 'Earthly Sacrifice and Heavenly Incense: The Law of the Priesthood in *Aramaic Levi* and *Jubilees*', in *Heavenly Realms and Earthly Realities in Late Antique Religions*, ed. Ra'anan S. Boustan and Annette Yoshiko Reed (Cambridge: Cambridge University Press, 2004), pp. 103–22; Silviu N. Bunta, 'A Misplaced Temple Question About Ezekiel's Visions', in *With Letters of Light: Studies in the Dead Sea Scrolls, Early Jewish Apocalypticism, Magic, and Mysticism*, ed. Daphne V. Arbel and Andrei A Orlov (Berlin: De Gruyter, 2011), pp. 28–44.

[118] *Hekhalot Zutarti*, 356, cited in Peter Schäfer, *The Hidden and Manifest God: Some Major Themes in Early Jewish Mysticism*, trans. Aubrey Pomerance (Albany, NY: SUNY Press, 1992), pp. 62–63.

[119] *Seder Rabba di-Bereshit*, pp. 782–84, cited in Peter Schäfer, 'In Heaven as It Is in Hell: The Cosmology of *Seder Rabba di-Bereshit*', in *Heavenly Realms* (2004): pp. 233–74, on p. 251.

[120] See Martin A. Sweeney's Introduction to Ezekiel in *The Jewish Study Bible*, pp 1042–45.

[121] Ezekiel 28:13–17.

[122] *Apocalypse of John*, 19–21.

The twelve gates of the celestial City honour the twelve Hebrew Tribes, but the gemstone foundations are embedded in a new narrative.

> And the wall of the city had twelve foundations, and in them the names of the twelve apostles of the Lamb.[123]

Many modern attempts have been made to relate the twelve apostles to the twelve gemstones. John unfortunately did not provide this information, and disagreements about the gemstones of the New Jerusalem have continued ever since.[124]

Although the High Priest's breastpiece continued to enjoy a powerful esoteric significance in early modern currents such as alchemy and Freemasonry, there is little Jewish literature in the intervening centuries that attributes specific occult properties to the twelve stones. A notable exception is a thirteenth-century work from the Rhineland called *Sefer Gematriot*, which describes the particular occult powers of each of the stones of the breastpiece.

> *Odem* appertains to Reuben... Its use is to prevent the woman who wears it from suffering a miscarriage. It is also good for women who suffer excessively in childbirth.[125]

The association of red gemstones with childbirth is common in the ancient world.[126] The medieval provenance of *Sefer Gematriot* suggests that this association found its way into Jewish magical lore at an early date, and

---

[123] *Apocalypse of John*, 21:10–14, *KJV*.

[124] For a modern attempt to correlate the twelve apostles with the twelve stones, see
http://overcomers.ca/blog_New_Jerusalem/The_New_Jerusalem_New_Creation_001.htm.

[125] *Sefer Gematriaot*, 43a–44b, cited in Joshua Trachtenberg, *Jewish Magic and Superstition: A Study in Folk Religion* (1939; repr. Philadelphia, PA: University of Pennsylvania Press, 2004), p. 137. The full Hebrew text of this work is given by Trachtenberg in Appendix II, pp. 265–68, and was more recently published as *Sefer Gematriot of R. Judah the Pious: Facsimile Edition of a Unique Manuscript*, ed. Daniel Abrams (Ashland, OH: Cherub Press, 2001). For more on *Sefer Gematriaot*, see Ronald H. Isaacs, *Divination, Magic, and Healing: The Book of Jewish Folklore* (Lanham, MD: Jason Aronson, 1998), pp. 77–86.

[126] For an example, see Timothy P. Harrison and Douglas L. Esse, *Megiddo 3: Final Report on the Stratum VI Excavations* (Chicago: Oriental Institute of the University of Chicago Press, 2004), p. 70.

syncretic traditions of the stones of the breastpiece emerged in medieval Germany in the circles of the German Jewish Pietists, and from there into Eastern Europe with the migration of the Ashkenazi Jews over the ensuing three centuries. In eighteenth-century Poland, Jewish gem cutters and traders, many of them aligned with the Hasidic movement and familiar with Kabbalistic themes,[127] seem to have generated the lore of the twelve gemstones as birthstones, and it is from this cultural matrix that the modern association of gemstones with the month of one's birth arose.[128] The belief that wearing the stone of one's birth-sign can confer good fortune is now found everywhere – even when the discrepancy between months and zodiacal signs creates confusion, and despite the fact that no agreement has been reached about the identity of the stones.

The imprint of modernity can be glimpsed in more recent permutations of this long tradition that reaches back to Exodus. The stones of the breastpiece originally seem to have represented the Tribes of Israel as a community, and not any individual's birth date. When Philo and Josephus related the breastpiece to the zodiac, they were not referring to anyone's natal horoscope. Even Marsilio Ficino, who complained about the melancholy his natal Saturn made him endure, advocated rituals using Venusian coral and Jupiterian chalcedony, not because he was born under Libra or Sagittarius – in fact, he was a Scorpio – but because these gemstones could help anyone suffering from Saturn's 'black bile'. It is not until the modern era that 'my birthstone' becomes a dominant feature in gemstone lore and gemstone marketing. It has been argued that awareness of an individual, isolated self is itself a signature of modernity.[129] If so, gemstones have made the transition smoothly and seamlessly, without abandoning the magic of their ancient lineage.

---

[127] For the dominance of Hasidism in Polish Jewry in the eighteenth century, see Glenn Dynner, *Men of Silk: The Hasidic Conquest of Polish Jewish Society* (Oxford: Oxford University Press, 2006). For the magical and Kabbalistic predilections of the Hasidim, see Moshe Idel, *Hasidism: Between ecstasy and magic* (Albany, NY: SUNY Press, 2012).

[128] See Lance Grande and Allison Augustyn, *Gems and Gemstones: Timeless Natural Beauty of the Mineral World* (Chicago: University of Chicago Press, 2009), p. 335; Kunz, *The Curious Lore of Precious Stones*, pp. 307–37.

[129] For this theme, see Alex Owen, *The Place of Enchantment: British Occultism and the Culture of the Modern* (Chicago: University of Chicago Press, 2004).

Conclusion

Poets, novelists, and playwrights have always sought inspiration in the lore of gemstones. Shakespeare's work is encrusted with references to their powers. In the poem called *A Lover's Complaint*, he praises

> ... The deep-green emerald, in whose fresh regard
> Weak sights their sickly radiance do amend,[130]

echoing Theophrastus' statement, in the fourth century BCE, that *smaragdos* 'is good for the eyes'.[131] John Milton, in *Paradise Lost*, writes of the towers of heaven 'with battlements adorned of living sapphire', mirroring Babylonian and Hebrew descriptions of *sappheiros* as the stone of heaven.[132] Literature can also generate new gemstone myths; the irresistible urge to weave narratives around the stones is not limited to the ancient world. In 1576, the French poet Rémy Belleau, drawing on the etymology of the Greek word *amethustos*, which means 'not intoxicated', published a poem about the god Dionysus and his pursuit of the nymph Amethyste. She refused the god's affections and was turned into a white stone; Dionysus wept in frustration, and, being the god of wine, his tears dyed the stone purple.[133] This story cannot be found in any Hellenistic, Roman, or medieval source, but it appears in modern descriptions of amethyst as though it were an ancient tradition. The sinister opal that disintegrates on contact with holy water in Sir Walter Scott's nineteenth-century novel, *Anne of Geierstein*, was entirely Scott's invention;[134] but for over fifty years his coupling of opals with sorcery and ill fortune almost single-handedly destroyed European trade in a gemstone which Pliny, in

---

[130] Shakespeare, *A Lover's Complaint* (1609), in *The Oxford Shakespeare*, ed. W. J. Craig (Oxford: Oxford University Press, 1914), p. 212.

[131] Theophrastus, *On Stones*, 24, p. 99.

[132] John Milton, *Paradise Lost* (London: Penguin Classics, 2003), 2:1049–50.

[133] Rémy Belleau, 'L'Amethyste, ou les Amours de Bacchus et d'Amethyste', in Rémy Belleau, *Les Amours det Nouveaux Eschanges des Pierres Precieuses* (Paris: Mamert Patisson, 1576), pp. 4–6. See also Kunz, *The Curious Lore of Precious Stones*, pp. 58–59.

[134] Sir Walter Scott, *Anne of Geierstein, or, The Maiden of the Mist* (Edinburgh: Cadell & Co., 1829). Kunz, in *The Curious Lore of Precious Stones*, pp. 143–44, noted in 1913 that 'much of the modern superstition regarding the supposed unlucky quality of the opal owes its origin to a careless reading of Sir Walter Scott's novel'.

the first century CE, described as possessing all 'the most brilliant qualities of the most valuable gems'.[135]

More recent narratives include the elvish gemstone rings – Narya, the red Ring of Fire; Nenya, the white Ring of Adamant; and Vilya, the blue Ring of Firmament – in J. R. R. Tolkien's *Lord of the Rings*. The names of the stones – Fire, Adamant, and Firmament – are very ancient, dating back to biblical literature as well as the Greek lapidaries, as Tolkien was well aware.[136] More recently, numerous magical gems have made their appearance in the Harry Potter novels, such as the rubies that adorn the hilt of the Sword of Godric Gryffindor, which makes its first appearance in *Harry Potter and the Chamber of Secrets*.[137] The gemstones of Middle Earth and Hogwarts, like Scott's opal, are magical but not explicitly celestial. But the interweaving of the traditions has resulted in literary tropes attaching themselves to astral gemstone lore, and vice versa. In the Greco-Roman world, the griffin was the creature of the Sun-god.[138]

The Sword of Godric Gryffindor, which alone can destroy the dreaded Basilisk, bears on its hilt blood-red stones redolent of strength and power, mirroring the red fire-stone Narya worn by Gandalf in *The Lord of the Rings*, and echoing the blood-red talismans of Egypt, Etruria, and Greece. Such stones seem to emanate solar light even when the name of the god has changed. However innovative the cultural adaptation, the perception that gemstones – uncut or faceted, plain or engraved – embody, through their colours, emanations of celestial divinity, is an idea with extraordinary agency and continuity.

---

[135] Pliny, *Natural History*, 37:21.80.
[136] For Tolkien's familiarity with biblical and ancient Greek, Norse, and Teutonic literature, see, among others, George Clark and Daniel Timmon, eds., *R. R. Tolkien and His Literary Resonances: Views of Middle-Earth* (Westport, CT: Greenwood, 2000); Verlyn Flieger, *Splintered Light: Logos and Language in Tolkien's World* (Kent, OH: Kent State University Press, 2002).
[137] J. K. Rowling, *Harry Potter and the Chamber of Secrets* (London: Bloomsbury, 2002).
[138] See Jamie Claire Fumo, *The Legacy of Apollo: Antiquity, Authority, and Chaucerian Poetics* (Toronto: University of Toronto Press, 2010), p. 33.

Fig. 11. Apollo riding on a griffin, Attic red-figure *kylix*, ca. 380 BCE, Kunsthistorisches Museum, Vienna IV 202.

I can think of no better way to conclude this paper than to cite a passage from the work of a sixteenth-century Kabbalist called Moshe Cordovero:

> The essence of divinity is found in every single thing – nothing but it exists... Do not attribute duality to God... Do not say 'This is a stone and not God'. God forbid! Rather, all existence is God, and the stone is a thing pervaded by divinity.[139]

---

[139] Moshe Cordovero, *Shi'ur Qomah*, Modena MS 206b, cited in Daniel Matt, *The Essential Kabbalah: The Heart of Jewish Mysticism* (Edison, NJ: Castle Books, 1997).

Investigating the Magical Practice found in *PGM* (*Greek Magical Papyri*) XIII

Claire Chandler

Abstract: *PGM* XIII is a Greco-Egyptian magical papyri dated to the mid fourth century CE. It contains at least two versions of a rite to summon the creator god and gain his name, which is then used in further spells also included in the papyrus. This paper examines the practices involved in this rite and explores their theoretical underpinning, investigating timing, writing and symbolism to expose the interconnectedness implicit in the ancient worldview and the place of magic within it. The magical papyri are documents which reflect the methods and experience of actual magical practitioners rather than literary depictions. These accounts and methods contextualise magic within an ontological world view.

The Greek Magical Papyri

PGM XIII is one of the Greek magical papyri that are surviving documents from Egypt which have been published as a modern collection.[1] This collection of documents, as published by Karl Preisendanz and his team, is known as the *Papyri Graecae Magicae* (*PGM*), *Die Griechischen Zauberpapyri* or *The Greek Magical Papyri* in English, and dates from the second century BCE to the fifth century CE.[2] An English translation was

___

[1] For recent studies of *PGM* XIII see Jacco Dieleman, *Priests, Tongues, and Rites: The London-Leiden Magical Manuscripts and Translation in Egyptian Ritual (100-300 CE)*, Vol. 153, *Religion in the Greco-Roman World* (Leiden/Boston: Brill, 2005); Dorian Gieseler Greenbaum, *The Daimon in Hellenistic Astrology* (Leiden/Boston: Brill, 2015), pp. 195, 200–5; Todd Klutz, 'Jesus, Morton Smith and the *Eighth Book of Moses* (PGM 13.1–734)', *Journal for the Study of the Pseudepigrapha* 21, no. 2 (2011): pp. 133–59; Todd Klutz, trans. 'The Eighth Book of Moses', in *Old Testament Pseudepigrapha: More Noncanonical Scriptures*, Vol. 1, ed. Richard Bauckham, James R. Davila and Alexander Panayotov (Grand Rapids, MI: Wm. B. Eerdmans, 2013).
[2] K. Preisendanz et al., eds., *Papyri Graecae Magicae: Die Griechischen Zauberpapyri* (Berlin and Leipzig: B. G. Teubner, 1928); K. Preisendanz et al., eds., *Papyri Graecae Magicae, Die Grieschischen Zauberpapyri*, Vol. 2 (Leipzig and Berlin: B. G. Teuner, 1931).

___

Claire Chandler, 'Investigating the Magical Practice found in *PGM* (Greek Magical Papyri) XIII', *Celestial Magic*, special issue of *Culture and Cosmos*, Vol. 19, nos. 1 and 2, 2015, pp. 87–97.
www.CultureAndCosmos.org

published in 1986.³ Hans Dieter Betz, the editor, begins his introduction to that volume as follows:

> The Greek magical papyri is a name given by scholars to a body of papyri from Greco-Roman Egypt containing a variety of magical spells and formulae, hymns and rituals.⁴

These documents present us with real working documents, 'direct from the magician's workshops' as William Brashear said in his exhaustive survey of the papyri.⁵ These are not literary accounts of magic, open to artistic license and imaginary flare, but actual working documents. The content of these papyri present us with material as used in Late Antiquity rather than an historical commentary or literary treatment. These documents have also managed to arrive in the modern world untouched by editorial influence. No one was sufficiently interested in them to cite them in another text or consider them interesting enough not to be thrown away; they were also fortunate not to have been destroyed by accident. Any textual errors introduced via the copying process are as potentially interesting as they are perplexing and these puzzles shed light on both the scribe and his environment.

PGM XIII was part of an ancient collection of documents which came to light in 1828. We know nothing about the archaeology of that discovery as the documents appeared on the antiquities market having being allegedly found by shepherds in a tomb near Thebes, which is modern Luxor, in Upper Egypt. No one knows these circumstances with any certainty, so anything we may deduce about the provenance of these documents must take this lack of evidence into account.⁶ This collection of

---

³ Hans Dieter Betz, ed., *The Greek Magical Papyri in Translation, including the Demotic Spells*, 2ⁿᵈ edition, Vol. 1 [*GMPT*] (Chicago, IL: University of Chicago, 1992).
⁴ Betz, *GMPT*, p. xli.
⁵ William M. Brashear, 'The Greek Magical Papyri: an Introduction and Survey; annotated bibliography (1928–1994)', in *Aufstieg und Niedergang der römischen Welt: Geschichte und Kultur Roms im Spiegel der neueren Forschung (ANRW) II.18.5*, ed. H. Temporini and W. Haase (Berlin: de Gruyter, 1995), p. 3400.
⁶ Brashear, 'Greek Magical Papyri', p. 3402.; Garth Fowden, *The Egyptian Hermes: a Historical Approach to the Late Pagan Mind* (Princeton, NJ: Princeton University Press, 1986), pp. 168–70; Jacco Dieleman, *Priests, Tongues, and Rites*, p. ix.; Pieter W. Van der Horst, 'The Great Magical Papyrus of Paris (PGM IV) and the Bible', in *A Kind of Magic: Understanding Magic in the New Testament*

Timing of the Rite

The first element I would like to look at is the timing of the Rite. The practitioner is instructed to begin a period of purification which will end on the Aries new moon, that is the new moon after the spring equinox, one of the turning points of the year. The new moon, having no light, is associated with times of secrecy or privacy. The rite includes many entreaties to the reader to keep both the book and knowledge of the rite secret.[17] The stress on secrecy was not only a precaution against those unsympathetic to magic. There were also 'issues of secrecy and strict limitation of both knowledge and practice to select individuals and circles'.[18] Even where these ritual practices were accepted and valued the element of secrecy was acknowledged and accepted.

Language

Language can be communicated in many ways. It can be written or spoken, and therefore heard. There is also the use of shapes and pictures to represent words and sounds and Egypt has a rich tradition of hieroglyphic writing. There is the sound that the letters and syllables make which may be connected to semantic meaning in a particular language, may be a word or name in another language, or may have no sensible translation. Some have described this as nonsense. A less judgemental term is non-semantic sounds.[19] Essentially we have a visual or an aural communication vehicle. There is also the idea that letters have numeric values, known as *gematria*, and therefore words can be represented by a number. This practice survives as modern numerology. Many ancient number schemes exist and they were by no means universally accepted.[20] We also find linguistic tricks such as palindromes, words which are spelt the same forwards as backwards, an example of visual communication, as the arrangement of letters is not apparent. There are palindromes in the multilingual papyri, in Demotic, which only make sense if they have been mistranslated back into Demotic from Greek.[21] This is an illustration of the complex intercultural connections indicative of this period.[22] Rhymes are spoken as are tones, which may be sung.

---

[17] Betz, *GMPT*, p. 179, l. 230–34; p. 189, l. 740–44.
[18] Naomi Janowitz, *Icons of Power: Ritual Practices in Late Antiquity*, (Pennsylvania, PA: Penn State University Press, 2002).
[19] Janowitz, *Icons of Power*, p. 45.
[20] Janowitz, *Icons of Power*, pp. 50–51.
[21] Dieleman, *Priests, Tongues and Rites*, p. 67.
[22] Dieleman, *Priests, Tongues and Rites*, p. 69.

Non-semantic sound is a characteristic of the magical voices or *voces magicae*. These are streams of words or characters, not obviously in the language of the rest of the text. They consist of names or gods, vowels and words of other languages, the meaning of which is difficult to penetrate. These magical or mystical voices appear in magical text around the beginning of the Christian era.[23] As the cultural mix of Egypt in this period is rich, it is difficult to say whether the presence of particular gods has anything to say about the cultural influence on the writer of the document. *Iaω*, one of the names for the Jewish god, is the most common deity found in the *PGM* but that does not make all documents containing it Jewish.[24] Known variously as *voces magicae* (magical voices), *ephesia grammata*, or *onomata barbara* (non-Greek names or words), these strings of names and words without a directly associated meaning are characteristic of magical texts from Late Antiquity.[25] Divine names have implicit meaning so these words may not have a readily apparent semantic meaning: they are the deity they represent. These streams of non-semantic sounds have several interesting features including the use of streams of vowels and the inclusion of divine names from many different cultures. These divine names have not been translated into Greek because of their nature. As the name *is* the deity it cannot be translated, so the original language remains.[26] Iamblichus explains that certain names have 'weightiness and great precision, participating in less ambiguity, variability and multiplicity of expression'.[27] When trying to convey the name of a deity the language used needs to convey an essentially unknowable concept.[28] For a language

---

[23] Brashear, 'Greek Magical Papyri', p. 3414.
[24] Betz, *GMPT*, p. lvii ; Dieleman, *Priests, Tongues and Rites*, p. 78.
[25] Crystal Addey, 'Assuming the Mantle of the Gods: "Unknowable" Names and Invocations in Late Antique Theurgic Ritual', in *Sacred Words: Orality, Literacy and Religion*, in *Orality and Literacy in the Ancient World*, ed. A. P. M. H. Lardinois, J. H. Blok, and M. G. M. van der Poel (Leiden: Brill, 2011), p. 279; Bohak, *Ancient Jewish Magic*, pp. 258–9; Brashear, 'Greek Magical Papyri', p. 3414; David Frankfurter, 'The Magic of Writing and the Writing of Magic: The Power of the Word in Egyptian and Greek Traditions', *Helios* 23, no. 2 (1994): p. 199.
[26] Iamblichus, *Di Mysteriis*, trans. Emma C. Clarke, John M. Dillon, and Jackson P. Hershbell (Atlanta, GA: Society of Biblical Literature, 2003), p. 299, VII.5.
[27] Iamblichus, *De Mysteriis*, p. 299, VII.5.
[28] Patricia Cox Miller, 'In Praise of Nonsense,' in *Classical Mediterranean Spirituality*, ed. A. H. Armstrong (London: Routledge & Kegan Paul, 1986), p. 482; Addey, 'Assuming the Mantle of the Gods', p. 282.

to do this successfully it needs to be able to convey meaning in a non-discursive way. Egyptian hieroglyphs are an excellent tool for this job as the word is pictorially represented and cannot be broken down. As Patricia Cox Miller explains in her exposition on the divine name in written form, logic and discursive language must be abandoned and paradox embraced.[29]

David Frankfurter contrasted the Egyptian and Greek approaches to language and demonstrated a difference in culture and approach.[30] The Egyptian worldview values writing as the tool of Thoth, the Egyptian scribe God, and sees it as a means for establishing harmony and cosmic order to the world.[31] With pictorial writing the message itself was present in the writing: as Frankfurter put it, 'the *medium* was the message – the writing by its very nature was efficacious, not just the content'.[32] The Greek language, by contrast, consisted of twenty four characters representing phonetic sounds which convey oral speech in written form.[33] The Greeks had little respect for the written word, believing it 'brought with it... deceit and laziness'.[34] Greek texts generally convey instructions that summarise the oral account, that is they outline what must be said and done.[35] Hermes and Thoth are the gods associated with writing and language. Hermes has both positive and negative qualities: provider of language and speech but also lies and deception, he is also responsible for the invention of the philtre or charm.[36] In *Phaedrus*, Plato describes the alphabet as Thoth's 'recipe for wisdom', and the term used for recipe is *pharmakon*, a term for magic dealing with poisons and herbal preparations used in healing. As this could denote a poison or a cure it reinforces the double-edged quality of an association with Hermes.[37] Hermes, or Mercury, is also the intermediary between gods and men.[38]

By Late Antiquity, after over three centuries of Hellenic influence, these two contrasting approaches to language appear to have had significant influence on each other: as Frankfurter wrote, 'oral and written

---

[29] Cox Miller, 'Praise of Nonsense', p. 481.
[30] Frankfurter, 'Magic of Writing'.
[31] Frankfurter, 'Magic of Writing', p. 190.
[32] Frankfurter, 'Magic of Writing', p. 192.
[33] Frankfurter, 'Magic of Writing', p. 194.
[34] Frankfurter, 'Magic of Writing', p. 191.
[35] Frankfurter, 'Magic of Writing', p. 191.
[36] Cox Miller, 'Praise of Nonsense', p. 492.
[37] Cox Miller, 'Praise of Nonsense', p. 492.
[38] Fowden, *Egyptian Hermes*, p. 31.

media converged uniquely'.³⁹ Coptic, the last stage of the Egyptian language, used, vowels, allowing the Egyptians to express their verbal pronunciation more accurately, which was extremely important as the sound of the name was part of the non-discursive nature of the language.⁴⁰ As Greek became the dominant culture and language, the streams of vowels and other non-semantic sounds in Greek script may be seen to be an attempt to introduce a non-discursive element into Greek.⁴¹ Cox Miller put it thus:

> When the God who is 'an invisible symbol' breaks into human speech, his sounds are the echoes of the alphabet, the vowels.⁴²

Vowels can be considered as single characters or as a word in themselves; this in turn can be spelt out by letters.⁴³ Each single character has symbolic associations, and by breaking down the name of the character those associations can see seen. Cox Miller cites Zosimus of Panopolis who broke down the characters in Adam, so exposing the association with the four elements and therefore the cosmos.⁴⁴ There is an equivalency between the letter and the cosmic association.⁴⁵ Vowels, notated in Greek script, have been associated with both the seven planets and the seven notes of the musical scale.⁴⁶ There was little agreement in antiquity on the scheme of association but Diane Touliatos, in her study of nonsense syllables in ancient Greek music, gives associations shown in Table 1. Egyptian priests were reported to sing the seven vowels during rites, so transcending both speech and writing as what is nonsemantic as a word becomes music.⁴⁷

---

[39] Frankfurter, 'Magic of Writing', p. 199.
[40] Addey, 'Assuming the Mantle of the Gods', p. 284.
[41] Frankfurter, 'Magic of Writing', pp. 199–201; Cox Miller, 'Praise of Nonsense', p. 483.
[42] Cox Miller, 'Praise of Nonsense', p. 483.
[43] Cox Miller, 'Praise of Nonsense', pp. 495–97. For example: A – L – P – H– A.
[44] Cox Miller, 'Praise of Nonsense', pp. 495–96.
[45] Janowitz, *Icons of Power*, p. 55; Cox Miller, 'Praise of Nonsense', p. 497.
[46] Frankfurter, 'Magic of Writing', p. 201; Cox Miller, 'Praise of Nonsense', p. 498; Dieleman, *Priests, Tongues and Rites*, p. 64.
[47] Dieleman, *Priests, Tongues and Rites*, p. 65.; Frankfurter, 'Magic of Writing', pp. 201–5.; Cox Miller, 'Praise of Nonsense', p. 493.; Betz, *GMPT*, p. 187, *PGM* XIII.630.

Name	Greek Upper	Geek Lower	Latin Text	Planet	Note
Alpha	A	A	A	Moon	D
Epsilon	E	E	E	Mercury	C
Eta	H	H	Ē	Venus	B flat
Iota	I	I	I	Sun	A
Omicron	O	O	O	Mars	G
Upsilon	Y	Y	Y	Jupiter	F
Omega	Ω	Ω	Ō	Saturn	E

Table 1.[48]

The following is an extract of some magical voices from PGM XIII.

205	[The pair] was then called DANOUP / CHRATOR BERBALI BALBITH IAŌ.
	'Lord, I imitate [you by saying] the 7 vowels; enter and hear me, A EE ĒĒĒ IIII
	OOOOO YYYYYY ŌŌŌŌŌŌŌ ABRŌCH BRAŌCH CHRAMMAŌTH PROARBATHŌ IAŌ
	OYAEĒIOYŌ'.

Table 2.

Here you can see a stream of names, including *Iaω*, and then the use of the seven vowels. On the second line you can see that the vowels increase in number as you move up the series, so alpha is only used once, but omega is used seven times so reflecting the order of the planets as seen from the Earth. See Table 1.

Materials used in the Rite
The Rite, which is found in both part A and part B of the papyrus, begins by gathering materials which will form part of that rite. Seven incenses and seven flowers are specified, matching the seven planets. These are dried, ground to a powder, and mixed with the milk of a black cow and wine which has not been mixed with seawater. This mixture is both used as ink to create a tablet and used as a drink later in the ritual. So here we have materials with corresponding symbolic value which have been mixed to create an ink which will be used to create a further level of symbolism. The directions then proceed as follows:

> Next, for the all-important meeting, have a square of natron on which you will write the great name with the seven vowels. Instead of the popping noise and

---

[48] Diane Touliatos, 'Nonsense Syllables in the Music of the Ancient Greek and Byzantine Traditions', *The Journal of Musicology* 7, no. 2 (1989).

96   Investigating the magical practice found in *PGM* XIII

the hissing [sound in the name] draw on the first part of the natron a falcon-faced crocodile and the nine formed god standing on him, for this falcon-faced crocodile at the 4 turning points of the year greets the god with the popping noise. For, coming up to breathe from the deep, he goes 'Pop, pop, pop,' and he of the 9 forms replies to him antiphonally. Therefore, instead of the popping noise, draw the falcon-faced crocodile, for the popping noise is the first element of the name. The second is a hissing. Instead of the hissing [draw] a snake biting its tail. So the two elements, popping and hissing, are represented by a falcon-faced crocodile and the nine-formed god standing on it, around these a snake and the seven vowels.[49]

The nine shaped one and using the tablet
A name is then created through a visual representation of sounds. Reinhold Merkelbach's paper shows an image of the god as drawn by Andreas Brodbeck.[50] This shows the two gods as they greet each other at the four quarters of the year, the nine formed god standing on the falcon faced crocodile, both surrounded by the snake and the vowels. Merkelbach recognises this nine formed god as the Egyptian Sun god and the crocodile as time and this can be seen as a representation of the passage of the sun around the zodiac.[51] In the above passage it also mentions the four turning points of the year – which are the solstices and equinoxes – which is also a reference to the Sun's journey. Another deity appearing in the magical voices is Abrasax (Abraxas), a god of equivalent stature to *Iαω*, whose name has a numerical value of 365, another reflection of the Sun's yearly passage. In addition to the visual depiction of sound, we have additional symbolic resonance from the associated deities to complete the whole message shown on the tablet, which is designed to bring the supreme god into the manifest world constrained by time and materiality.

Once we have our tablet, which is written with ink made of the symbolic ingredients mentioned above and showing a visual representation of the great name, as part of the invocation ceremony we do two things with the tablet. We first lick the tablet and then pour over the wine to wash off the text and then drink the wine, which has been caught in another vessel. So the final act is to imbibe the text within the body, and as the

---

[49] Betz, *GMPT*, p. 173, ll. 39–52.
[50] Reinhold Merkelbach, 'Kosmogonie und Unsterblichkeitsritus. Zwei griechisch-agyptische Weilherituale', in *Auferstehung und Unsterblichkeit*, ed. Erik Hornung and Tilo Schabert (Munich: Fink, 1993), p. 27.
[51] Merkelbach, 'Kosmogonie', p. 28.

wine is swallowed into the belly – which in Egypt was regarded as 'the power center of a person'.[52]

Conclusion

So we can see that many different methods of communication are used in this rite and that the symbolic elements reinforce them. The correspondences between the nature of the act, the deities involved, the physical characteristics of the materials chosen and the planetary attribution all reinforce the same message. Likewise it can be seen that the use of like correspondences can bridge the gap between the material and divine realms. The assumption is that the practitioner can become one with the god via the methods described in the text, that he becomes part of the god as the god links to him and by correspondence, to the cosmos. This stands in contrast to some interpretations of magical material as attempting to command the gods; rather it can be seen to align the practitioner with them and aid ascent to their level.[53]

---

[52] Jeremy Naydler, *Temple of the Cosmos: The Ancient Egyptian Experience of the Sacred* (Rochester, VT: Inner Traditions, 1996), p. 184.
[53] Cox Miller, 'Praise of Nonsense', p. 502; Addey, 'Assuming the Mantle of the Gods', pp. 291–92.

Alchemy and the Transgendering of Mercury

M. E. Warlick

Abstract: Within late medieval alchemical texts, Latin authors adopted both classical and Arabic concepts of physical matter. They assumed that metals were composed of two polarized substances – hot, dry and masculine Philosophic Sulphur, and cool, wet and feminine Philosophic Mercury – whose 'Chemical Wedding' within the laboratory produced the Philosophers' Stone. As visual illustrations developed in alchemical manuscripts and early printed books from the late fourteenth century onward, artists represented these substances with a variety of male and female characters, with Philosophic Mercury almost always depicted as a woman. At the same time, the planet Mercury, which oversaw the ripening of the metal Quicksilver within the earth, also played an important role within alchemical illustrations. This paper will examine how artists navigated this confusion by examining gendered images of the philosophical concept Mercury, the metal Mercury, and the planet Mercury, in light of shifting attitudes towards women in early modern science.

Alchemists use the term Mercury in many ways, including references to the planet Mercury, to the metal mercury, to the god Mercury, and, perhaps most importantly, to the concept of 'Philosophic Mercury'. Alchemical artists derived their images from astrological, religious and mythological visual precedents, although some alchemical images were truly innovative in their representations of alchemical substances and laboratory processes. These broader visual traditions influenced alchemical artists, who adapted their images of Mercury to the various kinds of Mercury they found in alchemical texts. This paper will investigate the complexity and contradictions surrounding representations of Mercury in alchemical imagery. It will trace the evolution of different visual representations of Mercury and examine the ways in which alchemical artists negotiated the gender differences between them. These observations are drawn from a larger study of images of women, gender and sexuality in alchemical manuscripts and early printed books. As alchemical imagery developed from the late fourteenth through the early seventeenth centuries, the transformations between these differing representations of Mercury reveal shifting attitudes towards gender both within alchemical philosophy and beyond.

M. E. Warlick,'Alchemy and the Transgendering of Mercury', *Celestial Magic,* special issue of *Culture and Cosmos*, Vol. 19, nos. 1 and 2, 2015, pp. 99–113.
www.CultureAndCosmos.org

Alchemical theories of physical matter descend from the Greeks, who described physical matter as consisting of the four elements of earth, water, air and fire with their shared oppositional qualities of cold, wet, hot and dry. In his *Meterologica*, Aristotle explained the formation of metals and minerals within the earth from 'exhalations', one vaporous and one smoky.[1] Dry exhalations produce infusible minerals and stones that are dug or quarried. Aristotle gave the examples of sulphur, realgar, ochre and ruddle, another red pigment. He also placed the composite ore cinnabar in this category. On the other hand, he explained that fusible metals are formed by moist vaporous exhalations, providing the examples of iron, gold and copper, which are mined. In the appended fourth chapter of the *Meterologica*, now ascribed to pseudo-Avicenna, the author explained the opposing qualities of substances by setting up a list of binary oppositions, both active and passive, that determine the ways in which the four qualities of cold or heat, moisture or dryness produce change in substances.[2]

As Greek theories migrated through the Arab world, a shift based on these teachings occurred, in which the cool, wet qualities of physical substances became more strongly contrasted to the hot, dry qualities, and these eventually polarized into the two philosophical concepts of Mercury and Sulphur. In Arab alchemical texts, the theory evolved that hot, dry, masculine Sulphur and cool, moist, feminine Mercury were the two component parts of all metals.[3] Alchemical texts often reiterate that these terms were not to be confused with the actual substances of sulphur and mercury, but rather they were conceptual properties of physical matter. In later alchemical illustrations, Philosophic Sulphur and Philosophic Mercury become the two main characters in alchemical narratives and they appear in a variety of male and female figural representations.

The relationship between alchemy and the seven planets visible to the naked eye also stems from ancient origins.[4] Each planet, including the Moon and the Sun, rules over the production of a metal within the earth in a continuing ripening process that evolves from lead to gold. The alchemist's task is to learn how to duplicate and quicken these natural processes. Lead is considered to be the least pure of all the metals, and thus it is ruled by Saturn, the slowest and outermost visible planet. The Moon

---

[1] Aristotle, *Meterologica*, trans. H. D. P. Lee (Cambridge, MA: Harvard University Press, 2004), Chap. III.vi.378a–b, pp. 286–87.
[2] Aristotle, *Meterologica*, Chap. IV.viii.384–85, pp. 338–43.
[3] John Read, *A Prelude to Chemistry* (London: G. Bell and Sons, 1939), pp. 8–21.
[4] Maurice P. Crosland, *Historical Studies in the Language of Chemistry* (New York: Dover, 1978), pp. 79–81.

and the Sun rule over the most refined metals of silver and gold. While early texts fluctuate somewhat in drawing relationships between the other planets and their metals, Mars was typically connected with iron, Jupiter with tin, and Venus with copper. The planet Mercury first ruled over electron, an alloy of silver and gold, but later came to be linked to the metal mercury, or quicksilver.

The metal mercury was well known in the ancient world.[5] Theophrastus described a simple technique to obtain mercury by crushing cinnabar ore (HgS), mercuric sulphide, a naturally occurring combination of sulphur and mercury. Over time, techniques were developed to produce vermillion, a synthetic version of cinnabar and a brilliant red pigment valued by painters.[6] Laboratory operations to separate mercury from cinnabar or to produce vermillion bear interesting parallels to descriptions of alchemical processes. While these artisan practices may have contributed to the development of alchemy's philosophical theories, alchemical philosophy drew from many other sources as well. Suffice it to say that the metal mercury does have quite curious properties, being the only metal that is liquid at room temperature and that has the ability to create alloys with most common metals, including silver and gold, but not iron. It was used in ancient times to colour other metals in amalgam gilding, and this may have influenced its reputation as an agent of transformation.

By the time that alchemy returned to the Latin West via twelfth century translations of Arabic texts, references to Philosophic Mercury, the planet Mercury and the substance mercury were common. In fact, Philosophic Mercury had been elevated to play a significant role in alchemical operations. The Latin author Geber, now identified as a Franciscan monk named Paul of Taranto, postulated a 'Mercury alone' theory, developed from the Sulphur-Mercury theory of the Arabs.[7] While accepting classical form/matter polarities, several late medieval alchemical texts asserted that masculine Sulphur played a crucial, but relatively minor role, while Mercury contained all that was necessary for the successful completion of the work. This view is expressed in another text, the *Liber secretorum alchimie*:

---

[5] Earle R. Caley, 'Mercury and Its Compounds in Ancient Times', *Journal of Chemical Education* 5, no. 4 (1928): pp. 419–24; Leonard Goldwater, *Mercury: A History of Quicksilver* (Baltimore, MD: York Press, 1972).
[6] Arie Wallert, 'Alchemy and Medieval Art Technology', in *Alchemy Revisited*, ed. Z. R. W. M. von Martels (Leiden: Brill, 1990), pp. 154–61.
[7] William R. Newman, *The Summa Perfectionis of Pseudo-Geber* (Leiden: Brill, 1991), p. 204.

> All strength and operation rests upon mercury, it being the mother and matter of all metals, just as hyle is the first cause... The material cause comes about through congealing as in the first hyle, the mother of all creatures, as established by the Supreme Artisan.[8]

This text was written in 1257 by Constantine of Pisa, a medical student who was collecting his university lecture notes on the natural sciences, including aspects of alchemical philosophy and practice.[9] Two versions of this manuscript have survived and both contain illustrations.[10] The Glasgow version was written in Germany in 1361. The Vienna version is a late fourteenth century Flemish adaptation of Constantine's text entitled, *The Secrets of My Lady Alchemy*.

Illustrations in early alchemical manuscripts were rare with the exception of vessels and pointy fingers in the margins. The Glasgow manuscript contains relatively simple cosmological diagrams that are largely unfinished. The Vienna manuscript embellished its diagrams with figural elements, and thus became the first alchemical manuscripts to do so. Throughout the text, Constantine explains the relationship between theological, cosmological and alchemical principles. The more elaborate illustrations in the Vienna manuscript represent the planets, their metals, the zodiac, and the creation of heaven and earth, drawing on *Genesis*. In two panels (Fig. 1), overlapping circles contain personifications of the planets in their medieval appearances, inscribed with the names of the planets and the metals they rule.[11] At the top left, the hand of God begins an unfolding cycle of creation. Below his hand is a crowned personification of the cosmos, followed by the planets Saturn, Jupiter, Mars and the Sun. The following folio continues with Venus, Mercury, Luna, the Earth, and the animals of the air, land and sea. The personifications of Jupiter and Venus are both regal, although their typical metals are reversed here, with Jupiter ruling copper and Venus ruling tin.

---

[8] Barbara Obrist, 'Cosmology and Nature in an Illustrated 13th Century Alchemical Tract: Constantine of Pisa, *The Book of the Secrets of Alchemy*', *Micrologus* I (1993): p. 135.

[9] Constantine of Pisa, *The Book of the Secrets of Alchemy*, ed. and trans. Barbara Obrist (Leiden: Brill, 1990).

[10] University of Glasgow Library, Sp. Coll. Ferguson Ms. 104; Vienna, Österreichische Nationalbibliothek, Middle Dutch Cod. Ms. 2372.

[11] Obrist, 'Cosmology and Nature', pp. 137–49; Jacques Van Lennep, *Alchimie* (Brussels: Crédit Communal, 1984), pp. 45–54.

Saturn is a three-headed personification of Time ruling lead, while Mars is a soldier, ruling iron.

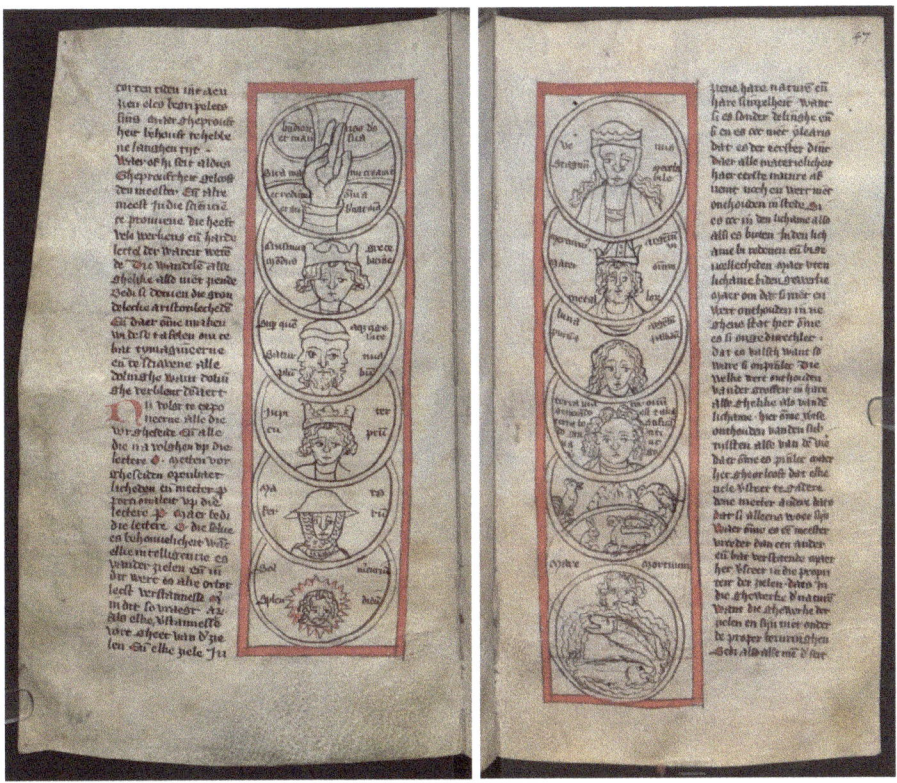

Fig. 1. Creation of the planets, metals and animals, Constantine of Pisa, *The Book of the Secrets of Alchemy*, ca. 1380, paper; ÖNB Vienna: Cod. 2372, fols. 46v, 47r; reproduced by kind permission of the Österreichische Nationalbibliothek, Vienna.

The next panel represents the planet Mercury as a bishop in the second circle from the top (Fig. 1, right). Jean Seznec charted the persistence of astrological personifications throughout the Middle Ages, demonstrating that they never really disappeared during the Christian era, but that their appearances certainly changed from Greco-Roman representations.[12] The curious representation of Mercury as a bishop extends back to the Babylonian god Nebo, who was a scholar. During a transitional period when astrological manuscripts were returning to the Latin west, artists often had only written descriptions of classical gods and goddesses rather than actual visual reputations. In some cases, Arabic artists had adapted western classical deities to representations of their own gods, or they had given them local attributes, as where Hercules wields a scimitar rather than a club.[13] Thus medieval artists merged Middle Eastern representations of the scholarly scribe god Nebo into a western clerical scholar surrounded by books, and then into a bishop. An alchemical manuscript at Cambridge depicts the planet Mercury as a bishop marrying the masculine Sun and the feminine Moon.[14] The planet's proximity in the sky to the Sun may have sparked Mercury's representation as an intermediary between them. Later there would be many alchemical representations of the so-called 'Chemical Wedding' of the Sun and Moon, but the appearance of the planet Mercury as a bishop is an early construct that would soon disappear. Planetary influence over the generation of metals within the earth and over laboratory processes will continue in alchemical texts long into the early modern period.

In the early fifteenth century, two new alchemical manuscripts appeared with abundant allegorical imagery.[15] Both would serve as models for much of the alchemical imagery that developed in later manuscripts and early printed books. A German Franciscan monk named Ulmannus produced the *Buch der Heiligen Dreifaltigkeit* (*Book of the Holy Trinity*) while he was attending the Council of Constance, 1414–1418. Written in the midst of strong religious debate and controversy, this manuscript weaves together alchemical theory and practical laboratory recipes within a matrix of religious and political allusions, delivered with the fervour born of a belief in the imminent threat of the Antichrist.

---

[12] Jean Seznec, *The Survival of Pagan Gods: The Mythological Tradition and Its Place in Renaissance Humanism and Art,* trans. Barbara F. Sessions (Princeton, NJ: Princeton University Press, 1981), pp. 156–60.
[13] Erwin Panofsky and Fritz Saxl, 'Classical Mythology in Mediaeval Art', *Metropolitan Museum Studies* 4, no. 3 (1933): pp. 228–80.
[14] Cambridge, Trinity College, Ms. 0.8.24, fol. 4r; Lennep, *Alchimie,* Fig. 80.
[15] Barbara Obrist, *Les débuts de l'imagerie alchimique (14e-15e siècles)* (Paris: Le Sycomore, 1982); Lennep, *Alchimie,* pp. 54–78.

Within the text, correspondences are drawn between the metals, the planets, virtues and vices.[16] The point is often made that Christ and Mary are unified, as Sulphur and Mercury are joined together in physical matter. At the end of the manuscript, the Crowning of Mary by the Trinity of Father, Son and Holy Spirit represents the feminine perfection of Philosophic Mercury. Christ's crucifixion and resurrection represents masculine perfection and the production of gold.

The other early fifteenth century manuscript is the *Aurora Consurgens* (*Rising Dawn*), of which the oldest version is in Zürich. Within the text, Sulphur and Mercury are presented as personifications of the Sun and the Moon in a variety of interactions. In one illustration, the male Sun is a knight jousting with his feminine opponent, the female Moon.[17] They ride on a Lion and a Griffin, symbols of masculine fixity and feminine volatility. Their shields contain small symbols of their opponents – he has the Moon, she has the Sun – as both Sulphur and Mercury were thought to each contain a small part of each other's essence. In another illumination from the same manuscript the two characters tie the legs of a dragon, representing the primal matter, the base material from which the two substances are purified into silver and gold. Primal matter must first be destroyed, as the volatility of Mercury is fixed, before further operations can continue. This manuscript also contains sexually explicit scenes of the couple's sexual union, drawing on the *Song of Songs*, and its romantic tale of a lover and his beloved, interpreted here as an allegory of chemical fusion in the laboratory.

Both manuscripts, the *Book of the Holy Trinity* and *Rising Dawn*, reflect philosophical and religious ideas of late medieval alchemical texts. Both contain many prominent images of women, influenced by the 'Mercury alone' theory. The late Gothic period saw the celebration of the cult of the Virgin Mary in abundant religious imagery. The alchemical emphasis on feminine Mercury is thus expressed in a variety of religious images of women within these early manuscripts, including the Virgin Mary, Eve, a female serpent and the Black Bride of the Song of Songs, in addition to the Moon. Both manuscripts also contain images of the alchemical androgyne, a half-male/half-female figural symbol of the Philosophers' Stone, the child of the union of Sulphur and Mercury, and this dual figure will prove to be one of the most enduring alchemical symbols.

---

[16] Barbara Obrist, 'Visualization in Medieval Alchemy', *Hyle* 9, no. 2 (2003): pp. 131–70, especially p. 133.
[17] Lennep, *Alchimie*, figs. 25, 44.

Later copies and adaptations of both manuscripts were produced into the mid-sixteenth century. Some developed the romance of Sulphur and Mercury even further, including the *Rosarium philosophorum* and *Donum Dei* series.[18] Artists adapted images from the *Book of the Holy Trinity* and the *Rising Dawn* in these newer illustrations. In one image, a woman, identified as 'Philosophic Mercury', stands on two fountains flowing beneath her feet. In the Glasgow version the fountains are labelled with glyphs for the Sun/gold and the Moon/silver (Fig. 2).[19]

She is nude to represent her purity. Her long loose golden hair represents her virginity, conveying a more secular representation of the virgin mother of the Philosophers' Stone. She holds a chalice of healing in her left hand and an encircling serpent in her right, objects held by earlier androgynous figures in the *Book of the Holy Trinity*. This image again reinforces the late medieval idea of the 'Mercury alone' theory, in which feminine Mercury contains all that is necessary for the completion of the work.

With the advent of printing, several compilations of earlier alchemical texts appeared, at first without illustrations. In 1550, an illustrated version of the *Rosarium Philosophorum* was printed with an illustrated title page and a narrative series of twenty woodcuts. The woodcuts are accompanied by a German poem, 'Sol und Luna,' whose author has not been identified.[20] The artist adapted again images from the *Book of the Holy Trinity* and the *Rising Dawn* into this new series that begins with the meeting, romance and sexual union of the Sun King and Moon Queen. The two figures then fuse into a half-male/half-female androgyne within a sarcophagus. Evaporation and condensation within the vessel are represented by a small male figure rising to the top and returning after a rain shower. The perfection of the feminine is achieved half way through the series, and is represented by an androgyne standing on a crescent Moon, to indicate the production of silver (Fig. 3). A second and more volatile conjunction follows, this time with a small female figure rising and descending after the rain. At the end of the series, the royal androgyne

---

[18] Lennep, *Alchimie*, pp. 54-150.

[19] Versions of this image can be found in Leiden, Universiteitsbibliotheek, Ms. Voss. Chym. F.29, fol. 95v; Paris, Bibliothèque Nationale, Mss. 7171, fol. 16r; Manchester, John Rylands Library, German Ms.1, fol. 6v. Paris and Manchester versions are illustrated in Lennep, *Alchimie*, figs. 146, 57.

[20] Joachim Telle, *Sol und Luna* (Hürtgenwald: Guido Pressler, 1980) and 'Remarques sur le *Rosarium philosophorum (1550)*', *Chrysopoeia* 5 (1996): pp. 265–320; Lennep, *Alchimie*, pp. 154–59.

stands triumphantly over a three-headed serpent, beside a tree with thirteen heads of the Sun. The final images of the Crowning of Mary and the Resurrection of Christ indicate the perfection of both Mercury and Sulphur.

Fig. 2. Philosophic Mercury, *Spruch der Philosophien* (*Rosarium Philosophorum* series), German, late sixteenth century, paper; University of Glasgow Library, Sp. Coll. Ferguson Ms. 6, Fol. 164v; reproduced by kind permission of the Special Collections Department of the University of Glasgow Library, Glasgow.

Within this series, the image of the androgyne on the Moon (Fig. 3) plays a similar role to the representation of 'Philosophic Mercury' (Fig. 2).

Fig. 3. Alchemical Androgyne, *De alchimia opuscula*, Part II: *Rosarium Philosophorum*, Frankfurt: Cyriacus Jacob, 1550, woodcut; University of Glasgow Library, Sp. Coll. Ferguson Al-y.18, fig. 10; reproduced by kind permission of the Special Collections Department of the University of Glasgow Library, Glasgow.

It would be inaccurate to say that such an evolution of the gendered imagery is strictly chronological, especially since the Glasgow drawing of female 'Philosophic Mercury' was created later than the woodcut, and both are based on earlier models. There are similarities in the objects held in the hands while the wings on the fountains of the Sun and the Moon are now attached to the androgyne. Although the androgyne is both male and female, its text indicates the perfection of the feminine has been achieved through an imperial birth (an Empress). The Moon is emphasized by a tree containing thirteen faces of the moon, in addition to the crescent moon on which the androgyne stands.

By the beginning of the seventeenth century, the Renaissance had inspired new transformations of the alchemical Mercury, depicted as a god in his Greco-Roman attire with winged hat and heels, and a caduceus entwined with two serpents (Fig. 4).

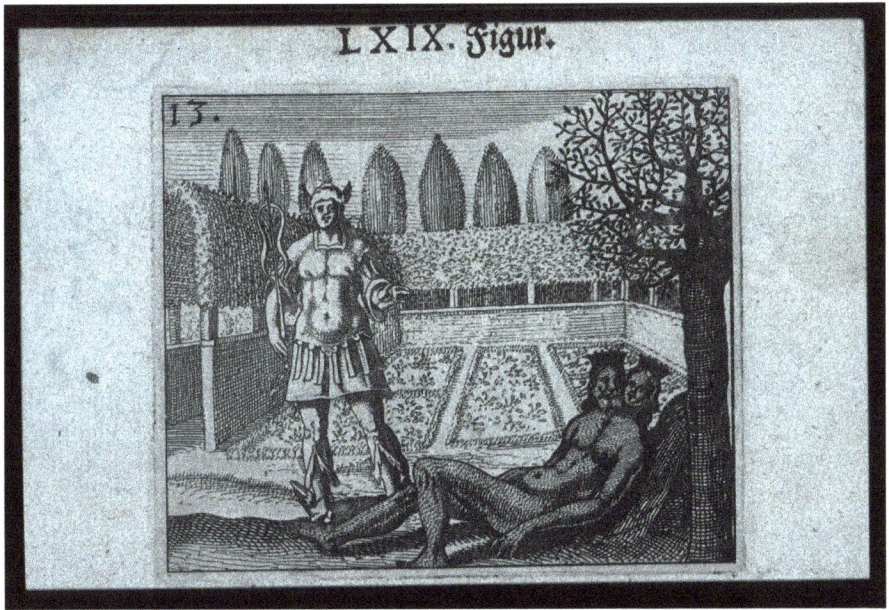

Fig. 4. Mercury and the Androgyne, Daniel Stolcius, *Chymisches Lustgartlein*, Frankfurt: Lucas Jennis, 1624, engraving by Baltazar Schwan; University of Glasgow Library, Sp. Coll. SM 1000, fig. LXIX; reproduced by kind permission of the Special Collections Department of the University of Glasgow Library, Glasgow.

Several factors influenced the return and appearance of this Mercury. One was the rise in the reputation of the Egyptian philosopher Hermes Trismegistus, a character whose reputation had evolved throughout the Middle Ages.[21] Hermes' fame as an ancient philosopher ranked him in some circles even higher than Plato and Aristotle. His role as the most important Hermetic philosopher secured his position as the founding father of alchemy. In 1488, soon after the appearance of Ficino's printed version of the *Corpus Hermeticum*, an image of Hermes Trismegistus, attributed to Giovanni di Stefano, was inserted into the mosaic pavement of the Siena Cathedral.[22] In alchemical texts, the ancient philosopher Hermes was often merged with the Greek god Hermes, and this would influence the role that the god Hermes/Mercury would begin to assume in alchemical imagery.

The second important person to shift the spotlight towards the classical god Mercury was the irascible Doctor Paracelsus, who lived in the early sixteenth century. His theories on alchemical medicine, or iatrochemisty, were especially influential. Paracelsus postulated a number of revisions to prevailing alchemical theory, but for the purpose of this paper, the most important was his shift from the duality of the Mercury-Sulphur theory to one that included Salt as a third essential component of physical matter. This trinity was not entirely new to alchemy as it paralleled other Trinitarian views, such as body, soul and spirit.[23] However, because of the emphasis that Paracelsus placed on three, rather than two, essential parts of primal matter, Salt became an equal partner to continuing representations of Philosophic Sulphur and Philosophic Mercury. For Paracelsus, Salt is the body or the physicality of matter, the ash left after a substance had been burned, Mercury was the volatile spirit of matter or escaping gases, and Sulphur became its soul, the essence that is collected.

The male god Mercury thus comes to represent Salt, the physical body that binds together male Sulphur and female Mercury. His caduceus encapsulates this notion, with its two serpents entwined on a single staff

---

[21] Antoine Faivre, *The Eternal Hermes: From Greek God to Alchemical Magus*, trans. Joscelyn Godwin (Grand Rapids, MI: Phanes Press, 1995).

[22] Bruno Santi, *The Marble Pavement of the Cathedral of Siena* (Florence: Scala, 1982), pp. 5–14; Carlos Gilly and Cis van Heertum, *Magic, Alchemy and Science 15th–18th Centuries: The Influence of Hermes Trismegistus,* exh. cat. (Venice: Biblioteca Nazionale Marciana and Amsterdam: Bibliotheca Philosophica Hermetica, 2002).

[23] Reijer Hooykaas, 'Chemical Trichotomy before Paracelsus?', *Archives internationales d'histoire des sciences* 28, no. 9 (1949): 1063–74.

(Fig. 4). This engraving appeared first in J. D. Mylius's *Philosophia Reformata* of 1622, one of several images in this text containing the god Mercury, now fully attired in his classical garb.[24] He represents not only the Hermetic wisdom that is necessary for completing the work, but he also functions as a guardian watching over the alchemical androgyne resting in the garden. Elsewhere in Mylius's book, the seven ancient planets with their traditional classical attributes are placed within a cavern to oversee the creation of their metals within the womb of the earth. Daniel Stolcius reprinted many of these illustrations in his *Chymisches Lustgärtlein* of 1624. The rising importance of Hermes Trismegistus and of Paracelsus within alchemical philosophy is suggested by the inclusion of both men on Stolcius's title page.

One the most important alchemical texts published in the early seventeenth century was Michael Maier's *Atalanta Fugiens*, which also contains several images of the new Mercury.[25] Maier was well versed in alchemical philosophy.[26] He wrote several texts that interpreted ancient myths and legends as alchemical allegories. The publisher J. T. De Bry probably engraved the images, although they have also been attributed to Mattaeus Merian. Whoever the artist, he was well versed in the artistic currents of the day, and had access to imagery from earlier alchemical manuscripts, upon which many newer illustrations were based. Mythological and gendered transformations took place within this Renaissance humanist environment, often inspired by Ovid's *Metamorphosis*.[27] The struggle described above between the knightly Sun, the feminine Moon and the Dragon in the *Aurora Consurgens*, is transformed in Emblem XXV of *Atalanta Fugiens* into a mythological scene, in which Apollo (Phoebus), god of the Sun, and Diana (Cynthia), goddess of the Moon, use the club of Hercules to destroy the dragon. In the distance, the celestial brother and sister are depicted in their mythic roles

---

[24] Stanislas Klossowski de Rola, *The Golden Game: Alchemical Engravings of the Seventeenth Century* (New York: George Braziller, 1988), pp. 167–82.
[25] H. M. E. de Jong, *Michael Maier's Atalanta Fugiens: Sources of an Alchemical Book of Emblems* (York Beach, ME: Nicolas Hays, 2002), pp. 191–95.
[26] Hereward Tilton, *The Quest for the Phoenix: Spiritual Alchemy and Rosicrucianism in the Work of Count Michael Maier (1569-1622)* (Berlin: Walter de Gruyter, 2003).
[27] Thomas Willard, 'The Metamorphosis of Metals: Ovid and the Alchemists', in *Metamorphosis: The Changing Face of Ovid in Medieval and Early Modern Europe*, ed. Alison Keith and Stephen Rupp (Toronto: Centre for Reformation and Renaissance Studies, 2007), pp. 151–78.

112 Alchemy and the Transgendering of Mercury

as archers. In Emblem XXXVIII, the winged god Hermes is represented in a passionate embrace with the goddess Aphrodite (Fig. 5).

Fig. 5. Emblem XXXVIII. Hermes/Mercury, Aphrodite, Eros, and the Hermaphrodite, Michael Maier, *Atalanta Fugiens*, Oppenheim: J. T. De Bry, 1618, engraving; University of Glasgow Library, Sp Coll Ferg Euing Bd 16.g-6, p. 161; reproduced by kind permission of the Special Collections Department of the University of Glasgow Library, Glasgow.

According to the Ovidian myth their child was a boy, Hermaphroditus, who later merged with the nymph Salmacis in a pool, to become a single figure of both sexes, the Hermaphrodite. In the motto of this image,

Hermes/Mercury becomes the Father of the androgynous child and Aphrodite/Venus its mother, as the alchemical allegory is retold, this time as a classical myth.[28]

Thus is happens that feminine Philosophic Mercury, mother of the alchemical androgyne and the Philosopher's Stone, becomes the masculine god Mercury, father of the Hermaphrodite. As feminine Mercury becomes masculine Mercury, the wider context of the increasing masculinization of early modern science seems to be a factor influencing these changes within alchemical imagery. More visual examples can be found, but it seems sufficient here to propose that gender is a most interesting filter to use when examining the evolution of alchemical imagery. Alchemy was a science of transformation, and its illustrations demonstrate just how mercurial those transformations could be.

---

[28] de Jong, *Michael Maier's Atalanta Fugiens*, pp. 251–55.

Teleological and Aesthetic Perfection in the *Aurora Consurgens*

Karen Parham

Abstract: This paper examines the concept of perfection in relation to the celestial magic described within the alchemical work *Aurora Consurgens*. This fifteenth-century illuminated manuscript has been erroneously attributed to Thomas Aquinas and was popularised by Carl Gustav Jung. It contains an entire section on 'astronomy', which is one of the keys to wisdom and perfection. Perfection, a multifaceted concept, proves useful in elucidating further philosophical understanding of the various traditions within Western esotericism. By identifying interpretations of this concept within *Aurora Consurgens*, I hope to demonstrate how this approach can aid in the understanding of both *Aurora Consurgens* and of alchemy and its relationship to celestial magic in general. This will then provide an opening to identifying concepts that are common to all Western esoteric traditions.

Aurora Consurgens, or 'morning rising', is an alchemical composite work consisting of two books written in Latin containing delectable illuminated emblems that caught the imagination of the early twentieth-century psychoanalysts C. G. Jung and Marie-Louise von Franz.[1] Chapter four in Book I provides reasons why the title *Aurora Consurgens* was chosen.[2] The *aurora*, or dawn, 'the Mother of the Sun', is the golden hour of the day, the end of all darkness, and has a typical display of red and yellow colours intermediating between the blackness of night and the whiteness of day. These same two colours are evidence of the transition between *nigredo* and *albedo* in the alchemical process' and 'the dawn soothes and relaxes all those who suffer from various night-time afflictions, so in the

---

[1] Marie-Louise von Franz, *Alchemy: An Introduction to the Symbolism and the Psychology* (Toronto: Inner City Books, 1980), pp. 177–272; Carl Gustav Jung, *Psychology and Alchemy* (1953; London: Routledge, 1993, repr.).
[2] *Aurora Consurgens*, trans. Paul Ferguson (Glasgow: Magnum Opus Hermetic Sourceworks No. 40, 2011), pp. 14–15.

dawn of this Science all the evil odours and vapours that afflict the Craftsman's mind will wither and diminish'.[3]

The *Aurora* is one of the earliest European emblematic alchemical manuscripts, and survives in ten late medieval versions/copies. The earliest dating for Book I is the fourteenth century; the emblems and the second book appear to have been added at the later date of 1420.[4] It was written by an anonymous cleric who some scholars, such as von Franz according to Andrea DePascalis, claim was the Scholastic philosopher Thomas Aquinas.[5] However, this has since been disputed and the consensus now is to refer to the author as Pseudo-Aquinas. Pseudo-Aquinas makes reference to various authorities in alchemy and philosophy, including Aristotle, Alphidius, Hermes and 'Senior'.[6]

For this paper, I have used a translation of the *Aurora* by Paul Ferguson, which is based on a printed edition made available by Dr Johann Rhenanus in 1625 and Conrad Waldkirch's 1593 version.[7] According to Jung, Waldkirch's edition omitted the first book because the printer perceived it as being sacrilegious.[8] The author of the *Aurora* unintentionally suggests that Scripture was composed in honour of alchemy. Entire paragraphs consist of linked paraphrases from various books of the Bible that explain the author's version of the alchemical process. In the opening paragraph, for example, there are three biblical references in the first sentence:

> Now all good things came to me (Wisd. 7:11) together with the first wisdom of the south (Matt. 12:42), which preacheth abroad, which uttereth her voice in the streets, which at the head of multitudes crieth out, and which in the

---

[3] *Aurora*, pp. 14–15. The 'evil odours and vapours' refer to the gaseous sulphur and mercurial fumes used during the *nigredo* processing.
[4] Adam McLean, 'The mystery of the *Aurora consurgens*', http://www.alchemywebsite.com/aurora_consurgens_extract.html [accessed February 2013]; *Aurora*, p. 1.
[5] Andrea DePascalis, *Alchemy The Golden Art: The Secrets of the Oldest Enigma* (Rome: Gremese International, 1995), p. 71.
[6] Alphidius was an ancient philosopher frequently quoted in alchemical literature such as the *Rosarium Philosophorum* and *Splendor Solis*. Senior is believed to be the acclaimed Arabic alchemist Mohammed Ibn Umail, see Jeffery Raff, *The Wedding of Sophia: The Divine Feminine in Psychoidal Alchemy* (Berwick, ME: Nicholas-Hays, Inc., 2003), p. 57.
[7] *Aurora*.
[8] Jung, *Psychology and Alchemy*, p. 376.

entrance of the gates of the city uttereth her words (Prov. 1:20-22) saying, 'Come ye to me and be enlightened (Ps. 33:6), and your enterprises shall not be confounded'.[9]

Jung and von Franz omitted Book II because of its more practical contents which failed to support their psychoanalytical approach which they applied to Book I. I am, therefore, approaching the work in its entirety with the assumption that there is some coherence and interrelatedness which Rhenanus, among others, recognised. To assist in the discussion of the various chapters from the two books, see the Table in Figure 1.

Alchemy is often described as the art of perfection where perfection is synonymous with successful transmutation.[10] However, there is more to this concept than meets the eye. Perfection is a relative and comparative term with many instantiations. The Australian philosopher John Passmore, for example, identified nine different types of perfection in his book *The Perfectibility of Man*.[11] Two of these types, teleological and aesthetic perfection, are most pertinent to the *Aurora*. According to Passmore, teleological perfection then 'consists in attaining to that end in which it is one's nature to find final satisfaction' and aesthetic perfection as 'the perfect performance of tasks in a flawless whole'.[12]

The aim of this paper is to identify any relationship there may be between the two books of the *Aurora* by analysing how teleological and aesthetic perfection is perceived. I will consider the text as an expression of universalism: the idea of a universal, inner understanding of reality proposed in pseudo-epigraphical works attributed to Hermes. This

---

[9] *Aurora*, p. 7.

[10] To give just two examples, Pseudo-Geber of the thirteenth century named one of his alchemical treatises *Of the Investigation or Search of Perfection*, and in the *Libellus de Alchimia* attributed to Albertus Magnus, it states that: 'Through this art, corrupted metals in minerals are restored and the imperfect made perfect', see Stanton J. Linden, ed., *The Alchemy Reader: From Hermes Trismegistus to Isaac Newton* (Cambridge: Cambridge University Press, 2003), p. 101.

[11] John Passmore, *The Perfectibility of Man* (Indianapolis: Liberty Fund, third edition, 2000), pp. 12–17. The nine types that Passmore recognises are: technical, moral, teleological, obedientiary, exemplary, deiform, immaculate, metaphysical and aesthetic. All of these types are evident in the *Aurora* but are less significant to the overall message wanting to be conveyed.

[12] Passmore, *The Perfectibility of Man*, pp. 15 and 24.

universalism is communicated in terms of teleological and aesthetic perfection. At the core of this universalism is the experience of gnosis.[13]

Book I		Book II	
I.	Introduction		Prologue
II.	What is wisdom?		Explanatory preamble to 'Treatise on Astronomy'
III.	Of those who are ignorant of this Science and refuse to accept it	I.	A Treatise on Astronomy
IV.	How this book got its name	II.	Arismetrica explained in the parabolical style
V.	The irritation of the foolish	III.	Natural phenomena explained according to the process of nature
VI.	First parable	IV.	The story of Mother Alchemy expressed in the parabolical style
VII.	Second parable	V.	Enigmatic discourse
VIII.	Third parable	VI.	Typical discourse
IX.	Fourth parable	VII.	How the Stone resembles the seed of man in the procreation of his descendants
X.	Fifth parable	VIII.	On the four things found in the human being
XI.	Sixth parable	IX.	On four internal organs within the human body
XII.	Seventh parable	X.	On the comparison of the Science with an egg
		XI.	On the comparison of the Science with the basilisk and other poisonous worms, due to the similarity of their nutriment
		XII.	On the minerals
		XIII.	On the multiplicity of quicksilver
		XIV.	On arsenic and orpiment
		XV.	On marcasite, magnesia and tutty
		XVI.	On the individual qualities of all the metals
		XVII.	On the four imperfect metallic bodies
		XVIII.	On the comparison of the Science with trees. Herbs, flowers, roots, and other vegetable matter
		XIX.	On the manifold and varied plurality of the Art
		XX,	On the varied character of the Work of the Philosophers
		XXI.	On the other modes of the operation
		XXII.	On the effects of this Medicine or Tincture
			The Tale of the Saracen and Protonotary

Fig. 1. Table.

---

[13] See Roelof van den Broek, 'Gnosticism and Hermeticism in Antiquity: Two Roads to Salvation', in *Gnosis and Hermeticism: From Antiquity to Modern Times*, ed. Roelof van den Broek and Wouter Hanegraaff (New York: SUNY Press, 1998), p. 120.

As defined by Hanegraaff, gnosis is ineffable and unverifiable and, according to its adherents, offers a more profound type of knowledge than reason and faith.[14] It is spiritual, as opposed to physical or worldly, and is experiential; for this reason it is said to surpass mere wisdom, which is reliant on the mundane. Therefore, gnosis is a more appropriate term to use with respect to the aims of the *Aurora*, rather than wisdom, which is the general term commonly applied.[15] It will become clear that celestial magic, understanding and replicating the powers of the seven planets, is an aspect of this gnosis in the *Aurora*.

Teleological Perfection: the realisation of gnosis
Originating from the Greek word *teleios*, meaning goal or purpose, teleological perfection relates to Aristotle's final cause.[16] Teleology suggests that things go through a process in fulfilling an unconscious or innate purpose which culminate in a natural end. As Passmore put it, teleological perfection implies a relationship between completion and the achievement of an inherent end.[17] In alchemy, teleological perfection is generally considered to be the successful transmutation of a base metal into gold. In the *Aurora*, I would argue that the true *telos* is to become an enlightened being. This is made possible by gnosis personified as the allegorical female figure of Sophia. She represents divine knowledge, gnosis, and her skill is in harnessing the powers of the four elements and the seven planets.

Book I draws heavily on wisdom literature originating from the ancient Near East, represented in the Bible in the canonical books of Job, Psalms, Proverbs, Ecclesiastes, Song of Songs, Wisdom, Ecclesiasticus and Hosea, and the Apocryphal books of Sirach and Wisdom of Solomon. Such wisdom/gnosis literature aims at providing insights and reflections into the human condition and an understanding of nature and reality acquired through observation and contemplation and expressed through daily practice, as opposed to sole reliance on the revelatory messages in

---

[14] Wouter Hanegraaff, *Western Esotericism: A Guide for the Perplexed* (London: Bloomsbury, 2013), p. 89.
[15] See for example, Raff, p. 45 or p. 53.
[16] Aristotle, *Physics*, trans. by Robin Waterfield (1996; repr. Oxford: Oxford University Press, 1999), p. 39. The final cause or 'fourth way' in which the word cause is used is 'for the end'. 'This is what something is for'.
[17] Passmore, *The Perfectibility of Man*, p. 15.

Scripture.[18] The *Aurora* takes this one step further by paraphrasing scriptural references, thus suggesting this wisdom is inspired and reliant on the revelations of the Holy Writ. This is confirmed in the second chapter of Book I of the *Aurora*, where seekers of wisdom are encouraged to 'a study of the Prophets, and will engross you in the subtleties of her parables, and will cause you to search out the hidden meaning of proverbs, and will persuade you to become conversant in the secret of parables (Ecclus. 39:1-3)'.[19] This combination of natural philosophy and revelation produces gnosis: divine, ineffable and unverifiable knowledge hidden but waiting to be discovered through transmutational experience.

Four of the five introductory chapters of the *Aurora* discuss the nature of gnosis, which is the key to understanding the sequential parables, and how this gnosis (translated using the generic term wisdom) is obvious but ignored by the foolish. In chapter one, the *Aurora* formulates it as follows: 'Who is wise that he shall understand that thing (Hos. 14:10) that Alphidius refers to as something that adults and children pass by regardless in the streets and highways and which mules and sheep every day tread into the dung?'.[20] I would argue that the parables pertain to the alchemical redemption processes that an individual's body, soul and spirit are subjected to in order to become enlightened. The process starts with the body and soul being in an initial state of corruption. After being cleansed the body and soul are united with the spirit, at which point the individual gains gnosis and become enlightened reaching his or her *telos*.

The first parable explains that the initial state is one of ignorance, lacking gnosis, when humankind was corrupted by original sin. It is as if the soul is covered by a 'huge cloud'.[21] The seven planets are the keys to the salvation of the soul. They appeared when 'the heavens opened and there thundered forth the voice of Him who has seven stars in his hand, which are the seven spirits (Apoc. 1:4) sent to the whole Earth to preach and bear witness'.[22] In order to be cleansed, extraction of the pure spirit hidden in the filth of the corrupted soul takes place. This is followed by the extraction of the individual soul from the body.[23] The soul must learn to rise above the density of matter with the aid of the seven planets and

---

[18] W. David Stacey, *Groundwork of Biblical Studies* (1979; repr. London: Epworth Press, 2000), p. 280.
[19] *Aurora*, p. 10.
[20] *Aurora*, p. 7.
[21] *Aurora*, p. 18.
[22] *Aurora*, p. 19, second parable.
[23] Raff, p. 76.

separate itself from the body. The removal of the corrupted soul, where the body is reduced to ashes, allows the soul to rise and be replenished by spirit, 'with innate humour'.[24] The Holy Ghost plays a vital part in this as it is responsible for causing the death of the corrupted body and reviving the soul through baptism using the three heavenly elements represented in water, blood (representing Air) and flame.[25] The author observes that these three forms of baptism are present in the three terms of pregnancy: 'in the first trimester of pregnancy it is water that nourishes the foetus in the womb, and in the second trimester air, while in the third trimester it is fire that nourishes and guards it... '.[26] This suggests that blood, the second form of baptism, is representative of Air. The Holy Ghost is the 'spirit of wisdom and understanding', the third aspect of the alchemical and Holy Trinity who exposes and inspires the soul (third parable).[27] Its gifts are only available to those who enter the house it has built based on fourteen virtues using the four elements as keys (fifth parable).[28] This now virtuous and wise soul returns to the ashes of its previous body generating a second Adam rid of any original sin (sixth parable). The newly embodied cleansed soul is ready then to unite with spirit eliciting the union between heaven and earth (the four elements), between God and the Holy Ghost (knowledge of the essence of God) and the generation of the philosopher's stone (seventh parable).[29] The end product is the embodiment of gnosis, an enlightened soul reborn into a purified body, 'that we should live in union and love' (p. 42). A similar process of sublimation (which involves a transition from solid to gas without the liquid state) in the alchemical vessel converts a dense element, a solid, into the element of air, a gas before, ultimately, becoming cinnabar (Book II, chapter twenty).

In the *Aurora*, the Holy Ghost or Spirit can be identified with Sophia or gnosis. The Spirit proceeds from both the Father and the Son and brings enlightenment through its sevenfold gifts (parable four). The Spirit is the means by which 'terrestrial things become heavenly', that is, defiled souls are purified of sin and imbued with the 'perfection of life'.[30] Similarly

---

[24] *Aurora*, p. 22.
[25] *Aurora*, p. 26, fourth parable.
[26] *Aurora*, p. 26.
[27] *Aurora*, p. 24.
[28] The fourteen virtues are: healing, humility, holiness, chastity, virtue, victory, belief, hope, charity, benignity, patience, temperance, spiritual discipline or intellect, and obedience.
[29] Raff, p. 134.
[30] *Aurora*, p. 26.

Sophia is 'the Medicine that puts poverty to flight', where poverty refers to an impoverished soul that is ignorant and scorns knowledge.[31] Sophia/Holy Spirit is the essence or goodness of God and infuses her perfection (gnosis) into a wise person's soul. An analogy is drawn between Sophia and the Queen of the south wind, the Queen of Sheba, an alchemist herself, who offered Solomon gold and precious stones (1 Kings 10:2).[32] The Queen of Sheba possesses knowledge of transmutation and by transmitting it to Solomon (representing the soul) he too becomes wise. Sophia is, therefore, the transmuting agent that inspires a soul to attain its *telos*, which is to hold knowledge of her and her transmuting principles. She is the philosopher's stone that actualises teleological perfection. Gnosis is the potential that is hidden in the corrupted soul. By eradicating all the obstacles, the corrupting influences, it is possible to uncover gnosis and become enlightened. However, it also needs that same gnosis in order to do so. This is made possible by the seven gifts of the Spirit, the seven celestial powers recognised in every microcosm on earth.

Book I is concerned with the teleological perfection of humankind, which is to actualise potential gnosis inherent from the beginning but buried. This seed of gnosis is the spirit which is only visible to the soul once it has been extracted from the body. As it ascends into the Hermetic errant spheres, it perceives the forces and qualities of the seven celestial powers and the four elements and the necessary phases and stages that will lead to their perfection. The teleological perfection of each phase and stage delivers aesthetic perfection; 'the perfect performance of tasks in a flawless whole'.[33] Sophia has the role of revealing this aesthetic perfection which is the key to teleological perfection.

The harmony of aesthetic perfection
Aesthetic perfection requires harmony, order, stability and unity: Passmore explains how the ideal State, which is aesthetically perfect, will have the characteristics of harmony, order, stability and unity and that the perfect citizen in that state will perform the tasks allotted to him thus contributing to total social harmony.[34] It entails a holistic notion that the harmonious whole depends on the successful completion of its

---

[31] *Aurora*, p. 11
[32] Aurora, Book I, introductory chapter five; see also Raff, p. 67.
[33] Passmore, p. 25.
[34] Passmore, p. 24.

contributory processes. The *Aurora* describes such processes that contribute to a harmonious whole, that is, the universe and everything in it.

Chapter nineteen of Book II in *Aurora* lists the numerous procedures of the 'celestial operation' that have been proposed. Some philosophers suggest the operation requires 'calcining, dissolving, distilling and coagulating', while others recommend 'sublimating, reiterating and fixing', 'inceration and imbibition', 'ablution or cleansing', 'killing and made white', 'quickening and nourishing', 'putrefying and corrupting', etc.[35] The list appears vast but Pseudo-Aquinas assures us that these all pertain to the same thing and an intelligent person 'would see them as interdependent and linked together like a chain, so that where one ends the other begins'.[36] These processes occur on a macrocosmic and microcosmic level and their correspondences are reflected in various synchronicities between the four elements, the Holy Trinity and the seven planets and life on earth, as I will now demonstrate.

Fundamental to the acquisition of gnosis in the *Aurora* are the four elements and the principles they represent. All elements are present in differing degrees in each other. They are also present in a human but require processing before they can produce an enlightened person. The general principle is that the element of Earth, mother of all elements, gave rise to the heavenly elements of Water, Air and Fire (Book I, sixth parable). Earth (the microcosm) with the aid of the same three elements (the macrocosm) was able to sustain life when the heavenly elements projected the powers of the seven planets into the centre of the Earth, making it possible for plants, animals and healing herbs to grow. The heavenly elements were separated from Earth and from one another through death and are returned to it by commingling with the aid of permanent water (philosophical mercury). Sophia enabled the union of these elements through transmutation, symbolised by the Moon and then the Sun that represent the actions of *albedo* and *rubedo*. Quoting Senior (Ibn Umail), Book II, chapter one explains how the Sun represents the hot and dry qualities of Fire in the element of Earth that conjoins with the Moon, the Water in the element of Air that is cold and moist, to create a united body and cleansed soul that is equipped to receive the 'light' (p. 54).[37] This is mirrored in a laboratory process of fixing soul, gaseous

---

[35] *Aurora*, p. 95.
[36] *Aurora*, p. 95.
[37] *Aurora*, p. 54.

sulphur, with the body of magnesia, mercury, to produce a sparkling sulphur-mercury composite cinnabar.[38]

The *Aurora* compares the alchemical process, which attempts to create a harmonious system, to an egg (Book II, chapter ten). The outer shell is Earth, the albumen is Water, the membrane joined to the shell is Air and the yolk is Fire, a system borrowed from the *Turba Philosophorum*.[39] Philosophers of the 'Science' are able to recognise the four elements in the egg and the fifth, represented as the chick in a bird's egg, as being comparable with the operations within alchemy. What the *Aurora* is suggesting here is that the alchemical operation focusing on balancing each element to produce the fifth is similar to the way the egg, containing the four elements, gives rise to the chick. An integral part of the alchemical process required the four elements and their four qualities of hot, cold, moist and dry to be perfectly balanced in order to give rise to the fifth element.[40] The author adds: 'although this analogy is not to be understood literally in the sense of the eggs that are produced by birds, but rather in terms of that egg of which the Philosophers speak'.[41] This Philosopher's egg probably refers to a hermetically sealed glass vessel shaped like an egg used by alchemists.[42] It was used to incubate the essential ingredients containing the four elements that would ultimately emerge as the philosopher's stone. The fifth element is a product of the perfection of the four and in this sense the four elements are contained in and constitute a whole (the fifth) that is aesthetically perfect. This ability to create aesthetic perfection involves Sophia: an understanding of the ubiquitous nature of the four elements and the insight and expertise required in proportioning them perfectly.

Another correspondence can be recognised in the four principal organs and fluids – the brain and phlegm, the heart and red bile, the liver and blood, and the testicles and black bile – that are governed by Water, Fire,

---

[38] Gabriele Ferrario, 'An Arabic Dictionary of Technical Alchemical terms: MS Sprenger 1908 of the Staatsbibliothek zu Berlin (fols. 3r–6r)', *Ambix* 56 (March 2009): p. 45. Magnesia was classified as a stone by the Arab alchemist Abu Bakr Mohammed Ibn Zakariyya al-Razi. Cinnabar is mercury sulphide.
[39] *Turba Philosophorum: A Complete English Translation by Arthur Edward Waite* (Seattle, WA: Ouroboros Press, 2006), fourth dictum.
[40] Lawrence M. Principe, *The Secrets of Alchemy* (Chicago: University of Chicago Press, 2013), pp. 37–44.
[41] *Aurora*, p. 75.
[42] John Read, *Through Alchemy to Chemistry: A Procession of Ideas and Personalities* (London: G. Bell and Sons, 1957), pp. 31 and 35.

Air and Earth (Book II, chapter nine). These four elements are conjoined by a quintessential principle that is life, which is 'neither hot nor cold, neither moist nor dry'.[43] This quintessential principle is the fifth element or life that together with the four elements produces aesthetic perfection.

The four elements and their four qualities are present in a manifest or concealed manner in all metals. The fiery hard Martian metal iron, for example, has a dry and hot manifestation but conceals cold and moist qualities that are difficult to extract and which are immediately absorbed by the dominance of Fire (Book II, chapter thirteen). Alchemical iron, with its prevailing heat, is described as 'the life of a roaring lion [or spirit]'.[44] Iron is able to 'constrain' tin or lead, two soft metals that are manifestations of the cold and moist qualities of Water.[45] Together they are capable of producing a Tincture, a sign that gnosis has been attained.

Of the three hypostases (Father, Son and Holy Spirit), the *Aurora* claims it is the Spirit that manipulates the three heavenly elements (Book I, fourth parable). The Spirit provides seven gifts with corresponding virtues projected onto the Earth that ensures salvation or alchemical transmutation. This same theme returns in Book II when discussing the views on the relationship between alchemy and astrology by the different authorities (Book II, chapter one). Aristotle, according to the *Aurora*, identified four main planets as governing the four elements: Saturn Earth, Mercury Water, Jupiter Air, and the Sun Fire.[46] In the same chapter, the *Aurora* explains how Saturn corresponds to the initial blackening phase when Earth lacks light. Mercury signals the blossoming of the whitening phase (*albedo*) that introduces Water and light. Jupiter with the element of Air represents the fruition of *albedo* that must subsequently undergo incineration in order for the completion to take place governed by the Sun. This same procedure is evident in plants; if a plant bears flowers not fruits, it is governed by Jupiter because it has reached the stage of whitening but not goldening that would produce the fruits.[47] The three heavenly elements of Water Air and Fire ensure that the plant can grow and reach its full potential. The *Aurora* suggests in Book I that the application of these same three elements leads to an enlightened soul; 'a living soul' infused with the 'perfection of life'.[48]

---

[43] *Aurora*, p. 73.
[44] Rhenaus refers to spirit (*spiritus*) whereas Waldkirch has lion (*leonis*), see *Aurora*, footnote on p. 90.
[45] *Aurora*, p. 89.
[46] *Aurora*, p. 50.
[47] *Aurora*, p. 53.
[48] *Aurora*, p. 47.

Thus, the heavenly elements and their corresponding planets (Mercury, Jupiter and the Sun) together with the element of Earth work to form an aesthetically perfect whole that allow or plants and souls to reach their *telos*.

Continuing in Book II, chapter one, an unnamed philosopher suggests that Fire's most successful results are yielded when the Sun is at its height in the three Fire signs consecutively: Aries, Leo and then Sagittarius. The Fire is in its most intense in Leo and attains 'true rest and tranquillity' in Jupiter.[49] It is in Jupiter that the 'earth holds onto the spirit, and from that moment does not allow him to escape'.[50] The attainment of 'true rest and tranquillity' suggests completion when the element of Fire and its corresponding planet, the Sun, has achieved its goal. The same is true of the element of Water and the Moon.[51] This is how the heavenly elements work their teleological perfection: their representative planets transit over the corresponding zodiacal constellations until they reach 'true rest and tranquillity' having played their role in perfecting whatever substance needed their aid. Again this suggests aesthetic perfection where the planets perform their task in a flawless whole.

Thus, it is through invoking the seven gifts of the Holy Spirit, the seven celestial powers of the three heavenly elements, by performing an alchemical process when the powers that drive the seven planets are at their highest, that the key to divine knowledge and knowing thyself is disclosed. The resultant gnosis is the realised physical, psychological and spiritual potentials of body, soul and spirit. The success of unleashing these powers, of actualising the potentials, and the attainment and application of gnosis relies on the aesthetic perfection of the alchemical system that was introduced when 'a huge cloud darkening the entire Earth' signalled the corruption of the soul.[52]

Concluding Remarks
Although Books I and II of the *Aurora* differ in topics and styles, they are related and deserve consideration as a whole, as the compilers intended. Book I focuses on gnosis, the *telos* of teleological perfection as revealed in Scripture. Book II provides the key, in the form of natural philosophy, to finding this *telos* within an aesthetically perfect system of interconnected,

---

[49] *Aurora*, p. 54.
[50] *Aurora*, p. 54.
[51] *Aurora*, p. 54.
[52] *Aurora*, p. 18.

interrelated parts and processes. Aesthetic perfection in the *Aurora*, therefore, refers to the ideas of universal correspondences and of living Nature, two characteristics of Western esotericism identified by Antoine Faivre.[53] Teleological perfection is concerned with Faivre's two remaining intrinsic characteristics of intermediaries and transmutation. The Holy Spirit's seven gifts, the seven celestial powers, are the intermediaries between heaven and earth, between the soul and the body, and are a tool of gnosis. This celestial tool is the knowledge of hidden forces in nature, a common medieval understanding of magic or *magia naturalis*.[54] It is these hidden forces that initiate transmutation.

The *Aurora*, I have argued, is concerned with teleological and aesthetic perfection expressed in alchemical terms. The *telos* of teleological perfection is gnosis, the successful transmutation of an individual into an enlightened being. Gnosis is an innate potential that can be realised by recognising and replicating the aesthetic perfection of the alchemical process revealed by Sophia. By examining teleological and aesthetic perfection, it can be ascertained that gnosis, within the context of the *Aurora*, can be defined, in universal terms, as the acquisition of a certain type of knowledge on how to actualise an inherent potential. Everything that is actualised can be said to be a potential that is realised through a combination of revelation and practice. This is analogous with extracting sulphur in order to solidify it in its purest form with the aid of mercury.

By assuming a belief in a universal inner dimension underlying material reality, it has been possible to recognise the relationship between gnosis and the idea of correspondences and living Nature crucial to aesthetic perfection. In highlighting the presence of an inner dimension, that is, a potentiality of gnosis waiting to be externalised or realised, the links between both books become clearer. Book I is concerned with the inner and its *telos* whereas Book II with how this *telos* can only be manifested if there is the presence of aesthetic perfection.

---

[53] Antoine Faivre, *Access to Western Esotericism* (New York: SUNY Press, 1994), pp. 10–15.
[54] Hanegraaff, p. 22.

Angelomorphism and Magical Transformation in the Christian and Jewish Traditions

Alison Greig

Abstract: This paper examines the concept of angelomorphism and magical transformation with reference to canonical and non-canonical Christian and Jewish beliefs. Magic, as loosely defined, is the attempt to engage with the world through the imagination or psyche in order to obtain some form of knowledge, benefit, or advantage, while celestial magic engages with the cosmos through stellar, planetary, or celestial symbolism, influences, or intelligences.[1] Angelification of an individual is linked to the concept of resurrection, where, in the eschaton, the physical body of the righteous is transformed into a glorious new body fit for eternal life in heaven, regaining its divine likeness and becoming androgynous like an angel. The Hebrew Bible and Merkabah traditions support the possibility of the exceptional transformation of a human being into an angelic entity. Qumran liturgical texts also suggest the formation of an angelomorphic identity among the priesthood. The Christian gospels state that the redeemed will become like angels in heaven. Gnostics, however, consider that scriptural references to resurrection refer symbolically to receiving spiritual knowledge (gnosis). The paper examines concepts and practices within the respective traditions that point to a radical magical transformation of the human being that is needed to secure access to the heaven realm and the divine.

The word angel is derived from the Greek *aggelos*, 'one going' or 'one sent', messenger.[2] The Latin version distinguishes the divine or spirit-messenger from the human, rendering the original Greek in the one case by *angelus,* and in the other either by *legatus* or by *nuntius*. *Aggelos* is then

---

[1] From the programme of the Eleventh Annual Sophia Centre Conference on Celestial Magic, 22–23 June 2013: 'Magic, loosely defined, is the attempt to engage with the world through the imagination or psyche, in order to obtain some form of knowledge, benefit or advantage. Celestial magic engages with the cosmos through stellar, planetary or celestial symbolism, influences or intelligences'.
[2] Hugh Pope, 'Angels', in *The Catholic Encyclopedia*, Vol. 1 (New York: Robert Appleton Company, 1907), at http://www.newadvent.org/cathen/01476d.htm [accessed 10 November 2014].

Alison Greig, 'Angelomorphism and Magical Transformation in the Christian and Jewish Traditions', *Celestial Magic,* special issue of *Culture and Cosmos*, Vol. 19, nos. 1 and 2, 2015, pp. 129–44.
www.CultureAndCosmos.org

sometimes used in scriptural translations for the Hebrew *mal'akh* 'messenger'. The distinctive biblical application of the word, both in Hebrew and Greek, is to certain heavenly intelligences whom God employs in the office of messengers. They act as God's messengers to humanity, and as agents who carry out His will, as in the angelic appearances before Hagar in Genesis 16:7, and Joshua at Gilgal (Joshua 5:13, 15). In addition, the angel Gabriel brings revelation, as in Daniel 8:15–16, and Gabriel also announces the coming birth of Jesus the Messiah in Luke 1:26; while in Genesis 19:13, two angels are sent to destroy Sodom.

According to Augustine,

> 'Angel' is the name of their office, not of their nature. If you seek the name of their nature, it is 'spirit'; if you seek the name of their office, it is 'angel': from what they are, 'spirit', from what they do, 'angel.'" ...the angels are servants and messengers of God.[3]

It is helpful to consider angelomorphic Christology within the context of pneumatology, the study of spiritual beings, in particular the Holy Spirit in Christian theology.[4] It has been defined as follows:

> Though it has been used in different ways by various scholars, without clear definition, we propose its use wherever there are signs that an individual or community possesses specifically angelic characteristics or status, though for whom identity cannot be reduced to that of an angel.[5]

---

[3] See the Catechism of the Catholic Church, Part One on the Profession of Faith, Section Two, The Profession of the Christian Faith, Chapter One, 'I believe in God the Father', Article I, Paragraph 5. Heaven and Earth, para. 329. Catechism of the Catholic Church (Citta del Vaticano: Libreria Editrice Vaticana, 1993), available at http://www.vatican.va/archive/ENG0015/_INDEX.HTM [accessed 10 November 2013], citing Augustine, *En. in Ps.* 103,1,15, J. P. Migne, ed. Patrologia Latina, 37,1348, available at http://ccc.usccb.org/flipbooks/catechism/index.html#102 [accessed 29 September 2016].
[4] See for example John McIntyre, *The Shape of Pneumatology: Studies in the Doctrine of the Holy Spirit* (London: Bloomsbury T&T Clark, 2004).
[5] Crispin H. T. Fletcher-Louis, *Luke-Acts: Angels, Christology and Soteriology, Wissenschaftliche Untersuchungen Zum Neuen Testament 2. Reihe 94* (Tübingen: Coronet Books, 1997), pp. 14–15.

Hekhalot and Merkabah traditions associated with Apocalyptic and Qumran texts

The texts of the Apocrypha and the Pseudepigrapha provide insights into Jewish ideas on the heavenly realm and later Christian beliefs. Jewish speculations in the *Hekhalot* ('palace') and *Merkabah* ('chariot') literature describe God as enthroned in a celestial palace.[6] The Apocrypha and the Pseudepigrapha are Jewish writings from the Second Temple Period (13th– 3rd centuries BCE) that are included in the Septuagint and Vulgate but excluded from the Jewish and Protestant canons of the Old Testament. The Apocrypha include the Book of Tobit, 1 Maccabees and 2 Maccabees, which are included in the Roman Catholic Canon; while 3 Maccabees and 4 Maccabees are examples of Apocryphal texts not included in the Roman Catholic Canon. The numerous texts of the Pseudepigrapha include the Apocalypse of Abraham and the Book of Enoch.[7]

These texts include accounts of the journeys of sages through heavenly palaces or utilize the image of God's chariot, examples of which are discussed below. This tradition includes three important elements: the qualities of the ideal mystic, the heavenly journey and a possible transformation at its conclusion.[8] Its literature is 'apocalyptic' as defined by Collins:

> ... a genre of revelatory literature with a narrative framework, in which a revelation is mediated by an otherworldly being to a human recipient, describing a transcendent reality which is both temporal, insofar as it envisages eschatological salvation, and spatial insofar as it involves another, supernatural world.[9]

It should be understood that while that apocalyptic literature is revelatory, it is not necessarily eschatological, even though eschatological literature is

---

[6] Gershom Scholem, *Major Trends in Jewish Mysticism* (1946; New York: Schocken Books, 1995), pp. 43–45. The first instances of this description are Isaiah 6.1 and Ezekiel 1.26.
[7] Michael E. Stone, 'Jewish Holy Scriptures: The Apocrypha and Pseudepigrapha', available at http://www.jewishvirtuallibrary.org/jsource/Judaism/apocrypha.html [accessed 25 September 2016].
[8] Martha Himmelfarb, *Ascent to Heaven in Jewish and Christian Apocalypses* (New York: Oxford University Press, 1993), pp. 9–46.
[9] J. J. Collins, *Apocalypse: Morphology of a Genre* (Missoula, MT: Scholars Press, 1979), p. 9.

invariably apocalyptic. In the apocryphal texts, heaven is seen as the resting place of the righteous who will 'have great joy like the angels of heaven'.[10] As Himmelfarb observes, according to Jewish thought, a person can become higher than angels; see, for example, Zechariah 3:7. See also Talmud Bavli, Shabbath 86a – 'take hold of My Throne and answer them'. In Christian apocalypses, ascent to heaven is the mode of revelation.[11] The Hekhalot and Merkabah traditions emphasize personal mystical encounters with God and the heavenly realm initiated by humans.[12] A model of the heavenly journey was provided by the prophet Ezekiel, who was lifted into a divine chariot and transported by the wind and Elijah: '...there appeared a chariot of fire, and horses of fire... and Elijah went up by a whirlwind into heaven'.[13]

After the destruction of the Temple in 70 CE, some Jews continued Temple worship by mystically visiting a surrogate heavenly Temple.[14] This experience was achieved through methodical meditation and mystical contemplation, as described for example in the manuals of Abulafia such as *The Book of Eternal Life* written in 1280 and *The Light of Intellect* written in 1285.[15] Scholem views this as a variation to second and third century CE Gnosticism and Hermeticism, with the ascent of the soul past hostile angels to its divine home, signifying redemption.[16] In the Hekhalot, the soul that completes the journey sees and hears all in the heavenly realm[17].

Fire was frequently associated with divine glory, purification and transformation. In Exodus, Moses went up to the mountain which was covered by a cloud of glory: 'The glory of the LORD rested on Mount Sinai... and He called to Moses from the midst of the cloud. And to the eyes of the sons of Israel the appearance of the glory of the LORD was like

---

[10] 1 Enoch 104:2, 4, in George W. E. Nickelsburg and James C. Vander Kam, *1 Enoch: A New Translation; Based on the Hermeneia Commentary* (Minneapolis, MN: Fortress Press, 2004), p. 161.
[11] Himmelfarb, *Ascent to Heaven*, p. 3.
[12] Vita Daphna Arbel, *Beholders of Divine Secrets: Mysticism and Myth in the Hekhalot and Merkabah Literature* (New York: SUNY Press, 2003), p. 144.
[13] 2 Kings 2:11. See also Ezek. 3:12–13 for a reference to 'wheels'.
[14] Rachel Elior, *The Three Temples: One the Emergence of Jewish Mysticism*, trans. David Louvish (Portland, OR: Littman Library of Jewish Civilization, 2005), p. 63.
[15] Scholem, *Major Trends in Jewish Mysticism*, p. 135.
[16] Scholem, *Major Trends in Jewish Mysticism*, pp. 48–49.
[17] Scholem, *Major Trends in Jewish Mysticism*, p. 55.

a consuming fire on the mountain top.'[18] Regarding the purification of the speech of the prophet Isaiah: 'Then flew one of the Seraphim to me, having in his hand a burning coal which he had taken with tongs from the altar. And he touched my mouth, and said: "Behold, this has touched your lips; your guilt is taken away, and your sin forgiven"'.[19]

The apocryphal book 3 Enoch records the transformation of the human Enoch into Metatron, the angelic Prince of the Countenance. Enoch sheds his human form, becoming a winged, glowing figure and is granted a place in the celestial hierarchy, along with profound wisdom that enables him to guide other Merkabah seekers.[20] 3 Enoch provides an account of Rabbi Ishmael's ascent to heaven, where he is guided by Metatron.

> This Enoch, whose flesh was turned to flame, his veins to fire, his eye-lashes to flashes of lightning, his eye-balls to flaming torches, and whom God placed on a throne next to the throne of glory, received after this heavenly transformation the name Metatron.[21]

Enoch becomes an angel in a kind of priestly investiture, donning special garments and being anointed with oil by the archangel Michael, and being enthroned, suggesting that the transformation stems from an understanding of heaven as a temple, where angels are priests.

The canonical basis for the belief that Enoch was transformed into an angel – since his death is not mentioned – is contained in Genesis: 'Enoch

---

[18] Exodus 24:15–17.
[19] Isaiah 6:6–7.
[20] Morton Smith, trans., *Hekhalot Rabbati: The Greater Treatise Concerning the Palaces of Heaven*, ed. Don Karr, corrected by Gershom Scholem (1943–47; Morton Smith Estate: Digital Brilliance, 2009); see also Hugo Odeberg, ed. and trans., *The Hebrew book of Enoch (Enoch 3) by R. Ishmael Ben Elisha, The High Priest*, in English, revised translation 1928, available at https://ia902606.us.archive.org/23/items/HebrewBookOfEnochenoch3/BookOfEnoch3.pdf [accessed 25 September 2016].
[21] Scholem, *Major Trends in Jewish Mysticism*, p. 67, cites *3 Enoch. Third Book of Enoch*, Chapter XLVIII (c), ALT 3 (6), which states in the words of God: 'I transformed his flesh into torches of fire, and all the bones of his body into fiery coals; and I made the appearance of his eyes as the lightning, and the light of his eyebrows as the imperishable light. I made his face bright as the splendour of the sun, and his eyes as the splendour of the Throne of Glory.'

134 Angelomorphism and Magical Transformation in the Christian and Jewish Traditions

walked with God after the birth of Methuselah three hundred years... Enoch walked with God; then he was no more, because God took him'.[22]

Wolfson observes that Jewish sources, beginning with the Apocalyptic and Qumran texts, may provide model of mysticism based on the 'angelification' of the human being who crosses the boundary of space and time and becomes part of the heavenly realm.[23] The mystical experience in this framework involves a two-step closing of the gap separating human and divine by the ascension into the heavens: (a) participation in the angelic liturgy in a standing posture, and (b) enthronement in the celestial realm, which represents the fullest expression of the mystical experience, an eschatological ideal of deification.[24] According to Wolfson, the ultimate secret of the prophetic experience is the imaginative representation of the divine as an anthropos. Only one who transforms the physical body into something spiritual – a transformation that is presented as angelification – is capable of imagining the divine form in bodily images.[25]

The Qumran liturgical texts provide insights into pre-rabbinic Judaism and the cultural background of early Christianity, including the earliest manuscripts of most of the Hebrew Bible books dating from the last centuries BCE or the 1st century CE.[26] The *Songs of the Sabbath Sacrifice* (4QShirShab), also known as the *Angelic Liturgy*, describes the Sabbath worship of the angelic priesthood in the heavenly temple.[27] Each of the seven firmaments have their own inner sanctuary which is administered by its own high-priestly chief prince. The final inner chamber, the central throne room, is inhabited by God himself.[28] The community believed that the righteous would be rewarded by 'eternal blessings and everlasting joy in the life everlasting, and a crown of glory and a robe of honour, amid

---

[22] Genesis 5:22–24.

[23] Elliot R. Wolfson, 'Mysticism and the Poetic-Liturgical Compositions from Qumran: A Response to Bilhah Nitzan', *Jewish Quarterly Review, New Series* 85, No. 1/2, Papers on the Dead Sea Scrolls (1994): p. 186.

[24] Elliot R. Wolfson, 'Yeridah la-Merkavah: Typology of Ecstasy and Enthronement in Ancient Jewish Mysticism', in *Mystics of the Book: Themes, Topics and Typologies*, ed. R. A. Herrera (New York: Peter Lang Publishing, 1993): pp. 13–44.

[25] Elliot R. Wolfson, *Language, Eros, Being: Kabbalistic Hermeneutics and Poetic Imagination* (New York, NY: Fordham University Press, 2005), pp. 120–21.

[26] James R. Davila, *Liturgical Works: Eerdman's Commentaries on the Dead Sea Scrolls* (Grand Rapids, MI: Eerdmans Publishing, 2000), p. 1.

[27] Davila, *Liturgical Works*, pp. 83–167.

[28] Davila, *Liturgical Works*, p. 84.

light perpetual'.[29] The angelomorphic status may have also implied the possibility of transport to what Corbin termed the imaginal realm.[30]

Fletcher-Louis argues that the purpose of the mystical participation at Qumran is angelification. 'The priesthood is a primary conceptual category for the formation of an angelomorphic identity'.[31] Segal observes that the Liturgy seems to map a seven-stage ascent to heaven to view God's throne and glory. Worship in the Heavenly Temple includes an example of angelomorphism in the blessing:

> May you be as an angel of the Presence in the Abode of Holiness to the Glory of the God of (Hosts).
> May you attend upon the service in the Temple of the kingdom and decree destiny in company with the Angels of the Presence, in common council (with the Holy Ones).[32]

For Nitzan, the mystical dimension in the liturgical writings from Qumran involves the harmony of communion of human beings and angels expressed in terms of the participation of individuals or the community in the angelic choir, which praises God in the heavenly temple.[33] This acknowledges that the pure 'may recite praises in company with the angels, and thus attain spiritual experience of communion with the celestial entourage'.[34]

Wolfson observes that the theoretical model for Nitzan is the description of the mystical experience offered by Scholem, which involves

---

[29] 1QS IV:7–8, see Geza Vermes, *The Complete Dead Sea Scrolls in English, Revised Edition* (London: Penguin Books, 2003), p.189. The scrolls are referred to by cave number and document number. The reference conventions are summarized in Craig Evans, *Holman QuickSource Guide to the Dead Sea Scrolls* (North Nashville: B&H Publishing Group, 2010.)

[30] James R. Davila, 'Heavenly Ascents in the Dead Sea Scrolls,' in *The Dead Sea Scrolls After Fifty Years*, Vol. 2, ed. P. W. Flint and J. C. Vander Kam (Leiden: Brill, 1999), pp. 461–85. For the imaginal, see Henri Corbin, 'Mundus Imaginalis: the Imaginary and the Imaginal', *Spring* (1972): pp. 1–19, available at http://www.hermetic.com/bey/mundus_imaginalis.htm [accessed 29 September 2016].

[31] Crispin Fletcher-Louis, *All the Glory of Adam: Liturgical Anthropology in the Dead Sea Scrolls* (Leiden: E.J. Brill, 2002), p. 56.

[32] 1QSb 4:24–28.

[33] Bilhah Nitzan, 'Harmonic and Mystical Characteristics in Poetic and Liturgical Writings from Qumran', *The Jewish Quarterly Review* 85 (1994): pp. 163–83.

[34] Nitzan, 'Harmonic and Mystical Characteristics', p. 166.

a direct and intimate consciousness of the divine Presence that, in the most extreme cases, eventuates in union with God.[35] The mystical aspect of Hekhalot literature, according to Scholem, involves the 'ascent of the soul to the celestial throne where it obtains an ecstatic view of the majesty of God and the secrets of His realm'.[36] However, according to Wolfson, rather than being merely a harmony between heavenly and earthly worshipers, mysticism involves the narrowing of the gap between human and divine and ultimately the ascension to heaven and transformation into an angelic being who occupies a throne alongside the throne of glory.[37] The mystical experience expressed in the Hekhalot thus involves a heavenly ascent culminating in the enthronement of the mystic that transforms him into an angelic being, a transformation that facilitates his vision of the glory and the powers of God.[38] In the *Songs of Sabbath Sacrifice*, one fragment, which, according to the reconstruction of Morton Smith, relates to the ascension and enthronement of an individual of the sect, would meet Wolfson's definition of 'mystical'.[39]

> Glorification Hymn A (4Q491, fr.11)
> ... the right(teo)us exult (in the streng)th of His might and the holy ones rejoice in... in righteousness...
> ... He has established it in Israel
> Since ancient times His truth and the mysteries of His wisdom (have been in al(l) power
> ... and the council of the poor into an eternal congregation
> ... the perfect ... (et)ernity a throne of strength in the congregation of 'gods' so that not a single king of old shall sit on it, neither shall their noble men...
> My glory is incomparable, and apart from me none is exalted.
> None shall come to me for I swell in... in heaven, and there is no...
> I am reckoned with the 'gods' and my dwelling-place is in the congregation of holiness.[40]

---

[35] Wolfson, 'Mysticism and the Poetic-Liturgical Compositions from Qumran', pp. 185–202, pp. 191–92.
[36] Scholem, *Major Trends in Jewish Mysticism*, p. 5.
[37] Wolfson, 'Mysticism and the Poetic-Liturgical Compositions from Qumran', p. 193.
[38] Wolfson, 'Yeridah la-Merkavah', p. 26.
[39] 1 of 4Q491; and see Wolfson, 'Mysticism and the Poetic-Liturgical Compositions from Qumran', p. 200.
[40] Vermes, *The Complete Dead Sea Scrolls in English*, pp. 341–42.

Furthermore, Wolfson states that in order to envision the 'glory', a term that signifies in Qumran fragments the heavenly world, 'one must become glorious, aglow with the glimmer of the divine image, the angelic splendor in whose likeness Adam was created'.[41] He refers to two epistemological principles, one traceable in the Greek philosophical tradition to Anaxagoras, 'like sees like', and the other to the occult wisdom of hermetic alchemy, 'like mirrors like', expressed in the Emerald Tablet attributed to Hermes Trismegistus, 'What is below is like that which is above, and what is above is like that which is below, to accomplish the miracles of one thing'.[42] A priest can behold the glorious light without only when he has become that light within, a transformation facilitated by faithful adherence to ascetic practices, especially sexual renunciation, intended to realize the ideal of ritual purity.[43]

Fletcher-Louis maintains that the purpose of entry into the sacred temple – with access to the heavenly world through the inner sanctuary – is transformation. The worshipper becomes closer to conformity to God's nature and modes of action. The liturgical anthropology of the temple tradition is essentially a matter of deification.[44] Furthermore, a ritual connection between the celibacy of some Essenes and their angelomorphic identity is possible.[45]

Angelification in the New Testament
The idea of angelification also finds support in the New Testament: St Paul described his ascension to the third Heaven, a revelation rooted in the Jewish apocalyptic traditions, as discussed above:[46]

---

[41] Elliot R. Wolfson, 'Seven Mysteries of Knowledge: Qumran Esotericism Reconsidered', in *The Idea of Biblical Interpretation: Essays in Honor of James L. Kugel*, ed. H. Najman (Leiden: Brill, 2003), p. 192.

[42] Jabir ibn Hayyan, 'The Emerald Tablet of Hermes Trismegistus', in E. J. Holmyard, *Alchemy* (Harmondsworth: Penguin Books, 1957), line 2, available at http://www.sacred-texts.com/alc/emerald.htm. See also Wolfson, 'Seven Mysteries of Knowledge', p. 192.

[43] Leviticus 15.17. See also Wolfson, 'Seven Mysteries of Knowledge', p. 193.

[44] Fletcher-Louis, *All the Glory of Adam*, p. 203.

[45] Alan F. Segal, *Life after death: A history of the Afterlife in the Religions of the West* (New York: Doubleday, 2003), p. 306.

[46] Also see the resurrected 'are like angels in heaven', Matt 22:30; Mark 12:25; Luke 20:36. The version of the Bible used is the *New Revised Standard Version Bible*, Division of Christian Education of the National Council of the Churches of Christ in the United States of America (San Francisco, CA: HarperCollins, 1989).

138 Angelomorphism and Magical Transformation in the Christian and Jewish Traditions

> I know a man in Christ who fourteen years ago was caught up to the third heaven – whether in the body or out of the body I do not know, God knows. And I know that this man was caught up into Paradise – whether in the body or out of the body I do not know... and he heard things that cannot be told, which man may not utter.[47]

Paul's ascension parallels the mystical experiences of apocalyptic Jews and is linked with the newly resurrected body, which resembles or is an angelic body, through a process of angelification. A master narrative of salvation is marked by the meta-schematization (change in the structure) of the body into a glorious body shared with Christ. For example, 'Lord Jesus Christ... will transform our lowly bodies so that they will be like his glorious body'.[48] And again,

> Jesus said to them, 'Those who belong to this age marry and are given in marriage; but those who are considered worthy of a place in that age and in the resurrection from the dead neither marry nor are given in marriage. Indeed they cannot die anymore, because they are like angels and are children of God, being children of the resurrection.[49]

Such themes were developed by the Apostle Paul, who stated that the body of glory or pneumatic body becomes androgynous, regains its divine likeness, its angelic completeness. In addition, he describes the primal combination of male and female that is lost in the Garden of Eden: 'There is no longer Jew or Greek, there is no longer slave or free, there is no longer male and female; for all of you are one in Christ Jesus'.[50] The message in the Gospels and in the writings of Paul with respect to believers being transformed into either angelic beings or beings analogous to angels implies that a believer will undergo a radical transformation, which is a prerequisite to becoming a full citizen of heaven.[51]

In Gnostic theologies, heavenly ascents are considered as a means to redemption. According to non-canonical Gnostic Christianity, exemplified by the texts discovered at Nag Hammadi and the *Pistis Sophia*, Jesus

---

[47] 2 Corinthians 12.
[48] Philippians 3:20–21.
[49] Luke 20:34–36.
[50] Galatians 3:28; also see Col. 3:11.
[51] 'But our citizenship is in heaven', Philippians 3:20.

Christ undertook a journey to heaven and defeated the planetary archons, thereby enabling his followers to undertake similar journeys.[52]

The Pistis Sophia, provides an account of Jesus Christ's journey to heaven, where he defeats the planetary spirits (archons) thus enabling his followers to undertake similar journeys, free from confines of earthly life and malevolent astrological influences. In the *(First) Apocalypse of James* from Nag Hammadi,[53] Jesus tells disciples that after his death he will return and 'appear for a reproof to the archons. And I shall reveal to them that he can not be seized. If they seize him, then he will overpower each of them'. The Gnostic is rescued from the dark powers and can depart from this world through the planetary spheres towards the pleroma. Similarly, the Gnostic text *Pistis Sophia* quotes Christ as saying:

> I flew to the height... And the gates of the firmament... all opened at the same time. And all the archons and all the powers and all the angels therein... looked upon the shining garment of light which I wore, they saw the mystery of their name within it... saying: "How has the Lord of the All passed through without our knowing?" And all their bonds were loosened, and their places and their ranks.[54]

In *The Gnostic Paul*, Pagels examines the way in which Paul's letters can be interpreted either antignostically or gnostically.[55] The Naasenes and Valentinians revered Paul as a Gnostic initiate, claiming that his receiving of the gnosis was a symbolic one, as set out in the Treatise on the Resurrection, which was discovered at Nag Hammadi:[56]

---

[52] G. R. S. Meade, trans., *Pistis Sophia*, 1921, available at http://www.sacred-texts.com/chr/ps/index.htm [accessed 15 September 2016].

[53] J. M. Robinson, ed., *The Nag Hammadi Library in English,* Fourth revised edition (Leiden: Brill, 1996), p. 264.

[54] Meade, *Pistis Sophia*.

[55] Elaine Pagels, *The Gnostic Paul – Gnostic Exegesis of the Pauline Letters* (New York: Continuum, 1992), p. 152.

[56] Pagels, *The Gnostic Paul*, p. 29, with reference to the *Treatise on the Resurrection*, a Gnostic text found at Nag Hammadi sometimes referred to as 'The Letter to Rheginos'. See Willis Barnstone and Marvin Meyer, eds., *The Gnostic Bible* (Boston, MA: Shambhala Publications, 2003); The Treatise on the Resurrection *(Nag Hammadi Codex I, 4)*, trans. Willis Barnstone, available at http://gnosis.org/naghamm/resurrection-barnstone.html [accessed 25 September 2016].

> The saviour has swallowed up death, so that you should not remain in ignorance [i.e., 'death']... and he has offered us the way of our immortality. Therefore, as the Apostle says, we suffered with him, and we arose with him, and we went to heaven with him.

According to Harrison, Paul's revelation is a paradigm for the Gnostic believer's ascent.[57] Furthermore, the motif of the heavenly journey can be seen in John 3:1–21. 'Jesus replied, " ...unless a person is born from above, he cannot see the kingdom of God".' The phrase 'born again' in the King James Version can be translated as 'born from heaven', indicating a heavenly journey and the transformation of the mystic.[58]

Paul describes Jesus Christ as 'a priest forever according to the order of Melchizedek', which could be connected to angelomorphism and the priesthood at Qumran.[59] Melchizedek is a mysterious figure in the Book of Genesis, who as 'a priest of God Most High', presents bread and wine to Abraham and blesses him.[60] Melchizedek does not belong to the traditional Levitical priestly caste of the Israelites. Early Church Fathers understood this as representing a pre-figuration of the priesthood of Christ and that of the Catholic Church.[61] Paul describes Christ as a high priest in the sanctuary and a true tabernacle, which was set up by God, i.e., in heaven.[62] The theme has been further amplified by Peter, who says: 'But you are... a royal priesthood... God's own people'.[63] While in Revelation, John writes ' ...you have made them to be a kingdom and priests serving our God'.[64] This is the notion that angelomorphism is linked to heaven as a temple with angels serving as heavenly priests.

Fletcher-Louis further discusses angelomorphism in Luke's Gospel and the Book of Acts. In Acts 6:15 the face of the martyr Stephen is explicitly likened to that of an angel; and in Acts 12:13–15 it is assumed that a person's guardian angel closely resembles them. He considers that those texts were constructed in conscious interaction with Jewish traditions of

---

[57] J. R. Harrison, 'In Quest of the Third Heaven: Paul & His Apocalyptic Imitators', *Vigiliae Christianae* 58, no. 1 (2004): pp. 24–55, p. 29.
[58] William C. Grese, '"Unless One Is Born Again": The Use of a Heavenly Journey in John 3', *Journal of Biblical Literature* 107, no. 4 (1988), pp. 677–93.
[59] Heb. 5:6, with reference to Psalm 110:4.
[60] Gen. 14:18–20.
[61] *The Catechism,* p. 1333.
[62] Heb. 8:1–2.
[63] 1 Peter 2:9.
[64] Rev. 5:10.

human angelomorphism.[65] According to Fletcher-Louis, 'the Lukan angelomorphic Christ brings an angelic identity and status to his followers'.[66] The relation between Jesus-followers and angels is one of 'substantive continuity of identity' and 'ontological affinity'.[67] However, for a contrary view, Sullivan stated that despite the similarity in appearance and the closeness of interaction, there does not seem to be any reason to suppose that there was any blurring of categories between angels and humans.[68] Sullivan considered that the transformation of Enoch into the Angel Metatron was a one-off event beyond the earthly sphere. In any case, according to Bucur, the depiction of eschatological humanity as angelic or angelomorphic should be understood as corresponding to the depiction of protological humanity. Thus, 2 Enoch 30.11 states that Adam was created as 'a second angel, honored and great and glorious', and so angelification signals a return to Paradise.[69]

Tertullian (ca. 160–225 CE) explained that, in the eschaton, the heavenly kingdom can be enjoyed when the righteous are changed into angelic bodies:

> This is the manner of the heavenly kingdom: within the space of its thousand years is comprised the resurrection of the saints, who arise either earlier or later according to their deserts: after which, when the destruction of the world and the fire of judgement have been set in motion, we shall be changed in a moment into angelic substance, by virtue of that supervesture of incorruption, and be translated into that heavenly kingdom... .[70]

Bucur considered that Clement of Alexandria (ca. 150–ca. 215 CE), another Christian theologian, saw the spiritual universe as hierarchical: the Logos is at the pinnacle, below which are the seven *protoctists* (the first

---

[65] Fletcher-Louis, *Luke-Acts*, p. 105; see also Fletcher-Louis, *All the Glory of Adam*.
[66] Fletcher-Louis, *Luke-Acts*, p. 254.
[67] Bogdan Gabriel Bucur, *Angelomorphic Pneumatology; Clement of Alexandria and other early Christian witnesses* (Leiden: Brill, 2009), p. 46.
[68] Kevin P. Sullivan, 'Wrestling with Angels: A study of the Relationship between Angels and Humans in Ancient Jewish Literature and the New Testament', (*Arbeiten zur Geschichte des antiken Judentums und des Urchristentums* 55) (Leiden: Brill, 2004).
[69] Bucur, *Angelomorphic Pneumatology*, p. 46.
[70] Tertullian. *Tertullian: Adversus Marcionem*, ed. and trans. Ernest Evans (London: Oxford University Press, 1972), III. 24, p. 249.

created angels), the archangels and the angels.[71] Advancement on the cosmic ladder leads to the progressive transformation of one level into the next at the end of the millennial cycle.[72] But Clement indicates that the time period indicated that the Gnostic ought to rise out of the sphere of creation and of sin. So the cosmic-ladder becomes an image of interior transformation. Bucur concludes that these texts present an ancient biblical and extra-biblical tradition – the transformation from human to angelic – that was eliminated, or de-emphasized, in mainstream Christianity.[73] According to McGrath, in a view that seems close to that in the *Songs of Sabbath Sacrifice*, whenever the Divine Liturgy is celebrated on earth, the boundaries between heaven and earth are removed with earthly worshippers joining in the eternal heavenly liturgy chanted by angels and '...worshipers have the opportunity of being mystically transported to the threshold of heaven'.[74]

Barker endeavours to reconstruct the worldview of the first Christians as including elements of Temple theology, arguing that these elements include: the Temple/Tabernacle as a microcosm of the creation; priests as angels and angels as priests, and where humans could become angels through resurrection or *theosis*.[75] Thus the fallen angels of scripture could be attributed to a corrupt priesthood.[76] According to 1 Enoch, the rebel angels brought their heavenly knowledge to earth and they made a covenant.[77] Since the temple priests had seen themselves as angels, according to Barker, the fallen angels were corrupted priests.[78] However, returning to angelification proper, in Psalm 110:

---

[71] Bucur, *Angelomorphic Pneumatology*, p. 42.
[72] Bucur, *Angelomorphic Pneumatology*, p. 42.
[73] Bucur, *Angelomorphic Pneumatology*, p. 46.
[74] Alister E. McGrath, ed., *A Brief History of Heaven* (Malden, MA: Wiley-Blackwell, 2003), p. 167.
[75] Margaret Barker, *Great High Priest: The Temple Roots of Christian Liturgy* (New York: Continuum, 2003), p. 105; see also http://www.margaretbarker.com/Temple/default.htm [accessed 26 September 2013].
[76] Genesis 6:1–4.
[77] 1 En.6.4.
[78] Margaret Barker, *Wisdom and the other Tree: A Temple Theology reading of the Genesis Eden Story* (Amsterdam: Society for Biblical Literature, 2012), p. 5, at http://www.margaretbarker.com/Papers/WisdomOtherTree.pdf [accessed 10 November 2013].

> The Lord says to my lord:
>   "Sit at my right hand until I make your enemies
>   a footstool for your feet."
> ² The Lord will extend your mighty scepter from Zion, saying,
>   "Rule in the midst of your enemies!"
> ³ Your troops will be willing
>   on your day of battle.
> Arrayed in holy splendor,
>   your young men will come to you
>   like dew from the morning's womb.
> ⁴ The Lord has sworn
>   and will not change his mind:
>   "You are a priest forever,
>   in the order of Melchizedek."

The investiture and symbolic birth of a Melchizedek-like figure – i.e., 'a priest forever in the order of Melchizedek' – in the holy of holies is described.[79] He is invited to sit on the throne: i.e., 'The Lord says to my lord: "Sit at my right hand"', which is the moment he takes his place as the divine son.[80] Margaret Barker, considering alternative translations of the text, considers that in this Psalm 'the heavenly birth and anointing of the king and birth into the life of heaven was what is meant by resurrection'.[81] Those who sit on the throne are reborn and live in heaven, equal to angels, sons of god, uniting the divine and human. The heavenly liturgy and the angel priesthood replicate the most ancient traditions of the Jerusalem Temple, and perpetuate them as a tradition in the Christian Church.[82]

Conclusions

Angelomorphism can be understood in various ways from literal to figurative, and has links to early liturgical practices, although the concept has been de-emphasized in current Christian teachings. The nature of the angelification can be understood in different ways: whether human beings join the angels' worship in heaven and thereby become more angelic by association; change into an angelic class of being through a process of

---

[79] Melchizedek is the king of Salem and priest of *El Elyon* ('God most high') mentioned in Genesis 14: 18–20. See footnote 61 above, regarding Paul's reference to Jesus Christ as a priest in the order of Melchizedek in Heb. 5:6.
[80] Barker, *Great High Priest*, p. 82.
[81] Margaret Barker, *Temple Mysticism, An introduction*, (London: Society for Promoting Christian Knowledge, 2011), p. 100.
[82] Barker, *Great High Priest*, p. 105.

transformation with divine fire; begin to function as messengers (*aggelou*) of the divine due to their faith; or become ontologically identified with Jesus Christ in the resurrection, the radical and magical transition from an earthly level to a heavenly one, aided by ritual, ascetic, prayer, or other religious practices, which has been equated with angelification in both Jewish and Christian earliest traditions. Being 'born from above' by mystical enthronement in sacred space is seen as another key to both the contemplation of the divine and the empowerment of the individual seer.

One result of the transference of the worshiper from the 'lower' to the 'higher' part of the continuum of life would be for individuals and communities to experience life more as the denizens of the heavenly realms would be imagined to experience it, i.e., to become more 'angelic', in resonance with the Hermetic dictum 'as above, so below'.[83] In this way, heaven becomes less a physical location in the sky, but rather an orientation towards the sacred in life. The dichotomy between heaven and earth, 'above' and 'below,' depends on the perspective and orientation of the person perceiving them. Life on earth includes experiences corresponding to periods of elevated awareness, which therefore, by analogy, are closer to the perceived heavenly powers. Similarly, life on earth may be perceived of as not completely disconnected from the heavenly realms, but rather as shaped by the thoughts and actions of individuals, which influence conditions while alive as well as those that are desired or imagined in the hereafter.

---

[83] Hayyan, 'The Emerald Tablet of Hermes Trismegistus'.

Celestial Magic as the 'Love Path': The Spiritual Cosmology of Ibn 'Arabi

Christine Broadbent

Abstract: Nature's secrets can be approached in a variety of ways and this paper explores celestial magic as the 'path of love' via the Sufi teachings of Muhyiddin Ibn al-Arabi (1165–1240 CE). Given the honorary title of 'the greatest master', *al-Shaykh al-Akbar*, he occupies a special place in the Sufi tradition, because his writings are by far the most extensive contribution to Islamic mystical philosophy. His terminology and works have become a main point of reference for most Sufi orders, partly due to the historical circumstances explored below. His teachings continue to be widely studied, and a range of contemporary Sufi schools, like *Beshara* in Scotland and *Karnak* in Northern Australia, have introduced westerners to the study, work, invocation and meditation of the Sufi path as passed down by Ibn 'Arabi.[1] This paper explores his use of astrological symbolism to illustrate Sufi cosmology, as for example, his 'orientations to spirit', which are a different way of viewing the 'quadruplicities'. In *Mystical Astrology According to Ibn 'Arabi,* translator and author Titus Burckhardt (1908–1984) calls attention to what Ibn 'Arabi calls the 'contemplative penetration of cosmic atmosphere'. Mystical correspondences, including 'eternal prototypes' and designated prophets, are linked to planets, like the symbolic chain he draws between the moon and Adam's prophetic role as the 'mirror' of divinity.[2] This may beg the question of an overlap between the mystical and the magical, yet any such engagement depends on cultural norms and social context for its nomenclature. Celestial 'magic', explored as an imaginative engagement with the cosmos for the production of knowledge, allows the Sufi 'love path', to be considered. Further, *Tasawwuf,* the mystical path of Sufism, is suggestive for the sociological discourse on the 'magical subject' and for the question that frames this paper: namely, what are the implications for our ways of knowing?

---

[1] Muhyiddin Ibn al-Arabi, *The Wisdom of the Prophets: Fusus al-hikam,* is the teaching resource most commonly used in Sufi schools. The *Karnak* Sufi school closed to students in 1991. I had the privilege of studying there in 1988.
[2] Titus Burckhardt, *Mystical Astrology According to Ibn 'Arabi,* trans. Bulent Rauf. (First published as *Une Clef Spirituelle de l'Astrologie Musulmane d'apres Mohyi-d-din Ibn 'Arabi',* 1950) (Sherborne, UK: Beshara Publications, 1977; repr. Louisville, KY: Fons Vitae, 2001), p. 9.

Christine Broadbent, 'Celestial Magic as the 'Love Path': The Spiritual Cosmology of Ibn 'Arabi', *Celestial Magic,* special issue of *Culture and Cosmos,* Vol. 19, nos. 1 and 2, 2015, pp. 145–66.
www.CultureAndCosmos.org

Introducing Ibn 'Arabi

Born in Murcia on 27 July 1165 CE in the medieval *Al-Andalus* of Islamic Spain, Muhyddin Ibn 'Arabi was known as the *Shaykh al-Akbar,* or 'greatest spiritual master'. Given that *Al-Andalus* had become 'one of the major intellectual centres in the Muslim world', this is high praise indeed.[3] His extensive writings recorded in detail the Sufi oral tradition that preceded him and ensured the survival of a rich mystical heritage, replete with technicalities, symbol systems and an extensive knowledge of the Islamic sciences of his day. With a formal Islamic education, a mother of Berber heritage, and a father from an ancient Arab lineage of high standing, Ibn 'Arabi chose not to follow his father's path of serving in the sultan's entourage, following instead the Sufi way. Sufis called the mystical sciences 'the knowledge of the Real' and Ibn 'Arabi studied under many different Sufi Shaykhs, starting in his youth.[4] These metaphysical studies included 'cosmology, esoteric exegesis, the science of letters and numbers and the stages of the [Sufi] Way itself'.[5] In addition, he learned practices like invocation, prayer, fasting, retreat and meditation, which tended to ripen the propensity to 'experiences of a supersensory nature'. 'Ibn 'Arabi seems to have had many such experiences... Among these were visions, foresight, spiritual communication with the living and the dead, and powers of healing'.[6]

Even within Sufism he chose the path which placed spontaneous revelation over philosophical speculation: 'If the speculative way can lead to divine knowledge, only the Prophetic Way allows God to be known in both His transcendence and His immanence...through inspiration (*ilham*) and theophanies'.[7] The frequency of openings to 'divine visions', Ibn 'Arabi

---

[3] Stephen Hirtenstein, *The Unlimited Mercifier: The Spiritual Life and Thought of Ibn 'Arabi* (Oxford: Anqa Publishing, 1999), p. 11. The birth date given is based on Ibn 'Arabi's own recorded statement: pp. 34, 252. NB: This book is most useful to learn about the historical context of Ibn 'Arabi's time and his place in the history of Sufism.
[4] William C. Chittick, *The Sufi Path of Knowledge: Ibn al-'Arabi's Metaphysics of Imagination*, compiled, edited and translated by Chittick from sections of *Al-Futûhât Al-Makkiya* (Albany, NY: SUNY Press, 1989), p. xi, cites 'a document dated 632/1234' in which Ibn 'Arabi 'mentions by name ninety masters of the religious sciences with whom he himself had studied'.
[5] R. W. J. Austin, trans., Introduction to *Sufis of Andalusia: The Ruh al-quds and al-Durrat al-fakhirah of Ibn 'Arabi* (Los Angeles: University of California Press, 1971), p. 24.
[6] Austin, Introduction to *Sufis of Andalusia*, p. 24.
[7] Muhyiddin Ibn 'Arabi, *Futûhât al-Makkiyya,* selected sections compiled and edited by Michel Chodkiewicz, published as *Les Illuminations des la Mecque* (Paris:

explained, was almost overwhelming, and he added: 'I could only put them from my mind by committing to paper what they revealed to me'.[8]

Perhaps revelation chose Ibn 'Arabi, since he was prone to powerful visions, starting with a near death experience as a child. In the biographical *Ruh al-quds*, he recounts the aged and famous philosopher, Ibn Rushd – known to Europeans as Averroes – asking to meet him, when he himself was only a 'beardless youth', but already known for his spiritual experiences. His account suggests that while having great respect for Averroes, he countered his 'speculative' thought with his own 'revelations', and Averroes 'became pale and I saw him tremble', praising God.[9] This occurred years before the time he claimed to have been initiated into the Sufi way, at age 20.[10]

Eighteen years after Ibn 'Arabi's death, Mongol invasions began the process of the disintegration of 800 years of Islamic civilisation. His legacy of over 350 written works meant that cultural knowledge was safe-guarded, ensuring an ongoing transmission of Sufi knowledge after widespread loss.[11],[12] It is to this legacy that Austin refers when he observes: '... he was the bridge or link between two historical phases of Islam and Sufism', adding, '... secondly he was the link between Western and Eastern Sufism'.[13]

To address this second point: Ibn 'Arabi was born in the western Muslim world of Spain and settled in the East after thirty years of extensive travel, during which time he criss-crossed between the western dominions of Spain

---

Sindbad, 1988; English translation by W. C. Chittick and J. W. Morris, published as *The Meccan Revelations*, Vol. II (New York: Pir Press, 2004), p. 90; here Vol. III, p. 177, 1.11–13, quoted by M. Chodkiewicz. NB: Chodkiewicz instances Ibn Tufayl, 'another [earlier] Andalusian', as an example of the 'speculative way', which Ibn 'Arabi resisted as a path, see pp. 89–90.

[8] Ibn 'Arabi, Introduction to the 'Memorandum', quoted by Ralph Austin in *Sufis of Andalusia: The Ruh al-quds and al-Durrat al-fakhirah of Ibn 'Arabi*, trans. R. W. J. Austin (1971; Sherborne: Beshara Publications, 1988), p. 48.

[9] Ibn 'Arabi, *Futûhât*, Vol. I, p. 153, quoted by Ralph Austin in *Sufis of Andalusia*, pp. 23–24.

[10] Ibn 'Arabi, *Futûhât*, II, p. 425, quoted by Austin, *Sufis of Andalusia*, p. 23.

[11] Hirtenstein, *Unlimited Mercifier*, p. 267: 'At least 350 works' is a conservative estimate. Osman Yahia, in his 1964 two volume classification, estimated that Ibn 'Arabi wrote 700 books, treatises and collections of poetry, of which 400 are extant. Even so, 'this inventory was necessarily full of omissions'.

[12] It is of interest that the works of Ibn 'Arabi have experienced a renaissance in the twentieth century Western world.

[13] Austin, *Sufis of Andalusia*, p. 48. For more on the East-West link see Chittick, *The Sufi Path of Knowledge* and Hirtenstein, *The Unlimited Mercifier*.

and Africa and the eastern Muslim world, with extended stays in many parts, including Iraq, Anatolia and the Levant.

In Konya he met Sadruddin al-Qunawi and took him as his disciple. Qunawi became his greatest proponent and compiler: 'It was through the latter's links with some of the most eminent Persian Sufis that Ibn 'Arabi's teaching reached the East'.[14] These eminent Sufis included Sufi poet Jalaluddin Rumi. 'Through Rumi in the East and Abu al-Hasan al-Shadhili in the West, two of the greatest Sufi orders were permeated by his teaching'.[15] It was in Qunawi's library that numerous original handwritten manuscripts and authenticated copies of Ibn 'Arabi's books were preserved for later times. Ibn 'Arabi's honorary title,'*Muhyid-din*', means 'animator of the religion', recognising the potency of his unique synthesis of Sufi knowledge.

The medieval Islamic worldview held spiritual teachers in high regard, and in *Al-Andalus* it was acceptable practice for these Shaykhs to publically criticise and 'awaken' even those of very high rank in worldly status: Ibn 'Arabi relates an anecdote in which his own paternal uncle awakened a king, in this way. When the king asked the Shaykh if it was lawful to pray in his fine clothes, part of the his fiery reply was: 'You are full of unlawfulness, and you ask me about your clothes, when the sufferings of men are upon your head'. The king renounced his position and served the Shaykh for his remaining years.[16] Ibn 'Arabi's social context, plus the cultural melting pot which was the *Al-Andalus* of his time, respected diverse ways of knowing. Hirtenstein adds: 'There was an extraordinary cultural interaction between Muslim, Christian and Jew, and many of the ideas that appeared later in Europe as the Renaissance, were formed and transformed in this crucible'.[17]

The Spiritual Praxis of Ibn 'Arabi: The 'Love Path'
The integration of 'knowledge' and 'love' in Sufism is intrinsic to its cosmology, and something that Ibn 'Arabi explored deeply. Sympathy with the 'effusion of being' and its fluid nature seem to have been natural to him, and 'unveilings' began early in his life. The *alam al-mithal*, or 'the world of imagination', was intensely real for Ibn 'Arabi, and he treated his experiences with respect, taking action based on those revelations.[18]

---

[14] Austin, *Sufis of Andalusia*, p. 49.
[15] Austin, *Sufis of Andalusia*, p. 49.
[16] Ibn 'Arabi, *Futûhât*, II, p.18, quoted by Austin, *Sufis of Andalusia*, pp. 21–22, gives one such example.
[17] Hirtenstein, *The Unlimited Mercifier*, p. 12.
[18] *alam al-mithal*, and the significance of this 'world of imagination' is explored further below.

Kashf, which means 'unveiling' or an 'opening' to higher orders of consciousness, is the praxis of the Sufi 'love path' and is considered a mode of gaining direct knowledge of the 'Real'.[19] The 'love path' is the path to that knowledge. In the spiritual context of his early experiences of *himma*, which refers to his ability to concentrate the energy of the heart; in the social context of the relative wealth and strong spiritual leanings of his extended family; and living in a social milieu that tended to respect revelatory experiences, Ibn 'Arabi realised his spiritual potential to a high degree'.[20] That this was also a realisation of intellectual potential is in complete accordance with the Sufi collusion of love and knowledge.

Burckhardt's statement that: 'the intoxication of love symbolically corresponds to states of knowledge, which go beyond discursive thought'[21] is a good starting point: for Ibn 'Arabi, the human heart is an organ of comprehension, since 'the heart is His Throne', and the experience of revelation opens the heart to knowledge.[22] What is considered truly natural to the heart is love as a quest for the divine, which is also a quest for knowledge in the Sufi lexicon. He describes the heart as: 'that which is delimited by fluctuation so that it never ceases undergoing transformation'. Chittick spells this out: 'In Islamic texts in general and Ibn 'Arabi in particular, the heart is a locus for knowledge rather than sentiments or feelings'.[23]

From these cultural roots Ibn 'Arabi developed a singular translation of the Sufi mystical tradition and the 'love path'. Campion describes him as 'the last major proponent of the synthesis of Islam with the mystery teachings of the classical world'.[24] Hermetic and Platonic ideas became a source of influence that can be seen as themes. This is attested by one of his honorary titles: *Ibn Aflatun* or 'Son of Plato'. Critchlow suggests that this title refers to his 'fundamental viewpoint' – 'the dependence of the sensible world on the

---

[19] Chittick, *The Sufi Path of Knowledge*, p. xii, explains the technical vocabulary of 'opening' (*futuh*) as being 'a near synonym for several other terms, such as unveiling, tasting, witnessing, divine effusion, divine self-disclosure and insight... mode[s] of gaining direct knowledge'.
[20] Hirtenstein, *Unlimited Mercifier*, pp. 37–39. His paternal uncle lived with the family in Seville and appears to have had a spiritual awakening at an advanced age. Through him Ibn 'Arabi met several Sufi masters.
[21] Burckhardt, *Introduction to Sufism: The Mystical Dimension of Islam*, trans. D. M. Matheson (1976; repr. Northamptonshire: Aquarian Press, Crucible, 1990), p. 31.
[22] Ibn 'Arabi, *Futûhât*, III, 129.17, quoted by Chittick, *Sufi Path*, p. 107.
[23] Ibn 'Arabi, *Futûhât*, III 198.33, quoted by Chittick, *Sufi Path*, pp. 106–7.
[24] Nicholas Campion, *Astrology and Cosmology in the World's Religions* (New York: NYU Press, 2012), p. 181.

150 Celestial Magic as the 'Love Path': The Spiritual Cosmology of Ibn 'Arabi

intelligible world, and the intelligible in return on the ontological principle of Unity'.[25] All goes back to Unity, on the Sufi 'love path'.

Astrological Signifiers on the Love Path
'So the cosmos is all lover and beloved, and all of it goes back to Him', said Ibn 'Arabi in *Al-Futûhât al-Makkiyya*, his opus.[26] As a symbolic language capable of many forms, astrology appeared within the *Futûhât*, integrated into his cosmology and serving to illustrate how 'it all goes back to Him'.[27] Titus Burckhardt compiled and translated the astrological fragments from the *Futûhât* for his 1950 French publication on mystical astrology.[28] With 560 chapters, it has been the source of many translations, compilations, separate books and treatises, *The Mystical Astrology of Ibn 'Arabi* being but one.[29] Ever faithful to the 'Unity of being', Ibn 'Arabi unfolded the Unity in a multiplicity of cosmological guises, in its play of subtle and material entities, of virtuality and of manifestation. He used a medieval cosmological schema constructed as concentric spheres, with a central Earth, plus sub-lunar and planetary spheres. The outer limit of the schema was 'the Sphere of the Divine Throne', considered to be the 'synthesis' of the cosmos. This descends to the next 'transcendent' sphere – the 'Pedestal' – the first differentiation where the 'divine longing' begins.[30] An intermediate zone is reached, with the third transcendent realm called the 'Sky of Zodiacal Towers'. Its focus is not physical, but it is the 'place of the archetypes'.[31] Like the archetypal *alam al-mithal,* or the world of imagination, the Zodiacal Towers are a threshold realm, accessible to the human imaginative faculty. Consciousness can undergo transformation in this realm.

The role of human consciousness is also part of the next descent, the 'sky of fixed stars' or 'stations'. A 'station' is a 'state' that has become permanent',

---

[25] Keith Critchlow, Forward notes to Burckhardt, *Mystical Astrology*, p. 7.
[26] Ibn 'Arabi, *Futûhât,* II 326.18, quoted by Chittick, *Sufi Path*, p. 181.
[27] Muhyiddin Ibn al-'Arabi, *Futûhât al-Makkiyya*, Cairo, 1329, 4 vol handwritten manuscripts. Compiled and edited by Osman Yahia, Cairo 1392–1413/1972–92 (14 volumes to date, corresponding to one third of Vol. I of the original *Futûhât*). Information from M. Chodkiewicz, ed., *The Meccan Revelations*, Vol. II, p. 251.
[28] Burckhardt, *Une Clef Spirituelle de l'Astrologie Musulmane d'apres Mohyi-d-din Ibn 'Arabi'* (see note 2, above).
[29] Hirtenstein, *Unlimited Mercifier*, Appendix 1, p. 272: Despite the length of the *Futûhât*, which was completed in 1231, a 'second version in thirty-seven volumes was completed in 1238 (636)'.
[30] Burckhardt, *Mystical Astrology*, pp. 26–29.
[31] Burckhardt, *Mystical Astrology*, p. 16.

as for example, the 'station of longing'.[32] This 'sky' is the place of the twelve zodiacal constellations, linked to spiritual 'stations' and depending in turn on the 'subtle order' of the archetypal zodiac preceding them.[33] From this point the seven physical planetary spheres descend from Saturn. Burckhardt suggests that this cosmological schema is 'a theoretical hierarchy according to the degrees of density'.[34] I find it useful to see it as a diagram of the potential ascent of the spiritual journey from its human centre – the visible world – to the subtle. The 'Unity' unfolds not as a linear flow, but in subjective time as moments of recognition and revelation (*kashf*), each moment timeless. Ibn 'Arabi's words from the *Futûhât* explain his perspective: 'the Real becomes qualified by wonder, receiving joyfully, laughter... and most of the attributes of engendered things. So return what belongs to Him, and take what belongs to you! He possesses descent, and we possess ascent'.[35]

Symbols as the Language of the Heart
When the transcendent sphere of the 'Pedestal' was described as the place where 'divine longing begins', this is a reference to 'the Most Beautiful Names' (also called the 'potentialities') – sorrowful in their unrealised potential and longing to be realised. Yet, human 'aptitude' to receive that spiritual union, Ibn 'Arabi explains, has no causal origin, rather: 'the aptitude of the potentialities [Names] is a specific state', and that in turn 'is a relationship subject to knowledge, and knowledge is a relationship subject to that which is known, and *the known is you and your states*' (italics added).[36] This is a typically elliptical statement, designed to challenge and transform the taken-for-granted worldview of the 'reader'. In the thirteenth century Islamic world, this was more likely the 'listener', since texts were read to a group.[37] Yet, when considered slowly, the message is quite clear that what we *can* know is conditioned and limited by our state of being. Immediately the emphasis is shifted from intellectual knowing to an experiential level,

---

[32] Burckhardt, *An introduction to Sufism*, p. 88.
[33] Burckhardt, *Mystical Astrology*, p. 15.
[34] Burckhardt, *Mystical Astrology*, p. 13.
[35] Ibn 'Arabi, *Futûhât*, I, 41.31, quoted by Chittick, *Sufi Path*, p. 181.
[36] M. Ibn al-'Arabi, *Fusus al-Hikam Vol II*, translated from Arabic to French by Ismail Hakki Bursevi, translated from French to English by Bulent Rauf (Oxford, Istanbul and San Francisco: Muhyiddin Ibn 'Arabi Society, 1987), p. 390.
[37] Hirtenstein, *Unlimited Mercifier*, p.156: 'As Arabic is normally written down without vowels... only an oral reading will determine which variant the author intends'.

sometimes called the wisdom of the heart. To reach this level a suitable symbolic language is needed to facilitate a shift in perspective.

Since for Ibn 'Arabi, love is the mechanism that receives knowledge, and the 'Most Beautiful Names' are the facets of knowledge, then the interaction between human longing and the 'divine longing' to be known are the dynamics of the 'love path'. Personal 'taste' opens the way to specific Names. Certain Names play leading roles, and tend to have complementary opposites. An example is 'beauty' (*jamal*), which is a deeply interior beauty and dialectical companion to *jalal*, majesty. These two Names feature strongly in *zhikr*, a spiritual practice of commemoration. Burckhardt notes: 'It is in the object, Beauty that love virtually coincides with knowledge'.[38]

Beauty, Love and Knowledge are three entwined symbols, which also indicate embodied potential. This understanding of the 'symbolic' as embodied, rather than just a 'sign', is an ancient one, as Liz Greene notes: 'the term 'symbol', in ancient Greek divinatory practice, carries the notion of a meeting, an encounter... This perception of symbols approaches them as both representations and embodiments of an objective reality that exists both within and outside the human being'.[39] The transformative nature of the symbol is such that it provides access to a realm beyond rational thinking where rational exclusions and boundaries cease to define reality.

The Divine Breath and its Symbols
Astrological Codes provide the symbolic ladder for Ibn 'Arabi's presentation of his concept of Being. Being is linked to the 'Breath': 'the substance of the cosmos is the All-merciful Breath, within which the forms of the cosmos become manifest'.[40] Ibn 'Arabi employed an astrological schema, translated and presented by Burckhardt, in which a correspondence between 'the 28 sounds which determine the lunar mansions' and 'the 28 letters or sounds of the sacred language', is established.[41] Here, the Arabic alphabet is conceived as the micro-cosmic form of the '28 cosmic degrees' of the divine 'Breath'. The 28 'mansions of the Moon' divide the tropical zodiac into 28 sectors.[42] Burckhardt translates this as the 'vehicle of spiritual revelation, in articulated language'; it starts with the silent hiatus of 0 degrees Aries, 'through the

---

[38] Burckhardt, *Introduction to Sufism*, p. 33.
[39] Liz Greene, 'Signs, Signatures and Symbols: The Languages of Heaven', in *Astrologies: Plurality and Diversity*, N. Campion and L. Greene, eds., (Ceredigion, Wales: Sophia Centre Press, 2011), p. 30.
[40] Ibn 'Arabi, *Futûhât*, II 404.9, quoted by Chittick, *Sufi Path*, pp.181–82.
[41] Burckhardt, *Mystical Astrology*, p. 35.
[42] Burckhardt, *Mystical Astrology*, p. 38.

guttural sounds, the labials, the palatals and the dental' sounds, as one reaches the last degree of Pisces. Burckhardt adds that this coding of the 'primordial sound' is 'carried by the physical breath' and relates to 'the double aspect of the role of the mediator proper to the human heart'.[43] This is 'double' in the sense that 'the subtle form of the heart changes all the time, successively answering all the directions or spiritual polarisations', yet also 'being always open to the transcendent Unity'.[44]

The Love Path and the Luminaries

Just as the Moon, its phases, and 'mansions', are used to code spiritual revelation, the fact that the Moon too has a 'double role', changing its form constantly while continuing to receive the light of the Sun, makes the Sun an equally important symbol for the 'Love Path'. Thus Burckhardt suggests: 'the relation between the Sun and the Moon is analogous to that which holds between Pure Intellect and its reflection in the human form'.[45] This symbolic correspondence of heart and Moon, Intellect and Sun, seems to resonate with the alchemical notion of the 'Hermetic Marriage' of Sun and Moon. Perhaps that is not surprising considering that the *Al-Andalus* into which Ibn 'Arabi was born was a period of high culture, percolating Alexandrine Hermeticism into Islamic sciences.[46]

The 'love path' then is a symbol of transformation, a consciousness open to knowledge: Ibn 'Arabi says of the transformed heart, 'The heart is his Throne and not delimited by any specific attribute. On the contrary it brings together all the divine names and attributes'.[47] The 'transformed heart' is repository of 'all' knowledge and Adam is the prophet who best represents this particular wisdom in Ibn 'Arabi's *Fusûs* or 'Wisdom of the Prophets'.[48] Both the Moon and Adam correspond to the level of consciousness, which is called the 'opening' of the heart to receive the 'essential revelation' (*at-tajalli*). The cosmic quality...which expresses itself in the role of mediator between "earth" and "Heaven"'.[49] For Ibn 'Arabi, the Moon has special importance to the 'love path' as a symbol of both receptivity and transformation, while Adam symbolises the prophet and prototype of the unique human potential to

---

[43] Burckhardt, *Mystical Astrology*, p. 35.
[44] Burckhardt, *Mystical Astrology*, pp. 38, 34–35.
[45] Burckhardt, *Mystical Astrology*, p. 30.
[46] See Hirtenstein, *Unlimited Mercifier*, pp. 33–36.
[47] Ibn 'Arabi, *Futûhât*, III 129.17, quoted by Chittick, *The Sufi Path*, p. 107.
[48] Ibn 'Arabi, *Fusus al-Hikam* I, focuses on 27 prophets, drawing together Islamic, Christian and Hebraic prophetology.
[49] Burckhardt, *Mystical Astrology*, pp. 34–35

develop an 'integral nature'; this nature is 'integral' precisely because it can comprehend diversity and also find synthesis in unity at the same time.[50]

Linking the ideas of lunar consciousness and Adamic consciousness is the following quote from Ibn 'Arabi's teaching manual, the *Fusûs*: 'Adam became the light itself of this mirror and the spirit of this form.'[51] Ibn 'Arabi links Adam's 'interior form' with the 'total of the Divine Names and Qualities', because he perfectly mirrors the divinity, as the Moon mirrors the Sun.[52] Both Adam and the Moon could be described as symbolic role models for entry to the 'love path' and also the potential for transformed consciousness that this represents.

This recalls the discussion of symbols by Greene: Symbols 'are generated by the human psyche through the organ of imagination rather than being constructed by the intellect... they are capable of inaugurating the transformation of psychic energy while at the same time describing that transformation'.[53]

Meccan Revelations and Symbolic Consciousness

That a symbol can inaugurate, as well as describe, transformation is a possibility that appears to be many times illustrated by the 'revelations' Ibn 'Arabi describes, and the life events that accompany them. His profound understanding of primordial Unity lives on through his writing, much of which is potentially transformative and clearly symbolic. The sheer number of his deeply nuanced works appears to support his claim that no reflective process interrupted his flow, as with the *Fusûs*, or 'Wisdom of the Prophets', his most widely read book.[54] He claimed this was 'revealed to him in a single dream'.[55] Of the *Futûhât*, his multi-volumed opus, he said: 'This book is not a place for that which is given by the proofs of the reflective powers, only for that which is given by divine unveiling'.[56] *Futûhât al-Makkiya* translates as the 'Meccan Revelations' because it was inspired by a mystical experience on a pilgrimage to Mecca in 1202. This journey sealed his eventual move to the East and was punctuated by continuous writing and visionary experiences.[57] Arriving in Mecca, he tells of an experience which revealed his life task:

---

[50] Ibn 'Arabi, *Fusus I*, pp. 12–13.
[51] Ibn 'Arabi, *Fusus I*, p. 10.
[52] Ibn 'Arabi, *Fusus I*, pp. 17–18.
[53] Greene, 'Signs, Signatures and Symbols', p. 30.
[54] Chittick, Introduction, p. xvii, discusses the historical trajectory of the *Fusus*.
[55] Austin, *Sufis of Andalusia*, p. 48.
[56] Ibn 'Arabi, *Futûhât,* II 389.6, as quoted in Chittick, *The Sufi Path*, p. xv.
[57] Hirtenstein, *Unlimited Mercifier*, pp. 146–47.

Christine Broadbent 155

> A vision of the Youth steadfast in devotion who is both speaker and silent, neither alive nor dead… He indicated to me by hint and sign that he was created to speak only in symbols… He revealed the reality of his Beauty to me and I understood… Then he said to me: 'Circumambulate in my footsteps, and observe me in the light of my moon, so that you may take from my constitution that which you write in your book and transmit it to your readers'.[58]

This seminal vision inspired a dedication to write the *Futûhât*, which was a dominant theme in the last 17 years of his life, when he settled in Damascus. In this he created an extensive compendium of Sufism, recording the oral traditions through his own lens of revelation, and demonstrating his profound respect for the Koran.[59]

Seeking the Possible: The Ternary of Spiritual Dynamics
The three 'orientations of the possible' on the journey of knowledge were defined by Ibn 'Arabi's treatment of the three astrological modes of operation, as translated and compiled by Burckhardt. Just as these modes define the most dynamic astrological 'aspects', so they are linked to a spiritual dynamic by Ibn 'Arabi.[60] The traditionally named 'cardinal', 'fixed' and 'mutable' signs were treated as the signs of 'mobility', 'fixation' and 'synthesis'.[61] These three modes were called the 'ternary of spirit', and considered to be 'superior' to the four astrological elements because they are closer to 'reintegration in the perfect [spiritual] synthesis'.[62]

Within this 'ternary', the 'mobile' signs of Aries, Cancer, Capricorn and Libra have an expansive movement which reaches out to measure the 'width of the possible'. They therefore embrace all that is manifest, relating to the 'states of this world'. The descending movement comes with the 'signs of fixation' (Taurus, Leo, Scorpio and Aquarius), which measure the 'depth of the possible'. In so doing, they are seen to regulate 'the relatively superior a-temporal world' and because of this 'descent', 'the world exists as such'. Finally are the 'synthetic signs' of Gemini, Virgo, Sagittarius and Pisces, which seek the height of the possible in the urge to return to 'the One'. They

---

[58] Ibn 'Arabi, *Futûhât*, I: 47ff and 1: 218ff (trans. O. Yahia), as quoted in Hirtenstein, *Unlimited Mercifier*, p. 152.
[59] Hirtenstein, *Unlimited Mercifier*, p.152: He says the *Futûhât* is 'a complete esoteric exposition of the Book of the Quran, both in structure and content'.
[60] The most dynamic aspects are the 'conjunction', 'opposition' and 'square'.
[61] Burckhardt, *Mystical Astrology*, p. 22.
[62] Burckhardt, *Mystical Astrology*, p. 21.

156   Celestial Magic as the 'Love Path': The Spiritual Cosmology of Ibn 'Arabi

therefore relate to the 'intermediary worlds' and to the 'synthesis' of spiritual and psychic elements in 'the world of corporality'.[63]

This treatment of the astrological signs gives interesting insights into an energetic dimensionality, further elucidating the dynamic aspect of the complementary action of 'Divine descent' and human 'ascent' which was integral to Ibn 'Arabi's cosmological schema.[64] As a model of spiritual possibilities, it adds transformative depth to the cosmology of the Sufi 'love path'.

Of Ways of Knowing: Knowledge and Love
Speaking for the position of a Gnostic or 'one of closeness', Ibn 'Arabi said: 'He accepts all kinds of beliefs, but does not remain tied to any figurative belief... knowing the kernel of all belief he sees the interior and not the exterior'.[65] The 'interior' is what he called the 'Real'. Love poetry is often the chosen mode of expressing Sufi mystical knowledge and one of the gifts this spiritual tradition has shared well beyond the bounds of the Islamic world. Ibn 'Arabi's unitary vision takes a passionate poetic form in the collection called *Tarjumâan al-ashwâaq*, or 'Interpreter of Ardent Desires'. One of its most well known verses follows:

> Oh marvel! A garden amidst the flames!
> My heart has become capable of every form:
> A pasture for gazelles and a monastery for Christian monks,
> a temple for idols and the pilgrim's Ka'ba,
> and the tables of the Tora and the book of the Quran.
> I follow the religion of Love: whatever way
> Love's camels take, that is my religion and my faith.[66]

Ibn 'Arabi was perhaps pushing against the doctrinal sensitivities in the politics of Islamic knowledge when he wrote such verses or made claims like the following: 'if a possessor of knowledge is cognisant of the being in his

---

[63] Burckhardt, *Mystical Astrology*, pp. 21–23.
[64] Burckhardt, *Mystical Astrology*, p. 12, suggests that Ibn 'Arabi's cosmological schema probably comes 'from the Andalusian Sufi Ibn Masarrah'.
[65] M. Ibn al 'Arabi, *Lubb'ul-Lub*, translated by Ismail Hakki Bursevi (1652–1728) into Turkish from Arabic; translated into English by Bulent Rauf as *The Kernel of the Kernel* (Sherborne: Beshara Publications, 1981), p. 1.
[66] M. Ibn al-'Arabi, *The Tarjumâan al-Ashwâaq: A Collection of Mystical Odes*, trans. R. A. Nicholson (London and Wheaton, IL: Theosophical Publishing, 1978), p. 56.

own ipseity, in all its meanings, he will not remain trapped in one belief'.[67] Ibn 'Arabi was no stranger to controversy: after his *Tarjumâan* collection of sixty-one love poems was made public, he was accused of improper behaviour, of writing erotica in the guise of poetry. The entire collection was dedicated to a beautiful young woman, *Nizam,* who represented for him 'the beauty of the Beloved' and the uproar that followed caused him to write a long commentary explaining his mystical allusions.[68]

Henri Corbin, citing these love poems, concludes that the 'love path' is mystical in the most passionate of ways. He calls this Ibn 'Arabi's 'dialectic of love', which he describes as: an 'invisible Beloved… whose actuality depends on an Active Imagination which makes physical love and spiritual love "conspire" in a single mystic love'.[69] Corbin sees this as an endless devotional dance, a lived experience facilitated by the creative imagination. Ibn 'Arabi's mystical odes assert the heart as the locus of knowledge, as the setting for spiritual possibilities, and also for transformation: the word *qalb* or 'heart' comes from the same Arabic root as *taqallub,* or 'transformation' and as Chittick notes, the two words can be used as virtual synonyms.[70]

Creative Longing
The locus Sufi practice circles around is love as the longing of the soul for mystical union, answering the longing of the 'Most Beautiful Names' to be known. Longing, in this two-way operation, is reminiscent of the 'As it is above, so it is below. And as it is below, so it is above' of the Emerald Tablet, whose alchemical operation describes 'the making of the One Thing'.[71] The 'ascent' and 'descent' of Ibn 'Arabi's cosmological schema also seem to evoke the Hermetic quest for the 'One Thing'. Taking his inspiration from the *hadith qudsi,* or sacred saying: 'I was a hidden treasure and I loved to be

---

[67] Ibn 'Arabi, *The Kernel*, p. 1.
[68] Ibn 'Arabi, *Tarjumâan*, was composed of 61 poems. Hirtenstein, *Unlimited Mercifier*, pp. 186–89, discusses the controversy, and notes that the final form of the *Tarjumâan*, with commentary, took 'ten years to come to fruition'. It is of note that the major controversy and critiques of Ibn 'Arabi's work came after his death, amid social turmoil and religious changes.
[69] Henri Corbin, *Creative Imagination in the Sufism of Ibn 'Arabi* (Princeton, NJ: Princeton/Bollingen, 1998), p. 291.
[70] Chittick, *The Sufi Path*, p. 106.
[71] Jabir ibn Hayyan, 'The Emerald Tablet of Hermes Trismegistus', in E. J. Holmyard, *Alchemy* (Harmondsworth: Penguin Books, 1957), pp. 97–98.

known, and I created the creation so that I be known', Ibn 'Arabi explains that the Divine longs to contemplate itself in the mirror of the human heart.[72]

His explanation describes the reciprocal relationship intrinsic to the inclusive nature of 'Unity', and can be interpreted as the transcendent-beyond-time requiring the conscious human to know itself.[73] This can be understood in the context of an inclusive notion of the 'Real', which transcends any polarity of consciousness.

The 'Most Beautiful Names', too, point to inclusion within diversity: 'the names are the names of the states… Likewise they have another relationship in which they name the Real'.[74] In this way, personal 'taste' can lead to a specific Name, yet, 'all have also a unique reference: the Divine Essence which they name'.[75]

In another of his works – *Anqâ Mughri* – Ibn 'Arabi describes a vision, foretelling a mystical union. This was experienced a short time before he left Spain and travelled to the East, where so much was to change, including his 'meeting' with the Youth who inspired him to write the *Futûhât*. Again this vision repeats the alchemical flavour of the inner 'marriage'. He recounts that he had a vision of a marriage but then realised: 'I did not find a "Bride" (*'irs*) or a "Husband" (*ba'l*) other than my own Essence, nor a dower other than my own Nature and attributes. For I was myself both the Husband and the Bride, and I married together the Intellect and the Soul'.[76]

The Primordial Unity of Intellect and Emotion
It is inward reality Sufis seek, and Sufi praxis is geared towards an integration of intellect and emotion, 'in their primordial unity'.[77] As we have seen, 'divine opening' and revelations are considered the true source of knowledge for Ibn 'Arabi and the 'Folk', as Sufis called themselves.[78] He clarified the difference between the Sufi path and intellectual path, when he said: 'The canon of the Folk of Allah ties together all parts of the cosmos, so they are taken from one

---

[72] Ibn 'Arabi, *Fusus I*, p. 378; this hadith is explored in 'The Wisdom of Ecstasy and Rapture in the Word of Abraham'.
[73] Ibn 'Arabi, *Fusus I*, p. 12; this is one of many examples of his interior exploration of Koranic text.
[74] Ibn 'Arabi, *Futûhât*, II 8:17, quoted by Chittick, *Sufi Path*, p. 188.
[75] Corbin, *Creative Imagination*, p. 302.
[76] M. Ibn 'Arabi, *Anqâ Mughrib* (*The Fabulous Gryphon*), trans. Gerald Elmore (Ibn 'Arabi Society), available at http://www.ibnarabisociety.org/articles/anqamughrib.html [accessed 24 May 2016].
[77] Burckhardt, *Introduction to Sufism*, p. 32.
[78] Chittick, *Sufi Path*, p. xxi.

thing to another, even if the scholar of outward appearances sees no relationship'.[79]

Henri Corbin speaks of an 'outside-of-time function', whereby 'openings' to the 'Oneness of Being' are experienced as: 'forever inexhaustible events of the soul'.[80] Above all other writers, Henri Corbin champions what he calls the 'imaginal' realm in Ibn 'Arabi's work. The 'imaginal' features as a world to be creatively accessed, in the form of the *alam al-mithal* – the intermediate zone of imagination. Acknowledging Corbin's role in opening Ibn 'Arabi's 'love path' to a wider audience, Chittick suggests that Corbin's work most vividly 'depicts the God of theophany [revelation] who can be grasped by imagination'.[81]

Alam al-mithal and Sophiology

The *alam al-mithal* refers to: 'the world in which occurs visions, apparitions, and in general all the symbolic histories'.[82] Corbin explored at length the notion of the soul's passion for the mystical union; and 'the nostalgia which is the secret of creation' is seen as a fusion of the divine and human longings.[83]

Ibn 'Arabi describes a spiritual alchemy where the Names are conceived as both the 'divine quality' and also the active agent of 'transformation'.[84] Only the imaginative faculty can perceive the fundamental nature of this world, which is an 'intermediary' between inner and outer events. The inner 'journeys' that Ibn 'Arabi reported in vivid details, he understood as embodied events in the *alam al-mithal*, the intermediate realm where the soul takes on form.[85]

Sophia and the archetypal feminine play an important role in the cosmology of Ibn 'Arabi: 'Universal Nature', as an active force, he depicts symbolically, as the 'Sigh of Compassion' – *Nafas Rahmani*.[86]: the 'Sigh' 'flows through the things of the world like the waters of a river and is unceasingly renewed,' said Corbin, paraphrasing the *Fusûs*.[87] He explored the symbolism of Ibn 'Arabi's experiences of *Sophia* or divine wisdom,

---

[79] Ibn 'Arabi, *Futûhât*, III 200.26.
[80] Corbin, *Creative Imagination*, pp. 291–92.
[81] Chittick, *Sufi Path*, p. xix.
[82] Corbin, *Creative Imagination*, p. 217
[83] Corbin, *Creative Imagination*, p. 152
[84] Ibn 'Arabi, *Fusus* II, p. 388.
[85] Many of these journeys are discussed in *Sufis of Andalusia*, which has an English translation of his personal accounts from the *Ruh al-Quds* of Ibn 'Arabi.
[86] Ibn 'Arabi, *Fusus* II, p. 354.
[87] Corbin, *Creative Imagination*, p. 201.

identifying some of the feminine presences therein. To do so he distilled some bibliographical details: Ibn 'Arabi's near-death experience as a youth, when a verse of the Koran appeared to him in the form of a beautiful being exhaling a sweet perfume; the two Sufi *shaikha* who strongly influenced him – Fatima of Cordova, and later, Yasmin of Marchena; also the vision of *Sophia aeterna* during his first visit to Mecca, and the meeting with *Nizam*, which inspired his collection of mystical odes, when he 'witnessed this station' [of Divine Love].[88] Also, in terms of astrological symbols, Ibn 'Arabi describes the mystic Moon and Venus as closest to the 'love path': the Moon is the 'mediator proper to the human heart', and Venus, in turn, is linked to 'the faculty of the creative imagination'.[89]

It can be seen that the Hermetic notion of gender as a primordial principle and natural polarity is common to both astrological and Sufi symbolism. For Sufi cosmology, the godhead is conceived as having a creative masculine aspect and also a feminine aspect. However, while the masculine is purely creative, the feminine aspect is considered both receptive and creative, which includes the maternal feature of what Ibn 'Arabi called the *Rahman*[90] or 'Divine Breath'.[91] Chodkiewicz summarises this as follows:

> It is from *rahma* [love] that the universe is born – it takes shape in the "breath of the *Rahman*" – it is through *rahma* that the universe is sustained, and it is to *rahma* that it will return: whence Ibn 'Arabi's denial that punishment will be eternal; whence his quest for the positivity…in every idea, in every belief.[92]

To summarise, the Sufi way goes beyond discursive boundaries; an integration of intellect and emotion is essential for knowledge, and integration is possible, because the heart is the organ of perception. Ibn 'Arabi explored, from many perspectives, the heart's 'natural' role as lover in the quest for the divine Beloved. Knowledge is treated as an interrelated whole, linked to states of consciousness and 'openings' to the 'Unity of Being', which can transcend cognitive limits. Again, those lines from the *Tarjumâan*, express Ibn 'Arabi's orientation: 'I follow the religion of Love: whatever way Love's camels take, that is my religion and my faith'.[93] This is close to what Campion calls

---

[88] Hirtenstein, *Unlimited Mercifier*, p. 149, quotes Ibn 'Arabi, *Futûhât*, IV:84.
[89] Burckhardt, *Mystical Astrology*, pp. 31–34.
[90] *Rahman* is pronounced 'Raakman'.
[91] Corbin, *Mystical Imagination*, p. 299.
[92] Chodkiewicz, Introduction to *Meccan Revelations II*, p. 42. Note that *rahma* also means 'compassion' but in this context, Chodkiewicz emphasizes that it means 'love'.
[93] Ibn al-'Arabi, *Tarjumâan*, p. 67.

'concrete magic', which seeks to merge with the greater whole, 'in a perhaps ecstatic union'.[94] The Sufi 'love path' creates no polarity between devotion and ecstasy that more ascetic, less passionate practices may do: the intoxication with the 'Beloved' knows no such bounds.

Sympathy as a magical and mystical principle
A human-divine *sympatheia* is a part of Ibn 'Arabi's understanding of the 'Real' and its ever-recurrent creation. Sympathy as a magical and mystical principle was originally a Stoic concept.[95] Further, 'an ontological link between symbol and symbolised reflects an idea of sympathies or correspondences that was clearly formulated in Stoic circles in the last two centuries BCE'.[96] It also accords with some modern therapeutic approaches, like Thomas Moore's suggestion that: 'To deal with the soul magically rather than heroically, requires an extreme sympathy with all that is taking place'.[97] As we have discussed, for Ibn 'Arabi it is 'sympathy' and 'aptitude' that open to a correspondence with certain Names or Qualities in the 'super-sensory' intermediary world of *alam al-mithal*. Sociologically this is also suggestive for the role of the 'Other', and the 'othering' of the one who looks, acts, believes, or thinks differently. Sympathy in Ibn 'Arabi arises from a deep exploration of the meaning of existence, and the 'love path' arises from the ability to be the 'mirror' of the divine. The very intention to reach for lunar or Adamic consciousness as a receptive 'mirror' means the 'other' is no longer other on that journey of integration.[98]

When the creative imagination is developed as the prime mode to comprehend the 'Real', 'normal' takes on new meaning. Out-of-body experiences, 'openings', extrasensory perception, telepathy and theophanic visions, were 'normal' within Sufi circles, and constant for Ibn 'Arabi, if his own journals and the records of those who knew him are to be believed.[99] What Jung calls 'meaningful coincidence' or 'synchronicity' may be

---

[94] Nicholas Campion, *The Medieval and Modern Worlds: History of Western Astrology* (New York and London: Continuum, 2009), p. 94.
[95] Diogenes Laertius, 'Biography of 'Zeno'', in *Lives of the Eminent Philosophers*, trans. R. D. Hicks (London: William Heinemann, 1925), Vol. 2, pp. 110–263.
[96] Greene, 'Signs, Signatures and Symbols', p. 31.
[97] Thomas Moore, *Dark Nights of the Soul: A Guide to Finding Your Way through Life's Ordeals* (New York: Gotham Books, 2004), p. 94.
[98] Ibn 'Arabi, *Fusus* I, p.10.
[99] Chittick, *Sufi Path*, p. xiii: 'It should be noted that "opening"… cannot be applied to any and every sort of "inrush"… Ibn 'Arabi, like other Sufis, provides many criteria for distinguishing among different types of paranormal perceptions'.

considered 'normal' within astrological circles.[100] Synchronicity certainly seems to be well exemplified by the seemingly super-human written output of Ibn 'Arabi and its role in saving hundreds of years of oral knowledge that may have otherwise been lost. For someone who saw time as 'imaginary', Ibn 'Arabi may not have been surprised by the timing of the Mongol invasion.[101] His interest and focus was the spiritual journey, the changing 'states' and timeless 'stations' he embodied in the 'world of the unseen'. As he says in the *Futûhât*: 'This is why the Presence of the Imagination is the vastest of presences: it combines the two worlds, the World of the Unseen and the World of the Visible'.[102] Through Ibn 'Arabi's works, Imagination as a 'Presence' allows sameness and otherness to be bridged, within an intermediate realm.

The Magical Subject
The modern category, 'magic', was born in colonial power relationships, developed conceptually as a counterpoint to 'rational' behaviour, and is far too politicized and complex to discuss here.[103] To focus more specifically on the human subject that employs 'magical thinking': Ibn 'Arabi as a magical subject is the pertinent example. In this context the 'magical subject' can be defined as the subject seeking knowledge in non-rational ways. In the case of the Sufi 'love path', there are specific applications of the imaginative faculty, a teacher is available as a guide to psychic and spiritual balance, and this is considered a path to knowledge of the 'Real'.

To consider Bruno Latour's assertion that via rational process we have erected a 'Great Divide' between 'Culture' and 'Nature', implies that the 'subject-object' Divide is a part of this.[104] That division appears in ways of knowing and in ways of applying knowledge to the larger environment. The

---

[100] See essay by C. G. Jung. *Synchronicity: An Acausal Connecting Principle*, trans. R. Hull (Princeton, NJ: Princeton University Press, 1973).
[101] Ibn 'Arabi, *Futûhât*, II 1.3: 'The moment is an imaginary portion in an existing source, which is the sphere and the star. The movement of that sphere and star is intersected by the portion allotted to it in an imaginary sphere which has no real existence, and which is called time'.
[102] Ibn 'Arabi, *Futûhât,* Chapter 311, 42.11, quoted by Chittick, *Meccan Revelations,* Vol. II, p. 172.
[103] Stanley J. Tambiah, *Magic, Science, Religion and the Scope of Rationality* (Cambridge: Cambridge University Press, 1990). This remains one of the best books on the subject of magic and rationality.
[104] Bruno Latour, *We Have Never Been Modern* (Cambridge, MA: Harvard University Press, 1993, pp. 97–137.

duality perpetuated between magical and rational thinking has not fallen far from the familiar divides of Nature versus Culture. Like that duality, it is open to Latour's critique that it is both asymmetrical and problematic. He suggests a solution: 'everything changes when, instead of constantly and exclusively alternating between one pole of the modern dimension and the other, we move down along the nonmodern dimension…where the work of mediation emerges…quasi-objects, quasi-subjects, proliferate in it'.[105] These unacknowledged 'hybrids', which he identifies as the demystified face of 'culture- nature', are likely to extend into rational-magical 'hybrids' as well.[106]

The Magical Subject as Other
When the magical subject is made Other, dismissed as 'irrational', one must ask: what actually comes before the rational gaze, what socially embedded assumptions of normalcy are themselves shot through with magical thinking? Meanwhile, magical thinking, as demonstrated by Ibn 'Arabi's body of work and life history, seems able to support high intellectual achievement. His important assertion, that one's 'state' determines what can be known, raises further questions: what outcomes may occur when magical thinking is unconscious and unacknowledged, or hidden in ambitious 'rational' plans? History debunks the myth that all rational thinking delivers desirable results.[107] It may also be a myth that magical thinking delivers only false results, or 'pseudo-science'. The question of the actual quality of knowledge hybrids is perhaps linked to consciousness and one's state, as Ibn 'Arabi's hermeneutics suggest. However, to make the magical subject 'Other' is to ignore, trivialise, stereotype, and often to repress, the knowledge that can be gained from a magical way of knowing.

'Othering' as a social process usually involves power relationships, and the political hegemony of a 'rational' worldview easily translates into economic advantage. Yet, the discourse on the 'Other' is expressed on a number of registers in the human sciences, and both psychological and ethical registers of 'othering' can be recognised, once that lens is applied.[108] Michel Foucault and his concepts of privileging, subjugation and concealment, as they appear

---

[105] Latour, *Never Been Modern*, p. 96.
[106] Latour, *Never Been Modern*, pp. 49–55, 140–42.
[107] Current development plans for the Amazon Basin could lead to even less desirable results than the 'rational' choice of drilling for oil in the Gulf of Mexico.
[108] Emmanuel Levinas, *The Levinas Reader*, ed. Sean Hand (New York: Library of Congress, 2001), p. 290. As a philosopher, he articulates the ethical Judaic perspective: 'Prior to any act, I am concerned with the Other and I can never be absolved from this responsibility'.

in the production of knowledge, and in the constitution of the modern subject, have played an important role.[109] He was acknowledged by Edward Said, who coined the term 'othering' to describe the process whereby ethnic others are stereotyped and homogenized, and who dedicated a book to this topic.[110]

Also acknowledging Foucault's influence, Peter Pels suggests: 'no present-day speculation about magic can escape the modern discursive boundary between the ideal modern subject that makes true perceptions and practises a rational discipline, and a magical subject that is set up in contrast as backward, immature, or dysfunctional'.[111] He adds that these are 'modernist myths that need to be scrutinized' and his edited compilation seeks to dispel these myths with situated ethnographies.[112] The socially constructed polarity, of the magical versus the 'rational' subject, is a boundary with great plasticity. It is thus open to manipulation. Yet, once that boundary is given ontological status, a knowledge system such as Ibn 'Arabi's, which moves seamlessly between spiritual epiphany and discursive logic, is not readily classified as being knowledge. In fact, once the magical subject is 'othered', an imaginative way of knowing is made irrelevant to serious knowledge pursuit.

Rationality, Disenchantment and Magic
Rationality and 'disenchantment' were drawn together by Max Weber at the turn of the twentieth century: he predicted disenchantment as the inevitable result of a capitalist culture of 'instrumental rationality', which is: 'dependent on the calculability of the most important technical factors'.[113] Weber explored the way in which rationalised science works against both magic and nature: 'rational empirical knowledge has consistently worked through to the disenchantment of the world and its transformation into a causal mechanism', and by refuting any search 'which asks for a "meaning" of inner-worldly occurrences'.[114] That double strategy of declaring the world 'causal', while

---

[109] See Michel Foucault, *Discipline and Punish: The Birth of the Prison* (London: Allen Lane, 1977).
[110] See Edward Said, *Orientalism* (London: Routledge and Kegan Paul, 1978).
[111] Peter Pels, Introduction to *Magic and Modernity: Interfaces of Revelation and Concealment*, ed. Birgit Meyer and Peter Pels (Stanford, CA: Stanford University Press, 2003), p. 31.
[112] Peter Pels, Introduction to *Magic and modernity*, p. 38.
[113] Max Weber, *Die protestantische Ethik und der Geist des Kapitalismus*, *1905* (*The Protestant ethic and the spirit of capitalism*), trans. Talcott Parsons (1930; Mineola, NY: Dover Publications, 2003), p. 24.
[114] Max Weber, *From Max Weber: Essays in Sociology*, translated and compiled by H. H. Gerth and C. W. Mills (1946; London: Routledge, 1991), pp. 350–51.

refusing to qualify inner-worldly events with meaning, resonates with Latour's more recent concept of 'purification' as the means of maintaining an artificial divide, while relations – 'mediations' – go on between the two 'sides'.[115] Spanos calls this: 'naturalising' a 'socially constituted hierarchical binary logic'.[116] The material, psychological and ethical implications of this double strategy are considerable, as is the capacity for reframing reality.

Modern enchantments tend also to be reframed and disowned, and as Pels suggests, this is 'because the content of *magic* is mostly defined in relation to a past superseded by modernity'.[117] Yet the 'rational enchantments' of 'consumer magic', described by the sociologist George Ritzer as the 'cathedrals of consumption' and the new 'hyper-realities' that keeps consumers, consuming, are ever expanding as a part of global business practice.[118] Pels speaks of a 'haunting of modernity by the magic it represses', and suggests this is wide-flung indeed.[119] He cites Martha Kaplan's ethnography on the printed word, which suggests that modern magic can also be 'enlightening, creative and progressive'.[120]

The magic that haunts modernity can even be found in the father of the sociology of religion, and of value-free social science, Max Weber. His own hybrid of the rational and magical was revealed in a 1917 lecture: *Science as a profession and vocation.* He exhorted each member of his student audience, to: 'find the *daemon* which holds the fibres of his very life'.[121] Sometimes known as the '*daemon* of the soul', in its link back to Plato, Goethe's usage was a likely source for Weber, with references to the *daemon* in both Heraclitus and Goethe. The translator defines *daemon* 'as the characteristic

---

[115] Latour, *Never Been Modern*, pp. 40–75.
[116] W. V. Spanos, 'Empire of the Gaze', in *Foucault and Heidegger: Critical Encounters*, ed. A. Milchman and A. Rosenberg (Minneapolis, MN: University of Minnesota Press, 2003), p. 238.
[117] Pels, Introduction to *Magic and Modernity,* p. 35, his italics.
[118] George Ritzer, *Enchanting a Disenchanted World: Continuity and Change in the Cathedrals of Consumption* (Los Angeles, CA: Sage Publications, 2010), pp. 22–31.
[119] Pels, Introduction to *Magic and Modernity*, p. 30.
[120] Martha Kaplan, 'The magical power of the (printed) word', in *Magic and Modernity: Interfaces of Revelation and Concealment*, ed. B. Meyer and P. Pels (Stanford, CA: Stanford University Press. 2003), pp. 183–99.
[121] Max Weber, *Wissenschaft als Beruf* ('On Some Categories of Interpretive Sociology'), in *Max Weber: Collected Methodological Writings*, trans. H. H. Bruun, ed. H. H. Bruun and S. Whimster (New York: Routledge, 2012), pp. 273–303. Weber's original lecture has had a number of translations with a mistaken translation of *daemon* into 'demon' by Talcott Parsons, here corrected by Hans Bruun, p. 353.

166   Celestial Magic as the 'Love Path': The Spiritual Cosmology of Ibn 'Arabi

and preformed essence of individual identity, the unchanging and self-directive "law" of destiny'.[122]

This notion of the *daemon* also seems to accord with Ibn 'Arabi's discussion of 'taste' and 'aptitude', which enables one to connect with certain of the Qualities or Names. While each of the Names relates to a different state, all relate back to the *Rahmin,* 'the universal Divine Compassion', or 'creative Feminine'.[123] A symbolic language is a suitable vehicle for the cosmology of Ibn 'Arabi, and as Bakhtiar suggests: 'Symbols are realities contained within the nature of things... Symbolism is perhaps the most sacred of the Sufi sciences, for it is through seeing symbols that one continues to remember, to invoke'.[124]

To conclude, I suggest that an interweaving of the rational and the magical occurs readily in the human search for meaning. Hybrids are common, but the multivalence of examples is not the prime issue. What Tambiah calls 'the translation of culture', is more important in understanding Ibn 'Arabi than the translation of the Arabic language, since misconceptions of the knowledge culture block accurate translation.[125] Likewise, the false divide between magic and rationality can be a genuine impediment to the journey of the creative imagination, whereas the everyday hybrids of the rational and magical are commonplace.

Where the search for meaning may lead is perhaps a matter of 'taste' and knowledge. Sufi knowledge, as expressed by Ibn 'Arabi, is in one way a spiritual manual for a journey through the states and stations of consciousness. This imaginative engagement with the cosmos has the goal of producing knowledge that comes from direct experience. In this context, consciousness itself is the frontier that the Sufi 'love path' most boldly explores, in the quest for union with 'the One'.

---

[122] Bruun and Whimster, *Max Weber,* Endnotes, p. 452. L. Scaff is cited for the definition.
[123] Corbin, *Mystical Imagination,* cites Ibn 'Arabi, *Fusus,* in 'Notes', p. 302.
[124] Laleh Bakhtiar, *Sufi Expressions of the Mystic Quest* (London: Thames & Hudson, 1976), p. 25.
[125] Tambiah, *Magic, Science, Religion,* pp. 35–58, discusses the 'translation of culture' and 'commensurability' as two prime concerns in ethnographic work and cultural anthropology. The translators whose work is cited here (Chittick, Burckhardt, Hirtenstein, Chodkiewicz, et al.) had great familiarity with the Sufi knowledge culture, prior to their translation work.

Bells and Spells: Rosicrucianism and the Invocation of Planetary Spirits in Early Modern Germany

Hereward Tilton

Abstract: This paper examines early modern theurgical techniques in the context of Christian anti-magical polemics and an associated marginalization of gnostic-emanationist religiosity. Particular attention is directed to the ritual invocation of planetary spirits in the Rosicrucian tradition, which involved artefacts (spirit-summoning bells, animated statues, etc.) manufactured from Paracelsian *electrum magicum*, a pervasive material in European ritual magical practice. Further light is cast upon this Christian Cabalistic theurgical tradition by the author's discovery of the Dutch Behmenist origins of the Gold- und Rosenkreuz.

Regarded as illicit by the major Christian confessions, the invocation of planetary spirits maintained a limited currency within a network of interrelated Paracelsian, Rosicrucian and Behmenist traditions in early modern Germany, primarily via a little-known Christian Cabalistic manuscript lineage I will address in the following paper. The value of these manuscripts within the economy of religious knowledge arose from their depiction of practical invocative techniques – fasting, prayer, entheogen use and quasi-Tantric ascetic practices – designed to cultivate altered states of consciousness. As post-Enlightenment historiographies of religion remain deeply informed by Protestant anti-enthusiasm, these techniques and their associated doctrines continue to be represented as a magical counter-category to both Christian faith and modern science; but for all their Neoplatonic and Jewish roots, they are more accurately described as marginalised forms of Christian religiosity. Within this suppressed form of Christianity the planetary intelligences constitute indispensable steps on an inner path to gnosis conceived as the reversal of an emanationist cosmogony. Despite the best efforts of Catholic, Lutheran and Calvinist authorities to abolish this alternative Christian worldview and way of life, the invocation of planetary spirits and the related theurgical animation of

---

Hereward Tilton, 'Bells and Spells: Rosicrucianism and the Invocation of Planetary Spirits in Early Modern Germany', *Celestial Magic*, special issue of *Culture and Cosmos*, Vol. 19, nos. 1 and 2, 2015, pp. 167–88.
www.CultureAndCosmos.org

statues persisted among inheritors of the inspirationist tendency of the so-called Radical Reformation.

Today there is a growing recognition among scholars that 'magic' has always been the religion of an Other.[1] The identity of that magical Other has remained surprisingly constant within the broader history of Christian discourse on magic, as has Christian orthodoxy's hegemonic concern with the preservation of institutional power and a monopoly on the valid expression of religiosity.

As a polemical category, the term 'magic' first arose amongst the ancient Greeks in reference to practices originating among the Persian priests (*mágoi*); while *mageía* could be envisaged as an exotic but entirely legitimate *prisca theologia*, it also possessed the negative connotation of fraudulent wonder-working techniques lacking any sophisticated theological superstructure or higher philosophical intent.[2] Similar positive and pejorative characterisations of *magia* persisted in pagan Rome: both are depicted side-by-side in the *Apologia* of Apuleius, for example, while the conception of magic as a set of barbarous, charlatanic techniques qualitatively different to religion was most influentially advanced in the work of Pliny.[3]

By contrast, the Church Fathers employed the term in a purely negative sense against the gnostic-emanationist pagan competitors of the early Christian Church. Thus Augustine (354–430) – utilizing magic as a synonym for Neoplatonic and Hermetic theurgy – condemned the summoning of celestial intermediaries between humankind and higher divinity, declaring that anyone who has recourse to such 'demons' has

---

[1] On magic and the demarcation of the boundaries of religion, see Randall Styers, *Making Magic: Religion, Magic and Science in the Modern World* (New York: Oxford University Press, 2004), pp. 96–116.

[2] E.g., the positive connotation of Plato, *Alcibiades* 1.121e–122a, in Plato, *Alcibiades*, ed. Nicholas Denyer (Cambridge: Cambridge University Press, 2001), p. 60, and the negative connotation of Euripides, *Orestes* 1497, in Euripides, *Orestes*, ed. and trans. Robin Waterfield (Oxford: Oxford University Press, 2001), p. 89.

[3] Apuleius, *Apologia*, pp. 25–26, in Apuleius, *Pro se de magia*, ed. Vincent Hunink (Leiden: Brill, 1997), pp. 86–90; Pliny, *Naturalis historia* 30.1–7, in Pliny, *Natural History libri XXVIII–XXXII*, ed. and trans. W. H. S. Jones (Cambridge, MA: Harvard University Press, 1963), pp. 279–83.

strayed from 'divine religion'.⁴ His words were aimed specifically at the statue-animating passages of the Hermetic *Asclepius*, which described the drawing down of celestial spirits into their artificial likenesses for divinatory purposes, and which was to inform subsequent Christian controversies regarding talismanic magic.⁵ Such astrological divination not only contravened Augustine's teachings on free will, but also posed the threat of a surreptitious pagan influence within the Church, as the pagan gods were linked to the heavenly bodies as their rulers.⁶ If these celestial beings existed at all, as rivals of the Church they could be nothing other than malevolent, and Augustine warned they must be distinguished clearly from the higher angels and other benevolent (Christian) powers of the supercelestial heavens.⁷

The defenders of nascent Christian orthodoxy also demonized gnostic-emanationist rivals within the early Church's own ranks by blackening their names – e.g., Simon Magus, Marcus, Marcus, Priscillian – with accusations of 'magic'.⁸ The purpose of this polemic was not only to segregate the divine from the natural realms, but first and foremost to obstruct access to the divine via emanationist conceptions of nature, thus establishing the priests, rites and doctrines of the Church as the sole legitimate avenue to God.⁹

---

⁴ Augustine, *De civitate Dei* 8.24, 10.9, in Augustine, *The City of God against the Pagans*, Vol. 3, ed. and trans. David Wiesen (Cambridge, MA: Harvard University Press, 1968), pp. 116–29, p. 287.
⁵ *Asclepius* 24, 37, in Brian Copenhaver, trans., *Hermetica* (Cambridge: Cambridge University Press, 2000), pp. 81, 89–90.
⁶ Augustine himself had 'worshipped' these stellar and planetary rulers in his Manichaean years: *Confessiones* 3.6, 4.3, in Augustine, *Confessions*, Vol. 1, trans. William Watts (London: William Heinemann, 1912), pp.114–21, pp. 153–57.
⁷ Augustine, *De civitate Dei* 10.26 (Augustine, *City of God*, pp. 369–70); in another place (*Ad Orosium contra Priscillianistas et Origenistas* 11.14) Augustine appeals to Sirach 3.22 ('what is hidden is not your concern') when considering the existence of planetary intelligences (Augustine, *Aurelii Augustini opera*, Vol. 15, No. 3 (Turnhout: Brepols, 1985), p. 177).
⁸ Acts 8.9–11; Irenaeus, *Adversus haereses* 1.15.6, 1.23.1, in Irenaeus, *Against the Heresies*, Vol. 1, No. 1, ed. and trans. Dominic Unger (New York: Newman Press, 1992), pp. 68, 81–82; Sulpicius Severus, *Historia sacra* 2.46, in Sulpicius Severus, *Historia sacra* (Leiden: Ex officinâ Elseviriorum, 1635), pp. 165–66.
⁹ This refusal of interaction with intermediary spirits is also evident among the Platonist Church Fathers; Origen, for example, anticipates Augustine when he declares 'all the heathen gods are demons' (*Contra Celsum* 7.69, cf. Psalms 96.5), and insists that 'the high priest' Christ is the only valid intercessor for prayer and

The close association of the polemic against magic with the marginalization of gnostic-emanationist religiosity persisted within medieval Christendom. Above all, it was the quest for sources of healing in the natural world that brought clerics and lay Christians alike into perilous proximity with marginalized texts and practices, particularly those of Hermetic provenance. Enduring problems for the Church hierarchies were posed by the twelfth- and thirteenth-century Christian reception of the Arabic *Picatrix*, which depicted the preparation of talismans in the context of a Neoplatonic natural philosophy coloured by Sabian-Hermetic star worship. As divine cosmogonic emanations, stellar and planetary spirits lend their occult powers to stones, rings or other objects engraved with their characters at the appropriate astrological moment. Usually worn as amulets, such talismans were employed for purposes of healing, fertility and the mitigation of various worldly travails.[10]

Responding to this increasingly popular practice, Thomas Aquinas (ca. 1225–1274) proscribed the use of *verba ignota* (unknown words) or talismanic characters.[11] For Thomas, all linguistic signs (words, characters, symbolic figures) are invocative (or 'addressative', to use Weill-Parot's neologism) – that is to say, they all address an autonomous intelligence to obtain its aid in performing the magical operation.[12] While Thomas' *Summa theologiae* states that textual amulets with Christian *verba divina* are a legitimate means of protection and healing, their efficacy derives from an understanding of the sense of those divine words rather than any

---

supplication (*Contra Celsum* 5.4) (Origen, *Contra Celsum*, ed. and trans. Henry Chadwick (Cambridge: Cambridge University Press, 2003), pp. 266, 452).

[10] *Picatrix* 1.5. in pseudo-Maǧrīṭī, *Picatrix: das Ziel des Weisen*, ed. and trans. Hellmut Ritter and Martin Plessner (London: Warburg Institute, 1962), pp. 24–34, 111–13.

[11] Thomas Aquinas, *Summa theologiae* 2.2.96, articles 1, 4, in Thomas Aquinas, *Summa theologica*, Vol. 3, Part 2, Section 2, trans. the Fathers of the English Dominican Province (New York: Cosimo Classics, 2007), pp. 1602–6.

[12] Nicolas Weill-Parot, 'Astral Magic and Intellectual Changes (Twelfth-Fifteenth Centuries): "Astrological Images" and the Concept of "Addressative" Magic', in *The Metamorphosis of Magic from Late Antiquity to the Early Modern Period*, ed. Jan Bremmer and Jan Veenstra (Leuven: Peeters, 2002), pp. 167–88, p. 169. See in particular Thomas Aquinas, *Contra Gentiles* 3.105.10–12, in Thomas Aquinas, *On the Truth of the Catholic Faith. Summa Contra Gentiles*, Vol. 3, ed. and trans. Vernon Bourke (New York: Image Books, 1956), p. 96.

power inhering in the form of their characters.[13] Thomas concedes the natural materials with which such amulets are created may indeed receive beneficial occult virtues from the heavenly bodies, but the use of talismanic characters resembles an act of prayer, and any such act directed beneath the divine (supercelestial) hierarchy is necessarily demonic.[14]

This segregation of the illicit invocation of celestial intelligences from the licit natural magical manipulation of occult sympathies and antipathies in nature went hand-in-hand with a 'dis-integration' of the cosmos and the disciplines used to investigate it, leading to the propagation of a form of the Scholastic 'double truth' (*duplex veritas*). Hence in his *De mineralibus* Albertus Magnus (1193–1280) praised not only the art of making talismans but also its founder, Hermes; through the engraving of images upon stones and metals one may lawfully receive occult virtues from their source in the divine *nous* via their intermediaries in the hierarchy of being, the stars and planets.[15] Yet in his theological writings Albertus makes the contradictory claim that 'the art of images is wicked', as it inclines to idolatry via the ascription of divinity to the stars themselves.[16] Techniques that may be licit in a natural philosophical context are illicit for any religious purpose: while occult virtues devolve from God, the stars are merely impersonal media in the natural process of the impression of forms (as are the talismanic images themselves, which will eventually become 'cold and dead' once the operation is finished).[17]

---

[13] Aquinas, *Summa theologiae* 2.2.96, article 4: 'Chrysostomus dicit... ubi est virtus Evangelii? In figuris litterarum, an in intellectu sensuum?', etc., in Thomas Aquinas, *Summa theologiae*, Vol. 3 (Ottawa: Impensis Studii Generalis O. Pr., 1942, p. 225; cf. Aquinas, *Summa theologica*, p. 1606.

[14] Aquinas, *Summa theologiae* 2.2.96, articles 2, 4 (Aquinas, *Summa theologica*, pp. 1602–6); note Thomas concedes planetary and stellar talismans may indeed produce their intended effects, but these are not natural physical effects, as they are achieved only indirectly via the intellectual natures (demons) they invoke; Aquinas, *Contra Gentiles* 3.104.7–12, 3.106.1–10 (Aquinas, *On the Truth of the Catholic Faith*, pp. 91–93, pp. 97–99).

[15] Albertus Magnus, *De mineralibus* 2.3.3, in Albertus Magnus, *Book of Minerals*, trans. Dorothy Wyckoff (Oxford: Clarendon Press, 1967), pp. 134–37.

[16] Albertus Magnus, *Super sententiarum* II 7.9: 'Sed imaginum ars ideo mala est, quia inclinans est ad idolatriam per numen quod creditur esse in stellis', in Albertus Magnus, *Opera omnia*, Vol. 27, ed. Stephan Borgnet (Paris: Ludovic Vivès, 1894), p. 158.

[17] Albertus Magnus, *De mineralibus* 2.3.3 (Albertus Magnus, *Book of Minerals*, p. 137).

This disintegrative astrologizing of natural philosophy was developed further by Pietro d'Abano (1250/1257–1316) in his *Conciliator* (ca. 1310), in which he attempted to explain the perceived efficacy of talismanic magic within a non-invocative Aristotelian framework. Subsequent generations came to associate d'Abano with the invocative magic of the *Picatrix*, in part due to his medical experimentation with a Hermetic solar talisman.[18] However, d'Abano rejected the intervention of planetary intelligences as conceived in Hebrew and Arabic magical texts; rather, he ascribed the efficacy of talismans merely to an intransitive psychosomatic force of the imagination.[19] Notwithstanding his considerable post-mortem reputation as a student of 'damned magic',[20] d'Abano's persecution by the Inquisition was probably inspired by the deterministic implications of his rational naturalistic approach, and specifically by a doctrine set forth in the *Conciliator* associating the seven planetary rulers with astrologically determined historical epochs.[21] The hostility of the authorities towards both astrological determinism and his textual sources led d'Abano to disguise this doctrine's origin:[22] it was not derived from Averroes – as implied in

---

[18] The operation in question was derived from two related Hermetic texts: see Nicolas Weill-Parot, 'Arnaud de Villeneuve et les relations possibles entre le sceau du lion et l'alchimie', *Arxiu de textos Catalans antics* 23/24 (2005), pp. 269–80, pp. 271–72). The amalgamated texts are to be found inserted within the Latin version of the *Picatrix* – a fact that gave rise to the suspicion (noted in later manuscript copies of the *Picatrix* itself) that the *Picatrix* had been d'Abano's source; David Pingree, ed., *Picatrix: The Latin Version of the Ghāyat Al-Ḥakīm* (London: Warburg Institute, 1986), pp. 82–85, 242.
[19] Pietro d'Abano, *Conciliator differentiarum philosophorum et medicorum* (Mantua: Johann Wurster and Thomas Septemcastrensis, 1472), f. 290r (*Diff.* 156); cf. Vittoria Perrone Compagni, 'La differenza 156 del Conciliator: una rilettura', *Annali del Dipartimento di Filosofia* 15 (2009): pp. 65–107, pp. 88–89.
[20] Brian Copenhaver, *Symphorien Champier and the Reception of the Occultist Tradition in Renaissance France* (The Hague: Mouton Publishers, 1978), p. 150.
[21] D'Abano, *Conciliator*, f. 20r (*Diff.* 9): 'Nam prima quidem est Saturni cassiel [sic]. Secunda Iovis sackiel. Tertia Martis sammael. Quarta Solis micael. Quinta Veneris anael. Sexta Mercurii raphael. Septima vero Lune Gabriel.' D'Abano's brief allusion to his persecution follows at the end of *Diff.* 9 (f. 21r).
[22] Witness, for example, Tempier's Parisian Condemnation of 1277, which threatens excommunication for the mere possession of invocative magical texts (*Chartularium universitatis parisiensis*, Vol. 1 (Paris: Delalain, 1889), p. 543), and which condemns a number of theses on astrological determinism and radical

the *Conciliator* – but rather from Eleazar of Worms' commentary on the *Sefer Yetzirah*.[23] As we shall see, Eleazar's angelic planetary rulers and epochs were to exert considerable influence on subsequent Christian practitioners of invocative astrological magic, chiefly via the works of d'Abano and Johannes Trithemius (1462–1516).

During the Renaissance Platonist revival, proponents of pagan theurgy sought to philosophically circumvent earlier medieval strictures against celestial invocations, creating cracks in the broader edifice of Christian orthodoxy that would contribute substantially to its widespread collapse in the course of the Reformation. Thus Marsilio Ficino (1433–1499) appealed to a work erroneously attributed to Thomas Aquinas (*De fato*) to claim that both the natural materials *and* the artificial graven images of a talisman are capable of drawing down occult virtues from the celestial realm – a notion in clear contravention of Thomas' genuine writings.[24] Indeed, the third book of Ficino's *De vita* ('On Obtaining Life from the Heavens') was essentially a commentary via Plotinus upon the theurgy of *Asclepius* – a text Thomas had specifically condemned.[25] Echoing the naturalism of d'Abano and Albertus, in *De Vita* Ficino emphasised that his astrological magic relied not upon the invocation of planetary and stellar intelligences, but rather upon the impersonal *spiritus mundi* mediating between the

---

Aristotelian themes, leaving a naturalist such as d'Abano exposed to persecution on a number of grounds.
[23] Eleazar ben Judah, פר יצירהס פירוש, London: British Library Add MS 27199, ff. 388v-470v (f. 438r); the same angels (קפציאל [Saturn], צדקיאל [Jupiter], סמאל [Mars], רפאל [Sun], ענאל [Venus], מיכאל [Mercury], גבריאל [Moon]) are given in Eleazar ben Judah's סודי רזיא, London: British Library Add MS 27199, ff. 1r–379v (f. 29r), a tract that was the chief source of the later grimoire *Sefer Raziel*. The Jewish provenance of the doctrine was well-known to d'Abano, as it also appears as an addendum to his translation of Abraham ibn Ezra's *Liber rationum: Abrahe Avenaris Iudei astrologi peritissimi in re iudicali Opera* (Venice: Petrus Liechtenstein, 1507), f. 43v. A similar list is to be found in Judah ben Barzillai's commentary (ca. 1200) on the *Sefer Yetzirah*, complete with the Babylonian planetary demons as attendant spirits, but there is no reference there to the 354-year epochs: Judah ben Barzillai, יצירה רפס פירוש (Berlin: M'kize Nirdamim, 1885), p. 247.
[24] Brian Copenhaver, 'Scholastic Philosophy and Renaissance Magic in the *De vita* of Marsilio Ficino', *Renaissance Quarterly* 37, no. 4 (1984): pp. 523–54, pp. 532–34.
[25] Thomas Aquinas, *Contra Gentiles* III 104.7–12.

anima mundi and the sensible world.[26] Elsewhere, however, he effectively mounted a defence of Orpheus and the *magi* against St. Paul himself; in so doing, he revealed that his resurrection of the *prisca theologia* was indeed concerned with the invocation of *numina* (spirits), each of which constituted a rung on a great ladder between heaven and earth.[27]

There is less dissimulation evident in the work of the great magical Reformers, Paracelsus (1493–1541) and Agrippa (1486–1535), with their 'overtly demonic, recklessly unorthodox magic'.[28] The Christian reception of Jewish Kabbalah and the Hekhalot literature by Pico, Reuchlin and their heirs contributed substantially to this 'reckless' tendency in late Renaissance magic, as did the emergence of various other inspirationist currents within the 'radical' wing of the Reformation, which took the newfound emphasis on individual religiosity, the priesthood of all believers, and direct, unmediated contact with the divine world to its furthest conclusion.[29] In this latter development lie the origins of magisterial Protestant and later Enlightenment polemics against

---

[26] Marsilio Ficino, *De vita libri tres* 3.25, in Marsilio Ficino, *Three Books on Life: A Critical Edition and Translation*, trans. and ed. Carol V. Kaske and John R. Clark (Tempe, AZ: Medieval and Renaissance Texts and Studies, 1998), pp. 37, 383. Cf. Plotinus, *Enneads*, 4.4.26, in Plotinus, *Enneads IV.1–9*, trans. A. H. Armstrong (Cambridge, MA: Harvard University Press, 1984), pp. 206–11; this spirit is the macrocosmic homologue of the fine material *spiritus* mediating between the soul and the body in the human individual; it transmits 'seminal reasons' (the Stoic *logoi spermatikoi*) which impress particular archetypal forms originating in the intellectual realm onto the world of matter: see Daniel Walker, *Spiritual and Demonic Magic: From Ficino to Campanella* (University Park, PA: Pennsylvania State University Press, 2003), pp. 112–13.

[27] Ficino, *In epistolas divi Pauli* VIII; cited in Walker, *Spiritual and Demonic Magic*, pp. 48–51.

[28] Walker, *Spiritual and Demonic Magic*, p. 75.

[29] On relevant figures such as the 'Platonic spiritualists' (e.g. Franck, Schwenkfeld, Weigel) see R. Emmet McLaughlin, 'Spiritualism: Schwenckfeld and Franck and their Early Modern Resonances', in *A Companion to Anabaptism and Spiritualism, 1521–1700*, ed. John D. Roth and James M. Stayer (Leiden: Brill, 2007), pp. 119–61; George Williams and Angel Mergal, eds., *Spiritual and Anabaptist Writers* (Louisville, KY: Westminster John Knox Press, 2006); and the classic study by George Williams, *The Radical Reformation* (Kirksville, MO: Sixteenth Century Journal Publishers, 1992).

'enthusiasm', which were closely allied to the modern polemic against magic.[30]

As gnostic-emanationist religiosity stemming from the Hermetic and Kabbalistic traditions remained widely illicit in the early modern period, its practical invocative techniques often went unprinted, circulating instead in oral and manuscript form. The value of such manuscripts within the economy of religious knowledge was derived in part from the very strictures of Christian orthodoxy against their dissemination; in some cases, however, access to this knowledge was restricted because it was deemed by practitioners to be properly esoteric in character, i.e. unsuitable for the uninitiated.[31] Although such restricted knowledge is less visible to the contemporary historian, it would be unwise to accept Hanegraaff's claim that esotericism is 'an imaginative construct in the minds of intellectuals and the wider public', as we are studying marginalized European religious practices with historically and functionally related homologues in Levantine Jewish, Islamic and Indo-Tibetan contexts.[32]

The Rosicrucian tradition is a particularly important conduit for manuscript collections of invocative magical texts, the contents of which were constantly edited and interpreted anew by practitioners. On the whole these manuscripts deal with the induction of altered states of consciousness through prayer, music, chanting, fasting and the ingestion of alchemically

---

[30] The paradigmatic text in this regard is Johann Christoph Adelung, *Geschichte der menschlichen Narrheit*, 7 vols (Leipzig: Weygand, 1785–1789); cf. Monika Neugebauer-Wölk and Markus Meumann, 'Aufklärung – Esoterik – Moderne. Konzeptionelle Überlegungen zur Einführung', in *Aufklärung und Esoterik: Wege in die Moderne*, ed. Monika Neugebauer-Wölk, Renko Geffarth, and Markus Meumann (Berlin: Walter de Gruyter, 2013), pp. 1–36.

[31] Although Richard Kieckhefer, *Magic in the Middle Ages* (Cambridge: Cambridge University Press, 1990), p. 140, uses the term 'occult' to characterise magical learning 'reserved for the few and concealed from the many', the term 'esoteric' is far more exact and less ambiguous; notwithstanding its loose contemporary connotations in popular culture, I use the term here in accordance with its etymology, i.e., to refer to knowledge that is communicable to – or intelligible by – a privileged circle of initiates alone. Compare with William Eamon, *Science and the Secrets of Nature: Books of Secrets in Medieval and Early Modern Culture* (Princeton, NJ: Princeton University Press, 1994), p. 43.

[32] Hereward Tilton, Review of Wouter Hanegraaff, *Esotericism and the Academy: Rejected Knowledge in Western Culture* (Cambridge: Cambridge University Press, 2012), *Journal of Religion in Europe* 6 (2013): pp. 491–93; Hanegraaff, *Esotericism and the Academy*, pp. 376–77.

produced entheogens – that is to say, psychoactive substances created in the laboratory that tend to elicit an experience of the divine.[33]

The Rosicrucian manifestos of the early seventeenth century bear traces of these invocative practices, although they are indistinctly expressed. Indeed, the manifestos' vacillation on this subject is suggestive of two redactional layers within the texts, the first stemming from a Paracelsian inclined to invocative magic and the second from a disinclined Lutheran. This fact accords well with the theory of their joint authorship by Tobias Hess (1558–1614) and Johann Valentin Andreae (1586–1654).[34] The *Confessio fraternitatis* is the more heterodox of the two works, as it elaborates more fully on Paracelsian practices that are only implied or mentioned cursorily in the *Fama fraternitatis*. Hence in the earliest known manuscript copy of the *Fama fraternitatis* it is said that the legendary medieval scientist-monk Christian Rosenkreuz learnt his arts from the 'Elementarische Inwohner' (elementary inhabitants) of Fez, which are specifically contrasted with human beings.[35] The *Confessio fraternitatis* goes on to state that Christian Rosenkreuz gained his knowledge 'through the service of angels and spirits'; it also refers to *nectromantia*, or the art of knowing other people's secrets by controlling their familiar spirits, and to *necrocomia*, or the prophetic interpretation of heavenly signs through the *evestrum* or astral spirit.[36] And there is a specific reference in the *Confessio*

---

[33] On this subject see Hereward Tilton, '*Alchymia Archetypica*: Theurgy, Inner Transformation and the Historiography of Alchemy', in *Transmutatio: La via ermetica alla felicità / The Hermetic Way to Happiness*, Quaderni di Studi Indo-Mediterranei V (Alessandria: Edizioni dell'Orso, 2012), pp. 179–216, pp. 187–92.

[34] The contribution of both Andreae and Hess to the manifestos has long since been established: see Martin Brecht, 'Johann Valentin Andreae. Weg und Programm eines Reformers zwischen Reformation und Moderne', in *Theologen und Theologie an der Universität Tübingen*, ed. Martin Brecht (Tübingen: J. C. B. Mohr, 1977), pp. 270–343, pp. 285–290. A third party is also implicated in the authorship of the manifestos: see Carlos Gilly, 'Die Rosenkreuzer als europäisches Phänomen im 17. Jahrhundert und die verschlungenen Pfade der Forschung', in *Das Rosenkreuz als europäisches Phänomen des 17. Jahrhunderts. Akten zum 35. Wolfenbütteler Symposium*, ed. Carlos Gilly and Friedrich Niewöhner (Amsterdam: In de Pelikaan, 2001), pp. 19–56, pp. 28–32.

[35] Pleun van der Kooij and Carlos Gilly, eds., *Fama fraternitatis: Das Urmanifest der Rosenkreuzer Bruderschaft* (Haarlem: Rozekruis Pers, 1998), pp. 11, 76, 104.

[36] *Confessio fraternitatis oder Bekanntnuß der löblichen Bruderschafft deß hochgeehrten Rosen-Creutzes/ an die Gelehrten Europae geschrieben* (Frankfurt am Main: Johann Bringer, 1615), pp. 59–60; cf. Adam Haslmayr, *Antwort an die*

fraternitatis to *Weltfürsten* or world rulers when it describes attracting spirits and 'entrancing the mighty sovereigns of the world' through a type of Orphic singing.[37]

Although the authors of the manifestos envisaged the integration of Biblical teaching with pagan philosophy and the abolition of the Scholastic *duplex veritas* – 'it shall not be said, this is true according to philosophy, but false according to theology', as the *Fama fraternitatis* has it – their ambivalence vis-à-vis invocative astrological techniques reflects a broader ideological struggle within early Rosicrucianism.[38] This fact is succinctly illustrated in an anonymous and undated *Hieroglyphic Portrait and Contrast of the True, Simple Brother of the Rosy Cross and the Falsely So-called Brother* (*Hieroglyphische Abbildung und Gegensatz der wahren einfaltigen und falschgenandten Brüder vom RosenCreutz*, ca. 1625–1630) (Fig. 1). The false Rosicrucian depicted here is evidently a Christian Cabalist, as he commands an angel with a wand and has Dee's hieroglyphic monad at his heart. A taloned foot betrays this diabolical impostor, whose gown is adorned with the names of Stoic philosophers – a reference to the pantheistic tendency of the Paracelsians to blur the distinction between the divine and natural realms.[39] To the left the sun is surrounded by the Zodiac and planetary signs, while an accompanying citation from the Book of Jeremiah implies that astrological magic leads back to the worship of the pagan gods.[40]

---

lobwürdige Brüderschafft der Theosophen von Rosencreutz (Frankfurt am Main: Johann Bringer, 1615), pp. 97–98; Paracelsus, 'Astronomia magna: oder die ganze Philosophia Sagax der grossen vnd kleinen Welt', in *Paracelsus: Sämtliche Werke*, Vol. 12, ed. Karl Sudhoff (Munich: Oldenbourg, 1929), pp. 1–507, pp. 148–157.
[37] 'Die mächtige Fürsten der Welt': *Confessio fraternitatis*, p. 62. The nature of these 'sovereigns' is certainly ambiguous: the Latin edition of the *Confessio* gives 'the mightiest sovereigns of the terrestrial realm' ('...potentissimos imperii terreri [sic] principes...'), though the contrast with Pluto – the king of the underworld – suggests an allusion to angelic powers; *Confessio fraternitatis R. C. ad eruditos Europae* (Kassel: Wilhelm Wessel, 1615), f. H2r.
[38] *Fama fraternitatis*, p. 99.
[39] Carlos Gilly, *Cimelia Rhodostaurotica. Die Rosenkreuzer im Spiegel der zwischen 1610 und 1660 entstandenen Handschriften und Drucke. Ausstellung der Bibliotheca Philosophica Hermetica Amsterdam und der Herzog August Bibliothek Wolfenbüttel* (Amsterdam: In de Pelikaan, 1995), pp. 170–71.
[40] Jer. 7.17–18: 'Do you not see what they are doing in the cities of Judah and in the streets of Jerusalem? The children gather wood, the fathers kindle fire, and the

178 Bells and Spells: Rosicrucianism and the Invocation of Planetary Spirits in Early Modern Germany

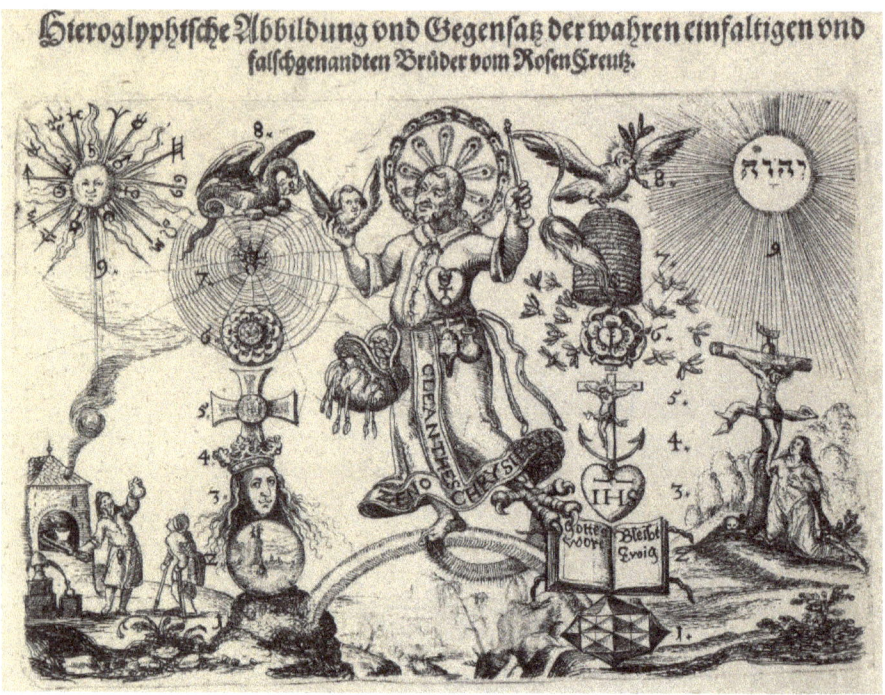

Fig. 1. *Hieroglyphische Abbildung und Gegensatz der wahren einfaltigen und falschgenandten Brüder vom RosenCreutz.* Anonymous broadside, ca. 1625–1630. Wellcome Library, London.

The persecution of ostensibly Rosicrucian groups in Hessen-Kassel, Hessen-Darmstadt and Württemberg during the early years of the Thirty Years War underlines the perceived threat to the social order posed by inspirationist Protestant currents – and specifically by those inspirationists inclined to invocative astrological practices. During his trial in 1619 the 'holy fool' Philipp Homagius was accused of distributing the late sixteenth-century Paracelsian grimoire *Arbatel* among a 'conspiratorial society' of Rosicrucians numbering over two hundred in Hessen-Kassel; he

---

women knead dough, to make cakes for the queen of heaven; and they pour out drink offerings to other gods, to provoke me to anger.'

was subsequently sentenced to 'perpetual imprisonment' as an enthusiast, a pantheist and a threat to state security.[41]

The invocation of planetary spirits and rulers within seventeenth- and eighteenth century Rosicrucianism occurred in the context of an art the *Arbatel* – utilising Paracelsian terminology – terms 'Olympic magic'.[42] In the genuine work of Paracelsus, 'Olympic spirits' are hypostases of the stars, their astral operations and their governance of the world; according to the treatise *De causis morborum invisibilium* they are the key to the Cabalistic art, and constitute the invisible power behind the visible stars in the heavens and the microcosmic stars within the human body.[43] Strangely, the *Arbatel* portrays the seven Olympic spirits as the visible stars themselves; they are 'governors of the cosmic machinery', and their duty is 'to determine fate and administer destiny, insofar as God permits it'.[44]

While the magic of the *Arbatel* – in keeping with most grimoires – is primarily directed towards miraculous worldly ends such as the attainment of invisibility or purses pouring forth gold, among seventeenth-century networks self-identifying as 'Rosicrucian' we find invocative astrological practices employed (in accordance with Hermetic and Jewish Kabbalistic antecedents) for decidedly gnostic purposes. That higher religious intent – a spiral ascent through the heavenly spheres, conceived microcosmically as seven qualities of the human soul (Fig. 2) – has been preserved in the manuscript traces of a Behmenist-Rosicrucian circle that became known to posterity as the Gold- und Rosenkreuz (Gold and Rosy Cross).

---

[41] Karl Hochhuth, 'Mitteilungen aus der protestantischen Secten-Geschichte in der hessischen Kirche', *Zeitschrift für die historische Theologie* 32, no. 1 (1862): pp. 86–159, pp. 87–88, 128–29, 131.
[42] *Arbatel de magia veterum* (Basel: Petrus Perna, 1575), p. 4.
[43] Paracelsus, 'De causis morborum invisibilium', in *Paracelsus: Sämtliche Werke*, vol 9 (Munich: Otto Wilhelm Barth, 1925), pp. 249–350, pp. 298–99.
[44] Named with the faux-Hebrew and faux-Greek neologisms 'Aratron', 'Bethor', 'Phaleg', 'Och', 'Hagith', 'Ophiel', and 'Phul'. Their appointment to particular historical periods (*Arbatel*, pp. 23–25) is indirectly derivative of the aforementioned Kabbalistic tradition transmitted by d'Abano; however, the fact their names are given in 'Olympic speech' – i.e., an angelic *Ursprache* uncoupled from a sacred language such as Hebrew – is reminiscent of Dee. *Arbatel*, p. 22.

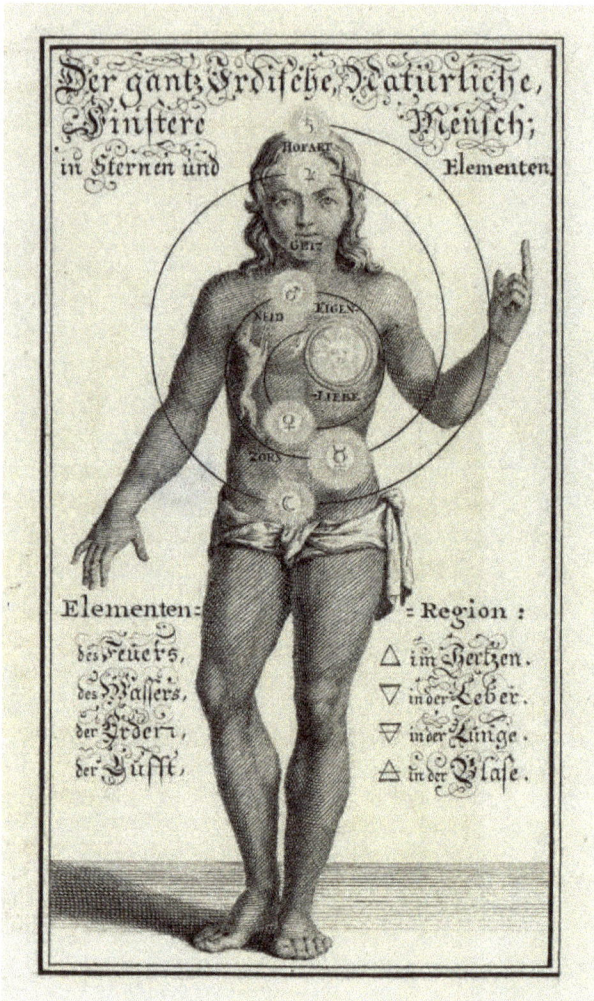

Fig. 2. The seven inner heavenly spheres, as depicted in Johann Georg Gichtel and Johann Georg Graber, *Eine kurtze Eröfnung und Anweisung der dreyen Principien und Welten im Menschen* (Leiden: [s.n.], 1696), figure IV.

The confluence of Behmenist and Rosicrucian currents dates to the earlier seventeenth century; an important intermediary was the Dutch engraver Michel le Blon (1587–1658), an associate of Erasmus Wolfart (fl. 1609),[45]

---

[45] Heinrich Khunrath's friend and editor.

Johann Arndt (1555–1621),[46] Paul Nagel (?–1624)[47] and Abraham von Franckenberg (1593–1652),[48] whose printed and manuscript works place invocative astrological magic within the framework of apocalyptic speculation on the seven angels of Revelations.[49] As a haven of relative religious tolerance, Amsterdam formed the heart of this union of Behmenist and Rosicrucian doctrine and practice, which by the later seventeenth century had coalesced around Ulrich Pfeffer (?–1680) and the Angelic Brethren of Johann Georg Gichtel (1638–1710).[50]

The alchemico-Cabalistic grimoires of the order of the Gold and Rosy Cross stem from the circle of Pfeffer and Gichtel; although they list a great number of techniques for the invocation of planetary intelligences, they rarely give any clear indication of their ultimate gnostic purpose (i.e., a *magia Metatrona* that had become the sole preserve of the order's highest grade of Magus).[51] The most important of the techniques in question deal

---

[46] The prominent proto-Pietist.
[47] A follower of Böhme and early distributor of the Rosicrucian manifestos.
[48] Publisher of Böhme and author of the first defence of the ancient Gnostics.
[49] Revelations 1.20. In his printed response to the manifestos (*Antwort oder Sendtbrief/ an die von Gott erleuchte Bruderschafft vom Rosen Creutz* (Amsterdam: [s.n.], 1615), le Blon confesses his chief interest is the fraternity's 'theological magic', while his manuscript *Tractatus magicus de Astronomia supernaturali* (Dresden: Sächsische Landesbibliothek – Staats- und Universitätsbibliothek Dresden, MS App. 736) touches upon the relation of the planetary rulers to Revelations and is signed with a Rosicrucian motto (f. 66v). On the early confluence of Rosicrucian and Behmenist currents, see Theodor Harmsen, 'The Reception of Jacob Böhme and Böhmist Theosophy in the *Geheime Figuren der Rosenkreuzer*', in *Offenbarung und Episteme: Zur europäischen Wirkung Jakob Böhmes im 17. und 18. Jahrhundert*, ed. Wilhelm Kühlmann and Friedrich Vollhardt (Berlin: Walter de Gruyter, 2012), pp. 183–206, p. 195.
[50] On Pfeffer, Gichtel and the origins of the Gold- und Rosenkreuz, see Hereward Tilton, 'The Urim and Thummim and the Origins of the Gold- und Rosenkreuz', in *Octagon: Die Suche nach Vollkommenheit im Spiegel einer religionswissenschaftlichen, philosophischen und im besonderen Masse esoterischen Bibliothek*, Vol. 2, ed. Hans Thomas Hakl (Gaggenau: H. Frietsch Verlag, 2016), pp. 4–70.
[51] Tilton, 'Urim and Thummim', pp. 46–54. The principal tracts in this regard are 'Jehova Jeschua Metatron, das ist, Magia Dei alba Jesu unsers Heylandes und Gnadenthrons', in *Septimus sapientiae: Liber verus ac genuinus* (Munich: Bayerische Staatsbibliothek, MS Kiesewetteriana 1e), pp. 399–421; 'Magia Metattrona [sic], das ist, die gute Heilige Geistkunst der cabalistischen weissen Magiae', *Septimus sapientiae*, pp. 422–25; 'Dei Magia, oder Magia divina, seu

182 Bells and Spells: Rosicrucianism and the Invocation of Planetary Spirits in Early Modern Germany

with the summoning of celestial and supercelestial spirits via the animation of statues (Figs. 3 and 4) and the striking of bells.

Figs. 3 and 4. Animated solar (left) and lunar (right) statues, from *Magia divina, oder gründ- und deutlicher Unterricht, von denen fürnehmsten Caballistischen Kunst-Stücken derer Alten Israeliten Welt-Weisen, und Ersten, auch noch einigen heutigen wahren Christen* ([s.l.]: L. v. H., 1745), pp. 58, 61.

Both classes of artefact – statues and bells – are manufactured from *electrum magicum*, an alloy of the seven alchemical metals that is uniquely

---

Praxis Cabulae albae et naturalis Theophrasti Paracelsi', *Septimus sapientiae*, pp. 426–556; 'Jesus spricht: In meines Vaters Hause sind viel Wohnungen', *Septimus sapientiae*, pp. 560–87; and *Das Buch mit sieben Siegeln* (Yale: Beinecke Rare Book and Manuscript Library, Mellon MS 110).

receptive to planetary influences.[52] A pervasive material in European ritual magical practice, *electrum magicum* first enters the historical record in the sixteenth-century pseudo-Paracelsian *Archidoxis magica*. There the author claims to have met a necromancer in Spain who engraved certain names and talismanic characters upon the interior of an electrum bell, which when rung would summon the corresponding intelligence; in this way the Olympic spirits exercise an influence upon the star (*astrum*) or 'invisible human' lying hidden in the mind and thoughts of the visible human being.[53]

Elaborating upon the practices referred to in the *Archidoxis magica* and the *Arbatel*, the texts of the order of the Gold and Rosy Cross effectively describe the *binding* of lower planetary spirits via the invocation of their commanding angels from the supercelestial realm.[54] Hence two types of magical electrum bell are described in the order's *De magia divina*: one for the summoning of 'the seven princes of the planets' (which are given the names of the Olympic spirits from the *Arbatel*), the other for summoning their angelic superiors.[55] The former 'bell of the lesser angel' (Fig. 5) is cast with Latinised Hebrew names of God: on the exterior, 'Saday' and 'Tetragrammaton', together with the planet and constellation of the operator's birth; on the interior, 'Elohim'; and on the clapper, 'Adonay'.

---

[52] On the production of *electrum magicum* see Hereward Tilton, 'Of Electrum and the Armour of Achilles: Myth and Magic in a Manuscript of Heinrich Khunrath (1560–1605)', *Aries* 6, no. 2 (2006): pp. 117–57, p. 119 n.7, pp. 128–31.

[53] Pseudo-Paracelsus, *Archidoxis magica*, in *Paracelsus: Sämtliche Werke*, Vol. 14, ed. Karl Sudhoff (Munich: Oldenbourg, 1933), pp. 437–98, p. 488.

[54] The centrality of Paracelsian Olympic magic to the order's practice is evident in 'Liber Theophrasti de septem stellis', *Septimus sapientiae*, pp. 182–342, pp. 227–28: '...der erste und oberste Fürst über die 7. Himmel... wenn er in seiner eigenen vom HERRN empfangenen Kraft in diesem Mysterio Magno, von einem magnetischen Lichte eines wahren Kindes GOTTES beweget wird, der thut alsdenn mehr, denn alle äußerliche sichtbare Sterne am Firmamente, so sich also in *descendente* erzeigen'; cf. *Liber de septem stellis dr. Philippi Theophrasti Paracelsi ab Hohenheim eigener hand abgeschrieben zu Saltzburg anno 1570* (Leipzig: Universitätsbibliothek Leipzig, Cod. mag. 39), f. 2r, where we find the same pseudo-Paracelsian tract without the order's Behmenist accretions.

[55] *De magia divina oder Caballistischer Geheimnüsse* (London: Wellcome Library, MS 4808), pp. 223–63, pp. 244–48. A third *electrum magicum* bell utilizing the characters of the moon and Aquarius to summon subterranean spirits is described in a version of the order's *Thesaurus thesaurorum* entitled γνῶθι σεαυτόν *seu noscete ipsum* (Munich: Bayerische Staatsbibliothek, MS Kiesewetteriana 1d), p. 291.

184 Bells and Spells: Rosicrucianism and the Invocation of Planetary Spirits in Early Modern Germany

Following ritual purification and prayer, the name of the planetary spirit to be summoned is written within the bell; a coloured ink matching the spirit's planetary provenance is used, and this ink is also laid out with paper and quill to receive the angel's answers (presumably a form of automatic writing is alluded to here).

Fig. 5 (left) and Fig. 6 (right). *Electrum magicum* bells from *De magia divina oder Caballistischer Geheimnüsse* (London: Wellcome Library, MS 4808), pp. 223–63 (pp. 246, 248).

The 'bell of the greater angel' (Fig. 6) is cast with 'Jesus', 'Tetragrammaton' and 'Adonay' upon the exterior, together with the names of 'the seven angels' (Oriphiel, Sachiel, Samuel, Michael, Aniel, Raphael and Gabriel). These are the *Angeli planetarum* of Trithemius and d'Abano,[56] although the order's texts describe them variously as archangels and thrones, and also associate them with Böhme's seven source spirits.[57] Likewise, the order's gnostic journey through the seven microcosmic celestial spheres corresponds to the opening of the seven seals, with all its apocalyptic repercussions (Fig. 7).[58]

---

[56] Hence the distinctive corruption of קפציאל as 'Oriphiel' via Trithemius' 'Oriffiel' and d'Abano's 'Caffiel'; cf. n.27, 29 supra and Trithemius, *Steganographia, hoc est, Ars per occultam scripturam animi sui voluntatem absentibus aperiendi certa* (Frankfurt am Main: Johannes Berner, 1606), p. 162.

[57] 'Liber Theophrasti de septem stellis', *Septimus sapientiae*, pp. 221–22.

[58] 'Liber Theophrasti de septem stellis', *Septimus sapientiae*, 283 ff.

Fig. 7. The closed book with seven seals, from *Das Buch mit sieben Siegeln* (Yale: Beinecke Rare Book and Manuscript Library, Mellon MS 110), f. 8r.

One curious instruction is of particular interest: 'a grain's weight of astral tincture' together with 'something fragrant' is to be placed under the operator's tongue while the bell of the lesser angel is struck and the invocation performed.[59] This detail is suggestive of the use of an alchemically produced entheogen; the operation is in any case an example of alchemically assisted theurgy, a category of magical practice I have described elsewhere.[60]

While the order's (mechanically) animated statues seem to be inspired – in part, at least – by Agrippa's citation of Ficino's various reflections on the *Asclepius*, the *electrum magicum* bells belong to an artefactual tradition that can be traced to the alchemico-Cabalist Heinrich Khunrath (1560–1605) via Ulrich Pfeffer.[61] Earlier incarnations of the order's bells are

---

[59] *De magia divina*, Wellcome Library, p. 246.
[60] Tilton, '*Alchymia Archetypica*', pp. 187–92.
[61] Agrippa, *De occulta philosophia* 1.39 (Heinrich Cornelius Agrippa von Nettesheim, *De occulta philosophia libri tres* (Venice: Curtius Navò, 1551), ff.

depicted in an emblem of Khunrath's *Amphitheatrum sapientiae aeternae* and a ritual magical tableau associated with Khunrath;[62] what is more, an *electrum magicum* planetary bell owned by Khunrath's protector Emperor Rudolph II is still in existence today (Fig. 8).[63]

Fig. 8. A replica of a spirit-summoning bell of Rudolph II, ca. 1600; the original is to be found at the Kunsthistorisches Museum, Vienna, KK 5969 (artist: Hans de Bull; dimensions: 7.8 x 6.3 cm; materials: the seven alchemical metals, gilded). Depicted on the bell's exterior are the seven planetary spirits, their characters and their constellations; around the bell interior and clapper are indecipherable spiralling strings of Greek and Hebrew *verba ignota*.

24v–25r); Ficino, *De vita* 3.20, in Ficino, *Three Books on Life*, pp. 348–55; *Picatrix* 3.5, pseudo-Maǧrīṭī, *Picatrix: das Ziel des Weisen*, pp. 193–97; *Asclepius* 24, 37 (Copenhaver, *Hermetica*, pp. 81, pp. 89–90; Tilton, 'Urim and Thummim', pp. 44–46, 51.
[62] *Tabulae theosophiae Cabbalisticae* (London: British Library, Sloane MS 181), ff. 1v–2r; cf. the work of the tableau's discoverer, Peter Forshaw, '"Behold, the dreamer cometh": Hyperphysical Magic and Deific Visions in an Early Modern Theosophical Lab-Oratory', in *Conversations with Angels: Essays towards a History of Spiritual Communication*, ed. Joad Raymond (Houndmills: Palgrave Macmillan, 2011), pp. 175–200, pp. 184–86.
[63] On Rudolph's *electrum magicum* planetary bell, see Beket Bukovinská and Ivo Purš, 'Die Tischglocke Rudolfs II.: Über ihren Urheber und ihre Bedeutung', *Studia Rudolphina* 10 (2010): pp. 89–104.

It is an intriguing fact that early seventeenth-century Rosicrucians were implicated in invocative magical practices closely related to those current among the eighteenth-century inheritors of the Rosicrucian mantle – yet the earlier circles were the bane of established religious and social hierarchies, while the Gold and Rosy Cross in its late quasi-Masonic phase became their staunch defender. Indeed, Prussia's Friedrich Wilhelm II himself became one of the seven Magi at the order's apex in April 1783 after consulting an *electrum magicum* 'Urim and Thummim', the order's most important ritual magical artefact.[64] The response to his subsequent ascent to the Prussian throne from a prominent Enlightened scientist is telling:

> Well may Europe lament the death of the great king [Frederick the Great]! For the glimmer of the Enlightenment and freedom of thought we had vainly cherished while his great example prevailed is extinguished. Now let us bow before the Magus Magorum and seek among the true sages – for whom the Philosophers' Stone is a mere trifle – the Urim and Thummim that grants a glimpse into the realm of the spirits. For we have another great paragon who encourages us to do just this, and who consigns that abominable freedom of thought to the abyss. All hail to an epoch in which Protestant Inquisitions, too, will be advancing the happiness of humanity![65]

Although Frances Yates portrayed the early Rosicrucian phenomenon as a proto-Enlightenment, by the dawn of modernity proper the inspirationist tendencies within Rosicrucianism constituted a reaction to the advance of mechanistic science and Enlightenment philosophy, which had discarded the ambiguous esoteric discourse of alchemy and rejected divine inspiration as a legitimate path to scientific knowledge. As the anti-

---

[64] See the letter from Johann Christoph von Woellner to Johann Rudolf von Bischoffwerder (Berlin: Geheime Staatsarchiv Preußischer Kulturbesitz, BPH Rep. 48 - König Friedrich Wilhelm II, Nr. 8, Bd. 1), f. 20r (22 April 1783).
[65] Brigitte Leuschner, ed., *Georg Forsters Werke*, Vol. 14 (Berlin: Akademie-Verlag, 1978), p. 557: 'Den Tod des großen Königs mag Europa nur beweinen! denn nunmehr ist der Schimmer von Aufklärung und Denkfreyheit wohl auf immer dahin, womit man sich einmal schmeichelte, solange seyn großes Beyspiel den Ton angab. Jetzt wollen wir uns vor dem Magus Magorum beugen und das Urim und Thummim, welches den Blick ins Reich der Geister öfnet, bey den wahren Weisen suchen, denen der lapis eine Kleinigkeit ist; denn wir haben ja ein anderes großes Beyspiel, welches uns dazu aufmuntert, und die abscheuliche Denkfreyheit in den Abgrund verdammt. Heil den Zeiten, wo auch protestantische Inquisitionsgerichte das Glück der Menscheit befördern werden!'

enthusiast polemic moved from a Reformation to an Enlightenment context, inspired knowledge evolved from the status of diabolical heresy to mere trickery: thus the divinatory art of animating statues of the planetary rulers detailed in the *Magia divina* was portrayed by the arch-enemies of the Gold and Rosy Cross, the Illuminati, as the epitome of religious manipulation of the masses.[66] In turn the inspired sciences of astrology and alchemy gave way to disciplines with no place for either heavenly influences or the investigation of poorly-understood psychosomatic phenomena, and the social response to the excluded modes of thought and practice shifted from prohibition to mere ridicule – a state of affairs that continues until the present day.

---

[66] Frances Yates, *The Rosicrucian Enlightenment* (New York: Routledge, 1972); Anon., *Der Rosenkreuzer in seiner Blösse* (Amsterdam: [s.n.], 1781), pp. 38–40; cf. Lucian, *Alexander* 26, in *Lucian*, Vol. 4, trans. A. M. Harmon (Cambridge, MA: Harvard University Press, 1961), p. 211; Hippolytus, *Refutatio* 4.28, in Hippolytus, *The Refutation of all Heresies*, trans. J. H. McMahon (Edinburgh: T&T Clark, 1868), pp. 93–97). For the Enlightenment reception of this ancient rhetorical topos, see Fontenelle's *Histoire des Oracles* (The Hague: Gosse et Neaulme, 1728).

Astral Ascent in the Occult Revival

Joscelyn Godwin

Abstract: The occult revival of the later nineteenth century inherited Neoplatonic and Hermetic ideas of astral ascent and commerce with the planetary spirits, but felt obliged to square these with contemporary discoveries in astronomy. In the 1850s, Andrew Jackson Davis adapted Swedenborgian ideas into a semi-scientific cosmology that served as the norm for spiritualists. In the 1870s, occultism separated from spiritualism and made its own pact with science, with results visible in the works of Emma Hardinge Britten, H. P. Blavatsky, and the Hermetic Brotherhood of Luxor. Outside these well-known movements, Cyrus Teed, known as Koresh, taught that the earth is a concave sphere with the heavenly bodies at the center. His system revived the themes of astral immortality through ascesis and an alchemical relation of humans to a closed cosmos. It was the basis for one of America's more successful utopian communities, which outlasted Teed for more than 50 years.

The ascent of the soul through the planetary spheres is one of the archetypal images of the Western esoteric tradition. The classic account is in the *Poimandres,* the first book of the Corpus Hermeticum, where the divine Mind explains to Hermes Trismegistus what happens to the human being before birth and after death.[1] The Hermetic ascent takes for granted the 'Standard Model' of how the cosmos is put together: a model that unites astronomy, psychology (the science of *psyche,* the soul), and metaphysics. Louis Rougier calls it the 'astral religion of the antique world', that was

> [f]ormulated by the Pythagoreans, developed in the winged myths of Plato, appropriated by Posidonius of Apamea to Stoic physics, permeated by Chaldaean astrology, expounded by Cicero in the form of a neo-Pythagorean apocalypse in the *Dream of Scipio Africanus,* celebrated in the Emperor Julian's *Discourse on the Sovereign Star* as the religious testament of Hellenism; hymned at paganism's close in Hierocles's *Golden Verses*; then,

---

[1] See *Hermetica: The Greek Corpus Hermeticum and the Latin Asclepius in a New English Translation,* ed. and trans. Brian P. Copenhaver (Cambridge: Cambridge University Press, 1992), pp. 1–7.

for more than ten centuries, after successively infusing the oriental salvation religions of Judaism, Gnosticism, Mithraism, Christianity, Manicheism, and Islam, it was the veritable faith of the elites of the Mediterranean shores. It survived the triumph of Christianity; it traversed the Middle Ages and inspired the *Divine Comedy,* and received its quietus only with Kepler's new astronomy and Galileo's modern mechanics.[2]

The Standard Model is spherical, geocentric and dualist. In its classic formulation by Aristotle and, following him, Ptolemy, it consists of a perfect world of eight celestial spheres, enclosing an imperfect world of four elements distinguished by their tendencies towards or away from the center of the system.[3] In principle the elements form four concentric spheres, with all the earth compressed in the center and all the fire on the outside, but in practice they are continually stirred up and mingling with each other: hence the mutable condition of the sublunary world. The celestial world, in contrast, is made from a subtle quintessence or aether. From the Moon's sphere outwards, all is self-moving, eternal, and perfect, and consequently all the motions of the stars and planets are circular. The Standard Model terminates with an eighth sphere carrying all the fixed stars, including the twelve constellations of the zodiac. Beyond that, nothing is visible; hence opinions differ. Aristotle posited a Prime Mover (*primum mobile*) as the necessary mechanism that spins the whole celestial world once a day around the static Earth.[4] Some Hermetic texts insert the thirty-six Decans between that all-encompassing sphere and the zodiac.[5] The Neoplatonism of Plotinus and Proclus extends the system with a hierarchy of Intelligibles;[6] Kabbalism does likewise with the ten

---

[2] Louis Rougier, *L'origine astronomique de la croyance pythagoricienne en l'immortalité céleste des âmes* (Cairo: Imprimerie de l'Institut Français d'Archéologie Orientale, 1933), pp. vi–vii. Author's translation.

[3] Aristotle, *Metaphysics,* XII.8 (1073b–1074a) on the planetary spheres, in *The Basic Works of Aristotle,* ed. Richard McKeon (New York: Random House, 1941), pp. 882–83; *On Generation and Corruption,* II.2 (330a–b) on the four elements (ed. cit., pp. 510–11); *On the Heavens,* I.2–3 (269b–270b) on æther (ed. cit., pp. 400–402); on all of these, Ptolemy, *Almagest,* Book I, in *Ptolemy's Almagest,* trans. and annotated G. J. Toomer (Princeton: Princeton University Press, 1998).

[4] Aristotle, *Metaphysics,* XII,7–8 (1072b–1074a), pp. 880–82.

[5] G. R. S. Mead, *Thrice Greatest Hermes* (London: John M. Watkins, 1949), vol. III, p. 46, quoting Stobaeus.

[6] Plotinus, *Enneads,* III.2.8, see *Plotinus, The Enneads,* trans. Stephen MacKenna (London: Faber & Faber, 1969), pp. 167–68; Proclus, *Commentary on Plato's Parmenides* I, 1, in *Commentary on Plato's Parmenides,* trans. Glenn R. Morrow

Sephiroth;[7] Christianity, with the nine orders of angels, makes a third, divine world above (or enclosing) the celestial and elemental worlds. Beyond that is infinite emptiness, or if you prefer, God.

Since the microcosm resembles the macrocosm, the human body corresponds to the elemental world, the soul to the celestial. At least, that is the exoteric version. In the Neoplatonism that became the mainstay of esoteric anthropology, the human being is threefold. To *soma,* the body, and *psyche,* the soul, it adds the *nous.*[8] That translates as 'mind', 'heart', 'soul', 'intellect', 'mood', 'reason', 'discretion' or 'judgment'; so evidently English has no word for something perfect and eternal, belonging to a state where knowledge and being are one. The *nous* has its home either among the stars, or beyond them. According to Trismegistus, we are here on Earth because our divine part has left that perfect condition to descend through the constricting spheres of the Standard Model.[9]

This is the astral *descent,* a necessary prelude to the present theme and the most imaginative rationale for natal astrology. On its way down through the spheres, the nous acquires seven vestures that constitute the psyche.[10] Each sphere stamps it with qualities and tendencies, which vary according to the planet's current position and aspects. By the time the soul enters the body with the baby's first breath, it bears the imprint of the celestial world as it stood at that moment, recorded in the natal horoscope. It then grows as body and soul, with the knowledge of its divine origin as a dormant potential.

---

and John M. Dillon (Princeton, NJ: Princeton University Press, 1987), p. 1, also the chart of the hierarchy on p. xxxiii.

[7] First appearing in the *Sepher Yetzirah,* see *The Book of Creation,* trans. Irving Friedman (New York: Samuel Weiser, 1977), pp. 1–2.

[8] The triad appears in Plato, *Timaeus,* 30b, see *Plato: The Collected Dialogues,* ed. Edith Hamilton and Huntington Cairns (Princeton, NJ: Princeton University Press, 1982), pp. 1162–63. For the meanings of *nous* or *noos,* see the searchable *Stanford Dictionary of Philosophy,*
http://plato.stanford.edu/search/searcher.py?query=nous [accessed 20 April 2016].

[9] See *Hermetica,* I, 12–15, p. 3. Compare Plotinus, *Enneads,* IV.7.13, IV.8, pp. 356–64.

[10] Elaborated in Aristeides Quintilianus, *De Musica,* II.17 (87), see *On Music, in Three Books,* ed. and trans. Thomas J. Mathiesen (New Haven: Yale University Press, 1983), p. 152; Macrobius, *In somnium Scipionis,* 12–13, see *Commentary on the Dream of Scipio,* ed. and trans. William Harris Stahl (New York: Columbia University Press, 1952), p. 136.

To the Hermetic philosopher, life on Earth is a preparation for the return to the pre-lapsarian state. The *Poimandres* describes the process.[11] At death, the physical body returns to the elements of which it was compounded. The vital energies dissolve in the general reservoir. The psyche, free from its material baggage, rises to the first celestial sphere, that of the Moon. Is it able to renounce or slough off those tendencies that it picked up from the Moon on its way down? If so, it continues upwards and outwards. If not, it wanders around in the sublunary region until it can incarnate again.

Continuing with the Hermetic account, at every celestial sphere the soul has to surrender one of its powers, or at least the negative aspect of it. To the Moon, ruler of generation, it surrenders the 'power of increasing and diminishing'; at Mercury's sphere, ingenuity turned to evil purposes; at Venus's, concupiscence; at the Sun's, desire for power and ambition; at Mars's, rashness and violence; at Jupiter's, the evil impulses that come from wealth; at Saturn's, falsehood and deceit. 'And then stripped of the effects of the cosmic framework, the human enters the region of the Ogdoad [the eighth sphere]; he has his own proper power, and along with the blessed he hymns the father.' Even that is not the end for such souls, for 'having become powers, they enter into god, which is the final good for those who have received knowledge: to be made god'.[12]

Thus the *Poimandres*. Less familiar is the *Apathanatismos*, a unique document from the cult of Mithras, preserved in a fourth-century papyrus manuscript now in Paris.[13] It instructs the initiate in a process resembling the Hermetic ascent, but in a much more active mode befitting the warrior mentality. When he faces the various hazards, trials and challenges he shouts 'Silence!' or bellows like a bull. On meeting each of the Seven Immortal Gods of the cosmos, who are the planetary gods, he does not submit to their judgment but conjures each one to 'Open the door!'. After passing their spheres he greets the Fates, who appear as seven virgins with serpent heads, and the Lords of the Pole, seven gods with the heads of black bulls. Finally Mithras himself appears, the polar divinity, whom the initiate commands to stay forever in his soul.

---

[11] *Hermetica*, I, 24–26.
[12] *Hermetica*, I, 26.
[13] English translation, with commentary, in Julius Evola and the UR Group, *Introduction to Magic: Rituals and Practical Techniques for the Magus*, trans. Guido Stucco, ed. Michael Moynihan (Rochester, VT: Inner Traditions, 2001), pp. 98–128.

Deification was not an option in the monotheistic traditions, nor did their concept of man require the *nous*. Exoteric Christianity and Islam kept the Standard Model as their cosmology, but modified the soul's history within it. Souls have no prehistory and only one life; the only judge is God; the only outcome an eternity in Hell, which is probably inside the earth, or in Heaven beyond the cosmic circuits. Dante compromised with the esoteric view in his *Divine Comedy*. He kept the purgative stages of the astral ascent as levels on the Mountain of Purgatory, and made the planetary spheres the lower circles of Paradise. But the fortunate souls in the monotheists' heaven are still souls, not gods or even angels.

With the Renaissance and the rediscovery of the Hermetic and Neoplatonic writings, the possibilities re-expanded. We can call this the first occult revival. The Renaissance magi, true to their Neoplatonic preceptors, saw the process as something to be attempted during life, rather than after it. György Szőnyi chooses the term *exaltatio* for the doctrine, 'according to which man—with the help of certain techniques, including magic—could bring himself into such a state that enables him to leave the body and seek the company of the Deity'.[14] He quotes Pico della Mirandola, who in his *Oration on the Dignity of Man*, declares that man can attain a state from which he can 'measure all things' and 'become He who made us', and Paracelsus, who claims that man is 'greater than heaven and earth' and that in his creative work he 'establishes a new heaven'.[15] Ficino, in his 'Praise of Philosophy', ended with the promise of the *Golden Verses*: that upon death, the devoted philosopher 'will go straight and free to the upper regions and will ascend beyond human form, having become God of life-giving heaven'.[16] Cornelius Agrippa devoted his *Three Books of Occult Philosophy* to the magics of the natural, celestial, and angelic worlds, all accessible because 'not only man being made another world [i.e. a microcosm] doth comprehend all the parts thereof in himself but also doth receive and contain even God himself'.[17]

The notion of human exaltation survived the trauma of the Reformation, uniting Protestants, Catholics, and Hermetists in a common esoteric vision.

---

[14] György E. Szőnyi, *John Dee's Occultism: Magical Exaltation through Powerful Signs* (Albany, NY: SUNY Press, 2004), p. 34.
[15] Szőnyi, *John Dee's Occultism,* p. 35.
[16] Marsilio Ficino, *The Letters of Marsilio Ficino,* trans. Members of the Language Department of the School of Economic Science (London: Gingko Press, 1985), Vol. III, p. 21 (Letter 13).
[17] Henry Cornelius Agrippa, *Three Books of Occult Philosophy,* trans. 'J.F.' (Hastings: Chthonios Books, 1986), p. 459 (Bk. III, ch. 36).

As examples we need only mention the English magus John Dee (1527–1608), the Hermetic martyr Giordano Bruno (1548–1600), the mystic and theosopher Jacob Boehme (1575–1624) and the enigmatic alchemist Cesare della Riviera (ca. 1538–1625). Riviera, writing while Bruno was awaiting martyrdom, conceives of a special type of man he calls the 'Hero'. His goal is the attainment of the second Tree of Life, i.e. the return to the state before the Fall of Man, whether the fall is from the Garden of Eden or through the planetary spheres.[18] Riviera's method is to construct a microcosm in the imagination, comprising both the elemental and the celestial world. Without leaving his chamber, the Hero observes the motions of the stars and the harmony of the spheres, unknown to the vulgar. He populates it with all the elemental and celestial species, free from all corporeality, and fixes them as though in transparent ice. Thereupon the incorporeal and intellectual forms are opened to him.[19] This sounds like the Hermetic initiate conversing with the blessed beyond the eighth sphere, except that the Hero, like the Mithraic initiate, has got there through his own will. Instead of being contained by the Standard Model, he contains it and controls its energies within himself.

Towards the end of this period the Hermetist Thomas Vaughan (1621–1666) writes in a related vein of an art by which a particular spirit can be united to the universal, and nature thereby 'strangely exalted and multiplied'.[20] His commentator A. E. Waite remarks that this implies the union of the individual spirit with universal consciousness.[21] In another work Vaughan advises the reader to 'know the region of light', to 'converse with spirits, and understand the nature of invisible things'; then he will know the Universal Subject.[22] In both cases, he seems to be defining the activation of the *nous* while still incarnate.

While these late Hermetists were at work, the Standard Model was breaking down. In 1543 Copernicus's heliocentric system was offered as a better basis for calculating planetary movements. Kepler, refining and testing that model, proved in *Harmonices Mundi* (1619) that the planets orbit the sun not in perfect circles but ellipses. After Galileo's telescope revealed the mountains on the Moon, the phases of Venus, the spots on the

---

[18] See Cesare della Riviera, *Il mondo magico de gli heroi: Edizione del 1605 in caratteri moderni* (Rome: Edizioni Mediterranee, 1986), p. 19.
[19] Riviera, *Il mondo magico*, pp. 93-4.
[20] Thomas Vaughan, *The Magical Writings of Thomas Vaughan*, ed. A. E. Waite (London: George Redway, 1888), p. 51.
[21] Vaughan, *The Magical Writings*, p. 157.
[22] Vaughan, *The Magical Writings*, p. 147.

Sun, the moons of Jupiter and the bulges on either side of Saturn, the heavens seemed more like the untidy, mutable world of the elements. Newton confirmed this in his *Principia* (1687) by proving that a single law, universal gravitation, obtains throughout the cosmos, and that the circular movements once thought to be so perfect are just the complex result of the straight-line pull of gravity. The whole cosmos, celestial and elemental worlds alike, was reduced to a uniform condition of materiality, a body without a soul, and so it remains. This I call the 'New Model' of the cosmos and the psyche. Coincidentally, social and political thought tended towards the end-point of Marxism, in which a soulless humanity is reduced to the lowest degree of its previous hierarchy: that of the material earth.

The esotericists of the post-Newtonian world could hardly deny the astronomical superiority of the New Model, and their spiritual cosmography easily adapted to it. That God should be at the center of the universe rather than at its circumference made metaphorical and metaphysical sense. Emanuel Swedenborg (1688–1772) learned in his spiritual conversations that the Creator resides in the Central Sun, around which there are three heavens: Celestial, Spiritual and Natural.[23] But the symbolism of the astral ascent was too good to lose. Swedenborg ascended without leaving his armchair, politely interviewing the inhabitants of the Moon, Jupiter and other 'earths in the universe' and sometimes being taken up in the spirit to view them himself.[24] The prospect for ordinary folk is that, on the leaving the body, each soul gravitates to the place suited to it, whether a heaven or a hell, and continues its life there much as it did on Earth. Yet since Swedenborg's angels claim that they were once humans, there must be some kind of progress in the heavens, and this idea was eagerly taken up by his successors.

A de-Christianized version of Swedenborg's system entered the popular forum in the late 1840s, thanks to Andrew Jackson Davis (1826–1910), the 'Seer of Poughkeepsie'. Already in his teens, Davis had absorbed much of Swedenborg's doctrine and tested it against his own visionary experiences. His writings, especially *The Principles of Nature* (1847), had a tremendous

---

[23] Emanuel Swedenborg, *Heaven and Hell,* trans. John C. Ager, http://www.sacred-texts.com/swd/hh/hh01.htm, sects. 29–31 [accessed 20 April 2016].
[24] Emanuel Swedenborg, *Earths in the Universe,* trans. John Whitehead, http://www.sacred-texts.com/swd/eiu/eiu03.htm, sects, 128, 134 [accessed 20 April 2016].

effect.[25] They supplied the metaphysical framework for the Spiritualist movement, and in some respects for the whole New Thought and New Age movements that evolved from it. Davis's cosmology, like Newton's, is unitary, except that the substance out of which everything is made varies in its coarseness or subtlety. It manifests in ascending order as Solids, Fluids, Vapors, Ether, Essences, Laws, Principles, Ideas, and finally, Deity.[26] Adjacent to the gross elemental states in which we live lies the 'Summer Land', to which we rise when we leave the body at death. Davis assigns it a definite astronomical location, on the opposite side of the Milky Way from the Earth. There it has its own stars, suns, and planets, and so closely resembles the material world that some souls cannot at first believe that they are dead. However, everything there is infinitely more harmonious, beautiful and wisely ordered than on Earth. Once there, we embark on an endless adventure of spiritual activity and development. Davis's Summer Land sounds like the True Earth described by Socrates in the *Phaedo,* or the world beyond the Cave in the *Republic*.[27] It also resembles Hūrqalyā, the 'imaginal world' of Persian theosophy that is described as objective but lacking a material substratum.[28] But there is a big difference: no particular effort or talent is needed to get to the Summer Land. It is simply the next stop on our evolutionary journey. The Universalists, most optimistic of Christian sects, had prepared the way thither by promising eventual salvation to every soul, either immediately on death or after a period of purgation. Such doctrines were in tune with the times, for the mid-nineteenth century believed in progress on Earth and liked to imagine it continuing in the heavens.

An important innovation in Swedenborg's system is the idea of marriage in heaven, not necessarily between those who were married on Earth but between 'twin souls'. The idea found a warm reception among the American spiritualists and social reformers such as Davis and his wife Mary, the presidential aspirant Victoria Woodhull (1838–1927) and

---

[25] See Antoine Faivre, 'Magnétisme et spiritisme aux États-Unis dans le milieu du XIXème siècle', in *Des Médiums: Techniques du corps et de l'esprit dans les deux Amériques*, ed. Silvia Mancini and Antoine Faivre (Paris: Imago, 2012), pp. 135–66.
[26] Andrew Jackson Davis, *A Stellar Key to the Summer Land* (Rochester: Austin Publishing Co., 1909), p. 51.
[27] Plato, *Phaedo,* 110b–111c, pp. 91–92; *Republic,* 515c–d, 748.
[28] See Henry Corbin, *Spiritual Body and Celestial Earth: From Mazdean Iran to Shī'ite Iran,* trans. Nancy Pearson (Princeton, NJ: Princeton University Press, 1977), pp. 75–79.

Thomas Lake Harris (1823–1906), of whom more below. It was a time when women's rights were in hot debate, and the idealized Victorian marriage was being criticized as sexual slavery. The doctrine taught that while every man and woman has a twin soul, few are lucky enough to have found, much less married, him or her. Most will have to wait until after death to reunite with their other half and continue their evolution as a 'bi-unity' or an androgynous angelic being. Meanwhile the Free Love movement demanded the right for men and women to seek their destined 'affinity'.[29]

Mormonism, which took doctrinal form in the same decade as Davis's revelations (1840s), had its own version of the ascent. In the later revelations of Joseph Smith (1805–1844), as with Swedenborg, there are three heavens. They are called, in ascending order, Telestial, Terrestrial and Celestial, and our spiritual condition determines the level to which we go when we die.[30] God (who is 'a man in flesh and bone'[31]) dwells with Jesus in the highest subdivision of the celestial heaven, and those who attain it will eventually become gods too, and rule universes of their own. The Mormon practice of baptism for the dead is part of the scheme. It offers to those who died without knowing the message of Jesus and Joseph Smith the opportunity of accepting it. If they do so, they may ascend from the lower heaven they currently inhabit to a higher one, there to rejoin their Mormon descendants. While for Mormons this is mainly a device for gathering one's ancestors and reuniting families, it recalls those spiritualists who made it their duty to educate and redeem lost and depraved souls, and help them forward in their evolution. Likewise there is an echo of the twin souls in the Mormon practice of 'sealing' marriages for all eternity. In Mormon doctrine, no one can attain the highest heaven without being thus married and sealed, and that presumably includes both Jesus and God, endowed like Hindu deities with their female *shaktis*.

The messages of the spiritualist mediums and the paranormal phenomena of the séance room satisfied their auditors for a while, reassuring them that there was a reality beyond the material world, that death is not the end, and that their loved ones were awaiting them in the

---

[29] See Cathy Gutierrez, 'Deadly Dates: Bodies and Sex in Spiritualist Heavens', in *Hidden Intercourse: Eros and Sexuality in the History of Western Esotericism*, ed. Wouter J. Hanegraaff and Jeffrey J. Kripal (New York: Fordham University Press, 2011), pp. 309–32.
[30] Joseph Smith, *Doctrines and Covenants of the Church of Jesus Christ of Latter-day Saints* (Salt Lake City, UT: Deseret Books, 1880), Section 76.70–98.
[31] Smith, *Doctrines and Covenants,* Section 120.32.

future state. But it did not give its believers anything more to do than to sit in circles, join progressive causes, and lead a moral life. The general banality of spirit communications and the unmaskings of fake phenomena gradually sapped the energy from the movement.

Two things changed during the third quarter of the nineteenth century. One was the emergence of mediums who were not passive channels, but asserted their own spiritual authority. Some examples, beside Davis, are Thomas Lake Harris (1823–1906) and John Murray Spear (1804–1887), who led communities on the strength of their daily commerce with higher worlds; Anna Kingsford (1846–1888), medical doctor and animal rights defender, who developed from her visions a new Christian Hermetism; and Lady Caithness, Duchess of Pomar (1830–1895), whose self-identification with Mary, Queen of Scots made her a prophet as well as a patron of the movement. The other was the second occult revival. During the 1870s a new movement emerged from a blend of Hermetism, Neoplatonism, Rosicrucianism, Kabbalah and Behmenist theosophy. Whether or not there was a hidden hand directing it, similar metaphysical schemes appeared from three independent and influential sources. They were Paschal Beverly Randolph (1825–1875), a black American clairvoyant; Emma Hardinge Britten (1823–1899), an English medium and inspired lecturer; and Helena Petrovna Blavatsky (1831–1891), co-founder of the Theosophical Society. All three had past histories as mediums under spirit control, but had become authorities in their own right.[32]

The system of this occult revival revolves around a central spiritual sun, the source of all.[33] It emanates rays that are co-eternal with it, but in some sense individualized as 'spirits' – presumably equivalent to Plato's *nous*. These set out on a journey through countless states and transformations lasting for aeons of cosmic time. Eventually they arrive at the human state, where the spirit makes a trinity with the soul and the body. Here we shift perspective from the spirit to the soul, the seat of consciousness both in life and after death. The soul is made from ethereal matter and is not naturally

---

[32] The definitive work on Randolph is John Patrick Deveney, *Paschal Beverly Randolph: A Nineteenth-Century Black American Spiritualist, Rosicrucian, and Sex Magician* (Albany, NY: SUNY Press, 1997). Marc Demarest's exhaustive research on Emma Hardinge Britten is available at the website 'Chasing Down Emma', http://ehbritten.blogspot.com/ [accessed 20 April 2016] and in his annotated edition of Britten's *Art Magic* (Forest Grove: Typhon Press, 2011).
[33] For comparative examples of the system, see Joscelyn Godwin, *The Theosophical Enlightenment* (Albany, NY: SUNY Press, 1994), pp. 295–96, 303–5.

immortal. It can only achieve immortality through union with the spirit. If it succeeds in this, after death the soul and the spirit form an inseparable and immortal individual who continues its pilgrimage as a god or angel and eventually returns to its source, yet even then is not annihilated. If however the soul has failed to make contact with the immortal spirit during life, the spirit abandons it at death. The soul is left to roam the elemental world like the impotent shades in the Graeco-Roman Hades, until it dissolves. Just as a corpse resembles the living person for while, so these cast-off souls may retain memories and opinions that make them seem conscious if they are evoked in the séance room. Randolph and Blavatsky greatly offended the spiritualists by telling them that the self-declared spirits of their loved ones were nothing but these 'astral shells', and Emma Hardinge Britten could never bring herself to believe it.[34] This doctrine of conditional immortality seems to me a re-formulation of the Hermetic ascent. There, too, it is the rare soul that succeeds in passing all seven planetary spheres to exit the cosmic round, escape the necessity of rebirth, and become a god. All the rest are recycled, body and soul.

The second occult revival was a group effort, for all the contentions between its members, by three prophetic types. First were those rare men and women who could put themselves into a clairvoyant or lucid state, control it to some degree, and report on what transpired there. Beside those already mentioned (Swedenborg, Davis, Randolph, Harris, Blavatsky, Kingsford), these include Charles W. Leadbeater (1854–1934), who dominated the second generation of the Theosophical Society, and Rudolf Steiner (1861–1925), who left it to form the Anthroposophical Society. All made the Hermetic ascent, or at least set foot on the threshold of higher worlds, while still alive (though whether there is any truth in what they report is another question entirely; Swedenborg, at least, says that the spirits often lie!). A second type acted as channel for higher intelligences through speech or automatic writing, but with a more critical and active participation than the common trance mediums. Such were Emma Hardinge Britten, John Murray Spear, the clergyman medium William Stainton Moses (1839–1892), Helena Roerich (1879–1955), wife of the

---

[34] See Sylvia Cranston, *HPB: The Extraordinary Life and Influence of Helena Blavatsky, Founder of the Modern Theosophical Movement* (New York: G. P. Putnam's Sons, 1984), pp. 131–32, 138; Deveney, *Paschal Beverly Randolph,* pp. 92–93, 110–12; Emma Hardinge Britten, *Nineteenth Century Miracles; or, Spirits and Their Work in Every Country of the Earth. A Complete Historical Compendium of the Great Movement Known as 'Modern Spiritualism* (New York: William Britten, 1884), pp. 2–5.

painter Nicolas Roerich, and Alice Bailey (1880–1949), whose channelled writings became a mainstay of the New Age.[35] A third type was equally influential in its revelations of the cosmic order and the destiny of man, but such people were not themselves gifted, and used mediums to obtain their information. Examples are Allen Kardec (1804–1869), founder of the French school of *spiritisme;* William H. Dower (1866–1937), founder of the Temple of the People and scribe of *Theogenesis*; Max Theon (1848–1927), founder of the 'Cosmic Philosophy', who experimented with over a hundred sensitives before finding the best medium in his wife, Mary Woodroffe (1843–1908); the magus Aleister Crowley (1875–1947), whose entranced wife Rose Kelly (1874–1932) opened the *Book of the Law;* and the poet William Butler Yeats (1865–1939), whose vision of the gyres and other poetic images were likewise given through his wife Georgie (1892–1968).[36] These examples, by the way, alert us to the varieties of sexual magic that were the great secret of many such figures and their cults.

Theon writes of the danger of this process to the sensitive medium, and of how she has to cross a region he calls the 'Hostile' in order to reach the higher regions of the spirit and soul.[37] (This might correspond, in Hermetism, to the trials of the planetary spheres.) Once across it, she arrives in the place where twin souls sleep, pending their incarnation.[38] One can hardly miss the parallel with Plato's myth of the androgyne as the primordial human condition.[39] Just as the Hermetic ascent awaits us all after death, while the initiate attempts it during life, some occultists enjoyed union with their twin souls here and now. Thomas Lake Harris, leader of the Brotherhood of the New Life in New York State and California, had a human wife who consented to a sexless marriage because his true bride was the Lily Queen, a spirit who dwelt in a sublime region

---

[35] Britten did not name her spirit guides. Spear claimed inspiration from the 'Association of Beneficents', Moses from 'Imperator+', Mme. Roerich from 'Morya', and Bailey from 'The Tibetan'.

[36] Kardec, Crowley and Yeats are amply documented. For the lesser-known examples, see *Theogenesis: The Third Section of the Ancient Stanzas of Dzyan* (Halcyon: Temple of the People, 1981), pp. xxv–xxvi; Christian Chanel, 'De la "Fraternité Hermétique de Louxor" au "Mouvement Cosmique": L'oeuvre de Max Theon' (unpublished PhD thesis, École Pratique des Hautes Études, 1993), p. 359.

[37] Chanel, 'De la "Fraternité Hermétique"', pp. 779–84.

[38] Joscelyn Godwin, Christian Chanel, John Patrick Deveney, eds., *The Hermetic Brotherhood of Luxor: Historical and Practical Documents of an Order of Practical Occultism* (York Beach: Weiser, 1995), pp. 15–16.

[39] Plato, *Symposium,* 189d–e, p. 542.

called Lilistan.[40] As an accomplished spirit traveller, Harris was able to visit her, and somehow or other they bred spirit children. Anna Kimball, an American physician, psychometrist and ex-Free Lover, was the first of many New Thought leaders enthused by the idea of sex with spirits.[41] It worked both ways: men could rise to the spirit worlds, like Harris, and father children there, while women could entertain spirit husbands, in which case their children would surpass their physical fathers. Randolph, too, taught that the highest goal of sexual magic was to bring down superior souls into one's children.[42]

The chief attraction of occultism was that it offered not just theory or consolation but practical instruction. The fruits of spiritualism were bland by comparison, nor did the Theosophical Society deliver on its early promise to investigate the occult powers of man and teach how to acquire them. Just as Socrates said that the philosopher practises dying here and now in order to be prepared for the event,[43] so practical occultism taught techniques for the separation of the soul from the body, astral travel and contact with higher beings. The methods of choice were the magic mirror, sex and drugs – the trio consecrated by Randolph and adopted by the Hermetic Brotherhood of Luxor[44] – and ceremonial magic, which reached its apogee in the Hermetic Order of the Golden Dawn. Both arose during the 1880s, and had an influence out of all proportion to their small membership.

Among twentieth-century occultists, Crowley experimented with another form of astral ascent when he set out to explore the thirty Aethyrs.[45] These are part of the Enochian system of magic revealed to the

---

[40] On Lilistan and its Lily Queen, see Arthur A. Cuthbert, *The Life and World-Work of Thomas Lake Harris, Written from Direct Personal Knowledge* (Glasgow: C.W. Pearce, 1908), pp. 217–19.

[41] On Anna Kimball, see 'Six Degrees of George Chainey' on Marc Demarest's website http://ehbritten.blogspot.com/2013/02/six-degrees-of-george-chainey.html [accessed 20 April 2016].

[42] See the first goal of the 'Mysteries of Eulis' in Deveney, *Paschal Beverly Randolph*, p. 337.

[43] Plato, *Phaedo*, 64a, p. 46.

[44] Godwin, Chanel, and Deveney, *The Hermetic Brotherhood of Luxor*, pp. 68–77.

[45] See Richard Kaczynski, *Perdurabo: The Life of Aleister Crowley* (Berkeley: North Atlantic Books, 2012), pp. 197–203.

Elizabethan magus John Dee in 1584 through his scryer Edward Kelley.[46] Each of the Aethyrs, or Airs as Dee called them, is a distinct zone between the Earth and the sphere of fire, inhabited by its own spirits. Each has a Call that enables the adept to ascend through it, beginning with no. 30 and ending with no. 1. In 1900, while he was in Mexico, Crowley started experimenting with the Enochian Calls using a crystal, but could not get beyond the first two Aethyrs.[47] Nine years later he succeeded in completing the course, with the help of Victor Neuburg, during a month-long magical retreat in the Algerian desert. The process was hazardous, especially when Crowley was possessed by the demon Choronzon and tried to kill Neuburg, but Perdurabo ('I will endure') lived up to his name. He was probably the first person since Enochian times to have run the gauntlet of all thirty Aethyrs. After that, he was in no doubt of his status as Magister Templi and vehicle for the law of the New Aeon.

Another place where old magical texts were put to experimental test was the Gruppo di Ur, an Italian association of the 1920s led by the Pythagorean mathematician and freemason Arturo Reghini (1878–1946) and the traditionalist philosopher Julius Evola (1898–1974). They published the Mithraic ritual mentioned above, with a commentary that sets it in a context of Kundalini yoga and Tantric practices.[48] By 'magic' they meant the science of self-realization, and the ritual and its commentary were intended as an aid to the process. Like the Enochian Calls, the Mithraic ritual makes high demands on the initiate, presupposing a strongly developed active imagination, so that whatever is commanded to appear before the inner senses appears with no less reality than the external world. Someone trained in the Spiritual Exercises of Ignatius Loyola might have an inkling of the process, though of course the purpose is very different: it is deification through defying the gods.

The whole question of the soul's ascent took on a new aspect in the teachings of Theosophy and its offshoots. In the Mahatma Letters[49] and

---

[46] See Meric Casaubon, ed., *A True and Faithful Relation of What Passed for Many Years, Between Dr. John Dee and Some Spirits* (New York: Magickal Childe Publishing, 1992), pp. 139–52.

[47] See Kaczynski, *Perdurabo*, p. 85.

[48] See Julius Evola and the UR Group, *Introduction to Magic*, pp. 98–128.

[49] *The Mahatma Letters to A.P. Sinnett from the Mahatmas M. & K. H. Transcribed and Compiled by A. T. Barker,* ed. Christmas Humphreys and Elsie Benjamin (Adyar: Theosophical Publishing House, 1979). See especially pp. 75–76 (Letter XIII).

Blavatsky's *Secret Doctrine*,[50] in Rudolf Steiner's writings on evolution,[51] and in Alice Bailey's communications from the Theosophical Mahatma Djwhal Khul,[52] human fate is intimately linked with that of the planets themselves. Blavatsky and her sources unfurl a formidably complex scheme of evolution through Root Races and Rounds. To simplify it for now, the main principle is an expansion of the Hermetic descent and ascent to a planetary scale, and even beyond. According to Theosophical prehistory, the whole of life on earth began in a purely spiritual state, and became progressively denser as the planet itself materialized. That is the point at which we find ourselves today. In the Theosophical system the other planets in the solar system seem dead and uninhabited to material science, because the life-waves on them are occupying their non-material counterparts. That is our destiny, too, as we become progressively more spiritualized and complete the cycle by returning to our original condition—but with the harvest of experience behind us.

In Rudolf Steiner's version of the Theosophical cosmogony, the present Earth is the middle of a sequence of seven planetary epochs, similarly defined as a descending and ascending cycle.[53] Behind us are the Saturn, Sun and Moon epochs; ahead, those of Jupiter, Venus and Vulcan. As the Earth itself evolved, extruding first the Sun, then the Moon from itself, various classes of cosmic beings provided the multiple vehicles with which the human being operates.

Alice Bailey's teachings speak more of the individual's experience of death, as a threefold process of Restitution, Elimination and Integration.[54] At death, the physical body is discarded, and so is the etheric body. The Restitution is the return of those bodies, with their atoms and cells, to their originating source. Elimination takes place in full consciousness, now centred in the astral body and the mental vehicle. This is probably the equivalent of the Hermetic ascent through the planetary spheres, since what is eliminated is the emotional and mental tendencies that have

---

[50] H. P. Blavatsky, *The Secret Doctrine: The Synthesis of Science, Religion, and Philosophy* (London: Theosophical Publishing Co., 1888).
[51] Rudolf Steiner, *Cosmic Memory: Prehistory of Earth and Man*, trans. Karl E. Zimmer (Hudson: Steinerbooks, 1987).
[52] For a brief summary, see Alice A. Bailey, *Initiation, Human and Solar* (New York: Lucis Publishing Co., 1922), p. 96.
[53] Steiner, *Cosmic Memory,* pp. 156–64.
[54] Alice Bailey's teachings on the subject are conveniently collected in *Death, the Great Adventure. Compiled by Two Students from the Writings of Alice A. Bailey and the Tibetan Master, Djwhal Khul* (New York: Lucis, 1985); here pp. 81–83.

accumulated around the soul. Integration seems to correspond to whatever happens once the Hermetic initiate has passed the eighth sphere.

Another strain of occultism treated the physical body not as rubbish to be discarded, but as a potential sharer in the soul's immortality. To believers in biblical authority there were the examples of Enoch, who lived 365 years and 'walked with God, and he was not, for God took him' (Genesis 5:24); Elijah, taken to heaven in a fiery chariot (II Kings 2:11); and of course Jesus, who could vanish and reappear at will in tangible form. (The Assumption of the Virgin Mary did not figure among the examples, probably because of anti-Catholic prejudice in the Anglo-Saxon world.) In 1814 the disciples of the English prophetess Joanna Southcott (1750–1814) were sure that she had achieved immortality and would be resurrected, until they were obliged to bury her corpse. The same happened in 1817 with Jemima Wilkinson (1752–1819), the 'Publick Universal Friend' regarded as God's feminine manifestation. The possibility of physical regeneration was the ultimate goal of the New Thought movement, exemplified by Cyrus Teed (1839–1908), the founder of Koreshanity, who disappointed his disciples by dying. Within living memory Mira Alfassa (1878–1973), a former pupil of Max Theon and, more famously, the 'Mother' of Sri Aurobindo's ashram, was believed by her disciples to be on the brink of achieving physical immortality and thus inaugurating a new type of humanity.

The case of Cyrus Teed is so curious and interesting that I will close with it.[55] He was a physician and alchemist in Utica, a flourishing city in Central New York, who was visited by an angel in 1869. The angel revealed a great cosmological secret: that the earth is a concave sphere, and that we live on the inner surface of it. The sphere is about 100 miles thick, and going outwards, or from our point of view downwards, it consists of seventeen layers: five geological strata, five mineral layers, and seven metallic shells, the outermost one being pure gold. Going inwards or

---

[55] Primary sources are Koresh [Cyrus R. Teed], *The Cellular Cosmology, or The Earth a Concave Sphere* (Estero: The Koreshan Unity, Inc., 1983); Sara Weber Rea, *The Koreshan Story* (Estero: Guiding Star Publishing House, 1994); Cyrus R. Teed, *Illumination of Koresh. Marvelous Experience of the Great Alchemist Thirty Years Ago, at Utica, N.Y.* (Estero: Guiding Star Publishing House [1900]). The following account is summarized from Joscelyn Godwin, *Upstate Cauldron: Eccentric Spiritual Movements in Early New York State* (Albany: State University of New York Press, 2015), pp. 217–27. The same book includes chapters on Jemima Wilkinson, Joseph Smith, Andrew Jackson Davis, John Murray Spear, Thomas Lake Harris, H.P. Blavatsky, and Paschal Beverly Randolph.

upwards from the surface on which we live, there are seven spheres corresponding to the planets, then a solar sphere, and at the center a star. This astral center has dark and light sides, and its rotation is the cause of night and day.

After his revelation, Teed assumed the name of Koresh and devoted the rest of his life to teaching his doctrine of 'Koreshanity' and gathering disciples.[56] If you raise objections to his cosmology, you can be sure he had an answer to them, and besides, in 1897 he proved by experiment that the earth's surface is concave.[57] On a long stretch of beach in Florida using state-of-the-art surveying technique, his team extended a perfectly straight 'air line'. It began eleven feet above the ground, and after four miles it met the surface, just as he predicted. More relevant to our subject is the Koreshan vision of a closed system in perpetual motion. When animal, vegetable, or mineral matter decays on Earth, its waste products flow upwards or inwards to the 'great alchemico-organic battery' of the central star, which sends them back as spiritual substances to the outer shells. The seven planetary spheres are loci at which this spirit-matter accumulates on its way up and down, or in and out.

In Koreshan doctrine, humanity is a microcosm of all this. Jesus Christ is its central star, and the seven planets correspond to seven types of man. When we die, our bodies join in the general alchemical interchange of matter and spirit, while our consciousness waits in the spirit world for its next embodiment. But our true destiny is to become as Jesus was. His bodily nature was unique because he had been conceived without sexual intercourse. At his death, his body was dissolved and became the Holy Ghost, to be absorbed by all who received it. In Koresh's Christology, as in Rudolf Steiner's, this was an event of cosmic importance, without which there would be no hope for the world.

As for method, forming a utopian community was more important to Koresh than any particular practice. He banned alcohol and tobacco, supported all the progressive causes, but the core of his method was sublimation of the sexual urge. The nineteenth-century horror of wasting or losing the semen found its explanation in the esoteric doctrine: that retaining the semen was essential for regeneration—at least for males. For

---

[56] There is no connection between Teed's movement and the Branch Davidian movement of David Koresh (1959–1993). Both adopted the biblical name of Cyrus, King of Persia and restorer of the Jews to Israel.
[57] There is an amusing account in John Michell, *Eccentric Lives and Peculiar Notions* (London: Thames & Hudson, 1984), pp. 41–50.

woman, Koresh promised that in time menstruation will cease and the substances now wasted will be used to improve her brain. To those who feared that without sex the human race would die out, Koresh only needed to point to Jesus's birth as proof that God was perfectly capable of peopling the earth by other means.

Like most prophets, Koresh saw himself as the herald of a new age. By his calculation it would last 24,000 years, corresponding to a precessional cycle. By the end of it, humanity will have rid itself of social, political, and economic ills and regained its birthright. The Koreshan emphasis on physical immortality puts it on the side of the non-dualist cosmologies, in which spirit and matter are different states of a Universal Substance. Otherwise his system has neatly turned the Standard Model inside out. Both are spherical and limited, the Standard Model by the central earth and the starry sphere, the Koreshan by the central star and the golden shell. Both contain planetary spheres through which the soul makes its ascent. From a scientific viewpoint, both models are as wrong as can be, but if there is truth in any of our sources, that is the last thing we need to worry about.

The Transformational Techniques of Huber Astrology

Sue Lewis

Abstract: While Bruno and Louise Huber were developing their Astrological Psychology, they assisted with the foundation of the Arcane School in Geneva and worked for three years with Roberto Assagioli at his Psychosynthesis Institute in Florence. Their non-predictive method blends astrology with psychosynthesis as a way to self-realization that resembles the pillars of ascent of Kabbalah and Neoplatonism. Like Jung, Assagioli concealed his esoteric interests to preserve his professional reputation, and Huber astrologers do not usually class themselves as magicians. Nevertheless their engagement with the evolution of the will through the shifting borders of the mind and its memories by way of learning triangles in the Natal Chart, as well as Moon Node Astrology, is similar to the use of celestial magic as a way to self-empowerment practised by members of the Hermetic Order of the Golden Dawn. This paper will examine the Hubers' astrology within the context of Neoplatonic, Kabbalistic and magical philosophy.

This is a revision of a paper presented at the Sophia conference on 'Celestial Magic' in June 2013, during the thirtieth anniversary celebrations of the English Huber School, now known as the Astrological Psychology Association (APA).[1] Astrological psychology is a direct translation of Astrologische-Psychologisches, the title given by Bruno and Louise Huber to the parent Astrologische-Psychologisches Institut (API) they founded in Zürich in 1964. The word 'magic' is not usually applied to Huber astrology, so my reasons for presenting its transformational techniques at this conference require some explanation.

Professor Wouter Hanegraaff of the University of Amsterdam has devoted some thirteen pages to unpicking what we might understand by magic under the subheading 'Tainted Terminologies'. The most relevant section of this overview draws on *De occulta philosophia* (1533), by the Renaissance magus Cornelius Agrippa (1486–1535):

---

[1] The English Huber School, now APA, was founded on 8 June 1983, at 12:30pm BST, in London, UK, at http://astrologicalpsychology.org.

Sue Lewis, 'The Transformational Techniques of Huber Astrology', *Celestial Magic,* special issue of *Culture and Cosmos*, Vol. 19, nos. 1 and 2, 2015, pp. 207–23.
www.CultureAndCosmos.org

Magic was explicitly presented here as the 'ancient wisdom', whose reputation needed to be purified from the common association with illicit practices of evil sorcery, superstition, and demonism. Agrippa adopted Reuchlin's categorization of the *ars miraculorum* as consisting of three levels (physics, astrology, and magic, the latter subdivided into a negative *goetia* and a positive *theurgia*), but he made *magia* into the umbrella term, subdividing it into (1) 'natural magic', concerned with the sublunary world of the elements, (2) 'celestial magic', pertaining to the realm above the moon but below the fixed stars, and mostly concerned with numbers and astrology, and (3) 'ceremonial magic', concerned with demonic and angelic entities above the fixed stars, and dominated by kabbalah.[2]

Professor Arthur Versluis of the University of Michigan has depicted astrology as 'standing midway between magic and mysticism… a complex union of Platonic philosophy with Christian herbal and astrological medicine, bound up together in what we might call an astrological mystico-magic'. His comment, that 'through astrology, the sage might glimpse aspects of the future, might even alter what before looked like destiny', suggests perhaps that the astrologer who uses a combination of technique and insight to open the way to self-knowledge and aspires to add something to the way of world may be slightly more deserving of the title of magician than the traditional practitioner of horary or judicial astrology who follows a set of rules to answer specific questions or predict the future.[3] Theurgy, the positive, goodwill magic that concerns us here, has been defined by the American magician Israel Regardie (1907–1985) as: 'a quest spiritual and divine… a task of self-creation and reintegration, the bringing into human life of something eternal and enduring'.[4] Regardie, who brought the secret workings of Hermetic Order of the Golden Dawn out of the closet and into the public domain, also made the connection between modern psychology and ancient wisdom, insofar as both concern

---

[2] Wouter J. Hanegraaff, *Esotericism and the Academy: Rejected Knowledge in Western Culture* (Cambridge: Cambridge University Press, 2012), pp. 164–77 (pp. 175–76); Henry Cornelius Agrippa of Nettesheim, *Three Books of Occult Philosophy*, trans. James Freake, ed. Donald Tyson (Woodbury, MN: Llewellyn, 2007). Hanegraaff also refers to *De verbo mirifico* (1494) by the Christian Kabbalist, Johann Reuchlin (1455–1522) as one of Agrippa's sources.
[3] Arthur Versluis, *Magic and Mysticism: An Introduction to Western Esotericism* (Lanham, MD: Rowman & Littlefield, 2007), pp. 96–97.
[4] Israel Regardie, *The Tree of Life: An Illustrated Study in Magic*, 3rd edition, ed. Chic Cicero and Sandra Tabatha Cicero (Woodbury, MN: Llewellyn, 2010), p. 19.

themselves with 'spiritual development and synthesis'.[5] With reference to the analytical psychology of the Swiss therapist Carl Gustav Jung (1875–1961), about whom more is written below, Regardie expressed the view that:

> Analytical psychology and magic comprise... two halves or aspects of a single technical system. Just as the body and mind... are... dual manifestations of an interior dynamic 'something', so psychology and magic comprise similarly a single system whose goal is the integration of the human personality.[6]

The psychosynthesis of Italian therapist Roberto Assagioli (1888–1974), which had a formative influence on Huber astrology, is less widely known but similarly concerned with self-integration. Bearing the above qualifications in mind, the astrological psychology of Bruno and Louise Huber merits consideration under the heading 'Celestial Magic'.

Louise Huber (1924–2016) studied astrology in Stuttgart immediately after World War Two, and found traditional techniques of astrological interpretation woefully inadequate to the task of helping her fellow Germans to rebuild their lives. In search of a spiritual dimension, she took a correspondence course with the Arcane School, which had been established by the English Theosophist Alice Bailey (1880–1949) in 1923. Her Swiss tutor, Anny Huber-Wuhrmann, was the mother of Bruno Huber (1930–1999), whom she met in 1952 and married in 1953. Bruno had been studying astrology since 1947, and the scope of his reading ranged from classical astrologers to the English Theosophist and founder of the Astrological Lodge, Alan Leo (1860–1917). In his late teens, Bruno started an undergraduate course in physics at the University of Zürich, but soon transferred his allegiance to psychology. By the time he met Louise, he had reached the conclusion that:

> It was the ancient wisdom which provided me with the most fruitful approach to research into astrology. Esotericists explore the underlying structure and the intent which underpin the outward phenomenal appearance of life. That's how they hope to gain a glimpse of the pattern and purpose of nature's ways.[7]

---

[5] Israel Regardie, *The Middle Pillar: The Balance Between Mind and Magic*, 3rd edition, ed. Chic Cicero and Sandra Tabatha Cicero (Woodbury, MN: Llewellyn, 2004), p. 4.
[6] Regardie, *The Middle Pillar*, p. 5.
[7] Bruno Huber and Louise Huber, *The Development of Astrological Psychology*, trans. Agnes Shellens and Heather Ross (Knutsford: API [UK], 2006), p. 5. The

210 The Transformational Techniques of Huber Astrology

Bruno and Louise shared an interest in non-predictive astrology that nourished psyche and soul, by illuminating those underlying patterns that give meaning and direction to an individual's life in a topsy-turvy world.

From 1956–58, Bruno and Louise administered the new European centre of the Arcane School in Geneva, and Bailey's esoteric astrology exerted a profound and lasting influence on their work: they adopted her introduction of esoteric as well as traditional planetary rulerships.[8] Louise's meditations across the zodiac sign axes (pairs of opposite signs) at Full Moon, and through the Moon signs, which aim to raise awareness and activity from the level personal rulership to the transpersonal level expressed through the esoteric ruler, owe much to Bailey, as do exercises with the ego and transpersonal planets discussed later in this paper.[9] The Hubers put into practice Bailey's observation that 'astrologers will eventually find it necessary to cast three horoscopes' by using Moon Node and House Charts along with the Natal Chart for comprehensive individual interpretations, reflecting on karma – meaning unfinished business we have brought into this life to complete – and extending insight into how we experience the attractions and stresses of our surrounding environment, revealing interweaving inner and outer paths on our journey to self-realization.[10] This triple vision was underpinned by a series of

---

two articles in this booklet are the primary source of historical background leading to the founding of API and are considered in greater detail in Sue Lewis, *Astrological Psychology, Western Esotericism, and the Transpersonal* (Knutsford: HopeWell, 2015), pp. 15–38.

[8] Alice A. Bailey, *Esoteric Astrology, A Treatise on the Seven Rays*, Vol. 3 (New York and London: Lucis, 1951), p. 68. The traditional (T), modern (M) and esoteric (E) rulers of the signs are: Aries: T Mars, E Mercury; Taurus: T Venus, E Vulcan; Gemini: T Mercury, E Venus; Cancer: T Moon, E Neptune; Leo: T Sun, E Sun; Virgo: T Mercury, E Moon; Libra: T Venus, E Uranus; Scorpio: T Mars, M Pluto, E Mars; Sagittarius: T Jupiter, E Earth; Capricorn: T Saturn, E Saturn; Aquarius: T Saturn, M Uranus, E Jupiter; Pisces: T Jupiter, M Neptune, E Pluto.

[9] For Full Moon meditations, see Louise Huber, *Reflections and Meditations on the Signs of the Zodiac*, trans. Moray Patterson (Tempe, AZ: American Federation of Astrologers, 1984); for 'The Moon as our Feeling Nature', and 'The Moon in the Zodiac Signs', see Bruno Huber and Louise Huber, *The Planets and their Psychological Meaning: Capabilities and Tools of the Personality*, trans. Heather Ross, ed. Barry Hopewell (Knutsford: HopeWell, 2006), pp. 239–84.

[10] Alice A. Bailey, *A Treatise on White Magic or The Way of the Disciple* (New York and London: Lucis, 1951), p. 439. For 'Working with the Three Charts', see Joyce Hopewell, *The Living Birth Chart: Astrological Psychology: A Practical Workbook* (Knutsford: HopeWell, 2008), pp. 183–214.

Theosophical concepts; karma, reincarnation, the existence of Akashic records of past lives, the belief in the divine fragment at the central core of each human being, and the understanding of the Will as a 'principle of abstract eternal motion, or its ensouling essence'.[11]

Notwithstanding their inspirational content, Bruno was not entirely satisfied with Bailey's channelled astrology nor with the lofty spiritual orientation of the Arcane School in Geneva, whose leading initiates were reluctant to engage with the psychological needs of their disciples. He found the more grounded approach he was seeking in Assagioli's psychosynthesis and, from 1959–62, the Hubers worked at his Istituto di Psicosintesi in Florence, where they had many opportunities to talk to clients and undertake statistical tests using case histories.

Assagioli's Jewish mother and Catholic wife were both Theosophists, and he was attuned to religious mysticism or spirituality that extended beyond the boundaries of any particular dogma or faith, although he kept his meditative practice in a separate compartment from his therapeutic work, which he approached from a scientific perspective.[12] In 1930, he shared a platform with Bailey at a pre-Eranos summer school in Ascona on the banks of Lake Maggiore.[13] Seven years later, he and the pioneering astrologer Dane Rudhyar (1895–1985) became friends, following publication of Rudhyar's seminal work, *The Astrology of Personality* (1936), which brought together astrology and analytical psychology.[14] Rudhyar, writing about astrology and Regardie about magic independently made comparisons with analytical psychology, the term adopted by Jung, in 1913, to distinguish his psychological science from the psychoanalysis of Sigmund Freud (1856–1939), whereas Assagioli replaced analysis by

---

[11] Alan Leo, *The Art of Synthesis*, 6th edition (1912; New York: Astrologer's Library, 1978), pp. 255–84.

[12] Jean Hardy, *A Psychology with a Soul: Psychosynthesis in Evolutionary Context* (London: Arkana, 1989), pp. 2, 11, 15.

[13] Hans Thomas Hakl, *Eranos: An Alternative Intellectual History of the Twentieth Century*, trans. Christopher McIntosh with Hereward Tilton (Montreal and Kingston: McGill University Press, 2013), pp. 28–30.

[14] Deniz Ertan, *Dane Rudhyar: His Music, Thought, and Art* (Rochester, NY: Rochester University Press, 2009), p. xxiv; Dane Rudhyar, *The Astrology of Personality: A Re-formulation of Astrological Concepts and Ideals in Terms of Contemporary Psychology and Philosophy*, 3rd edition (Garden City, NY: Doubleday, 1970), pp. 85–113.

synthesis.[15] Both Jung and Assagioli studied and learned from Freud's sexual theory but reacted to its limitations by developing therapeutic methods for working with the whole person, body, mind and soul.

It is important to recognize that, as Assagioli and the Hubers worked together in the late 1950s, psychosynthesis was incorporated into the Huber method at inception, and that the subsequent influence of Jung resulted largely from posthumous publication of his *Memories, Dreams, Reflections* (1961).[16] This provided the Hubers with an autobiographical journey against which to demonstrate the effective working of their method of Age Progression through the twelve houses, spending six years in each over a seventy-two-year cycle, during which intensity curves through the quadrants and houses highlight periods of introspection at low points and increased outgoing activity around the cusps of houses, with a surge of pressure immediately before each of the four cardinal angles.[17]

Given his appreciation of Rudhyar's alignment of analytical psychology with modern astrology, Assagioli was naturally interested in the possibility of an astrological psychosynthesis and readily contributed to the Huber project. As a doctor and psychiatrist, he built up profiles of human consciousness through experiment and observation, and devised exercises balancing polarities and using triangles to achieve 'synthesis between the

---

[15] Andrew Samuels, Bani Shorter, and Fred Plaut, *A Critical Dictionary of Jungian Analysis* (London and New York: Routledge and Kegan Paul, 1986), p. 21, dates Jung's adoption of the term 'analytical psychology' referred to by Rudhyar in The *Astrology of Personality* and Regardie in the *The Middle Pillar*. Hardy describes the development of psychosynthesis in the 1920s and 1930s on pp. 17–18 of *A Psychology with a Soul*.

[16] Carl Gustav Jung, *Memories, Dreams, Reflections*, ed. Aneila Jaffé, trans. Richard and Clara Winston, 3rd edition (Glasgow: Collins Fount, 1977).

[17] Bruno and Louise Huber, *LifeClock: The Huber Method of Timing in the Horoscope* (York Beach, ME: Samuel Weiser, 1994), Vol. 2, pp. 173–204. Jung was born on 26 July 1875 in Kesswil, Switzerland. The Rodden Rating C reflects a birth time span from 17:20, with a Capricorn Ascendant to 17:29 with 3 degrees Aquarius ascending. Huber places the Ascendant on the cusp of Aquarius. For more on Age Progression and cosmic cycles, see *LifeClock*, pp. 23–52. The house intensity curve uses Golden Mean proportions, and stress points behind the angles of the Ascendant, Midheaven or Medium Coeli, Descendant, and Imum Coeli correspond to the Gauquelin effect – see Bruno Huber and Louise Huber, *Transformation: Astrology as a Spiritual Path*, trans. Heather Ross, ed. Barry Hopewell (Knutsford: HopeWell, 2008), pp. 44–47.

stages, qualities, and levels of love and will'.[18] As a scholar, he drew analogies with the insights of great philosophers.[19] In a collection of basic writings on psychosynthesis, published in 1965 but written over many years, Assagioli introduced the allegory of the cave, in which Plato (ca. 428–ca. 348 BCE) depicts unenlightened humanity as prisoners chained in a dark cavern, unable to endure the light.[20] This state of being precedes the arduous process of transmutation through which the individual must pass before opening up to the light of self-realization, 'a state of consciousness characterized by joy, serenity, inner security, a sense of calm power, clear understanding, and radiant love'.[21] Similarly, Huber astrology recognizes three tiers of planetary operation – asleep when reacting automatically, awakening with the dawning awareness of a need for change, and fully awakened at a level of integrity and discernment, in alignment with the soul.[22]

Kocku von Stuckrad begins his study of Western esotericism with 'Footnotes to Plato' and ends with Assagioli, initially observing that:

> Symbolic correspondence—the ties of the soul in Plato—remains a prominent part of astrology right up to the present day. Even the conception of the cosmos as a living being in which all parts are interconnected is an unshakeable foundation of esotericism and philosophy of nature ever since Plato.[23]

Von Stuckrad concludes by stating the intention of Assagioli, and the transpersonal movement he joined in the 1960s, 'to replace the predominant medical approach of psychology, even more so of psychiatry, with a model that emphasizes the healthy rather than the pathological person' and that 'sees the person's spiritual needs as an indispensable

---

[18] See the foreword by Piero Ferrucci on his study of human consciousness in Hardy, *A Psychology with a Soul*, p. xi; Roberto Assagioli, *The Act of Will: A Guide to Self-Actualization and Self-Realization* (Woking: David Platts, 1999), pp. 100–5, on polarities and synthesis. Assagioli's fundamental archetypes are love and will.
[19] See Hardy, pp. 121–23 on Assagioli's debt to Plato.
[20] Plato, *Republic*, 2 Vols, trans. Paul Shorey (Cambridge, MA: Harvard University Press, 1937), VII.I–II.
[21] Roberto Assagioli, *Psychosynthesis: A Manual of Principles and Techniques*, 2nd edition (Wellingborough: Turnstone, 1975), pp. 48–49.
[22] Huber and Huber, *The Planets*, pp. 154–57.
[23] Kocku von Stuckrad, *Western Esotericism: A Brief History of Secret Knowledge*, trans. Nicholas Goodrick-Clarke (London: Equinox, 2005), p. 13.

aspect of their total personality'. Stuckrad categorizes this movement as one of the contemporary fields of discourse taking forward the esoteric project.[24] This is the context into which I place Huber astrology.

Like the psychological astrology of Liz Greene, which interfaces with Jungian psychology and is referred to by Patrick Curry, Huber grew out of the Theosophical astrology of Leo to meet the needs of the New Age, while also bearing characteristics of earlier Neoplatonic and Hermetic astrologies that crystallized in and around Alexandria during the first centuries CE with their emphasis on self-knowledge and self-transformation.[25] Notably, Curry cites Hermetic rather than Gnostic influence, with which I incontestably agree, but this choice needs clarification. Whereas Hermeticists and Gnostics were equally concerned with 'gnosis' – meaning revealed knowledge not obtained through systematic reasoning – the Gnostic view that 'our world is the result of a tragic split within the divine world' has been described by Roelof van den Broek as 'anticosmic': 'Gnostics considered the planets and the signs of the zodiac as evil powers, which the soul on its way back to its origin could pass only if it had true gnosis', by being one of a chosen few granted access to divinity.[26] In contrast, Hermetic philosophical doctrine 'became the core of a cosmic religiosity, which could lead to the mystical experience of falling together with the universe', and 'the Hermetic way finally led to initiation in the divine mystery'.[27] So, from the Hermetic viewpoint, humanity could be empowered, capable of self-recovery and of contributing to world regeneration through self-will, with the planets and signs of the celestial world acting as helpful intermediaries.

Huber astrology extends the five relational aspects between zodiac signs of the 360-degree circle established by Ptolemy, the second-century Alexandrian astronomer and geographer, to include not only the 0-degree conjunction, 60-degree sextile, 90-degree square, 120-degree trine, and

---

[24] Stuckrad, *Western Esotericism*, pp. 145–46.
[25] Patrick Curry, 'Varieties of Astrological Experience', in Roy Willis and Patrick Curry, *Astrology Science and Culture: Pulling Down the Moon* (Oxford and New York: Berg, 2004), pp. 65–76 (pp. 72–73), explores the correlation between Neoplatonic/Hermetic astrology and psychological astrology without mentioning Huber.
[26] Roelof van den Broek, 'Gnosticism and Hermetism in Antiquity: Two Roads to Salvation', in *Gnosis and Hermeticism: From Antiquity to Modern Times*, ed. Roelof van den Broek and Wouter J. Hanegraaff (Albany, NY: SUNY Press, 1998), pp. 1–20 (pp. 1, and 9).
[27] Broek, pp. 10, 12.

180-degree opposition of which he approved, but also the 30-degree semi-sextile and the 150-degree quincunx brought into the correspondence between musical instruments and zodiacal aspects by Marsilio Ficino (1433–1499).[28] Huber attributes consciousness-raising qualities to semi-sextiles and quincunxes, which pave the way to psychosynthesis, but does not use the divisive semi-squares and sesqui-quadrates introduced by Johannes Kepler (1571–1630) and favoured by many modern astrologers. The Huber figure of 30-degree aspects fanning out to the circumference from the conjunction of Cancer and Leo, traditionally ruled by Moon and Sun, extending 30 degrees to Gemini and Virgo ruled by Mercury, 60 degrees to Taurus and Libra ruled by Venus, 90 degrees to Aries and Scorpio traditionally ruled by Mars, 120 degrees to Pisces and Sagittarius traditionally ruled by Jupiter, and 150 and 180 degrees to Aquarius and Capricorn ruled by Saturn, creates a symmetrical pattern connecting signs, planets, and aspects.[29] This is especially effective if coloured to highlight the elements of the sign glyphs – red for fire, green for earth, yellow for air, and blue for water – and the lines of the aspects – orange for conjunction, green for semi-sextile and quincunx, blue for sextile and trine, and red for square and opposition. Artistic presentation, attracting the gaze inwards to illuminate underlying patterns, plays an important part in Huber interpretation, but the inconjunct green aspects it introduces deviate from Ptolemy's preoccupation with perfect cosmic order, signalling a dynamic shift of emphasis to encourage growth and transformation.

After Alexandria comes Florence, where Ficino was a towering figure of the Renaissance. The son of a doctor, he transferred his allegiance from Aristotelian medicine to Plato's philosophy, and became the Medicis' translator of Greek texts into Latin, to which he added commentaries. These included the *Corpus Hermeticum*, *Dialogues* of Plato, *Hymns* of Orpheus, *Sayings* of Zoroaster and works by the pagan Neoplatonists of the third to fifth centuries CE.[30] Besides being a scholarly translator, Ficino was a priest, musician, astrologer, and writer, who presented himself as a

---

[28] Claudius Ptolemy, *Tetrabiblos*, trans. F. E. Robbins, Loeb Classical Library, 435 (Cambridge, MA: Harvard University Press, 1940; repr. 1994), I, 12–16, pp. 69–79; Angela Voss, ed., *Marsilio Ficino*, Western Esoteric Masters Series (Berkeley, CA: North Atlantic Books, 2006), pp. 184–86.

[29] Bruno Huber, Louise Huber, and Michael Alexander Huber, *Aspect Pattern Astrology: A New Holistic Horoscope Interpretation Method*, trans. Heather Ross (Knutsford: HopeWell, 2005), pp. 23–24, 47; Lewis, *Astrological Psychology*, pp. 8, 86–87.

[30] Voss, *Marsilio Ficino*, pp. xiii–xv.

'doctor of souls' in the foreword to his *Liber de Vita* (1489).[31] In part three, 'On Making your Life Agree with the Heavens', he encourages the use of powerful colours for creating a talismanic map of the universe to attract auspicious planetary energies:

> There are three universal and singular colours of the world: green, gold, and sapphire, and they are dedicated to the three Graces of heaven. Green, of course, is for Venus and the Moon, moist, as it were, for the moist ones, and appropriate to things of birth, especially mothers. There is no question that gold is the colour of the Sun, and no stranger to Jove and Venus either. But we dedicate the sapphire colour especially to Jove, to whom the sapphire itself is said to be consecrated. This is why lapis lazuli was given its colour (sapphire), because of its Jovial power against Saturn's black bile. It has a special place among doctors, and it is born with gold, distinct with gold marks, so it is a companion of gold just as Jupiter is the companion of the Sun. The stone ultramarine has a similar power, possessing a similar colour with a little green.[32]

Given Christian distrust of astrology, 'as a manifestation of human pride that seeks to understand destiny and the hand of God in ways that human beings allegedly were not meant to', in the words of Versluis, it is no surprise that Ficino struggled to get his astral magic past Papal inspection, and hid behind classical authorities.[33] Notwithstanding, this was an influential book in the sixteenth century, and again in the twentieth. Ficino inspired the healer and medical theorist Paracelsus (1493–1541), much of his *Book of Life* was reproduced in Agrippa's *Occult Philosophy* and, in 1548, a translation from Latin into Italian was marketed in a pocket edition as an everyday guide to healthy living.[34] Referring to the revival of interest in Ficino during the twentieth century, Michael Allen alludes to 'striking parallels to current new age therapies' and notes 'his holistic approach to health and to the importance of our inner sense of well-being and of well-

---

[31] Marsilio Ficino, *Book of Life*, trans. Charles Boer, 2nd edition (Woodstock, CT: Spring, 1996), p. 1.
[32] Ficino, *Book of Life*, p. 153.
[33] Versluis, *Magic and Mysticism*, p. 96; 'The Apology of Marsilio Ficino', in *Book of Life*, pp. 184–89.
[34] Nicholas Goodrick-Clarke, *The Western Esoteric Traditions: A Historical Perspective* (New York, NY: Oxford University Press, 2008), p. 58 on Agrippa and Ficino, and pp. 80–81 on Paracelsus and Ficino; Sandra Cavallo and Tessa Storey, *Healthy Living in Late Renaissance Italy* (Oxford: Oxford University Press, 2013), pp. 18–19.

being's power over the external world'.³⁵ It is easy to find correspondences between Ficino and Huber regarding their use of all seven aspects, emphasis on relationships between planets and colours, and concern for the health of body and soul. Both astrologies belong to the Neoplatonic and Hermetic streams. Ficino's 'astrological powers and influences, ever-changing in their dance', as Allen describes them, become Huber learning triangles, although Bruno and Louise credited more immediate sources of inspiration.

Florentine art had such an impact on Bruno that he toyed with the idea of becoming an artist. This experience awakened him to the importance of the initial visual impression of the astrological chart. Like a lotus, it opens out from the centre, and its five levels from the centre to the periphery can be seen in the charts of Bruno and Louise, who always introduced themselves to their students by sharing their horoscopes. According to Leo, whose advice the Hubers followed:

> Every human being is a 'Divine Fragment', a centre within the universal divine consciousness, inseparably united with every other centre, and all blended in one ultimately by the universal Life and Consciousness in which they are centred... The 'Divine Fragment'... may be represented as a small blank circle in the centre of every horoscope...³⁶

Moving outwards from the divine fragment in the centre, the innermost circle contains the aspect structure representing inner motivation, and here the astrologer ponders for a few minutes to allow a picture of the person behind the chart to emerge before starting to analyse coherence, colour, shape, and aspect patterns. Bruno's chart conveys a mountain range, while Louise's displays a large plateau, although the dominant triangles in Bruno's extend into four-sided figures, emphasizing his urge to convert research and learning into a system, while the incomplete trapeze in Louise's stimulated her drive 'to create something active and enduring from her understanding of the processes of life'.³⁷ Both display significant green quincunxes, minds working together to solve problems and raise awareness.

---

³⁵ Michael J. B. Allen, 'Ficino, Marsilio, b. 19.10.1433 Figline, d. 1.10.1499 Careggi (Florence)', in *Dictionary of Gnosis and Western Esotericism*, ed. Wouter J. Hanegraaff, with Antoine Faivre, Roelof van den Broek, and Jean-Pierre Brach (Leiden: Brill, 2006), pp. 360–67 (p. 364).
³⁶ Alan Leo, *Esoteric Astrology* (Rochester, VT: Destiny, 1983), pp. 241–42.
³⁷ Huber et al., *Aspect Pattern Astrology*, p. 208.

218 The Transformational Techniques of Huber Astrology

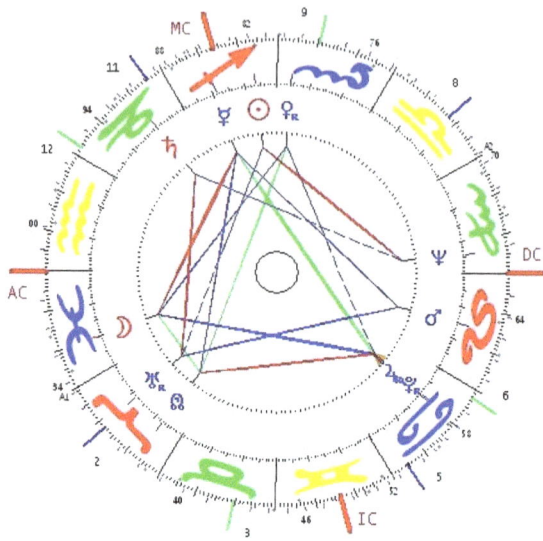

Fig. 1: Bruno Huber, b. 29 Nov. 1930, 12:55, Zürich, Switzerland (RR:A).[38]

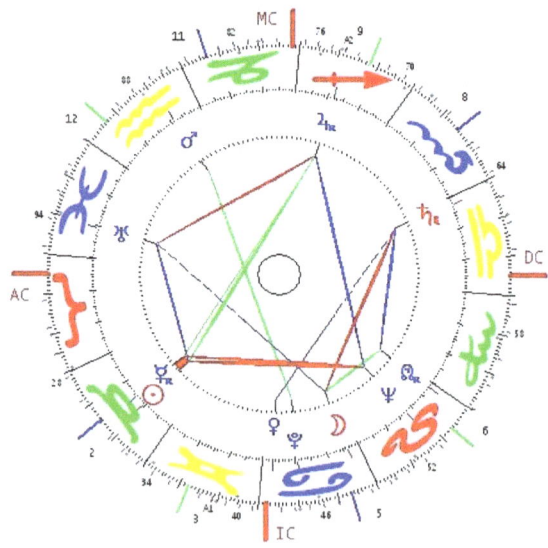

Fig. 2. Louise Huber, b. 10 May 1924, 03:15, Bamberg, Germany (RR:A).[39]

---

[38] Repr. using MegaStar from www.catharsoftware.com.
[39] Repr. using MegaStar from www.catharsoftware.com.

On the psychological effect of colour, Bruno and Louise cite Johann Wolfgang von Goethe (1749–1832), Friedrich Wilhelm Ostwald (1853–1932) and Aemilius Müller as creators of the colour wheel, and a key source of inspiration was *Concerning the Spiritual in Art* (1911) by Wassily Kandinsky (1866–1944), the Russian abstract artist working in Germany.[40] Kandinsky described the founder of the Theosophical Society, Helena Petrovna Blavatsky (1831–1891), as a torchbearer and had much to say about colour, shape, movement, and the inner person:

> Colour provides a whole wealth of possibilities of her own, and when combined with form, yet a further series of possibilities. And all of these will be expressions of inner need.[41]
> The life of the spirit may be fairly represented in diagram as a large acute-angled triangle divided horizontally into unequal parts with the narrowest segment uppermost.
> The whole triangle is moving slowly, almost invisibly forwards and upwards.[42]

The mobile state described by Kandinsky corresponds to the three-coloured learning triangle, an innovation of astrological psychology that illuminates the cycle of growth. There are four sizes, the smallest affecting a specific segment of life and the largest expressing the core personality.[43] A person with a small learning triangle, comprising a red square, a blue sextile, and a green semi-sextile, often experiences inner tension that results in a need to change something in the outer environment. Someone with a medium learning triangle, comprising a blue trine, a square, and a semi-sextile, may be nudged out of complacency by conflicts and problems in the environment. A large learning triangle, comprising a green quincunx, a sextile, and a square, suggests preoccupation with expansion of consciousness, learning and development, and an ambivalent attitude to the environment. A dominant triangle, comprising a quincunx, a trine, and a square, encompasses the centre of the chart, so that issues of growth and learning are wholly life-transforming. A point of conflict arises where the square aspect meets either the sextile or the trine, and the green aspect acts as a trouble-shooter, seeking a solution. If the sequence of blue/red,

---

[40] Huber and Huber, *Transformation*, p. 154.
[41] Wassily Kandinsky, *Concerning the Spiritual in Art*, trans. M. T. H. Sadler (Mineola, NY: Dover, 1977), pp. 13, 33.
[42] Kandinsky, *Concerning the Spiritual in Art*, p. 6.
[43] Huber et al., *Aspect Pattern Astrology*, pp. 198–209.

red/green, green/blue angles runs clockwise the learning process will take longer than if it runs in an anticlockwise direction – which is direct in astronomical time.

Beyond the inner circle of the aspect structure is the circle of the planets, and here Huber interpretation of Saturn radically differs from Ficino's reflections on the melancholy scholar.[44] The Huber Saturn represents the body and the mother figure, and bears a striking similarity to the *Shekhinah*, as the 'lower waters' of *Malkhut* rising to the 'upper waters' of the 'sea of *Binah*', the two feminine poles of Kabbalah.[45] In Bruno's model of an amphora – a narrow-necked open flask – the three ego planets, Saturn, Moon, and the Sun, rise sequentially up the middle pillar with Saturn at the base, while in the illustrated hierarchy of planets, the three ego planets occupy a central band, with Saturn on the fixed column or pillar of form, one rung lower than Binah on the Tree of Kabbalah. Professor Les Lancaster has highlighted similarities between the Tree of Kabbalah and the psychosynthesis egg diagram:

> Emphasis on integration is a primary imperative in Kabbalah. Unification of the levels of the soul is just one dimension of that global process of transformation that is seen by kabbalists as their major task...
> The name that Assagioli gave to his system of therapy, psychosynthesis, suggests that its goals bear comparison with those more cosmological objectives of Kabbalah... Assagioli seems to have drawn on the kabbalistic understanding of the divisions of the soul. He posited three realms of the unconscious: a lower unconscious, identified with bodily functions, a middle unconscious dealing with present experiences and their relation to 'I'; and a higher unconscious concerned with intuitive and spiritual functions. Psychosynthesis is directed to the integration of these levels, and especially to forging synthesis between the personal self and the transpersonal self.[46]

Lancaster's comparison can be extended to the Huber hierarchy of planets with its three tiers. The lower life-sustaining functions correspond to Venus in the fixed column to the left, expressing a love of harmony, Mars in the cardinal column to the right, epitomizing action, and Mercury and Jupiter in the middle, mutable column, representing the learning and

---

[44] Ficino, *Book of Life*, pp. 6–33; Raymond Klibansky, Erwin Panofsky, and Fritz Saxl, *Saturn and Melancholy: Studies in the History of Natural Philosophy, Religion and Art* (London: Nelson, 1964), pp. 250–59.
[45] Brian L. Lancaster, *The Essence of Kabbalah*, 2nd edition (London: Arcturus, 2006), p. 110.
[46] Lancaster, *The Essence of Kabbalah*, pp. 40–41.

experience that underpin growth. In the central tier are the three ego planets, Saturn corresponding to the body and sense of security, Moon to the feelings and desire for contact, and Sun to the mind and sense of self. Along the upper tier are the transpersonal planets, Uranus as creative intelligence, Neptune as unconditional love, and Pluto as spiritual will.

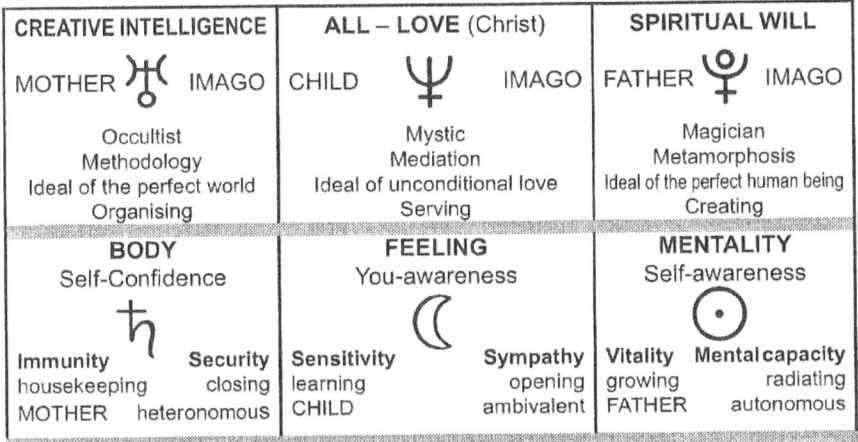

Fig 3. Planetary Table, representing (from left to right) at the higher, spiritual level, the transpersonal planets, Uranus, Neptune, and Pluto and, at the middle level, the personal, ego planets, Saturn, Moon, and Sun.[47]

Citing Assagioli's psychosynthesis and Bailey's esoteric astrology, Huber asserts that 'transformation of the threefold personality is an important precondition for spiritual development', and adapts the first three of five initiations related by Bailey to the life of Christ: '1. Birth in Bethlehem; 2. Baptism in Jordan; 3. Transfiguration on Mount Carmel; 4. Crucifixion on Mount Golgotha; and 5. Resurrection and Ascension'.[48] According to Bailey:

> At the first initiation, the control of the Ego over the physical body must have reached a high degree of attainment... The second initiation forms the crisis in the control of the astral body...[49]

---

[47] Repr. Huber, *The Planets*, p. 97.
[48] Huber and Huber, *The Planets*, pp. 91, 106.
[49] Alice A. Bailey, *Initiation Human and Solar*, 8th edition (1967), pp. 82–83, 85–86, repr. in *The Soul: The Quality of Life*, compiled by a student from the writings

At the third initiation the control of the soul-illumined mind is finally established, and the soul itself assumes the dominant position and not the phenomenal form.[50]

The first initiation, which describes the passage from Saturn to Uranus, was likened by Bruno and Louise to the Damascus experience, when sceptical Saul is transformed by a lightning flash into the apostle Paul; it is about letting go of personal fear and becoming responsible for more than just oneself.[51] The second initiation, from Moon to Neptune, engages with the feelings, and the sense of abandonment felt by Christ in the Garden of Gethsemane, when Judas sold him for thirty pieces of silver, Peter denied knowing him, and other disciples slept; by abandoning hope at one level, the initiate lets go of emotional attachment, accepts what comes along, is forgiving, attuned to the universe, and transmits unconditional love.[52] The third initiation, from Sun to Pluto, was compared to the Way of the Cross; it forces us to understand what is happening mentally, control our thoughts, and stride towards the top of the mountain where we discover a new light of understanding.[53]

While retaining Christian analogies, these three initiations adapt the path of spiritual ascent up the Jacob's ladder of kabbalists, or the ladder of St John Climacus of the Byzantine Church, to the transition from ego-centred to transpersonal or soul-centred living with the personal and transpersonal planets of the celestial sphere as intermediary guides. By incorporating three rather than five initiations, the Hubers followed the guidance of Assagioli, who clearly stated: 'Psychosynthesis does not aim nor attempt to give a metaphysical nor a theological explanation of the great Mystery – it leads to the door, but stops there'.[54]

Returning now to the five levels, beyond the centre, aspect structure, and planetary cycle, are the circles of signs connected with inheritance, and houses determining the sequence of age progression in relationship to planets and signs. Through the axes of the signs and houses more transformational journeys can be made.

---

of Alice A. Bailey and The Tibetan Master, Djwhal Khul (London and New York: Lucis, 1974), pp. 256–57.
[50] Alice A. Bailey, *The Rays and the Initiations, A Treatise on the Seven Rays*, Vol. 5, 2nd edition (1965), p. 674, repr. in *The Soul*, p. 259.
[51] Huber and Huber, *The Planets*, pp. 108–10.
[52] Huber and Huber, *The Planets*, pp. 111–14.
[53] Huber and Huber, *The Planets*, pp. 115–17.
[54] *Psychosynthesis*, pp. 6–7.

The aspiration to contribute to an eventual triumph of unity and light over separation and darkness has been repeated throughout history. This paper demonstrates ways in which, according to the Hubers, the planets of the celestial sphere can be instructive intermediaries, helping us to build bridges between ourselves, our planet, and the infinite space beyond, and how astrological psychology provides some modern solutions to an eternal quest.

Ancient Necromantic Rituals in Contemporary Celestial Magic

Jane Burton

[Selene the Moon cries:] 'How many times ... have you [the witch Medea] disorbed me with your incantations, making the night moonless so that you might practise your beloved witchcraft undisturbed'. Apollonius Rhodius, *Argonautica* 4.55.[1]

Baying [of Hounds] loud as that which rings at the grim gate of Dis [Haides] or from Hecate's escort [of black hounds] to the world above. Valerius Flaccus, *Argonautica* 6.110.[2]

Abstract: This paper explores how witches and spiritual mediums both focus on solar and lunar events as important times for their magical rituals, and also the importance they place upon zodiacal influences. Additionally, it will investigate if blood, either the practitioners own or symbolic, is utilised in basic magical rituals for necromantic purposes such as spirit divination. Necromantic rituals from Ancient Greek magical texts were compared with contemporary rituals employed by the informants, using primary and secondary sources. This is an ethnographic report of participant observation of spiritual mediums and witches living in the Valencia region of Spain. It was conducted over a one-year period of fieldwork study. Data was collected by way of a questionnaire and in a series of interviews with spiritual mediums and witches who practice spirit invocation for divinatpurposes.

Introduction

Pagans observe and celebrate the eight Sabbats of the 'Wheel of the Year' but there are indications that other celestial events are just as important. Nicholas Campion writes that a pagan astrology 'deals with magical ritual,

---

[1] Apollonius Rhodius, *Argonautica*, 4.55, available at https://frankzumbach.wordpress.com/2013/11/17/hekate-ii-via-theoi-greek-mythology/ [accessed 11 November 2016].
[2] Valerius Flaccus, *Argonautica*, 6.110, available at https://frankzumbach.wordpress.com/2013/11/17/hekate-ii-via-theoi-greek-mythology/ [accessed 11 November 2016].

Jane Burton, 'Ancient Necromantic Rituals in Contemporary Celestial Magic', *Celestial Magic*, special issue of *Culture and Cosmos*, Vol. 19, nos. 1 and 2, 2015, pp. 225–50.
www.CultureAndCosmos.org

intended to heal the self, or the community, through the use of astrological principles, calendar festivals, and auspicious timings.' Campion indicates that generally, pagan cosmology tends to be concerned less with which zodiac sign the Moon resides in at a given moment of magic ritual, but focuses more 'with "drawing down the moon" the invocation of benign lunar power.'[3] However, astrological tradition also suggests that when the Moon is in specific zodiac sign, its energies can be utilized in a certain ways, as a guide to action.

In 1959 Gerald Gardner, the founder of modern witchcraft, wrote a source book, *The Meaning of Witchcraft*, for witches from a witch's viewpoint. After being misquoted by reporters claiming 'that he'd [Gardner] admitted, too, that some witches find great power in new spilled blood', he reiterated in this text that witches did not use blood in their rites.[4] Gardner wrote, ' to clear up any possible misunderstanding, now or in the future, I will say it yet again; witches do not use the blood of sacrificed animals, birds, or any other living things in their rites'.[5] However, Gardner did go on to say that 'blood was sometimes used in ceremonial magic, but this is a different thing from witch rites'.[6]

In this study my informants are of Northern European and Spanish nationalities, are predominantly female, and are all living in the Valencia region of Spain. They consist of one small group of spiritual mediums and two small groups of witches; all three groups practice either magic and/or spiritual divination on a regular basis. The focus of this investigation is to explore the significance of celestial influences and the use of blood within their rituals for spirit divination.

Witches and Witchcraft
Gardner, along with fellow witch and co-founder of Gardnerian Wicca Doreen Valiente, was instrumental in bringing the contemporary pagan religion of Wicca to the attention of the general public. He was to write about Wicca's rituals and beliefs – and the reasons behind them – and to

---

[3] Nicholas Campion, *Astrology and Cosmology in the World's Religions* (New York: NYU Press: 2012), p. 198.
[4] Gerald Gardner, *The Meaning of Witchcraft* (England: IHO Books 2000), p. 226.
[5] Gardner, *The Meaning of Witchcraft*, p. 227.
[6] Gardner, *The Meaning of Witchcraft*, p. 227. See also Ronald Hutton, *The Triumph of the Moon: A History of Modern Pagan Witchcraft* (Oxford: Oxford University Press, 1999), especially pp. 241–71.

emphasise how these rituals and beliefs were harmless. Although there were some secrets, he insisted that he mustn't reveal these to the world.[7]

The term 'witch' for the purpose of this research is defined in the context described by Crowley along with Valiente's discussion of practitioners of magic. When trying to define the word 'witch', High Priestess Vivien Crowley suggests, 'Witches practice what is known as *the Craft*, a tradition of wisdom and ancient lore'.[8] And when discussing practitioners of magic, Doreen Valiente states,

> There is nothing really supernatural or supernormal, in the strict sense of these words. All is part of nature; but much of the realm of nature is 'occult', that is, hidden. The occultist, therefore, is one who ventures into these hidden realms in search of their secrets. He is not some wild eyed crank who goes around dressed in eccentric clothes in order to attract attention to himself.[9]

Wiccan witches adopted the eight Sabbats., the significant points in the solar year on which witches celebrate and connect with natural, psychic, solar, lunar and planetary tides and cycles.[10] One way in which they connect with nature and celestial bodies in their celebrations is in the energy-raising ritual of the 'cone of power'.[11] This is a ritual that the research subjects I investigated practised during the Sabbats and at other key celestial times when performing their magical divination. The ritual of the 'cone of power' involves forming a circle around lighted candles or fire. The participants dance around the circle until they feel that they have raised enough energy from the Moon. They then form a line with linked hands and rush towards the fire shouting the thing they desire most. This movement is repeated until they are exhausted, when they believe they have sent the spell to its destination.[12] With this in mind it can be considered that the witch and psychic medium may be one and the same, as

---

[7] Gerald Gardner, *Witchcraft Today* (1954; New York: Citadel Press, 1970, 2004), p. 13.
[8] Vivianne Crowley, *Wicca* (London: Thorsons, 1996), p. 3.
[9] Doreen Valiente, Forward to *Natural Magic* (1975; Sevenoaks: Robert Hale Limited, 2007), p. 7.
[10] Janet Farrar and Stewart Farrar, *The Witches' Bible, The Complete Witches' Handbook* (1981; London: Robert Hale Limited, 1984), p. 13.
[11] Doreen Valiente, *The Rebirth of Witchcraft* (Custer, WA: Phoenix Publishing, 1989), p. 45.
[12] Valiente, *The Rebirth of Witchcraft*, p. 45.

it has been suggested that they harness the influences of the universe to connect with the dead in the spirit world.[13]

Necromancy

There have been recent scholarly debates surrounding the history of necromancy in antiquity. Sarah Iles Johnston argues that the ancient Greeks and Romans almost always favoured a consultation with their chosen deities rather than communication with the dead and hardly ever, if at all, performed the art of necromancy.[14] Daniel Ogden maintains there is enough evidence to suggest that the ancient Greeks practiced necromancy, although possibly not altogether approved of by ancient Greek society. He states,

> The Greeks in general probably felt that one could not do much serious or lasting harm by the practice of necromancy proper other than to one-self. In certain modes and contexts, the ghosts may find the process undesirable and uncomfortable, but there is a limit to the damage one could do to those already dead.[15]

Within the *Greek Magical Papyri*, there is a specific spell for invoking the dead, simply titled the 'Eighth Book of Moses'.[16] In this ancient magical text it is suggested that necromancy was best performed at night, and also when the moon is full or at significant astrologically influenced times.[17]

Furthermore, the ancient Greek Homeric hymns, *The Odyssey* and *The Iliad*, mention the invocation of the dead and of the gods for the sole purpose of attaining knowledge of the future.[18] An example of this comes from *The Odyssey*, in which Odysseus made his journey to the underworld

---

[13] David Gordon Wilson, *Redefining Shamanisms: Spiritualist Mediums and other Traditional Shamans as Apprenticeship Outcomes* (London: Bloomsbury Publishing, 2013), p. 30.

[14] Sarah Iles Johnston, *Ancient Greek Divination, Blackwell Ancient Religions* (Malden, MA, and Oxford: Wiley-Blackwell, 2008), p. 97.

[15] Daniel Ogden, *Greek and Roman Necromancy* (Princeton, NJ: Princeton University Press, 2004), p. 267.

[16] Hans Dieter Betz, ed., *The Greek Magical Papyri in Translation including the Demotic Spells,* Vol. 1, second edition (1986; Chicago: University of Chicago Press, 1992), PGM XIII.1–343.

[17] Betz, *The Greek Magical Papyri*, PGM XIII.1–343.

[18] Homer, *The Iliad,* trans. George Chapman (Hertfordshire: Wordsworth Classics, 2003); and Homer, *The Odyssey*, trans. E. V. Rieu (Middlesex: Penguin Books, 1951).

in order to consult the ghost of the Theban prophet Tiresias.[19] Odysseus dug a ceremonial ditch as a method of entering and exiting Hades. Milk, honey, wine, or possibly the blood of a ram was offered as a libation to the ghosts. When other ghosts appeared, the urge to drink the blood was strong, wanting to taste life once more; however, Odysseus managed to restrain them with his sword. As soon as Tiresias appeared, Odysseus put away his sword and the seer he invoked delivered the prophecy; after the prophecy was delivered the restrained ghosts were allowed to drink the blood.[20]

Ogden defines necromancy as a way to gain information from the dead by invoking its spirit for the purpose of divination.[21] As Ogden records, the main features of necromantic rituals are that rituals take place at night and outdoors; are centred around a pit or a fire; libations of wine, water, honey, or oil are offered to the ghost/spirit; a sacrifice (usually a black sheep) is burnt as an offering; blood from the sacrificial animal is also offered to the ghost as a drink to restore them with the life force in order to aid communication with the living; prayers or incantations are said to aid their transition into this world from the spirit world; and, lastly, a sword is kept to hand to restrain the spirit (it is believed that ghosts are frightened by the bronze and iron of the sword).[22]

Whilst discussing magical rituals Campion proposed that, 'the basis of magic, including astral magic, is therefore that by uttering or writing a word, one actively invokes the thing that the word represents'.[23] Therefore, the ritual is not necessarily designed to invoke a human form, deity, demon or spirit for magical purposes. Thus, spiritual divination used by the members of the three study groups is defined as calling upon spirits for the purpose of foretelling the future, similar to Campion and Ogden's suggestions.

---

[19] Homer, *Odyssey*, 10.488, 11.13–149 (extracts). Cited from Daniel Ogden, *Magic, Witchcraft and Ghosts in the Greek and Roman Worlds: A Sourcebook* Oxford: Oxford University Press, 2002), pp. 179–82, source number 144.
[20] Georg Luck, trans., *Arcana Mundi: Magic and the Occult in the Greek and Roman Worlds: A Collection of Ancient Texts* (1985; Baltimore, MD: The John Hopkins University Press, 2006), p. 223.
[21] Ogden, *Greek and Roman Necromancy*, pp. xviii, xxii.
[22] Ogden, *Magic, Witchcraft and Ghosts*, p. 179.
[23] Campion, *Astrology and Cosmology In The World's Religions*, p. 93.

Literature Review

Arthur Edward Waite makes references to rituals using blood in conjunction with lunar and planetary cycles in his interpretation of various ancient and medieval magical rituals translated in *The Book of Ceremonial Magic*.[24] This nineteenth century text was republished in 1972 for the contemporary student of the occult. After explaining the table for planetary hours, Waite writes that the hours of Saturn and Mars – when they are in conjunction with the Moon – are best for preparation of rituals; he also suggests 'the hours of Saturn Mars and Venus are good for communication with spirits' and 'the hour of Saturn is best for invoking souls in hell'.[25] Therefore, Waite is suggesting that the employment of celestial timings, using specific planetary aspects, are the most favourable time to perform magical rituals to give the spell the added powerful essence it needs to fulfil the desired outcome.[26]

In 1989, seventeen years after the republication of Waite's translation, Melita Denning and Osbourne Phillips, former Grand Masters of the Aurum Solis, wrote about the invocation of the powers of the planets in planetary magic. Denning and Phillips devote a chapter to planetary days and hours and their attributions to contemporary magical rituals.[27] According to Denning and Phillips, the workings of Planetary Magick are begun during a planetary hour dedicated to the celestial body which is the subject of the working, and for full efficacy, on the day of the week the celestial body rules.[28] They believe that Planetary Magick not only harnesses the energies of the sun and the moon, but also the other five luminaries in our solar system and the archetypes associated with them, to empower rituals. When discussing ancient necromancy and divination through spirit or deity, Waite suggested that recently necromantic rituals had been adapted and become less barbaric thanks to Eliphas Levi and Pierre Christian; Waite emphasised the powerful link blood had with this type of magic. He claimed that blood was thought to be the 'medium of

---

[24] A. E. Waite, *The Book of Ceremonial Magic* (Eastford, CT: Martino Publishing, 2011), pp. 304–33.
[25] A. E. Waite, *The Book of Black Magic* (1972; San Francisco, CA: Red Wheel/Weiser, 2008), p. 147.
[26] Waite, *The Book of Black Magic*, pp. 145–48.
[27] M. Denning and O. Phillips, *The Magical Philosophy Book IV. Planetary Magick. Invoking and Directing the Powers of the Planets* (1989; Woodbury, MN: Llewellyn Publications, 2011), pp. 105–15.
[28] Denning and Phillips, *The Magical Philosophy Book IV. Planetary Magick*, p. 107.

physical life' and necessary in this type of ritual, suggesting that blood could be considered as a powerful tool with which to boost the power of the spell.[29]

More recently Occult author Seth (a pseudonym) explained that blood in itself held no power; however, in blood magic the practitioner draws on the energy found so abundant in blood that the sorcerer can unlock the energies within.[30] As recently as 2011, contemporary necromancer Sorceress Cagliastro argued that divination is often considered the main reason for communicating with the dead, and that blood is the bait to help call on the spirit you wish to communicate with.[31] She also outlined the different types of blood, or Sacred Elixir as she refers to it, and how the different types can be used for magic along with their specific attributes to the ritual.[32] This notion supports my research of contemporary practitioners of magic and spirit divination who utilise ancient practices employing blood in some of their magical rituals, especially when calling upon spirits. Therefore, contemporary practitioners of magical rituals do consider employing astrological influences and blood, which they feel could give efficacy to their ritual.

The significant ethnographic works of Tanya Luhrmann, Susan Greenwood and Jeanne Favret-Saada have been taken into consideration when conducting this research, as they are regarded as some of the most influential academics of contemporary pagan studies.[33] They are identified by their use of a reflexive attitude towards their research subjects when involved in fieldwork over several years. In the mid 1980s Tanya Lurhmann focused her research on a small group of Wiccan witches living in London, England, immersing herself into their secret world to understand why they are drawn to witchcraft and it practices. Susan Greenwood conducted an ethnographic study of contemporary pagan and ceremonial groups that practiced magic in London during the 1990s. She

---

[29] Waite, *The Book of Ceremonial Magic*, pp. 323–24.
[30] Seth, *Blood Magick* (Lincoln, NE: iUniverse Inc., 2003), p. 7.
[31] Sorceress Cagliastro, *Blood Sorcery Bible. Volume 1: Rituals in Necromancy. A Treatment On The Science Of Blood & Magnetics As They Pertain To Blood Sorcery And Necromancy* (Tempe, AZ: The Original Falcon Press, 2011), p. 122.
[32] Cagliastro, *Blood Sorcery Bible*, pp. 53–77.
[33] T. M. Lurhmann, *Persuasions of the Witch's Craft: Ritual Magic in Contemporary England* (London: Picador, 1994); Susan Greenwood, *Magic, Witchcraft and the Otherworld: An Anthropology* (Oxford: Berg, 2000); Jeanne Favret-Saada, *Deadly Words: Witchcraft in the Bocage* (Cambridge: Cambridge University Press, 1980).

too shifted between the worlds of academia and a small pagan witch community, employing an insider/outsider perspective in her study. Greenwood investigated how Pagans connected with the 'otherworld' and examined issues of identity, gender and morality amongst them. Favret-Saada focused on the region of the Bocage in France for her study. She encountered different types of practitioners of magic and recalls how she encountered professional magicians, or un-witchers, who undo the curse of the witch. The witch can cast a spell and bring misfortune onto the bewitched with a thought, a word or a look.[34] Favret-Saada says 'Now, witchcraft is spoken words; but these spoken words are power, and not knowledge or information.'[35] The un-witcher uses the power of the word to undo the misfortune, but it is difficult for the un-witcher to pass on the knowledge of witchcraft to the ethnographer just for the sake of knowing; to the un-witcher the word is capable of cursing or curing, it is formidable.[36]

Methodology
Greenwood, Favret-Saada and Lurhmann adopted an insider's perspective for their studies. Greenwood claimed that 'if an anthropologist wants to examine magic then he or she must directly experience the otherworld', thus demonstrating the need to immerse oneself fully into the world of the research subject in order to win trust and gain a greater understanding.[37] Lurhmann read magic books, took workshops to learn magical exercises, and studied Tarot in order to become more like her research subjects. She stated, 'Very early on in the study I realized that the new subjective experience involved in learning to practice magic was crucial to an individual's decision to become further involved'.[38] Furthermore, Favret-Saada argued that 'there is no room for uninvolved observers' in this type of research whilst investigating witchcraft beliefs in Normandy's Bocage.[39] She felt as though she could not understand the phenomenon until she fully submerged herself in its practices.[40] However, Tamzin Powell embarked upon her own MPhil thesis investigating the pagans and witches of the Wye Valley and Forest of Dean and their folklore as a native, and I found

---

[34] Favret-Saada, *Deadly Words*, p. 3–12.
[35] Favret-Saada, *Deadly Words*, p. 9.
[36] Favret-Saada, *Deadly Words*, p. 9.
[37] Greenwood, *Magic, Witchcraft and the Otherworld*, p. 12.
[38] Lurhmann, *Persuasions of the Witch's Craft*, p. 18.
[39] Favret-Saada, *Deadly Words*, p. 10.
[40] Favret-Saada, *Deadly Words*, pp. 10–12.

myself in the same position.[41] Powell is a High Priestess of the coven she researched, making her an established member of the group.[42] I have been a practicing witch for over fifteen years and a friend and acquaintance of all the members of the three study groups for nearly eight years. I have also been practicing witchcraft with one of the group of witches on a regular basis for the past six years. As an astrologer I appeared on a local radio station in this area of Spain presenting weekly horoscopes to the listeners. I also wrote horoscopes and articles for a number of magazines in the region. I am known on a personal and professional level by most of the members of the groups. Powell too had gained the trust of her informants, as she was already one of them. Unlike Greenwood and Lurhmann, neither Powell nor I had to learn magic from books or attend workshops in order to become an insider and become like our research subject at the start of our study, we were already entrenched in our insiderness.

Ethnographic research relies on some type of social interaction or participant observation with the chosen group of people. Davies claims that participant observation is more than a unitary research method, in that it employs various methods to gather data.[43] For this reason participant observation has played an important part in this study to date. One advantage of my long-standing relationship with the spiritual mediums group and the two groups of witches was that it appeared to help the respondents feel more comfortable with giving up information for this study. The interviewees' willingness to share their experiences with me was due to this relationship. Another advantage was that I found myself in a good position to interpret survey responses and interviews, thanks to the familiarity and trust between the study group and me.

As a result of talking to a small focus group of six people, I designed a questionnaire in order to ascertain whether any celestial factors influenced their magic or spirit divination. The research was also intended to look for any connection between their magic or spirit divination rituals and ancient necromantic rituals employing blood. The survey data was collected at meetings of spiritual groups on the Costa Blanca, Spain, which consisted

---

[41] Tamzin Powell, 'Between The Severn and the Wye: A Contemporary Reflexive Ethnography of Rural Pagans; the Folklore, Otherworld and the Continuity of Cunning-Folk and Witches in the Wye Valley and the Forest of Dean' (MPhil, University of Wales Trinity Saint David, 2014).
[42] Powell, 'Between The Severn and the Wye', p. 5.
[43] C. A. Davies, *Reflexive Ethnography: A Guide to Researching Selves and Others* (London: Routledge, 1999), p. 67.

of one group of spiritual mediums and two groups of witches who also utilised mediumship within their 'magical' practices.

The spiritual mediums were chosen as a distribution point for a short questionnaire, as it was believed there would be a large number of people within this group who had an interest, some knowledge and varying degrees of experience with using magic, spirit divination and astrology. The intention of the study and what is meant by celestial influences and necromancy was explained to the group before the questionnaire was given to them. I explained celestial influences from moon phases and planetary positions in the sky to planetary aspects usually attributed to astrology, for example, a new moon in Leo or a full moon in Pisces. Necromancy was defined simply as a form of magic involving communication with the deceased for divination.

The questionnaire was distributed to approximately sixty attendees, thirty-seven of whom completed the survey. The respondents answered questions ranging from the practice of magical rituals to their general involvement in spirit divination and any attitudes to celestial influences. To complement the survey data, personal interviews were conducted. The interviewees in this study are referred to by fictional names only. These interviews expanded upon areas of interest that were seemingly limited by the questionnaire in order to enrich the data already discovered.[44]

In the same way that Powell discusses her remaining a native after her study was completed, I am and hope to continue to involve myself in spirit divination with some members of this group of witches, both academically and personally, which can only enhance the study.[45] John McLeod suggests that the qualitative method of research can take months, if not years, to come to a 'satisfactory end point' with a 'convincing conceptualisation' of the researcher's material.[46]

I began this study as a deep insider, being a witch of a similar age to some in the study groups; I live as a non-native in the Valencia region of Spain, as do most of the research study subjects. Most members of the spiritual mediums group, having frequented their regular weekly meetings over the past eight years, know me; I have also occasionally spoken on

---

[44] Judith Bell, *Doing Your Research Project*, 4th edition (London: Open University Press, 2005,) p. 157.
[45] Powell, 'Between The Severn and the Wye', p. 83.
[46] John McLeod, *Qualitative Research in Counselling and Psychotherapy* (London: Sage Publications, 2001), p. 135.

esoteric subjects for them at their request. As a researcher, I neither carried a notebook nor recorded conversations; any notes were written in private.

My account of the 24ᵗʰ of May 2013

As my research methodology involved participant observation, I participated in the creation of a magic circle for spirit divination with a small group of witches. One such occasion was when the full moon was in Scorpio on 24 October 2013.

On 24 of May 2013, when the full moon was in Scorpio, Luna, Lily, Paulo and I went up to the Cap de San Antoni, Costa Blanca Spain, to perform magic. I drove up to the lighthouse at around 8:30pm with Lily after picking her up, arriving a little early to find Luna and Paulo waiting for me. We walked along the dirt track from the car park into the grounds of the lighthouse. From there we descended a little way alongside the cliff face to a secluded and sheltered spot. We have used this place, a favourite of ours, to perform our magic for the past five years. We chose this position as it is a beautiful setting with a stunning view. It is sheltered from visitors to the lighthouse, making it a favourite haunt for lovers in the evenings. The view over the sea and of the expanse of sky is inspiring.

Luna laid out her altar cloth and we placed our items on the cloth: a cauldron, a charcoal burner, an athame, a ritual knife used in modern witchcraft, a chalice and a bottle of wine. As a form of libation, we also took a large, white candle for Hecate and some almonds and roses. We placed a candle in each of the four corners to represent the guardians of the watchtowers. We sometimes place additional coloured candles in certain places to correspond with the elements; for example, to represent water we would place a blue candle, to represent earth it would be brown or green. However, due to the uncharacteristically cold and windy weather we chose not to do this during this ritual. After placing the candles in the four corners, we lit them along with incense sticks. We were now ready to call on the guardians of the watchtowers, either for protection or to give energy to our magic. If we required protection, we asked the guardians to stand facing outwards from our circle to watch over us, protecting us from negative entities or energies. If we required help to energise our magic, we asked them to stand facing inwards into our circle. Paulo is usually the one who calls in the guardians.

We all faced east and chanted:

> Hail Guardian of the Watchtower East
> Powers of Air
> As you carry the seeds of the plants across the land
> As you bring the moisture of the storms to the shore
> Join us, in all your gentle and powerful ways
> We bless the elements of Air
> And call upon you to gather here with us.

We all faced west and chanted:

> Hail Guardian of the Watchtower of the West
> Powers of Water
> Water, soft and yielding, formless and flowing
> You are the blood coursing through our veins
> We bless the elements of Water
> And call upon you to gather here with us.

We all faced south and chanted:

> Hail Guardian of the Watchtower of the South
> Powers of Fire and Feeling
> Flaming One
> Apollo, Bright Warrior
> Wild courage
> Lion strength
> We bless the elements of fire
> And call upon you to gather here with us.

We all faced north and chanted:

> Hail Guardian of the Watchtower of the North
> Powers of Mother and Earth
> Changeless power of unending change
> In steadfastness and strength
> We bless the element of Earth
> And call upon you to gather here with us.

Then Luna took over and opened the circle, calling on Hecate to stand by us and aid us in our magic.

> We cast this circle with a white light to you Hecate asking you to stand by us and to add power to our magic on this full moon in Scorpio. Hecate we welcome you to our circle – so mote it be.

All the time whilst this invocation was happening, Lily, Paulo, Luna and I visualised the guardians sending us energy with Hecate standing by. We raised the energy by meditating and rubbing our hands together. We then took it in turns to light our own small candles, which had been inscribed with our desire, using the flame from the main large white candle that we had dedicated to Hecate. My candle is always inscribed with sigils. I like to code my requests using these sigil symbols instead of writing them in full. Sigil magic is often associated with and used in chaos magic. We burnt our mixtures of incense we had made up and energised beforehand and passed the spell written in dragon's blood, a resin or powder extract from a variety of plants, on paper through the scented smoke. This paper can sometimes be marked with menstrual blood if desired. Whilst suffumigating our desires we recited the words; 'through scent smoke and magic candle fire I send the universe my desire'. Lighting the paper with our candles, we then let it burn in the cauldron and contemplated, waiting for our answers.

We gave our offering of nuts and wine, enjoying them too. We did not, however, discuss what we had just asked for, for fear of it not working. The spell casting is never discussed, but we did exchange stories of past successes and formulas that have worked, for future references which are passed around the group if and when needed.

We then asked Paulo to reverse the order of the calling of the guardians of the watchtowers, adding thanks for their protection or energy. We then let Luna close the circle, giving thanks to Hecate, and with these final words from us all,

> As above so below our magic is done strong good and true so mote be.

We spend a good 20 minutes contemplating the stunning view of the full moon over the Mediterranean Sea and expressing our feeling about the ritual just performed. Lily and Luna explain how they felt the power and energy so much stronger this time than they have of late. They both felt that lately there has been a lull in the energy in their magic. Paulo and myself have had the complete opposite experience – we felt the energy has been strong for sometime and hoped that it continued for us both. We then packed up our belongings and headed into the old town for tapas and a few cold beers, spending the evening drinking, eating, socialising and planning for the next time we will meet up at the lighthouse for magic. We all agreed to meet for the next one, the new moon in Gemini on the 8th of June 2013, as we discussed how Hecate is the female counterpart of Hermes, the guardian of the gateway to the underworld, and Hermes is the Greek counterpart of Mercury and Mercury is the ruler of Gemini. It was agreed that this date would be an excellent time for communication with spirit and Hecate for our magic.

Survey Results
Questionnaire & Discussion
Below are the questions on the questionnaire put to the spiritual mediums.

Q1. When performing spirit divination/magic do you place any importance on celestial or astrological aspects, i.e., the moon phases and position of the planets?

Q2. Do you have a ritual you perform before during and after your spiritual divination/magic, i.e., food or drink offerings, the lighting of specific candles or giving thanks to your chosen spirit or deity?

Q3. Some people offer a sacrifice of some kind; something of theirs they value to give up as a sacrifice to their chosen spirit or deity?

Q4. Do you or did you feel that your menstrual cycle had any significance on your sensitivity in your spirit divination/magic?

Q5. Have you either used your menstrual blood, blood from another part of yourself, i.e., finger, from somewhere else such as animal blood or imitation blood such as red ink?

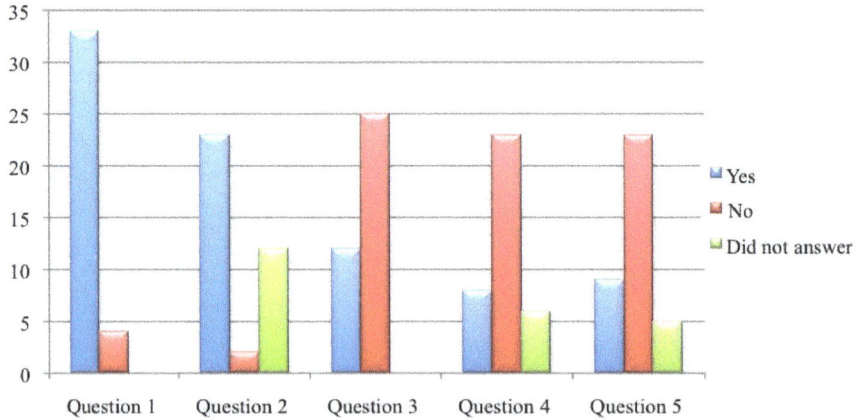

Fig. 1: Survey results

Question 1. When performing spirit divination/magic do you place any importance on celestial or astrological aspects, i.e., the moon phases and position of the planets?
Of the thirty-seven respondents who completed the short survey, thirty-three answered 'Yes' when asked if they placed any emphasis on celestial movements when performing their magic or spirit divination. The main celestial body with which they felt a connection was the moon and its different phases. All thirty-three who answered 'Yes' felt that the energies within and around them were much stronger and more powerful during a full or new moon than at any another time of the moon's cycle. Six of the thirty-seven respondents said they noted which zodiac sign the full moon was in at the time of their magic, using that influence or energy for their divination. Interestingly, three of the four surveyed who said they did not place any emphasis on celestial movements indicated that they will now take more note of planetary activity whilst performing magic or spirit divination to 'test the energy' and see if it has any bearing on their performance. I have to point out here that my question has clearly influenced and possibly changed the future behaviour of the three respondents. Regardless of what a researcher does to ensure he or she does not influence the study there will always be some aspects that have not been taken into account. In this instance it shows that reflexivity does have its limits. However, according to Hertz, having limits is not of great importance because reflexivity is 'ubiquitous'.[47] Although my question did make three of them rethink their own thought patterns when it comes to their spiritual divination and celestial influences we cannot be sure that they will take notice of such influences next time they perform their magic.

Question 2. Do you have a ritual you perform before, during and after your spiritual divination/magic, i.e., food or drink offerings, the lighting of specific candles or giving thanks to your chosen spirit or deity?
Of the thirty-seven respondents only two said that they did not perform rituals of any sort before calling on spirits for divination purposes. Twenty-three respondents had their own rituals consisting of protection, burning candles and incense, using crystals and also giving offerings to appease their chosen spirit or deity. The rituals they perform show a similarity, albeit a vague one, with necromantic rituals. However, twelve who performed spirit divination and magic employed rituals that showed a very

---

[47] Rosanna Hertz, ed., *Reflexivity and Voice* (Thousand Oaks, CA: Sage Publications, 1997), p. viii.

strong correlation with necromantic rituals that involved the offering of food and wine.

Considering that this study is examining possible connections between spirit divination and ancient necromantic rituals, the question of a sacrifice was put to the respondents. It was explained that the sacrifice could be something personal to be given up as an offering. Of the thirty-seven, only twelve respondents answered 'Yes', signifying that they offer up a sacrifice of some kind.

Question 3. Some people offer a sacrifice of some kind; something of theirs they value to give up as a sacrifice to their chosen spirit or deity?
The final two survey questions were added due to a suggestion mentioned in the initial focus group, that menstrual cycles and menstrual blood are very significant in magic or spirit divination rituals. Some even noted that when they performed whilst menstruating they felt more powerful; others noted that their menstrual cycle coincided with different moon phases. This was significant to them as they felt it affected the energies in their magic. The blood aspect was offered up not only as a sacrifice similar to that in necromantic rituals but also as the ultimate, life-giving force. In ancient necromantic rituals blood is offered to the spirit in order to give the spirit a 'taste' of life.

Question 4. Do you or did you feel that your menstrual cycle had any significance on your sensitivity in your spirit divination/magic?
Of the thirty-seven respondents, eight answered with 'Yes' that their menstrual cycle had any impact on their sensitivity. It has to be taken into consideration that of the thirty-seven surveyed four were males and nineteen were over the age of 60 and therefore, possibly past menopause, although this cannot be verified.

Question 5. Have you either used your menstrual blood, blood from another part of yourself, i.e., finger, from somewhere else such as animal blood or imitation blood such as red ink?
Notably, three of the thirty-seven surveyed who answered 'No' said that if they had thought about it, they would have used their menstrual blood in their magic had they not reached menopause. They felt using their own blood might have had a powerful influence on their spiritual and 'magical' work, although they had no experience of it. Of the four male respondents three answered 'No' to the question of using menstrual blood in their

magic; however one did state that he had used blood from his finger for his magic or spirit divination.

The survey results do suggest that there is a connection with necromantic rituals and celestial influences within their spirit divination and magic. In retrospect, this short questionnaire was limited. This is a typical finding in this kind of research, which is why semi-structured interviews with eight willing respondents of the survey were conducted. The interviews discussed the use of rituals, celestial influences and blood rituals within their magic and the connection with ancient necromantic rituals in much more detail.

I am aware that I influenced the behaviour of my sample, when I gave them the questionnaire, precisely because of the nature of the questions; some now are more aware, both of the Moon's zodiacal sign of the power of their menstrual cycle and will be more so the next time they perform their magic.

Interviews and Discussion
Celestial Influences
All eight of the interviewees were in agreement that the full moon was a significant time for their spirit divination or magic. Luna, a witch who practices spirit divination, says,

> When the moon is full and, to me, at its most powerful I reflect this in my casting. I also cast my circle smaller when the moon is full because I like to cone a stronger, more powerful energy. I have stood outside many times barefoot and drawn down the full moon's energy before I begin.

Luna suggests she likes to 'cone the power of the moon', a ritual performed by many witches who, in some form, follow the Wiccan path.[48]

The extant evidence from the *The Greek Magical Papyri* suggests that astrology plays an important role in necromancy. 'Libra: perform invocation… spell of release… necromancy'.[49] There are also instructions as to which astrological sign holds host to the most preferential time for certain rituals to attain a specific outcome.

---

[48] Gerald Gardner, 'Drawing Down the Moon', in *The Gardnerian Book of Shadows*, available at http://www.sacred-texts.com/pag/gbos/gbos01.htm [accessed 2 February 2015].
[49] Betz, *The Greek Magical Papyri*, PGM III.275–818.

> Orbit of the Moon: Moon / in Virgo: anything is rendered obtainable. In Libra: necromancy. In Scorpio: anything inflicting evil. In Sagittarius: an invocation or incantations / to the sun and moon. In Capricorn: say whatever you wish for best results. In Aquarius: for a love charm. Pisces: for foreknowledge. In Aries: fire divination or love charm. In Taurus: incantation to a lamp. Gemini: spell for winning favour. In Cancer: phylacteries. Leo: rings or binding spells.[50]

Quite limited in detail, this text still indicates that favourable times to perform magic using astrological timings were used. The ancient Greeks and Romans believed festivals of the dead to be excellent times to perform necromancy. The main festivals considered as auspicious times for rituals are the thrice-yearly opening of the 'mundus', the hole in the underworld from which spirits of the dead could emerge: the Anthesteria and Genesia were held in Athens and the Parentalia and the Lemuria were held in Rome.[51]

The interviewees were in agreement on the significance of the full moon; also that on certain Sabbats, such as Halloween and the winter and summer solstices, the energy is stronger than at any other times in the calendar. Luna explained that she always acknowledges Halloween, a festival to celebrate and remember the dead, as a time for magic and connecting with the spirit world:

> I make much more of a deal of Halloween. It is the start of the Witch's year, and the night where the veil between the living and dead is at its thinnest point. I feel empowered doing magic on this night! I have meditated on Halloween purposefully to connect with my spirit guide, and have asked for their help in performing magic.

For Saoirse, in her magic or divination, the planetary hours play a big part in the planning of 'magical' rituals. Saoirse claims,

> I'd say the moon phases and planetary hours have more of an effect on my magic making it stronger.

---

[50] Betz, *The Greek Magical Papyri*, PGM VII.284–999.
[51] W. Warde Fowler, 'Mundus Patet', available at http://penelope.uchicago.edu/Thayer/E/Journals/JRS/2/Mundus*.html [accessed 26 March 2014]; Ogden, *Greek and Roman Necromancy*, pp. 167–68.

Lily, an artist, witch and spiritual medium who is influenced by Waite's literature, goes further when discussing celestial influences on her magic; here, she explains

> The day of the week is important as different Gods and planets rule certain days. Say, for example, I wanted guidance on my career, I would chose a green candle as that symbolises money for me and I'd choose a Thursday as this is ruled by Jupiter the planet of abundance. For love I would use pink or red and choose a Friday as this day is ruled by the planet Venus symbolising love and passion. I do take notice of planetary activities more and more and how it affects my spirit magic.

Here she suggests that she takes note of astrological meanings for each day before embarking on her magic. For Lily, the day determines what kind of magic and which spirit she will call upon for divination purposes.

According to Waite, favourable timings for spirit divination using astrological events were in the planetary hours of Saturn and Venus.[52] Whereas in more recent times instructions for invoking spirits using planetary magic and archetypes can be found in literature about planetary magic by David Rankin and Sorita d'Este and Denning and Phillips.[53] Planetary hours use the so-called Chaldean system to divide diurnal time. A different planet rules each planetary hour of each planetary day. The planet that rules the first hour of the day is also the ruler of the whole day and gives that day its name. Therefore the first hour of Sunday is ruled by the Sun, the first hour of Monday is ruled by the Moon and so on.[54]

Libations and Locations
All of the interviewees had a ritual they enacted every time they commenced their magic for spiritual divination; Luna, Saoirse, Lily and Rosa all followed a similar path. The process they all employed was very similar to that of necromancy. They all said, weather permitting, they preferred to be outdoors with their magic rather than being confined indoors as they felt it was more powerful under the energy of the moon and stars. Ancient necromantic rituals have been described as being typically

---

[52] Waite, *The Book of Black Magic*, p. 147.
[53] Denning and Phillips, *The Magical Philosophy Book IV. Planetary Magick;* David Rankine and Sorita d'Este, *Practical Planetary Magick. Working Magick of the Classical Planets in the Western Mystery Tradition* (London: Avalonia, 2007), pp. 76–93.
[54] Waite, *The Book of Black Magic*, pp. 146–47.

carried out in caves, by marshes or lakes and in dense forests. It was also commonly practised on battlefields, at graves, or in tombs as these were considered to be gateways to the Underworld and these were the places most abundant in ghosts.[55] The ritual ideally begins at midnight and continues until daybreak, because it is believed that the ghosts must return to the underworld when the process is over and the prophecy delivered. Furthermore, for the best results this ritual should be performed on a full moon.[56] There are typical tomb-side libations or offerings to pacify and appease the dead, usually consisting of honey-milk, wine, water and sometimes olive oil with a sprinkle of barley. Author and healing practitioner Christopher Penczak discusses the need for appeasing potentially disruptive spirits he calls 'outdwellers' during a necromantic ritual. 'Outdwellers' he says are unwanted spirits that can make the ritual area quite hostile.[57] American witch Christian Day writes about these types of libations or offerings and how they can be used to appease the spirit invoked. In one incantation he commands 'Let these offerings appease you, spirit of [name of spirit here]! Come forth and provide the answers I seek!'[58] When questioned about offerings Rosa explained,

> At certain phases of the moon, but most certainly the when the moon is full I put out some honey and garlic and an apple.

Luna and Saoirse also said they have offered food and drink. In describing her particular offering to Hecate, her chosen goddess for spirit divination magic, Saoirse declared,

> I will offer a raw egg and almonds, but only to Hecate, the egg signifying a new life, the almonds because they are plentiful. I don't drink during magic work but I will have coffee and biscuit after, to show appreciation. To indicate the magic bit is over, I eat and drink after I have closed the circle.

Luna goes into great detail about her libations to her chosen spirit for her divination magic:

---

[55] Ogden, *Greek and Roman Necromancy*, pp. 3, 25.
[56] Ogden, *Greek and Roman Necromancy*, pp. 166–68.
[57] Christopher Penczak, *The Mighty Dead. Communing with the Ancestors of Witchcraft* (Salem, NH: Copper Cauldron Publishing, 2013), p. 100.
[58] Christian Day, *The Witches Book of the Dead* (San Francisco, CA: Red Wheel/Weiser, 2011), p. 120.

The raw egg is a symbol of fertility, womanhood and growth. It is also a representative of the goddess to me so I use a raw egg as an offering to the goddess when I am working outdoors. It's also for me away of saying thank you! I suppose I feel it's giving something back to the earth to crack a raw egg around the root of a tree etc. Nuts, especially almonds, which are related to Hecate who is the goddess I always call on. Sometimes I use a branch from an almond tree as well. Coins, silver coins were told to me by Saoirse to be good to leave as an offering, and we have left them in an almond tree before up at the lighthouse when going up there to work together.

Sacrifice
Usually a black sheep or cow was offered to the underworld in the form of a sacrifice. The throat of the animal was cut, the blood was drained into the pit for the ghosts to drink from, and afterwards the carcass was burnt whole. This was said to aid the ghost's communication with the living.[59]

Interviewee Lily has an interesting opinion on sacrifice within the bounds of magic:

> I do find that if something is sacrificed, an animal, the actual act of killing creates certain energy. I don't have the words for what that energy is. But it can enhance spiritual 'magical and ritual work. Ok, I am not one for sacrificing. Sacrificing living creatures is not for me as I am a little bit squeamish. I do, however sacrifice blood. That is my only sacrifice.

In necromancy the sacrificed animal is burnt whole, but in other ancient Greek sacrifices the carcass was distributed amongst those present with a view to the animal being eaten; sometimes a portion of the carcass was left on the altar for the Gods.[60] Whilst none of the interviewees actually sacrificed living creatures, one of the interviewees did offer a sacrifice of her own in the form of menstrual blood. Saoirse explained,

> I use my menstrual blood 98% of the time, only if I don't have any do I not call on Hecate, she is the Queen of witches, therefore is top cat, why go lower. When I call on anyone else it is for something very specific, they are called to help me, in Hecate's name. The blood is connected to Hecate obviously and I

---

[59] Ogden, *Magic, Witchcraft and Ghosts in the Greek and Roman World*, p. 179.
[60] Christopher A. Faraone and F. S. Naiden, eds., *Greek and Roman Animal Sacrifice: Ancient Victims, Modern Observers* (Cambridge: Cambridge University Press, 2012), p. 65.

don't offer it to anyone else. When I call on others, Hecate is involved first so the blood is for her.

Lily on the other hand had a different use for her sacrifice of menstrual blood. She continues:

> I generally use it in my painting and my magic. I think it is a very powerful thing and a very magical thing in itself. Certainly whether I am painting/ channelling, I find the act of using it enhances my magic. I used it for invoking the goddess Aphrodite when I painted her and other Goddesses for inspiration.

She continues to expand on her use of her menstrual blood within her magic:

> Part of it is that it's easier than cutting yourself and more natural. I used the blood to connect with the goddess I am working on to evoke that specific Goddess for inspiration. For my pendulum work blood is my obvious sacrifice if I don't have menstrual blood my magic fluid available I will cut myself although I'd prefer not to. I use the blood to make my mark on the paper, I prefer to use my pure fresh blood as it's easier to use, it's much more potent, it's the first blood on the first day and it's the most painful. So it's more meaningful.

It is noteworthy that this study showed that menstrual blood, in particular, was used as a sacrifice and offering to a chosen spirit or deity as opposed to blood from a small cut to the finger, for example. Luna describes the use of blood in her magic:

> My menstrual cycle affects my magical ability, it makes me feel much more attuned to the moon and the planet, therefore I use my menstrual blood in my spells. It's part of me so why not!

Furthermore, blood was used in a sacrificial way in that it was offered as a part of oneself to a chosen spirit or deity and as the ultimate life force energy to aid communication with spirit. Both contemporary necromancers, Day and Cagliastro, discuss the use of blood in their spirit divination. Day uses the blood from a prick to his finger, Cagliastro mentions blood harvested from three different body parts/areas for invoking ancestors, menstrual blood being one of them.[61]

Hecate the Guardian of the Gateway
The main Goddess that witches call upon for spirit divination and magic is Hecate. This connects spirit divination to necromancy and celestial magic, yet again. Hecate is mentioned numerous times within the *Greek Magical Papyri*, for example, in spell casting for necromantic purposes or calling on her to aid communication with the dead in order to perform magic.[62] According to Sara Iles Johnson, Hecate's role is to guide disembodied souls back to Hades and the otherworld, a role similar to that of Hermes who guided dead souls on their journey to the otherworld and who was guardian of the gateway.[63] Hecate is also likened to the moon in the *Chaldean Oracles*, fragments of Hellenistic texts from the second century CE.[64] When asked about Hecate and her importance to her magic Saoirse responds,

> I call on Hecate whenever I'm doing anything magical or spiritual. I cast my circle then ask Hecate to stand with me, to protect me and strengthen my magic. Doing Tarot cards, I call on Hecate and after that, I call on any spirit guides I may have to aid my work, but it's always Hecate first.

Jacob Rabinowitz discusses Hecate's role as the Guardian of the Gateway for the dead and as a 'bridge between both realms'. Rabinowitz examines numerous ancient texts to clearly establish Hecate's role as the keeper of the keys that open the door between realms and as the intermediary between the worlds of dead and the living.[65] Lily recalls a celebration to honour Hecate with menstrual blood:

> In the autumn time there is a celebration when you meditate, draw down the power of the moon and literally paint yourself with your menstrual blood. You

---

[61] Day, *The Witches Book of the Dead*, p. 120; Cagliastro, *Blood Sorcery Bible*, p. 55.
[62] Betz, *The Greek Magical Papyri*, PGM IV.2708–84, PGM IV.2785–2890.
[63] Sara Iles Johnson, *Hekate Soteira* (Atlanta, GA: Scholar Press, 1990), pp. 26, 31, 146, 147; Jacob Rabinowitz, *The Rotting Goddess: The Origin of the Witch in Classical Antiquity* (New York: Autonomedia, 1998), pp. 22–39.
[64] Ruth Majercik, trans., *The Chaldean Oracles: Text, Translation, and Commentary by Julianus the Theurgist* (Leiden: E. J. Brill, 1989), pp. 163, 180.
[65] Rabinowitz, *The Rotting Goddess*, pp. 24, 25.

then lay on the earth; this is how my friends from Safron's coven celebrate each year.

Lily's friend Safron is part of another local coven which follows the Witches of Avalon School of witchcraft. Safron travelled from her home in Spain to Glastonbury, England, in 2009 to learn from the Priestess of Avalon known as Kathy Jones.[66] The date for this particular ritual that many of the witches encountered perform is 16 November, a day to celebrate and honour the triple-headed goddess Hecate. Gillian Macdonald discusses myths, taboos and the use of blood in tribal rituals. She devotes a chapter to menstrual blood, detailing one particle ritual she uses to invoke the energies of the Goddess Hecate using food libations and menstrual blood.[67]

Protection
There are prayers to release the ghosts of the dead who, in ancient necromantic rituals, must be managed with a sword, as the dead are believed to be frightened of bronze and iron.[68] Only Luna and Anna used a sword of some kind in their 'magical' rituals for spirit divination. Day says he employs a bronze dagger in his necromantic ritual to form a circle to protect him form evil.[69] Luna used an athame for protection and for opening and closing her circle. An athame is a ceremonial knife used in magical rituals. Luna says she feels safe with the athame asserting,

> Never ever would I open a circle in the first place if I didn't have my athame with me, it stays on my lap or close by me the whole time the magic is being performed.

She also goes into more detail about casting her circle just before calling on spirit for divination work:

> When I open my circle with prayers of protection I imagine a blue light coming out the end of my athame and completely surrounding me, then I feel safe within my 'bubble' to work. I have more or less always done this, but

---

[66] Glastonbury Goddess Temple, available at http://www.goddesstemple.co.uk [accessed 22 June 2013].
[67] Gillian Macdonald. *Blood Mysteries* (Somerset: Green Magic Publishing, 2013), pp. 30–34.
[68] Ogden. *Magic Witchcraft and Ghosts in the Greek and Roman World*, p. 179.
[69] Day, *The Witches Book of the Dead*, p. 119.

didn't realize how important it was until I was working with someone else and was probably complacent about this ritual. I know for a fact that something dark entered my space, and stayed in the house. It was very frightening and affected other members of the family. I had to do a lot of demanding it left and lighting candles everywhere before I felt it calm down and will never really know if it ever left that house as we moved out soon after. I have always taken my protection ritual to be very important after that. I also tend to ask the four corners to stand guard and offer protection now as opposed to asking them to lend strength to my magic.

Although a carcass is not burned, a form of symbolism of burning to appease a chosen spirit and for protection is apparent during the ritual. All interviewees seemed to burn incense and candles mindfully chosen for the purpose and the spirit they wish to call on. Artist Lily uses smudge sticks and Palo sticks, amongst other things, for her protection whilst painting. Before she channels the influences of the goddess she will cleanse and protect her ritual space with the smudge and Palo sticks, then call upon her chosen goddess and paint her image. A Palo Stick, or 'Holy Stick', is a natural wood infused with incense, used for centuries by the indigenous people of South America as a spiritual remedy for purifying and cleansing, as well as to get rid of evil spirits and misfortune. Here Lily clarifies how she feels she protects herself with Palo and incense sticks:

> I am using something to control the energy that I am calling upon in some way with protection from my Palo and incense sticks, light, bubbles and my positivity.

Luna conveys how she lights something for her chosen spirit:

> I always have a white candle lit for my chosen deity. I also burn my paper with my desires written on in dragon's blood or my menstrual blood; whichever is readily available at the time of my magic. Once the circle is closed I sometimes throw the ashes into the air.

Additionally, Rosa and Saoirse indicated they also throw the ashes into the wind when they have finished their magic.

Conclusion

There is an indication from the questionnaire replies and the interviews that my informants placed an emphasis upon celestial timings and positions according with their knowledge of astrology. Many of the survey respondents were much more aware of celestial influences within their magic although some only focused on lunar phases and lunar influences. Additionally there is evidence of ancient necromantic rituals employed within the researched groups and their contemporary magic and spirit divination practices, in particular the use of blood within their magical rituals when invoking spirit for divination, contradicting Gerald Gardner's statement that blood is never used in rituals by witches.

The interviewees were a little more knowledgeable of astrology, more so than those surveyed with the questionnaire. The interviewees, who also answered the questionnaire, seemed to place more importance on planetary positioning and the influences this bestowed upon their 'magical' practices. Whilst they do perform their magic outdoors, some of the time there was no emphasis upon this, or the location, being of importance. They offer libations of raw egg, nuts, honey and wine in order to appease and give thanks to a spirit or Hecate, their chosen goddess, when performing spirit divination. It has been shown that they also offer some kind of sacrifice, preferably their menstrual blood as they feel it is the ultimate life force and much more potent than the blood from a self-inflicted cut. Although they do not have a fire, they do have a representation of this with the candles and incense sticks that they burn during their rituals, the ashes of which are then scattered into the wind at the end of their rituals. They also offer up prayers of protection, invocation and thanks during their magic. It became apparent that whilst this study evolved, the respondents of this group were not aware that they followed any kind of ancient necromantic ritual whilst performing their spirit divination; they said 'they just did it intuitively', claiming to have no knowledge of necromancy before the study began although classical text and references are readily available to them.

My data was gathered from one study and will therefore be more or less applicable to all spiritual mediums and witches. Nonetheless, this pilot study based on this small group of people has proved extremely interesting, giving an insight to their spiritual divination and magical practices and their correlation with celestial bodies and necromantic rituals of ancient times.

South Indian Ritual Dispels Negative Karma in the Birth Chart

Lilan Laishley

Abstract: This paper examines the practice of celestial magic in contemporary South India as it relates to the individual birth chart. Specific celestially oriented rituals are understood to minimize the unpleasant effects of the birth chart and positively influence the planetary deities. The rituals incorporate various magical objects and actions including *puja*, *mantras*, prayers, *yantras*, ceremonial offerings, icons, gemstones, and shrines. This paper is based on participant observation during a research trip to Tamil Nadu, South India, where an astrologer suggested a ritual was needed to clear the negative *karma* he saw in my birth chart. This led to a multifaceted ritual at a ninth-century snake temple that I documented with photos and interviews. This specific site was chosen because the celestial snake *Rahu /Ketu* in the Indian astrological system was identified as the cause of the difficult *karma* and would need to be approached for help in clearing it. I will share the stages of this ritual, including the symbolic meaning of the objects used and actions taken. I conclude with my proposal that ritual is both a container and vehicle for celestial magic.

In the summer of 2004 I went to Tamil Nadu in South India for six weeks on an educational research trip with two other professors and twelve students. We based ourselves in Madurai, a traditional city that is both physically and spiritually situated around the site of the ancient and beautiful temple dedicated to the goddess Meenakshi. During those six weeks I researched Jyotish, the form of astrology that is practiced in South India. The term Jyotish, often translated as 'science of light,' refers to the light from the Sun, Moon, planets and stars.[1] Jyotish is also referred to as Indian Astrology or Vedic Astrology, though Jyotish is a more accurate term since it is practiced in countries other than India and by people that are not necessarily rooted in Vedism such as Buddhists, Sikhs, Jains, Muslims and Christians.[2]

---

[1] Hart de Fouw and Robert Svoboda, *Light on Life: An Introduction to Astrology of India* (Twin Lakes, WI: Lotus Press, 2003) p. xxii.
[2] de Fouw and Svoboda, *Light on Life*, p. 4.

252 South Indian Ritual Dispels Negative Karma in the Birth Chart

As an American astrologer trained in the Western European tradition I knew very little about Jyotish and was curious how it was practiced in India. I did not concentrate on the technical workings of Jyotish which are different from Western astrology in many ways, including in its use of the stars (sidereal) instead of the Sun (tropical) to orient to the night sky. Instead I was interested in observing how astrology was part of the life of the Tamil people and how it was integrated into their society. I was pleased to discover that astrology in Madurai was widespread. Astrologers commonly held consultations outside of temples. Astrological *yantras*, diagrams for magical incantation, were for sale in sidewalk markets, and planetary shrines were prominently placed in all the temples.[3]

My research during those six weeks led me to the conclusion that the rich and varied ritual practices currently found in South India provide a window into the types of astrological magic that were part of ancient, medieval, and Renaissance astrology in Western Europe. It felt like I had tapped into fertile ground that, if explored further, could lead to a better understanding of how ritual magic can still be a potent force in the practice of Western astrology.

Some define magic as the belief that supernatural or spiritual forces can be controlled through rituals and incantations with the goal of power over nature and the circumstances of life; in this way magic can be understood as a technology since it aims for change or manipulation, not just for knowledge.[4] Others reject magic as simply a technology of rites but instead understand magic as a worldview of living in an enchanted world of participation, where persons and things have sympathy and correspondence to each other.[5] Celestial magic directs its worldview and rites toward the cosmos through stellar, planetary or celestial symbolism, influences or intelligences.[6] As Keith Thomas wrote,

> ... the astronomers of the ancient world had been impressed by the regular behaviour of the heavens, in contrast with the flux and mutation of life on

---

[3] For *yantra*, see *Tamil Lexicon* (Madras: University of Madras, 1963), Vol. 3, p. 3393.
[4] Dan Burton and David Grandy, *Magic, Mystery, and Science* (Bloomington: Indiana University Press, 2004), pp. 36–37.
[5] Wouter J. Hanegraaff, *New Age Religion and Western Culture* (Leiden: E. J. Brill. 1996), p. 394.
[6] Conference Programme for Sophia Centre for the Study of Cosmology in Culture's Eleventh Annual Sophia Centre Conference 'Celestial Magic' 22–23 June 2013 at Bath Royal Literary and Scientific Institute, Bath, England.

earth. They accordingly assumed a division of the universe whereby the superior, immutable bodies of the celestial world ruled over the terrestrial or sublunary sphere, where all was mortality and change.[7]

Astrology is based on the idea that what happens in the celestial world corresponds to, reflects or influences earthly events. This relationship between heaven and earth is a doctrine of universal sympathy. As Diogenes Laertius put it:

> The world has no empty space within it, but forms one united whole. This is a necessary result of the sympathy and tension which binds together things in heaven and earth.[8]

This finds its expression in the Emerald Tablet's aphorism 'As Above/So Below', a shorthand way of saying that all that happens in the realms of the universe above us, such as the doings of the gods or the movements of the stars and planets, is directly reflected in what happens down here on Earth, and vice versa.[9] This macrocosmic/microcosmic connection is one way we are able to know the universe, since we are like it and have an affinity with it.[10] One of the benefits of celestial magic is to create a link between the interconnected dual realities of As Above and So Below, Macrocosm and Microcosm, Spiritual and Physical, or Heaven and Earth, thereby providing a way for individuals to engage actively with the cosmos and establish a meaningful placement in and relationship with that cosmos.[11]

The ritual in which I participated was intended to influence positively the planetary deities in order to clear the *karma*, fruits of my past deeds, in my astrological birth chart.[12] This intention clearly fits into the definition of celestial magic. Since the ritual took place within the broader context of

---

[7] Keith Thomas, *Religion and the Decline of Magic* (New York: Charles Scribner's Sons, 1971), pp. 284–85.

[8] Diogenes Laertius' biography of 'Zeno' in *Lives of Eminent Philosophers*, trans R. D. Hicks (London: William Heinemann, 1925), Vol. 2, pp. 110–263 (para. 140).

[9] Jabir ibn Hayyan, 'The Emerald Tablet of Hermes Trismegistus' in E. J. Holmyard, *Alchemy* (Harmondsworth: Penguin Books, 1957), pp. 97–98. See also Richard Tarnas, *The Passion of the Western Mind* (New York: Ballantine Books, 1991), p. 82; and Burton and Grandy, *Magic, Mystery, and Science*, p. 43.

[10] Burton and Grandy, *Magic, Mystery, and Science*, p. 47.

[11] Lilan Laishley, *Religious Diversity on the Labyrinth: Rituals that Engage a Sacred Cosmos* (Saarbrucken: LAP Lambert Publishing. 2011), p. 76.

[12] For *karma*, *Tamil Lexicon* (Madras: University of Madras, 1963), Vol. 1, p. 762.

astrology in India, specifically Tamil Nadu, I will first provide some general observations about astrology in Tamil Nadu and then describe the ritual.

Astrology has been part of the social and religious fabric of India since the second millennium BCE. It remains of paramount importance for traditionally minded Hindus and an astrologer is consulted before any trip, activity, or ritual.[13] Astrology has status in the culture because it is part of scripturally sanctioned Sanskrit literature and is recognized as orthodox in the Brahmanical tradition. Astrology is also offered at the Master's and Doctorate level at various universities. The planets are not just celestial bodies but are considered anthropomorphic deities that protect or afflict humans.[14] They are referred to as *Navagraha*, or nine planets. These *Navagraha* are the seven visible planets of Sun-*Surya*, Moon-*Chandra*, Mercury-*Budha*, Venus-*Shukra*, Mars-*Mangala*, Jupiter-*Guru*, and Saturn-*Shani* as well as the Moon's north node, *Rahu*, and the Moon's south node, *Ketu* (the nodes are two points where the Moon's orbit intersects the ecliptic and they lie at opposite points in the birth chart). *Rahu* and *Ketu* have no physical substance since they are positions on the ecliptic, but are given equal status with the planets due to their impact on the Sun, Moon, and Earth through eclipses.[15] The *Navagraha* are considered deities and are as respected and worshipped as other divine beings in India.

In Tamil Nadu most temples, from the very large temple in the city to the small village temple, have a shrine to *Navagraha* (see Fig. 1, Village Shrine to the planets). When visiting a temple I was told to first visit the Shrine of *Navagraha*, even before I went to any of the other deities, even the main deities of Shiva, Ganesh, or Meenakshi. There are also major temples in South India that are dedicated to each of the *Navagraha*, so the planets have their own dedicated places of worship as well as being represented in other temples.

In the United States people who engage astrologers will go for a consultation maybe once a year to understand current planetary cycles and

---

[13] Stephen Markel, *Origins of the Indian Planetary Deities* (Lampeter: The Edwin Mellen Press, 1995), pp. 3, 5.
[14] Caterina Guenzi, 'The Allotted Share: Managing Fortune in Astrological Counseling in Banaras', in *Cosmologies of Fortune: Luck, Vitality and the Contingency of Daily Life*, ed. G. Da Col and C. Humphrey, Special Issue of *Social Analysis* 56, nos. 1 and 2 (2012): pp. 41–42.
[15] Komilla Sutton, *Indian Astrology: How to Discover the Secrets of your Vedic Star Sign* (New York: Penguin Group, 2000) p. 15.

get a pulse on what is happening in their lives.[16] There is also interest in using astrology as a psychological system of self-knowledge and to gain new perspectives and insight.[17] Typically, astrologers in the West are expected to describe a problem, lay out a timeline of planetary significance, and suggest some possible course of action; but they are not expected to fix the problem.

Fig. 1. Village Navagraha shrine.[18]

In India, however, astrology attaches great import to fixing the problem that is seen in the birth chart. In India, astrology not only points out what the problem is so that a client can understand and accept it, but it also suggests corrective curative opportunities. It offers a remedy. Judy Pugh in her study of astrological counselling in contemporary India sees consultation with an astrologer (diviner) as a therapeutic process which not only includes identifying client ailments and obstacles but also includes remedial measures. Pugh states:

---

[16] For an in-depth analysis of the popularity and practice of astrology in Western culture, see Nicholas Campion, *Astrology and Popular Religion in the Modern West* (Farnham: Ashgate, 2012), especially Chapters 11 and 12.
[17] Nicholas Campion, *Astrology and Cosmology in the World's Religions* (New York: NYU Press, 2012), p. 197.
[18] All images in this essay were taken by the author.

While diviners may in fact send clients to other healers, there are also many cases in which the diviner himself takes sole responsibility for the client's ailments and problems. Not only does the diviner engage the client in a communicative interaction in which problems can be explored and clarified, but he may also use the dialogue to organize for the client ameliorative patterns of thought and behavior. In addition, he may recommend and actually prepare for the client various amulets, potions, and other protective devices;...[19]

In Joytish there are many remedial measures.[20] These measures include: *yoga* postures; *pranayama*, the use of controlled breath to access the life force; meditation; *mantras,* sacred formula for the invocation of a deity; and *yantras*, diagrams of numbers, words and symbols that contain the energy of a particular planetary quality (see Fig. 2, *Yantra* of Navagraha).[21] A *yantra* is made more powerful if a *mantra* is chanted in association with it. There are also icons, which are visual representations of the planetary deities and *puja*, which is worship and adoration of gods with proper ceremony.[22] A very simple *puja* I often saw in India was the lighting of an oil lamp in front of the icon of a deity; an act which reminded me of lighting a candle in front of a statue of Mary, Mother of God, in many Christian churches. Another remedial action is a visit to the temple on the day that is dedicated to a planetary deity. For example, if you are having trouble with Saturn, you would go to the temple on Saturday, Saturn's day and do *puja* for Saturn. Another remedy is the use of gemstones that have associations with particular planetary deities. Using Saturn as an example, one might wear Saturn's stone, a blue sapphire, to help alleviate a negative Saturn influence. These remedies are a type of celestial magic since they are actions directed to the planetary intelligences – deities – to gain knowledge, benefit, or advantage.

---

[19] Judy Pugh, 'Astrological Counseling in Contemporary India', *Journal of Culture, Medicine, and Psychiatry* 7, no. 3 (1983): p. 280.
[20] Komilla Sutton, *The Lunar Nodes: Crisis and Redemption* (Bournemouth: The Wessex Astrologer Ltd., 2011) pp. 149–53.
[21] For *mantra*, see *Tamil Lexicon*, Vol. 3, p. 3068.
[22] For *puja* see *Tamil Lexicon*, Vol. 3, p. 2826.

Fig. 2. *Yantra* of Navagraha.

While in Tamil Nadu I had decided that in addition to observing evidence of astrology in Tamil culture I would also have my chart analysed by several astrologers. This led to a total of three astrological consultations. The first was by an astrologer who was seated on the ground outside of a temple, which is a fairly common sight in South India. He had with him a parrot and a deck of cards. If I had been Tamil he would have talked to me about my astrological chart, but since I was a foreigner he utilized his parrot to discover my fate. The astrologer spread out the cards in front of him and had the parrot walk over all the cards and peck at one to indicate that was the chosen card for my reading. The astrologer then described the meaning of the card through our group's interpreter. The interpretation was very broad and general, but had a positive note about the influences of Venus, which was then prominent in the night sky.

My second chart reading was from a professor in the Mathematics Department at a local university. I asked him if there was a conflict with him being both an astrologer and a mathematics professor, but he assured me there was not, since astrology is linked to mathematics in India. He spoke excellent English and no interpreter was needed. We met in his home in a suburban area and the whole visit had a very utilitarian feel to it, almost as if I was visiting an accountant. I did not get any major insights into my chart or find any mystery in the reading that I received from the professor, but I did enjoy the fact that astrology was accepted in an academic environment.

For my third reading, our group's interpreter, a college age woman from Madurai, introduced me to her family astrologer. He was a caste astrologer, which means that he came from a family of astrologers from a specific caste and learned his skill from a guru. There were four generations of astrologers in his family: his grandfather, father, himself and his son were all astrologers. His extended family had three children who had also learned astrology. The reading with the caste astrologer took place in a meeting room at the hotel where we were staying. He only spoke Tamil, so everything was translated for me. I took notes and recorded the consultation. When he examined my astrological chart he immediately focused on what he termed my difficult *karma* in dealing with relationships. He said that relationships do not stick to me and that they roll right off me. It was true that I had multiple unsuccessful relationships and had been divorced twice. I was then in the second year of my third marriage.

The astrologer said that the problem with my relationships was due to *Rahu* and *Ketu*, the Moon's North and South nodes. In Jyotish, *Rahu* and *Ketu* are symbolized by a *Naga*. *Nagas* are like snakes but they stand erect; they are thought to be evolved beings, and due to the shedding of their skin they symbolize the transformation of death and rebirth and as snakes they also signify poison and wisdom and are able to influence events both positively and negatively.[23] Given the great antiquity and the immense corpus of Indian mythology there are contradictory stories about the origins of *Rahu* and *Ketu* but the most well known myth is the story of the 'Churning of the Ocean'.[24] The story has variants, but basically relates how the gods and demons were fighting over who would first discover the hidden nectar of immortality. The gods did not want the demons to get it,

---

[23] Sutton, *The Lunar Nodes*, pp. 2, 10.
[24] Markel, *Origins of the Indian Planetary Deities*, pp. 57–58.

since it would make them immortal. Once the nectar was found, *Rahu* tricked the gods and drank the nectar, making himself immortal. The Sun and Moon found out about *Rahu*'s trick and told Lord Vishnu, who was so furious that he cut *Rahu* in half. But since *Rahu* was now immortal he could not be killed and remained alive in two separate parts which remain in the sky as two separate halves, *Rahu*, the head of the serpent, and *Ketu*, the tail of the serpent. Since the Sun and Moon were the ones who reported the deception, they became *Rahu* and *Ketu*'s enemies. The ability of *Rahu* and *Ketu* to create eclipses and darken, even devour, the Sun and Moon is one reason why *Rahu* is considered the Demon of Eclipses and they are particularly powerful in the birth chart (see Fig. 3, *Rahu* – the serpent's head, and Fig. 4, *Ketu* – the serpent's tail).[25]

Fig. 3. *Rahu* – the serpent's head (from author's shrine).

---

[25] Sanjay Patel, *Hindu Deities* (London: Plume, 2006), pp. 117–19.

260 South Indian Ritual Dispels Negative Karma in the Birth Chart

Fig. 4. *Ketu* – the serpent's tail (from author's shrine).

The position of *Rahu* and *Ketu* in the birth chart is associated with *karma*, the 'action' we take in past, present and future lives and the consequences of that action. *Rahu* and *Ketu* indicate internal struggles with our *karma*. It is through our struggles with *Rahu* and *Ketu* that we have the opportunity to uncover the hidden wisdom of our past life experiences. According to Komilla Sutton, *Rahu* and *Ketu* are the karmic axis of our lives.

> Like beads on a necklace, previous lifetimes are interconnected by an invisible thread – which is *Rahu/Ketu*. As the indicator and the Lords of Karma in the birth chart they represent the stumbling blocks which, when overcome, eventually lead to liberation and maturity of the soul. *Ketu* deals with the past karma and *Rahu* with the need to create new karma.[26]

---

[26] Sutton, *The Lunar Nodes*, p. 4.

The remedial measure for my relationship troubles that the astrologer suggested was a clearing ritual at a temple well known in the region to dispel the problems created by the karmic issues of *Rahu* and *Ketu*. As Judy Pugh suggested, the astrologer not only diagnosed my trouble, he was also taking responsibility for the remedy.[27] This remedy included referring me to a specialist, since only a Brahmin priest could enact the ritual. But the astrologer also took on the responsibility of the remedy by organizing the ritual in all aspects, from deciding the place of the ritual, securing the specialist, and creating the ritual offering.

In the study of religion, my field is Ritual Studies, which means that I view religious phenomena through the lens of ritual. Ritual Studies is a complex field since there is a vast variety of rituals throughout history in multiple cultures that express the psychic, social and religious world of its participants. Different types of rituals include festivals, celebrations, healing, and rites of passage (such as marriages and funerals).[28] I define ritual as a structured series of symbolic, embodied actions that are directed with intention toward a specific goal. The goal of a ritual varies based on the type of ritual and can be to transform (rite of passage), cure, celebrate, empower, and engage in physical and metaphysical realities. Ritual Studies is a multi-disciplinary field in that one must engage many different disciplines in order to understand a ritual. There will often be philosophical/religious meanings, historical significance, a special text from which the ritual is drawn, material objects that are used, art that is representative of the event, as well as the community context which includes social implications and political hierarchies; see for example the work of Victor Turner, who studied the Ndembu.[29]

Ritual Studies has a strong association with Anthropology and utilizes ethnographic fieldwork in research, which includes the methodology of participant observation.[30] Participant observation is a method whereby the researcher is both a participant in and an observer of a ritual. There are challenges to being both a participant and an observer, in maintaining both

---

[27] Pugh, 'Astrological Counseling', p. 280.
[28] Fred Clothey, 'Ritual, Nature and Theories', *The Perennial Dictionary of World Religions*, ed. Keith Grim (San Francisco, CA: Harper San Francisco, 1989), pp. 624–28.
[29] Victor Turner, *The Ritual Process: Structure and Anti-Structure* (1969; Chicago: Aldine de Gruyter, 1995).
[30] Russell Bernard, ed., *Handbook of Methods in Cultural Anthropology* (Walnut Creek, CA: AltaMira Press, 1998)

an insider and an outsider perspective at the same time.[31] Holding these dual perspectives can be like walking a narrow path since it can be difficult to keep an objective, intellectual awareness of an event in which one is subjectively and emotionally involved. The researcher can take an etic approach and analyse a ritual while the ritual is occurring using existing theories, but this tends to emphasize the outsider point of view. Or the researcher can engage in a emic approach and let go of preconceived notions and engage fully in the ritual, carefully documenting the ritual as a phenomenon by keeping field notes, collecting photos, gathering material objects, and conducting interviews in order to analyse the data after the fact. This is the approach that I took. I was interested in the subject of Jyotish and brought an open-minded curiosity to the ritual, an ideal attitude for engaging in ethnographic research.

A simple way to analyse this ritual, or any ritual for that matter, is to break it down into its component parts. I will examine this karmic dispelling ritual by looking at 1. The Goal, 2. Place/Time, 3. Participants, 4. Material Objects, 5. Structured Actions, and 6. Conclusion.

1. The Goal
The caste astrologer who suggested the ritual made clear that the goal of the ritual was to clear the negative *karma* in my birth chart caused by *Rahu* and *Ketu*, especially surrounding marriage. Before the ritual began I very clearly set my intention that my *karma* be cleared so that I have a stable, joyous, and long-lasting marriage. I silently repeated this intention to myself during planning, preparation, and implementation of the ritual.

2. Place/Time
The place for the main ritual was the Peraiyur Sree Naganathar Temple near Pudhukottai in Tamil Nadu. This is a Snake Temple dated ca. 9–12th century (see Fig. 5, Snake Temple). Lord Shiva, known by the name *Naganathar*, the Snake Lord, resides at the temple with his Royal Consort. This temple is considered a holy place. It is a '*parigara thalam*' which means it is a place of intercession where one can plead to get rid of *tosham,* which is a fault, blemish, or transgression.[32]

---

[31] Barbara Tedlock, 'From Participant Observation to the Observation of Participation: The Emergence of Narrative Ethnography', *Journal of Anthropological Research* 47 (1991): pp. 69–94.
[32] *Tamil Lexicon*, Vol. 2, p. 2508.

Fig. 5. Snake Temple.

The temple is well known in the region for rectifying any malefic effect in an individual's horoscope by the offering of prayers. The temple is especially good at rectifying the ill effects caused by *Rahu* and *Ketu*, as well as problems such as hindrance in marriage and delays in childbirth. People come to the temple on their own to worship the deities and it is also possible to pay for a special ceremony led by a priest.[33] The astrologer set up such a special ceremony with a priest for my ritual. The date and time for the ritual was 3 July 2004. We left Madurai at 7:30 in the morning for the approximately two-hour drive to the temple. The timing for this event

---

[33] YouTube video of the Sri Naganathar temple near Pudakkottai http://www.youtube.com/watch?v=o-d6_OHQuqg [accessed 1 June 2016].

appears to be one of convenience for all participants since it was scheduled on a Saturday, not Thursday which is the special day dedicated to *Rahu/Ketu* at the temple.

3. Participants

I was the main participant since it was my *karma* that was negatively effected and needed to be cleansed. The astrologer was a central participant in that he made the observation that such a ritual would be beneficial to me. He also organized the entire ritual, which was quite elaborate. In many ways he acted like a producer. He made the arrangements for the pre-ritual of prayers and *mantras* by Brahmin priests that occurred in Madurai the day before we left for the temple, and he made arrangements for the priest to lead the ritual at the temple. The astrologer did not lead the ritual; rather the Brahmin priest associated with the temple led the ritual. The astrologer also gathered the items needed for the offering, many of which were purchased near the temple, and he prepared the offering. The astrologer's son, who was around twelve years of age, accompanied us an observer. There was also a college-age Hindu woman who was our translator and had connected me to the astrologer. My husband Bill also accompanied us to the temple. I had thought Bill would simply be an observer and we were both surprised when the astrologer let us know that Bill was to be a participant in the ritual. Neither of us had expected this, but the astrologer explained that since a successful marriage was one of my desired outcomes, it was important for my husband to go through the ritual with me. This fits with Pugh's contention that the astrologer and 'client participate together in an integral process which weaves supportive continuities between the scene of the advisory session and the scene of the client's everyday life'.[34]

An interesting question is whether to consider the deities as participants in the ritual. Represented materially by stone icons, someone might consider them objects, rather than participants. But since they were the deities to whom the prayers, *mantras*, offerings and requests were made, many would consider them participants. The main deities at the temple were two forms of Shiva – *Naganathar*, the Snake Lord and *Kasi Vishvanathan*, and his Royal Consort, *Parvati*. There were other deities worshipped at the temple including *Rahu* and *Ketu*.

---

[34] Pugh, 'Astrological Counseling', p. 281.

4. Material Objects

The offering that was made to the deities was the main object in this ritual. The offering was a collection of items arranged on a brass platter; some items we brought with us and some were purchased at a small stand outside the temple (Fig. 6, Author and husband with offering). Each of the items in the offering had a symbolic meaning. Victor Turner calls symbols the basic building-blocks of ritual. He also states that analysis of the symbols needs to be based on the culture that designed the ritual, an emic/insider perspective, not the symbolism that an outsider like myself might attribute.[35]

Fig. 6. Author and husband with offering.

For this reason I interviewed the astrologer a few days after the ritual and asked him about the meaning of the material objects and the ritual actions. These meaning are: bananas represented food for the deities; limes drive away debt and keep good friends coming and bad ones going; coconut brings in links with government related things; and Beetle Leaf brings in a good relationship with God and asks God to accept what the priest says that I deserve, which is good health and wealth. There was a small brass snake that sat in the palm of our hands that was used during the ritual. We

---

[35] Turner, *The Ritual Process*, pp. 9,14.

also had flowered garlands to place on the deities as an offering, and flowered garlands for my husband and me after the ritual was completed. There were costs involved including a fee for the Brahmin priests who did the pre-ritual, a fee for the temple priest who led the ritual, and a fee for the astrologer. I also paid fees for the translator, car rental, and purchase of items in the offering.

5. Structured actions
Ritual action is embodied, which means it engages the body through the five senses of sight, hearing, taste, smell and touch and includes what is said, done, and seen.[36] The actions of a ritual, which also have symbolic meaning, form the ritual's structure. Turner has shown how these ritual elements combine into patterns that essentially blaze a trail that 'connects the known world of sensorily perceptible phenomena with the unknown and invisible realm… It makes intelligible what is mysterious.'[37] Ritual structure weaves together the goal, place, participants, and objects, bringing the separate parts into a meaningful whole.

The first action was a pre-ritual done by Brahmin priests prior to going to the temple. Ideally I should have done *puja* and recited a *mantra* for 108 days as a preparation for this ritual. But since I was not going to be in India for 108 more days, the astrologer retained priests to do a condensed version of the *mantra* and *puja* for me by repeating the *mantra* 108 times over a 24-hour period. The *mantra* they chanted was *Om. Srim. Su. Saravana Bhava Nama Om.* This means 'Blessed Goodness Divine'. I was not with the priests, and I did not see this take place. But the ash from the prayers and burnings were placed on a small metal *yantra* that had the symbols for the *Navagraha* on it. The ashes and *yantra* were folded neatly together into a paper envelope. This ash was meant to drive away all evil things of the snake, and to bring in all good things. The priests used sacred water from Alagarkoil (an ancient healing site) in their ritual, which was also part of the offering.

On the morning of the ritual we rented a car and driver to take the astrologer, his son, the translator, Bill and me to the snake temple. We left at 7:30 in the morning and drove several hours to the temple. The temple was in a rural setting with small street markets geared to temple visitors. From these markets we bought the bulk of the objects for our offerings, such as the coconut, garlands, and limes. We entered the stone temple and

---

[36] Clothey, 'Ritual, Nature and Theories,' p. 625.
[37] Turner, *The Ritual Process*, pp. 10, 15.

sat in a quiet place while the astrologer arranged the offering. We said prayers over the offering, asking for a successful ritual and clearing. After our offering was arranged on a brass plate the temple priest joined us and led the main ritual.

For the main ritual we went to the three main deities who each had their own section in the temple. First we went to *Naganathar* the Snake Lord, who was the central deity of the temple and the focus of the ritual. *Naganthar* was a stone image about five feet tall and similar in appearance to the smaller snake icons that surround the temple as seen in Figures 6, 8 and 9. Bill and I sat cross-legged in front of *Naganathar*, each holding in the palm of our hand a small brass snake. We said a *mantra* for 108 times while holding the little snakes. The *mantra* was *Om Nagarajaya Nama Ha* which means 'Praise to the name of the Snake King'. This *mantra* was asking the snake to reside in me and do good things for me. Bill and I lost count of how many times we said the *mantra* and were stopped by the priest, who seemed surprised that we did not know when we had reached 108 repetitions.

Then the priest poured oil over the Snake Lord. The oil is to keep things from sticking to the snake and to help block evil things and to abolish evil things. Then the priest poured the water from the fountain at the centre of the temple over the Snake Lord. This action was to take evil from my past lives and help guide me in the future. Next the priest poured the water the Brahmin priests had charged in the pre-ritual from Alagarkoil, which was to connect me to the snake. The next step was that the priest poured milk over the Snake Lord to give us long life and grant all my wishes. After that, a paste of rice flour mixed with water was rubbed over the Snake Lord. This was to release all evil things I have done in this life, even if I did not know about them or know they were evil, and also to release all the evil things done in past lives. Then turmeric powder mixed with water was rubbed on the Snake Lord. This was to bring good friendship, a bright face and blessings from the goddess. Then rose and sandalwood were put on the Snake. This was to protect my body since sandalwood is a luxury and brings a sense of satisfaction. Then a garland was placed over the Snake, which was meant to please the God so he will be happy and bless me. After this conclusion we went to the two other deities and did a smaller version of the offering and worship (*puja*).

After we finished with *puja* at all three deities, the very last act was to go to the *Navagraha* shrine, which was positioned prominently in the temple.

268 South Indian Ritual Dispels Negative Karma in the Birth Chart

Fig. 7. Snake Temple Navagraha shrine.

At the shrine the astrologer placed the *yantra* and ash from the pre-Brahmin ritual (see Fig. 7, Snake Temple Navagraha shrine). The astrologer prayed to the *Navagraha* and told the nine planets that we had just finished a ritual to take away the bad things related to my past lives. He told the *Navagraha* that we did this ritual for the best of intentions and we did it the best that we could. However, he asked the planets, if we did something wrong with the ritual, please make it right for me. This final appeal to the planets gave me a sense of how important the planets were in the scheme of things. The astrologer told me that the *Navagraha* have the power even to shake the gods and goddesses, who each have their own horoscope. The astrologer's description of the primacy of the planets is different from Guenzi who states the planetary deities are hierarchically subordinate to the major gods and goddess of the Hindu pantheon.[38]

6. Conclusions
There is usually an assumption that rituals will be effective in meeting their intended goal. It is not common to question whether a ritual was a success or not. But Ron Grimes is a ritual scholar who believes it is important, even necessary, to be critical of ritual and to question whether or not it was successful.[39] Was the ritual efficacious? Did it accomplish what it set out to accomplish? And how does one decide if a ritual 'worked'? There is a very clear way to judge whether a ritual at the Snake Temple was considered efficacious. If the goal of a ritual participant was successful, for example a marriage took place or a baby was born, then the satisfied ritual participant will return to the temple and offer a snake icon as a symbol of success and gratitude.

Fig. 8. Snake Icons at street market.

---

[38] Guenzi, 'The Allotted Share', p. 43.
[39] Ronald Grimes, *Ritual Criticism: Case Studies in its Practice, Essays on its Theory* (CreateSpace Independent Publishing Platform, 2010).

270 South Indian Ritual Dispels Negative Karma in the Birth Chart

These icons are available for sale at the street markets near the temple, and are miniature versions of the larger Snake Lord in the temple (see Fig. 8, Snake icons at market).

The temple's apparent success in taking away negative *karma* and hindrances is seen in the large number of snake icons that are placed everywhere around the temple, along the walkways and on top of walls, which you can see in Figure 5. There are also snake icons outside of the temple walls and underneath trees around the temple (see Fig. 9, Icon offerings under tree).

Fig. 9. Snake icon offerings under tree.

There are so many snake icons adorning the temple that there is not enough room to display them all, leaving many icons in piles around the temple (see Fig. 10, Author after ritual in front of icons).

It has been over twelve years since I participated in this ritual to dispel the negative relationship *karma* associated with *Rahu* and *Ketu* that the astrologer identified in my chart. Do I consider it a success? Yes, I do. I am grateful for the care and attention to detail that was given to this ritual. I am grateful for the effort that was taken on my behalf. I am in a happy, prosperous marriage that has outlived in years any of my previous relationships, combined. Is this a coincidence? Is it the result of the ritual?

I will never know. But if I were to go back to India I would return to this temple, purchase a snake icon and place it as an offering.

Fig. 10. Author after ritual with icons behind her.

In summary, there are many ways to participate in celestial magic. In South India today celestial magic is found in the numerous remedial practices, including meditation, *mantras, yantras* and *puja*, which are used to counter negative influences in the birth chart. These remedies become a ritual when they are combined into a structured series of symbolic embodied actions that are intentionally directed toward a specific goal. Ritual is a container for celestial magic because it provides an overarching structure that brings together and organizes the participants, objects, and actions. Ritual is also a vehicle because ritual takes this container of celestial magic and blazes a trail with symbolic, embodied, and progressive actions toward a *telos,* an end result that links the participant with their cosmos.

NOTES ON CONTRIBUTORS

Christine Broadbent is a professional astrologer with an active consulting practice in both Sydney and Auckland. Her special interest in Ibn 'Arabi was first sparked in 1988 when she spent a year studying his *Fusus-al-Hikam* and discovered his lesser known mystical astrology at Karnak Sufi school in Northern Queensland. Her prior academic background includes postgraduate studies in the sociology of knowledge and work as a tutor in Sociology at the University of NSW, Sydney, where she gained MA qual. and Hons degrees, first class. She more recently completed two years of postgraduate research at Massey University in Auckland. Her enduring interest in knowledge studies led her back to Sociology to research the 'othering' of astrology as a knowledge system, and the shifts occurring with the renewal of astrological scholarship since the late twentieth century. Her current research focus is Maori cosmology, in particular the maramataka Moon calendars and celestial navigation. Active in Australian and New Zealand astrological education, Christine also holds a graduate teaching diploma from Sydney University.

Jane Burton graduated with the MA in Cultural Astronomy and Astrology at the Sophia Centre for The Study of Cosmology in Culture at the University of Wales Trinity Saint David in July 2012. Her dissertation was titled 'Is the 2012 Awakening/Ascension a progressive or catastrophic millenarianism? An investigation into the social and environmental doctrine of a 21st Century Apocalyptic Prophecy'. She is currently researching witches and goddess worshippers, and has spent time 'going native' as a deep insider with specific covens and goddess worshipping groups in Spain, Malta and in Staffordshire in England. Her research will continue to investigate whether or not her research groups place any emphasis upon blood within their magical and spiritual rituals, and furthermore, whether they believe celestial timings and the location of the ritual have any efficacy upon their rituals.

Claire Chandler received her MA in Cultural Astronomy and Astrology from the Sophia Centre in 2014 having focused on the themes of history and archaeoastronomy. Her thesis investigated the cultural context of magic and astrology in Greek Magical Papyrii (PGM) XIII. She is continually fascinated by how different cultures make sense of the cosmos and how ideas of the divine are shown in the cultural assumptions made about the material world and how magic can be seen to move between the two. She has been a practising astrologer and a previous president of the Astrological Lodge of London.

Joscelyn Godwin, educated at Magdalene College, Cambridge and Cornell University, is Professor of Music at Colgate University, USA. His research and publications concern speculative music (*Harmonies of Heaven and Earth, Music, Mysticism and Magic, J. F. H. von Dalberg, Harmony of the Spheres, The Mystery of the Seven Vowels,* etc.), Western esotericism (*Robert Fludd, The Theosophical Enlightenment, Arktos, The Golden Thread, Athanasius Kircher's Theatre of the World, Atlantis and the Cycles of Time,* etc.), and translations in those fields (*The Chemical Wedding, Splendor Solis, Hypnerotomachia Poliphili,* and works by Fabre d'Olivet, René Guénon, Julius Evola, Antoine Faivre, etc.).

Liz Greene is a Jungian analyst and professional astrologer, and has been director of the London-based Centre for Psychological Astrology since 1982. She holds doctorates in psychology and, from the University of Bristol, in history, and taught on the MA in Cultural Astronomy and Astrology at Bath Spa University and, from 2007 to 2013, at the University of Wales, Lampeter. She has been a tutor on the training programme of the Association of Jungian Analysts, London, since 1983. She is the author of numerous books and academic papers on psychological, mythological, astrological, and historical themes.

Alison Greig has an MA in Cultural Astronomy and Astrology from the Sophia Centre for the Study of Cosmology in Culture, University of Wales, Trinity Saint David. Her dissertation was on concepts of heaven in the history of western religions. Originally from New Zealand, she has been working abroad for many years in Austria and the USA. She holds an MA in International Relations from Webster University (Vienna), a Bachelor in Social Sciences from Waikato University and a Bachelor of Laws from Auckland University, New Zealand, where she was admitted as a Barrister and Solicitor.

Mike Harding is an existential psychotherapist and consultant astrologer. He is a Senior Lecturer and supervisor at the School of Psychotherapy and Psychology at Regent's University, London. Over the years he has chaired the Astrological Association of Great Britain, the Association of Professional Astrologers and the Society for Existential Analysis. He is the author of *Hymns to the Ancient Gods* and co-author with Charles Harvey of

Working With Astrology, as well as authoring articles on both the technical and philosophical aspects of astrology for the *Astrological Journal* of the Astrological Association of Great Britain. His paper 'Astrology as a Language Game', given at the Inaugural Conference of the Sophia Centre at Bath Spa University College in 2003, is published in *Astrology and the Academy* (Bristol: Cinnabar Books, 2004).

Lilan Laishley earned her doctorate in Religious Studies at the University of Pittsburgh, PA, USA with a focus on symbol and ritual. She has taught philosophy and religion at several universities and has presented numerous academic papers at the American Academy of Religion. She has been a consulting and teaching astrologer for thirty years and has written extensively on astrology. Her article, 'Astrology as Religion: Theory and Practice' in the *Journal for the Study of Religion, Nature, and Culture* (2007) examines the intersection between astrology and religion. More recently she presented a five-week lecture series on Astrology and Christianity at the Thorne Sparkman School in Chattanooga. She is author of *Religious Diversity on the Labyrinth: Rituals that Engage a Sacred Cosmos* (Lambert Academic Publishing, 2011), which examines how ritual expresses the cosmological beliefs of the participants.

Sue Lewis has a MA in Western Esotericism from the University of Exeter, Diplomas from the Faculty of Astrological Studies and the Astrological Psychology Association, of which she is a tutor, and a Certificate in Transpersonal Perspectives from the Centre for Transpersonal Psychology. She has published two books, *Astrological Psychology, Western Esotericism, and the Transpersonal* (HopeWell, 2015) and *Astrology and Juan de Mena's 'Laberinto de Fortuna'*, Paper of the Medieval Hispanic Research Seminar, 21 (Queen Mary London, 1999).

Karen Parham lectures in Philosophy and Religious Studies at Birmingham Metropolitan College and is a freelance writer and course designer for various institutions. Karen completed her PhD at the University of Hull in Philosophy and Dutch Studies, focusing on the philosophical study of mysticism and concepts of perfection. She has also worked for the Open Universiteit in Heerlen, The Netherlands, as a researcher into 'Methodologies in the Humanities' and for the Literary and Linguistic Computing Centre at the University of Cambridge as a researcher in Middle Dutch texts. She is currently studying another MA in European Philosophy at the University of Wales Trinity Saint David.

José Manuel Redondo was awarded his PhD with a thesis on Proclus's theurgy, under Dr Gregory Shaw ('*The celestial imagination*: Proclus on the hieratic art of the Greeks or theurgy'). While specializing in Neoplatonism, Redondo teaches Medieval and Renaissance philosophy and about Greek religion, divination and magic in classical and late antiquity at the Universidad Nacional Autónoma de México (U.N.A.M). He has also been teaching at diverse psychological institutes, particularly those working a 'Jungian' approach, on Greco-Roman mythology and the symbolism of astrology and the tarot, and has also published articles in academic and alternative publications. Redondo is also currently involved with several research and translation projects of works on philosophy, divination and magic from Late Antiquity up to the Renaissance.

Hereward Tilton has lectured on early modern Rosicrucianism, Christian Cabala and alchemy at the Ludwig-Maximilians-Universität in Munich, the department for the History of Hermetic Philosophy and Related Currents at the University of Amsterdam, and the Exeter Centre for the Study of Esotericism at the University of Exeter. His most notable publication to date is a biography of Michael Maier, *The Quest for the Phoenix*. He is currently writing a new book incorporating his research on restricted teachings of the Gold- und Rosenkreuz and the Christian Cabalistic employment of entheogens.

M. E. Warlick is a Professor of Art History at the University of Denver, Colorado. She is author of *Max Ernst and Alchemy: A Magician in Search of Myth* (Austin, 2001), *The Alchemy Stones* (London, 2002), and has published articles within *The Art Bulletin*, *The Art Journal*, *Glasgow Emblem Studies*, and within conference proceedings for the Association for the Study of Esotericism. She teaches classes on European Art from the 18th through the 20th centuries with a special emphasis on Surrealism and on Art and the History of Science.

BACK ISSUES OF CULTURE AND COSMOS
http://www.cultureandcosmos.org/backIssues.html

Contents, Vol. 1 no 1 (spring/summer 1997)
Robin Heath: *An Astronomical Basis for Solar Hero Myths;* **Norris Hetherington**: *Ancient Greek Cosmology and Culture: a Historiographical Review;* **Alan Weber**: *The Development of Celestial Journey Literature, 1400 - 1650;* **Ken Negus**: *Kepler's Tertius Interveniens;* **John Durant** and **Martin Bauer**: *British Public Perceptions of Astrology: an Approach from the Sociology of Knowledge.*

Contents Vol. 1 no 2 (autumn/winter 1997)
Otto Neugebauer: *On the History of Wretched Subjects;* **Nick Kollerstrom**: *The Star Zodiac of Antiquity;* **Robert Zoller**: *The Hermetica as Ancient Science;* **Edgar Laird**: *Christine de Pizan and Controversy Concerning Star Study in the Court of Charles V;* **Jürgen G.H. Hoppman**: *The Lichtenberger Prophecy and Melanchthon's Horoscope for Luther;* **Elizabeth Heine**: *W.B.Yeats: Poet and Astrologer.*

Contents Vol. 2 no 1 (spring/summer 1998)
J. McKim Malville and **R. N. Swaminathan:** *People, Planets and the Sun: Surya Puja in Tamil Nadu, South India;* **Carlos Trenary:** *Yaxchilan Lintel 25 as a Cometary Record;* **Graziella Federici Vescovini:** *Biagio Pelacani's Astrological History for the Year 1405;* **Frank McGillion:** *The Influence of Wilhelm Fliess' Cosmobiology on Sigmund Freud;* **Nicholas Campion:** *Sigmund Freud's Investigation of Astrology.*

Contents Vol. 2 no 2 (autumn/winter 1998)
Giuseppe Bezza: *Astrological Considerations on the Length of Life in Hellenistic, Persian and Arabic Astrology;* **Angela Voss:** *The Music of the Spheres: Marsilio Ficino and Renaissance harmonia*; **Robert Zoller:** *Marc Edmund Jones and New Age Astrology in America.*

Contents Vol. 3 no 1 (spring/summer 1999)
Michael R. Molnar: *Firmicus Maternus and the Star of Bethlehem*; **Roger Beck:** *The Astronomical Design of Karakush, a Royal Burial Site in Ancient Commagene: an Hypothesis*; **Chantal Allison:** *The Ifriqiya Uprising Horoscope from* On Reception *by Masha'alla, Court Astrologer in the Early 'Abassid Caliphate.*

Contents Vol. 3 no 2 (autumn/winter 1999)
Robin Waterfield: *The Evidence of Astrology in Classical Greece;* **Remo Catani:** *The Polemics on Astrology 1489-1524*; **Claudia Rousseau**: *An Astrological Prognostication to Duke Cosimo de Medici of Florence.*

Contents Vol. 4 no 1 (spring/summer 2000)
Patrick Curry: *Historical Approaches to Astrology*; **Edgar Laird:** *Heaven and the Sphaera Mundi in the Middle Ages*; **George D. Chryssides:** *Is God a Space Alien? The Cosmology of the Raëlian Church.*

Contents Vol. 4 no 2 (autumn/winter 2000)
David J. Ross: *The Bird, The Cross, and the Emperor: Investigations into the Antiquity* of

The Cross in Cygnus; **Angela Voss:** *The Astrology of Marsilio Ficino: Divination or Science?;* **Patrick Curry:** *Astrology on Trial, and its Historians: Reflections on the Historiography of 'Superstition'.*

Contents Vol. 5 no 1 (spring/summer 2001)
Demetra George: *Manuel I Komnenos and Michael Glykas: A Twelfth-Century Defence and Refutation of Astrology,* Part I; **Richard L. Poss:** *Stars and Spirituality in the Cosmology of Dante's* Commedia.

Contents Vol. 5 no 2 (autumn/winter 2001)
Arkadiusz Sołtysiak: *The Bull of Heaven in Mesopotamian Sources;* **Demetra George:** *Manuel I Komnenos and Michael Glykas: A Twelfth-Century Defence and Refutation of Astrology,* Part 2; **Garry Phillipson** and **Peter Case:** *The Hidden Lineage of Modern Management Science: Astrology, Alchemy and the Myers-Briggs Type Indicator.*

Contents Volume 6 Number 1 (spring/summer 2002)
Ari Belenkyi: *A Unique Feature of the Jewish Calendar - Dehiyot;* **Demetra George:** *Manuel I Komnenos and Michael Glykas: A Twelfth-Century Defence and Refutation of Astrology,* Part 3; **Germana Ernst:** *The Sky in a Room: Campanella's Apologeticus in defence of the pamphlet* De siderali fato vitando; **Tommaso Campanella:** *Apologia for the opuscule on* De siderali fato vitando.

Contents Volume 6 Number 2 (autumn/winter 2002)
Jesse Krai: *Rheticus' Poem 'Concerning the Beer of Breslau and the Twelve Signs of the Zodiac';* **Anna Marie Roos:** *Israel Hiebner's Astrological Amulets and the English Sigil War;* **Nicholas Campion:** *Surrealist Cosmology: André Breton and Astrology.*

Contents Volume 7 Number 1 (spring/summer 2003) GALILEO'S ASTROLOGY
Nick Kollerstrom: *Foreword: Galileo as Believer;* **Nicholas Campion:** *Introduction: Galileo's Life and Work;* **Antonio Favaro:** *Galileo, Astrologer;* **Germana Ernst:** *Astrology and Prophecy in Campanella and Galileo;* **Nick Kollerstrom;** *Galileo as an Astrologer: Antonino Poppi: On Trial for Astral Fatalism: Galileo Faces the Inquisition;* **Guiseppe Righini:***Galileo's Horoscope for Cosimo II de Medici;* **Mario Biagioli:** *An Astrologico-Dynastic Encounter; Galileo's Correspondence; Galileo's Letter to Dini, May 1611; On the Character of Sagredo: Galileo's judgements upon his nativity; Galileo's Horoscopes for his Daughters; Rome, 1630;* **Bernadette Brady:** *Four Galilean Horoscopes: An Analysis of Galileo's Astrological Techniques; A Sonnet by Galileo.*

Contents Volume 7 Number 2 (autumn/winter 2003)
Günther Oestmann: *Tycho Brahe's Geniture;* **Bernard Eccles:** *Astrological physiognomy from Ptolemy to the present day;* **James Brockbank:** *Planetary signification from the second century until the present day;* **Julia Cleave:** *Ficino's Approach to Astrology as Reflected in Book VII of his Letters.*

Contents Volume 8 No 1/2 (spring/summer autumn/winter 2004)
Valerie Shrimplin *Organising INSAP;* **Rolf Sinclair** *Foreword: INSAP IV in Oxford: A Summary;* **Nicholas Campion** *Introduction: The Inspiration of Astronomical Phenomena;* **Hubert A. Allen, Jr.** *Hawkins' Way: Remembering Astronomer Gerald S. Hawkins;* **Hubert A. Allen, Jr. and Terry Edward Ballone** *Star Imagery in Petroglyph National*

Monument; **Mark Butterworth** *Astronomy and the Magic Lantern*; **Ann Laurence Caudano** *Sun, Moon, and Stars on Kievan Rus Jewellery (10th – 13th Centuries)*; **Nicholas Campion** *The Sun is God;* **Anne Chapman-Rietschi** *Cosmic Gardens*; **Deborah Garwood** *Paris Solstice*; **N. J. Girardot** *Celestial Worlds In the Work of Self-Taught Visionary Artists With Special Reference to Howard Finster's Vision of 1982*; **John G. Hatch** *Desire, Heavenly Bodies, and a Surrealist's Fascination with the Celestial Theatre*; **Holly Henry** *Bertrand Russell in Blue Spectacles: His Fascination with Astronomy*; Ronald Hicks *Astronomy and the Sacred Landscape in Irish Myth*; **Chris Impey** *Why Are We So Lonely?*; **Bernd Klähn** *The Aberration of Starlight and/in Postmodernist Fiction*; **Nick Kollerstrom** *How Galileo dedicated the moons of Jupiter to Cosimo II de Medici*; **Arnold Lebeuf** *Dating the five Suns of Aztec cosmology*; **Andrea D. Lobel** *Trailing the Paper Moon: Astronomical Interpretations of Exodus 12:1-2*; **Stephen C. McCluskey** *Wordsworth's 'Rydal Chapel' and the Astronomical Orientation of Churches*; **David Madacsi** *Sky: Atmospheres and Aesthetic Distance in Planetary and Lunar Environments*; **Daniel R. Matlaga** *A Journey of Celestial Lights: The Sky as Allegory in Melville's Moby Dick*; **Paul Murdin** *Representing the Moon*; **R. P. Olowin** *Robinson Jeffers: Poetic Responses to a Cosmological Revolution*; **David W. Pankenier** *A Brief History of Beiji (Northern Culmen)*; **Richard Poss** *Poetic Responses to the Size of the Universe: Astronomical Imagery and Cosmological Constraints*; **Barbara Rappenglück** *The material of the solid sky and its traces in cultures*; **Brad Ricca** *The Night of Falling Stars: Reading the 1833 Leonid Meteor Storm*; **Patricia Ricci** *Lux ex Tenebris: Etienne-Louis Boullée's Cenotaph for Sir Isaac Newton*; **Sarah Richards** *Die Planetentheorie: its uses and meanings for the Saxon mining communities and the culture of the Dresden Court 1553-1719*; **William Saslaw and Paul Murdin** *The Double Apollos of Istrus*; **Petra G. Schmidl** *Dusk and Dawn in Medieval Islam; On the Importance of Twilight Phenomena with Some Examples of Their Representations in Texts and on Instruments*; **Valerie Shrimplin** *Borromini and the New Astronomy: the elliptical dome*; **Joshua Stein** *Cicero's Use of Astronomy as Proof of the Existence of the Gods*; **Antje Steinhoefel** *Art and Astronomy in the Service of Religion:Observations on the Work of John Russell (1745-1806)*; **Burkard Steinrücken** *An interpretation of the 'Sky Disc of Nebra' as an icon for a bronze age planetarium mechanism with parallels to the moving world-soul in Plato's* Timaeus; **Gary Wells** *Daumier and The Popular Image of Astronomy.*

Contents Vol. 9 no 1 (Spring/Summer 2005)
Gennadij Kurtik and Alexander Militarev *Once more on the origin of Semitic and Greek star names:an astronomic-etymological approach updated*; **Prudence Jones** *A Goddess Arrives: Nineteenth Century Sources of the New Age Triple Moon Goddess*; **Louise Curth** *Astrological Medicine and the Popular Press in Early Modern England.*

Contents Vol. 9 no 2 (Autumn/Winter 2005)
Marinus Anthony van der Sluijs *A Possible Babylonian Precursor to the Theory of ecpyrōsis*; **Liz Greene** *Did Orphic Beliefs Influence the Development of Hellenistic Astrology?*; **Ariel Cohen** *Astronomical Luni-Solar Cycles and the Chronology of the Masoretic Bible*; **Tayra Lanuza-Navarro** *An Astrological Disc from the Sixteenth Century*; **J.C. Holbrook** *Celestial Navigators and Navigation Stories.*

Contents Vol. 10 no 1 and 2 (Spring/Summer, Autumn/Winter 2006)
Lucia Dolce *Introduction: The worship of celestial bodies in Japan: politics, rituals and icons*; **Lucia Dolce** *The State of the Field: A basic bibliography on astrological cultic*

practices in Japan; **Hayashi Makoto** *The Tokugawa Shoguns and Yin-yang knowledge (onmyōdō)*; **John Breen** *Inside Tokugawa religion: stars, planets and the calendar-as-*method; **Mark Teeuwen** *The imperial shrines of Ise:An ancient star cult?*; **Lilla Russell-Smith** *Stars and Planets in Chinese and Central Asian Buddhist Art from the Ninth to the Fifteenth Centuries*; **Matsumoto Ikuyo** *Two Mediaeval Manuscripts on the Worship of the Stars from the Fujii Eikan Collection*; **Tsuda Tetsuei** *The Images of Stars and Their Significance in Japanese Esoteric Buddhist Art*; **Meri Arichi** *Seven Stars of Heaven and Seven Shrines on Earth: The Big Dipper and the Hie Shrine in the Medieval* Period; **Gaynor Sekimori** *Star Rituals and Nikko Shugendô*; **Meri Arichi** *The front cover image: Myōken Bosatsu.*

Contents Vol. 11 no 1 and 2 (Spring/Summer, Autumn/Winter 2007)
Micah Ross *A Survey of Demotic Astrological* Texts; **Francis Schmidt** *Horoscope, Predestination and Merit in Ancient Judaism*; **Stephan Heilen** *Ancient Scholars on the Horoscope of Rome*; **Joanna Komorowska** *Philosophy among Astrologers* ; **Wolfgang Hübner** *The Tropical Points of the Zodiacal Year and the* Paranatellonta *in Manilius' Astronomica;* Aurelio Pérez Jiménez *Hephaestio and the Consecration of Statues*; **Robert Hand** *Signs as Houses (Places) in Ancient Astrology*; **Dorian Gieseler Greenbaum** *Calculating the Lots of Fortune and Daemon in Hellenistic Astrology*; **Susanne Denningmann** *The Ambiguous Terms* ἑῴα *and* ἑσπερία, ἀνατολή, *and* ἑῴα *and* ἑσπερία δύσις **Joseph Crane** *Ptolemy's Digression: Astrology's Aspects andMusical Intervals*; **Giuseppe Bezza** *The Development of an Astrological Term – from Greek* hairesis *to Arabic* ḥayyiz; **Deborah Houlding** *The Transmission of Ptolemy's Terms: An Historical Overview, Comparison and Interpretation.*

Contents Vol. 12 no 1 (Spring/Summer 2008)
Liz Greene *Is Astrology a Divinatory System?*; **James Maffie** *Watching the Heavens with a 'Rooted Heart': The Mystical Basis of Aztec Astronomy*; **J.C. Holbrook** *Astronomy and World Heritage.*

Contents Vol. 12 no 2 (Autumn/Winter 2008)
Mark Williams *Astrological Poetry in late medieval Wales: the case of Dafydd Nanmor's 'To God and the planet Saturn'*; **Scott Hendrix** *Choosing to be Human: Albert the Great on Self Awareness and Celestial Influence*; **Graham Douglas** *Luis Vilhena and the World of Astrology.*

Contents Vol. 13 no 1 (Spring/Summer 2009)
Josefina Rodríguez-Arribas *Astronomical and Astrological Terms in Ibn Ezra's Biblical Commentaries: A New Approach*; **Andrew Vladimirou** *Michael Psellos and Byzantine Astrology in the Eleventh Century*; **Marinus Anthony van der Sluijs** *The Dragon of the Eclipses—A Note*; **Patrick Curry** *Response to Liz Greene's 'Is Astrology a Divinatory System?'*

Contents Vol. 13 no 2 (Autumn/Winter 2009)
Liz Greene *Mystical Experiences Among Astrologers*; **Peter Pesic** *How the Sun Stood Still: Old English Interpretations of Joshua and the Leap Year*; **Doina Ionescu** *Virginia Woolf and Astronomy*; **Carlos Ziller Camenietzki and Luis Miguel Carolino** *Astrologers at War: Manuel Galhano Lourosa and the Political Restoration of Portugal, 1640–1668*; **Nick Campion** *Astrology's Role in New Age Culture: A Research Note*

Culture and Cosmos

Contents Vol. 14 no 1 and 2 (Spring/Summer, Autumn/Winter 2010)
Dorian Gieseler Greenbaum *Introduction*; **Friederike Boockmann** *Johann Kepler's Horoscope Collection*; **J. Cornelia Linde (trans.)** *Helisaeus Röslin's Delineation of Kepler's Birthchart, 1592*; **J. Cornelia Linde and Dorian Greenbaum (trans.)** *David Fabricius and Kepler on Kepler's Personal Astrology, 1602*; **Dorian Greenbaum (trans.)** *Kepler's Delineation of his Family's Astrology*; **J. Cornelia Linde and Dorian Greenbaum (trans.)** *Kepler and Michael Mästlin on their Son's Nativities, 1598*; **J. Cornelia Linde and Dorian Greenbaum (trans.)** *Kepler's Methods of Astrological Interpretation for Rudolf II, 1602*; **J. Cornelia Linde and Dorian Greenbaum (trans.)** *Kepler's Astrological Interpretation of Rudolf II by Traditional Methods, 1602*; **J. Cornelia Linde and Dorian Greenbaum (trans.)** *Kepler's Letter to an Official on Rudolf II and Astrology, 1611*; **J. Cornelia Linde and Dorian Greenbaum (trans.)** *Excerpts from Kepler's Correspondence and Interpretation of Wallenstein's Nativity, 1624-1625*; **J. Cornelia Linde and Dorian Greenbaum (trans.)** *The Nativities of Mohammed and Martin Luther, 1604*; **J. Cornelia Linde and Dorian Greenbaum (trans.)** *The Nativity of Augustus*; **John Meeks** *Introduction: Kepler and the Art of Weather Prognostication*; **John Meeks (trans.)** *Kepler's Weather Calendar of 1618*; **John Meeks (trans.)** *Excerpts from Kepler's Weather Calendar of 1619*; **Patrick J. Boner (trans.)** *Astrology on Trial: Kepler, Pico and the Preservation of the Aspects De stella nova: Chapters 7-9*; **J. Cornelia Linde and Dorian Greenbaum (trans.)** *On Directions*; **J. Cornelia Linde and Dorian Greenbaum (trans.)** *David Fabricius and Kepler on Astrological Theory and Doctrine, 1602*; **J. Cornelia Linde and Dorian Greenbaum (trans.)** *David Fabricius and Kepler on Fabricius's Directions, 1603-1604*; **J. Cornelia Linde and Dorian Greenbaum (trans.)** *On Aspects, 1602*; **Appendix** *A Selection of Kepler's Handwritten Charts*

Contents Vol. 15 no 1 (Spring/Summer 2011)
Miguel Querejeta *On the Eclipse of Thales, Cycles and Probabilities*; **Nicholas Campion** *The Shock of the New: The Age of Aquarius*; **Alejandro Gangui** *The Barolo Palace: Medieval Astronomy in the Streets of Buenos Aires*; **Nicholas Campion and John Frawley** *Research Note: A Horoscope by André Breton*

Contents Vol. 15 no 2 (Autumn/Winter 2011)
Liz Greene *Heavenly Hosts: Angelic Intermediaries as Soul-Gates*; **Pamela Armstrong** *Ritual Ornamentation—From the Secular to the Religious*; **Paul Cheshire** *William Gilbert: Macrocosmal Astrologer in an Age of Revolution*; **Sylwia Konarska-Zimnicka** *Astrologia Licita? Astrologia Illicita? The Perception of Astrology at Kraków University in the Fifteenth Century*; **John Frawley** *Research Note: William Blake and Antares*

Contents Volume 16 No 1/2 (Spring/Summer Autumn/Winter 2012)
Nicholas Campion, *Editorial: The Inspiration of Astronomical Phenomena*; **Chris Impey,** *The Inspiration of Astronomical Phenomena*; **Ulisses Barres de Almeida,** *What are these sparks of infinite clarity? And what am I? So I pry*; BATH AND THE HERSCHELS: **Michael Hoskin,** *William Herschel's Wonderful Decade, 1781–1790*; **Francis Ring,** *The Bath Philosophical Society and its influence on William Herschel's career*; **Roberta J.M. Olson and Jay M. Pasachoff,** *The Comets of Caroline Herschel, Sleuth of the Skies at Slough*; HISTORY AND CULTURE: **V.F. Polcaro and A. Martocchia,** *Guidelines for a social history of Astronomy*; **Euan MacKie,** *A new look at the astronomy and geometry of Stonehenge*; **Leonid Marsadolov,** *Archaeoastronomical Aspects of the Archaeological Monuments of*

Siberia; **Christian Etheridge**, *A systematic re-evaluation of the sources of Old Norse astronomy*; **Aidan Foster**, *Hierophanies in the Vinland Sagas: Images of a New World*; **Inga Elmqvist Söderlund**, *Inspiration from antique heroic deeds: Hercules as an astronomer*; **Patricia Aakhus**, *Astral Magic and Adelard of Bath's Liber Prestigiorum; or Why Werewolves Change at the Full Moon*; **David Pankenier**, Astrology for an Empire: The 'Treatise on the Celestial Offices' (ca. 100 BCE); **Steven Renshaw**, *The Inspiration of Subaru as a Symbol of Values and Traditions in Japan*;b **Daniel Armstrong**, *Citing The Saucers: Astronomy, UFOs and a persistence of vision*; **Alberto Cappi**, *The concept of gravity before Newton*; **Paul Murdin**, *Artilleryman to head of state—how astronomy inspired Francois Arago*; **Paolo Molaro and Alberto Cappi**, *Edgar Allan Poe's cosmology in* Eureka; **Voula Saridakis**, *For 'the present and future happiness of my dear Pupils'": The Astronomical and Educational Legacy of Margaret Bryan*; **Michael Rowan–Robinson**, *The invisible universe*; THE ARTS: **Arnold Wolfendale**, *The Inter-Relation of the Visual Arts and Science in General and Astronomy in Particular*; **Lynda Harris**, *Changing Images of the Milky Way during the Greco-Roman and Medieval Periods*; **Lucia Ayala**, *The Universe in images: Iconography of the Plurality of Worlds*; **Tayra M. Carmen Lanuza-Navarro**, *Astrological culture before its public: the representation of astrology in Golden Age Spanish Theatre*; **Emily Urban**, *Depicting the Heavens: The Use of Astrology in the Frescoes of Rome*; **Michael Mendillo**, *The Artistic Portrayal of the Medicean Moons in Early Astronomical Charts, Books and Paintings*; **Rolf Sinclair**, *Howard Russell Butler: Painter Extraordinary of Solar Eclipses*; **Beatriz Garcia, Estela Reynoso, Silvina Pérez Alvarez and Rubén Gabellone**, *Inspiration of Astronomy in the movies: a history of a close encounter*; **Gary Wells**, *The Moon in the Landscape: Interpreting a Theme of 19th Century Art*; **Clive Davenhall**, *The Space Art of Scriven Bolton*; **Matthew Whitehouse**, *Astronomical Organ Music*; **Aaron Plasek**, *Between Scientists, Writers and Artists: Theorising and Critiquing Knowledge-Production at the Interstices between Disciplines*; ARTISTS: **Merja Markkula**, *The Way I See the Stars: fibre art inspired by astrobiology*; **Govinda Sah**, *Beyond the Notion*; **Gisela Weimann**, *Above all the stars*; **Courtney Wrenn**, *Nebulae (emission / absorption)*; **Toby MacLennan**, *Presentation of Playing the Stars*; **Felicity Spear**, *Extending vision: sky-situated knowledge and the artist's eye*; **Vanessa Stanley**, *Surveillance-Surveillance-Surveillance*; **Jim Cogswell**, *Molecular Delirium*.

Contents Vol. 17 no 1 (Spring/Summer 2013)
Clifford J. Cunningham and Günther Oestmann *Classical Deities in Astronomy: The Employment of Verse to Commemorate the Discovery of the Planets Uranus, Ceres, Pallas, Juno, and Vesta*; **Dorian Knight** *A Reinvestigation Into Astronomical Motifs in Eddic Poetry*; **Karen Smyth** *'I specially note their Astronomie, philosophie, and other parts of profound or cunning art': The Use of Cosmos Registers by Chaucer and Others*; **Kirk Little** *Spellbound: The Astrological Imagination of Washington Irving*; **Guiliano Masola and Nicola Reggiani** *Σελήνη Τοξότη: Business and Astrology in the Papyri*; **Reinhard Mussik** *Research Note: Weltall, Erde, Mensch and Marxist Cosmology in East Germany*

Contents Vol. 17 no 2 (Autumn/Winter 2013)
Daniel Brown: *The Experience of Watching:Place Defined by the Trinity of Land-, Sea-, and Skyscape*; **Pamela Armstrong:** *Skyscapes of the Mesolithic/Neolithic Transition in Western England*; **Olwyn Pritchard**, *North as a Sacred Direction? Traces of a Prehistoric North-South Route Across Pembrokeshire*; **Tore Lomsdalen:** *The Islandscape of the Megalithic Temple Structures of Prehistoric Malta*; **Fernando Pimenta,**

Nuno Ribeiro, Anabela Joaquinito, António Félix Rodrigues, Antonieta Costa and Fabio Silva: *Land, Sea and Skyscape: Two Case Studies of Man-made Structures in the Azores Islands*

Contents Vol. 18 no 1 (Spring/Summer 2014)
César Esteban, *Struggling for Interdisciplinarity: Reflections of an Astrophysicist Working in Cultural Astronomy*; **Ronald Hutton,** *Prehistoric British Astronomy: Whatever Happened to the Earth and Sun?*; **Nick Kollerstrom,** *Galileo and the Astrological Prophecy of Manuel Rosales*; **Clive Davenhall,** *Dr Katterfelto and the Prehistory of Astronomical Ballooning*; **Nicholas Campion,** *Celestial Art: An Interview with Geoff MacEwan.*

Contents Vol. 18 no 2 (Autumn/Winter 2014)
Roger Beck, *The Ancient Mithraeum as a Model Universe. Part 2*; **Helena Avelar and Charles Burnett,** *The Interpretation of a Horoscope Cast by Abraham the Jew in Béziers for a child born on 29 November 1135: An Essay in Understanding a Medieval Astrologer*; Lindsay Starkey, *Creation, Providence, and the Limits of Human Knowledge of the World: Mellin de Saint-Gelais and John Calvin on Astrology*; **Scott Hendrix,** *The Contextual Rationality of Galileo's Astrology*; **Richard Angelo Bergen, Paradise Lost and the Descent of Urania: from Astrology to Allegory** R. Hakan Kirkoğlu, *Ilm-i nudjum and 18th century Ottoman Court Politics*; **Graham Douglas,** *Trystes Cosmologiques: When Lévi-Strauss met the Astrologers.*

www.ingramcontent.com/pod-product-compliance
Lightning Source LLC
Chambersburg PA
CBHW042113100526
44587CB00025B/4035